MAKING
THE BLACK JACOBINS
| | | | |

THE C. L. R. JAMES ARCHIVES

MAKING
THE BLACK JACOBINS

C. L. R. James and the Drama of History

| | | | |

RACHEL DOUGLAS

DUKE UNIVERSITY PRESS   DURHAM AND LONDON   2019

© 2019 Duke University Press
All rights reserved

Designed by Amy Ruth Buchanan
Typeset in Arno Pro and Gill Sans Std.
by Westchester Publishing Services

Library of Congress Cataloging-in-Publication Data
Names: Douglas, Rachel, [date] author.
Title: Making the Black Jacobins : the drama of C. L. R. James's history / Rachel Douglas.
Description: Durham : Duke University Press, 2019. | Series: The C. L. R. James archives | Includes bibliographical references and index.
Identifiers: LCCN 2019002423 (print)
LCCN 2019009129 (ebook)
ISBN 9781478005308 (ebook)
ISBN 9781478004271 (hardcover : alk. paper)
ISBN 9781478004875 (pbk. : alk. paper)
Subjects: LCSH: James, C. L. R. (Cyril Lionel Robert), 1901–1989. Black Jacobins. | James, C. L. R. (Cyril Lionel Robert), 1901–1989—Criticism and interpretation. | Toussaint Louverture, 1743–1803. | Haiti—History—Revolution, 1791–1804.
Classification: LCC F1923 (ebook) | LCC F1923 .D684 2019 (print) | DDC 972.94/03—dc23
LC record available at https://lccn.loc.gov/2019002423

Cover art: Édouard Duval-Carrié, *Le Général Toussaint Enfumé*, 2001. © Édouard Duval-Carrié. Courtesy of Rum Nazon, Cap Haïtien.

THIS BOOK IS DEDICATED TO
CATRIONA AND LEILA

CONTENTS

Acknowledgments ix

Introduction 1

1 Toussaint Louverture Takes Center Stage: The 1930s 29

2 Making History: *The Black Jacobins* (1938) 69

3 Rewriting History: *The Black Jacobins* (1963) 102

4 Reshaping the Past as Drama (1967) 133

5 Afterlives of *The Black Jacobins* 178

Notes 215

Bibliography 265

Index 295

ACKNOWLEDGMENTS

This book is based on research conducted in Trinidad and New York funded by a British Academy Small Research Grant (SG-51932) and a Small Research Grant from the Carnegie Trust for the Universities of Scotland. The book was written while I was in receipt of an Arts and Humanities Research Council Early-Career Fellowship (AH/I002662/1). I gratefully acknowledge the support of the AHRC, the British Academy, and the Carnegie Trust. During the project, I moved to the University of Glasgow from the University of Liverpool, and I would like to thank colleagues at both institutions for their contributions, especially Charles Forsdick, Michael Syrotinski, and Jackie Clarke.

In addition to the AHRC and the universities of Glasgow and Liverpool, I am very grateful to the following organizations for their assistance with the October 2013 conference, *The Black Jacobins* Revisited: Rewriting History: International Slavery Museum, National Museums Liverpool, the Bluecoat, Society for the Study of French History, Association for the Study of Modern and Contemporary France, Society for French Studies, Royal Historical Society, Alliance Française de Glasgow, and the Haiti Support Group. Participants at that event, including the keynote speakers Yvonne Brewster, Selwyn R. Cudjoe, Rawle Gibbons, Robert A. Hill, Selma James, Nick Nesbitt, and Matthew J. Smith, made invaluable contributions to C. L. R. James scholarship there.

This book has been a long time in the making and many people have collaborated with me to help bring it to fruition. To each of the following people I owe more than I can say, and so let me warmly thank David Abdullah, Michel Acacia, Katie Adams, Foz Allan, Tayo Aluko, Adisa "Aja" Andwele, Yoshio Aoki, A. James Arnold, David Austin, David A. Bailey, Martin Banham, Aisha Baptiste, Carla Bascombe, Madison Smartt Bell, Anthony Bogues,

Sergio Bologna, Yvonne Brewster, Hans-Christoph Buch, Margaret Busby, Jhon Picard Byron, Raj Chetty, Sandro Chignola, Rocky Cotard, Selwyn R. Cudjoe, Raphael Dalleo, Claudy Delné, Mike Dibb, Ceri Dingle, Farrukh Dhondy, Marilyn Dunn, Natalia Ely, Laurent Dubois, Grant Farred, David Featherstone, Kate Ferris, Charles Forsdick, Maria Cristina Fumagalli, Ferruccio Gambino, Marvin George, Rawle Gibbons, Corey Gilkes, Maurisa Gordon-Thompson, Katie Gough, Donna Hall-Commissiong, Emma Hart, Leila Hassan, Kathleen Helenese-Paul, Yuko Hirono, Kate Hodgson, Raphael Hoermann, Christian Høgsbjerg, Sean Jacobs, Selma James, Ulrick Jean-Pierre, Kwynn Johnson, Aaron Kamugisha, Rochelle Kapp, Louise Kimpton-Nye, Kwame Kwei-Armah, Jean-Pierre Le Glaunec, Adrian Leibowitz, Hongling Liang, Rosa López Oceguera, Filippo del Lucchese, Danielle Lyndersay, Roy McCree, Peter D. McDonald, Llewellyn McIntosh (Short Pants), F. Bart Miller, Lukanyo Mnyanda, Sumita Mukherjee, Jenny Morgan, Stephen Mullen, Martin Munro, Philip Murray (Black Sage), Lorraine Nero, Nick Nesbitt, Aldon Lynn Nielsen, Tadgh O'Sullivan, Raffaele Petrillo, Bryony Randall, Ciraj Rassool, Alan Rice, David Rudder, Marina Salandy-Brown, Catherine Spencer, Corinne Sandwith, Bill Schwarz, Marika Sherwood, Richard Small, Andy Smith, Matthew J. Smith, Terry Stickland, Patrick Sylvain, Glenroy Taitt, Afonso Teixeira Filho, Harclyde Walcott, Elizabeth Walcott-Hackshaw, Ozzi Warwick, Zoë Wilcox, and Eugene Williams. Without their generous help, none of this would ever have been possible.

Frank Rosengarten, Darcus Howe, and Dapo Adelugba, who all contributed to this project, sadly died before the book was finished. Robert A. Hill, C. L. R. James's literary executor and close associate, shared his unparalleled extensive knowledge of James's life and work. After my own two trips to the C. L. R. James Papers archive at Columbia University, New York, Jeremy Glick was an enormous help with archival research assistance. There could not have been a better-qualified navigator of that archive. I appreciate how quickly he stepped into the breach when some archive photos were lost. I am forever indebted to Rianella Gooding for taking such good photographs of James's open-book gravestone in Tunapuna cemetery, Trinidad, for me at short notice. Very special thanks to three people in Barbados—Alissandra Cummins, William St. James Cummins, and Anderson Toppin—who moved heaven and earth at short notice to take a high-resolution photo of Ras Akyem-i Ramsay's artwork. Many thanks to the artist Édouard Duval-Carrié, and to the owners Rum Nazon, Cap-Haïtien for allowing me to use the 2001 portrait of *Le Général Toussaint enfumé* (General Toussaint wreathed in smoke) for the cover. This directly James-inspired artwork reclaims *The Black Jacobins* for the land of its inspiration: Haiti. Warm thanks also go to Ramsay, Kimathi Donkor, Lubaina Himid, and the Middlesbrough Institute of Modern Art for granting me permission to reproduce their artworks in the following pages.

Most of the actual writing of this book happened at the National Library of Scotland, Edinburgh. Staff there and at the interlibrary loans department at Glasgow University Library were very efficient and enabled me to access many rare documents. Librarians and archivists from around the world have provided me with an abundance of rare materials about C. L. R. James. I would particularly like to thank staff in special collections departments at the University of the West Indies, St. Augustine, Trinidad; Columbia University, New York; the Walter P. Reuther Library of Wayne State University, Detroit, Michigan; the Tamiment Library of New York University Library and the Oral History of the American Left materials set up by Paul Buhle and Jonathan Bloom; the Schomburg Center for Research in Black Culture in New York City; the Penn State University Libraries; the Moorland-Spingarn Research Center at Howard University, Washington, DC; the Errol Hill Papers at Dartmouth College, New Hampshire; the Richard Wright Papers at the Beinecke Library, Yale University; the Sir Learie Constantine Collection, National Library Information Services (NALIS), Trinidad; the Andrew Salkey Archive, British Library; the Quinton O'Connor Memorial Library, Oilfield Workers' Trade Union (OWTU), San Fernando, Trinidad; the Institute of Commonwealth Studies, Senate House Library, University of London; Glasgow Caledonian University Archive of the Trotskyist Tradition, Glasgow; the Talawa Theatre Company Papers at the Victoria and Albert Theatre and Performance Archives, London; and the Labour History Archive and Study Centre, Manchester.

Thanks to editor Gisela Concepción Fosado and to everyone at Duke University Press for their support. I am grateful to the readers for their incisive and thought-provoking comments. A different version of sections of chapter 4 appeared in *The Black Jacobins Reader*, edited by Charles Forsdick and Christian Høgsbjerg (2017). I acknowledge the permission given by the editors and Duke University Press to draw on the material in the context of this broader analysis.

I would like to thank my family, especially Stephen—my first reader—who has been so supportive of this project, who has lived with the book for a long time, and who has gone out of his way to help at every stage of the process. This book is dedicated to Catriona and Leila, who arrived during the book's making. Both have been very patient while I have been working on the mysterious book. They both probably know a great deal now about C. L. R. James, *The Black Jacobins*, and the Haitian Revolution, as these were subjects of conversation in our house for so long. Their drawings and doodles often adorned many of the pages as I was writing them. I hope that one day soon they too will read and discover *The Black Jacobins* for themselves.

INTRODUCTION

There is no drama like the drama of history.
—C. L. R. James, *The Black Jacobins*

If there is no drama like the drama of history, according to C. L. R. James himself, what was the role of actual drama in shaping his own accounts of the Haitian Revolution across versions of *The Black Jacobins*? This question guides the present book, which takes James's own representation of the past of the Haitian Revolution as drama into account by examining both his plays, *Toussaint Louverture* in 1936 and *The Black Jacobins* in 1967. Clichés about links between drama and history abound. References to the drama of history, the great drama of a revolution, and descriptions of historical characters as tragic protagonists on the stage of world history are commonplace. Publisher Secker and Warburg's 1938 advertisement for *The Black Jacobins* referred once to "romance" and twice to "drama": "The romance of a great career and the drama of revolutionary history are combined in CLR JAMES' magnificent biography of TOUSSAINT LOUVERTURE. [. . .] The drama of his career is here brilliantly described in a narrative which grips the attention."[1] But beyond such analogies where historical events can be said to resemble drama, what happens when the past is actually turned into drama?

Making The Black Jacobins*: C. L. R. James and the Drama of History* charts the trajectory of C. L. R. James's multiple engagements with the Haitian Revolution throughout his lifetime, including his pioneering history *The Black Jacobins*. By uncovering the mobile and organic transformations of *The Black Jacobins* in both its theatrical and historiographical versions, this book illuminates the genesis and evolution of James's Haitian Revolution–related writing over a period of almost sixty years, from the 1930s to his death in 1989. *The Black Jacobins* is shown in chapter 5 on future directions to have lived on in a series of afterlives where others have made the work speak to new circumstances and issues in their turn.

The Black Jacobins is one of the great works of the twentieth century and remains today the cornerstone of Haitian Revolutionary studies. *Making* The Black Jacobins investigates the complex transformations through which the work came to be, via the first comparisons of the two plays and two versions of the history, while taking the reader on a tour of the significant paratexts—book covers, interviews, talks, and reviews—that document the work's multiple becomings. This book investigates the vital significance of *The Black Jacobins* as a work of history and of theater by bringing the revisions and their meanings to the attention of general readers of James. It is based on discussion of hitherto all but completely neglected manuscripts of James's first and second plays, and his correspondence about these plays and history editions, together with special attention to the ways in which James rewrote and rethought *The Black Jacobins* history over the course of his life in many different contexts and periods. The book surveys for the first time in its entirety the history of James's masterpiece and its transformations as history and play. As a whole, *Making* The Black Jacobins compares and contrasts the changing historiographic narrative with the relative freedom of theater to refashion understanding of the revolution, in the absence of any conclusive documentation in the historical archive.

Despite its importance as the classic history of the Haitian Revolution, there is relatively little knowledge of the eventful history of *The Black Jacobins* itself, and of key changes made by James and others, both during and after the author's lifetime. Rewriting—the subject of this book—links James's topic, his writing methods, and the events of the Haitian Revolution. James's history helped to change the way colonial history was written from presenting the colonized as passive objects to active subjects. Added to this, James kept telling and retelling how the Haitian Revolution rewrote world history as the first and only slave revolution to fight against the great powers of the day and win.

Rewriting, it will be argued, is an important part of James's working methods from the beginning and throughout his whole career. James's other early rewritten works include *The Life of Captain Cipriani* (1932) and *The Case for West Indian Self-Government* (1933), with the condensed latter title cutting out most of the biographical material about the Trinidad labor leader Cipriani.[2] *Mariners, Renegades, and Castaways: The Story of Herman Melville and the World We Live In* (1953) was first privately published by James in a bid to appeal against deportation from the United States, with a copy sent to every member of Congress. Its evolution saw James rewrite one chapter and cut out another.[3] James also rewrote *A History of Negro Revolt*, first published in 1938, publishing it again in 1969 with a new title—*A History of Pan-African Revolt*—and an extra epilogue, focusing like the 1963 *Black Jacobins* history revisions on bringing the 1938 history up to date.[4] Other slight changes were made to that text when James was revising it, including the removal of references to Franco's Moors.[5] However, there were also occasions when not a single word was changed. *World Revolution*, for example, was first published in 1937 and later reprinted unchanged in 1973.[6] Another updated statement was James's pamphlet *State Capitalism and World Revolution*, which went through four editions during James's lifetime: 1950, 1956, 1968, and 1984.[7] In this way, other works too, beyond *The Black Jacobins*, were reshaped by James during his lifetime and reframed in order to respond to new circumstances across the world.

This book is about the nature and significance of changes throughout James's Haitian Revolution writings from the 1930s up to his death in 1989, and beyond. James was, above all, a profoundly political person. In a 1980 interview, he said he wanted to be remembered as one of the important Marxists for his serious contributions to Marxism.[8] This book examines what happens as James keeps traveling further along the road of *The Black Jacobins* in his Haiti-related writing. From the start, James's writings about the Haitian Revolution can be thought of as reworking Marxism and Trotsky's notion of permanent revolution. Examining James's Haiti-related writings, the book reads the changes as reflections of James's own political evolution. It is productive to think of the different history editions, plays, and articles as drafts or working documents, offered up for discussion and further elaboration by James's political groups. Looking at what changes over time also allows us to chart James's serious and original contributions to Marxism through the prism of his Haiti-related works.

The Black Jacobins must be read alongside James's defining political experiences and the great strides in terms of Marxist theory and practice made in America from the 1940s onward. Under the pseudonym J. R. Johnson, James was organizing a political group in the United States from the early 1940s onward, which became known as the Johnson-Forest Tendency. This was formed of a small core, including Raya Dunayevskaya, originally from Russia, one of Trotsky's secretaries, and whose pseudonym "Freddie Forest" became part of the group's name. There was also Grace Lee, a Chinese American who had studied German and helped the group to study Marx's writings from the original German, while Dunayevskaya enabled them to study other Marxist works from the original Russian.[9] Increasingly, James and his group drew attention to the spontaneous self-activity of the masses and to more popular alternative leaders.

While *The Black Jacobins* is famed as the classic history of the Haitian Revolution, the trajectory of James's wider Haitian Revolution–related writings also includes two plays that bookend the two editions of the more celebrated history. It is crucial to study these plays in conjunction with the history versions because they give us some of the first and last words on the Haitian Revolution, according to James. The 1936 performance of the first play, *Toussaint Louverture*, antedates the initial 1938 publication of the history *The Black Jacobins* by two years, while the second play, *The Black Jacobins* (1967) comes more than four years after the revision of the history for its second 1963 edition. The script for the 1936 play *Toussaint Louverture*—previously feared by many to have been lost for good—has only recently been published, thanks to Christian Høgsbjerg's 2013 critical edition. Surprisingly, less seems to be known about the 1967 play *The Black Jacobins* than would be expected, despite the script for this second play appearing twice in print and being performed across a number of countries over the decades since its December 14–16, 1967, premiere by the Arts Theatre Group, University of Ibadan, Nigeria.

Theater occupies a special place in this study, especially the connection between the activities of doing theater and doing politics. Theater can be thought of as politics-ready, and James's use of theater's specific political qualities is examined, including its potential to propose alternatives to the present realities, to show people images of themselves through live performance, and to perform revolution in action.[10] Drama has further advantages for representing the past, which will be explored, including dialogic drama's multivoicedness, enabling alternative characters, of whom there is little archival trace, to speak more audibly and to take center stage.[11]

The final section addresses the afterlives of *The Black Jacobins*, including key translations, monuments and exhibitions dedicated to James, and the trajectory of his Haitian Bible in Haiti itself, the country of James's inspiration, and across other political situations including apartheid South Africa. The book ends by examining how *The Black Jacobins* is a book always kept open by others beyond James himself, with multiple components of *The Black Jacobins* acting as a guide and catalyst for political action.

Rethinking the Rethinking: Work on James and *The Black Jacobins*

Across the wealth and breadth of existing scholarship on James, it is striking how many prominent references there are, often even in titles, to the need to rethink James, *The Black Jacobins*, and the audacity of his achievements.[12] This book builds on Susan Gillman's conceptualization of *The Black Jacobins* as a "text-network," which she expresses as an equation: "from Columbus to Toussaint + Toussaint to Castro = from Columbus to Castro," arguing that the resulting revised edition of James's history even outdoes Eric Williams's 1970 book by the same title.[13] To this equation, I would add that *The Black Jacobins* is always already itself more than the sum of its parts: a constantly changing whole with shifting coordinates, which grows in size as James continues to relocate and reorient his most famous work. Already the history in itself is a text-network, if we look beyond the history to consider the multiple versions and revisions of the different editions and sprawling drafts of the two plays, which multiply, becoming even more multilayered as the coordinates of the protean *Black Jacobins* text-network shift.

David Scott's groundbreaking study *Conscripts of Modernity* (2004) has analyzed a number of key additions to the 1963 revised edition of the history. His interpretations are based largely on one set of added paragraphs as Scott reads through James's *Black Jacobins* to make wider arguments about the romance of anticolonial pasts and the tragedy of postcolonial presents/futures. This project tries to fill the gap, which Scott himself acknowledges, namely telling the story of the actual writing of *The Black Jacobins*—a story that, Scott indicates, urgently needs to be told. This book takes his analysis of anticolonial pasts and postcolonial presents/futures in new directions, both forward and backward across the writing of *The Black Jacobins*, including the plays. This book also builds on studies of James's plays by Nicole King, Frank Rosengarten, and Reinhard Sander, which all predate Høgsbjerg's discovery and publication of the Hull manuscript of the first play, *Toussaint Louverture*, and which make astute observations about James's playwriting based on published versions of the second play, *The Black Jacobins*, from 1976 and 1992.[14] Here all the versions of the plays and history are compared for the first time.[15]

Palimpsests, Paratexts, and Methods

This book argues that *The Black Jacobins* should be seen as a palimpsest with its successive layers of rewriting as it reuses the same story of the Haitian

Revolution for different purposes: articles, plays, histories. Resembling a palimpsest, James's multiple text-network related to Haiti contains manuscript inscriptions where new writing is superimposed on top of previous writing, often leaving behind visible traces of the rewriting. My case for calling *The Black Jacobins* a palimpsest is strengthened by James's own conviction that his 1938 history's "foundation would remain imperishable."[16] It is the very fact that the vast bulk of the history itself remains unchanged for the subsequent editions that makes it a palimpsest. Palimpsests are layered repositories of embedded vestiges, meaning that earlier inscriptions remain and are never erased, because "these narrative inscriptions become part of the whole."[17]

French narratologist Gérard Genette's famous work *Palimpsestes* is centered on his notion of hypertextuality, whereby a later text (the hypertext) grafts itself palimpsestually onto a hypotext, an earlier text that it transforms.[18] Such transformative visions of palimpsests/rewriting underpin my book, as do Genette's theories of paratexts or textual outsides—everything connected with the book that is not the text proper.[19] For this study, it is sometimes necessary to judge the works in question by their covers, and their prefaces, notes, appendixes, epilogues, and bibliographies, which James uses to reframe his Haiti-related work throughout its long evolution. While Genette's work on palimpsests and paratexts is very usable for this book, it is also necessary to break with his decontextualized, inward-looking approaches to textuality, and with his rigid typologies of hypertextuality and paratexts. Such approaches need to be adapted and decolonized to look outward at the political contexts that are so important to a fundamentally political person like James.[20]

For my examination of the making of *The Black Jacobins*, materialist methodologies for tracking manuscript and textual versions from genetic criticism and book history have also been useful. Book history offers methods for analyzing the material aspects of a book's construction—be that its cover, format, packaging, or typography—and the circumstances of literary production, dissemination, and reception. Traditionally, book history's methodologies have been applied primarily by those working on the medieval and early modern periods, with scholarly attention to postcolonial and modern book history still in its infancy.[21] Inspired by perspectives from book history, I pay closer attention to the material conditions of textual production, transmission, and reception of *The Black Jacobins* throughout its long genesis.

Where methods are concerned, the book seeks to decolonize genetic criticism and to build on the postcolonial genetic criticism established by

Richard Watts, A. James Arnold, and others. The book attempts to look both backward to investigate the complex genesis of these texts and also, crucially, beyond the dominant genetic paradigm, refusing the fetishization of the earliest beginnings that can mar works of genetic criticism, which sometimes pay little attention to what happens after publication.[22] *Making* The Black Jacobins also looks forward beyond initial publication to consider the impacts, the becomings, and afterlives of James's magnum opus. This results in a type of genetic criticism that tries to be politically informed and forward-looking, as befits one of the greatest and most original thinkers of the Marxist tradition.

With genetic criticism, the genetics in question are those of manuscripts.[23] Genetic criticism is a youngish, predominantly French phenomenon that offers a method for reading and ordering all drafts of a literary work intelligibly and is concerned with the genealogies of its textual beginnings. It offers a useful model for approaching the dynamics of the long genesis and evolution of James's plays and history based on the Haitian Revolution. On theater, genetic criticism sheds invaluable light on the many layers that make up the creative process of writing the plays in particular.[24] Specifically, I have used genetic criticism methods for performing archival work and establishing the relative chronology of all the manuscripts and typescripts consulted for both the 1936 *Toussaint Louverture* and the 1967 *Black Jacobins* plays.

These genetic criticism and book history approaches have been fruitful for illuminating the plays' geneses from new angles, and have formed a useful theoretical framework for approaching and making sense of all the play drafts. Genetic criticism involves a search for origins, and empirically genetic criticism and book history typologies try to set themselves apart from the traditional domain of literary criticism by stressing the material dimension of the work at hand. This is a genetic field that seeks archival reality based on more materially concrete empirical evidence. Genetic criticism has given me a how-to guide with which to document the handling of archive boxes, folders, and their dusty contents, fragile manuscript and onionskin typescript pages, the examination of every blot and mark, and even analysis of various paper and notebook types. How-to guides by Almuth Grésillon and others have helped me to work out the relative chronologies of drafts.[25] *Avant-texte* is the central notion around which genetic criticism revolves. It is often translated into English as pre-text or genetic dossier, or indeed the term can be left in French. Protocols elaborated by genetic critics dictate how to put archival documentation into a readable and intelligible form. The avant-texte or genetic dossier chronologically works out the various stages as the writing progresses from first manuscript or typescript draft to last, before publication of the book proper.

For my analysis of the evolution of James's *Black Jacobins* project, empirical work on variants is only ever a means to an end. In the case of the *Toussaint Louverture* and *The Black Jacobins* plays, I have sought at a preliminary stage of my work to establish the relative chronology of all the scripts consulted. But the cataloging of variants in their own right is not the aim of this book. Rather, establishing all the different versions of the typescripts and of the published texts themselves has been the essential first stage of my research, providing a more authoritative basis from which to develop wider points about James's *Black Jacobins*. Genetic criticism and book history methodologies have certainly been enabling for reconstructing and clarifying the complex story of *The Black Jacobins* throughout the decades, which is the aim of this book.

Trying to make genetic criticism and book history methodologies talk to a work like *The Black Jacobins* has led me to think about the problems and unacknowledged assumptions of these models. Hallmarks of genetic criticism that I found rather alien to James's *Black Jacobins* project included the method's usually narrow French-Francophone application—a type of genetics that, despite its major impact in France, has not traveled so well to other countries outside its *appellation d'origine contrôlée*. It is also important to think about changes made after first publication of works like *The Black Jacobins*. Genetic criticism rarely pays attention to the trajectory of a work after first publication. Traditionally, there has been a strict cutoff point between the manuscript pre-text and the published text, with the latter normally seen as fixed, and variants studied only up to the point of publication.[26] As will be shown, however, the published form of *The Black Jacobins* is never fixed. Here, I use genetic criticism's methods to read variants across published versions of the work too.

Recently, considerable strides have been made to widen the scope of genetic criticism beyond France, to Francophone authors and to literature written in other languages from elsewhere. For instance, 2011 saw the publication of an important collection of genetic criticism on works by African and Caribbean writers. This was a special issue, "Afrique–Caraïbe," of the official journal *Genesis*, of genetic criticism's Paris-based institutional home: the Institut des textes et manuscrits modernes (ITEM).[27] Prior to this publication in 2011, geneticist readings of Francophone literature had been given a platform within ITEM when in 2009 a team dedicated to the Francophone manuscript was set up, embarking on a bimonthly seminar program from which many of the *Genesis* articles took shape. Since then, the group now has shifted its focus toward the global south.

This work by the Francophone subsection of ITEM in Paris is a key reference point for my work. Recently, the scope of genetic criticism has been widened in new thematic directions, such as theater, autobiography, letter writing, and photography. Further afield, the emphasis has occasionally been on a particular geographical location (Argentina, Russia), or a language (Hispanic), but the Francophone manuscript focus entrenches the monolingualism of genetic criticism. Such a Francocentric approach could divide James's *Black Jacobins* in English from the likes of Aimé Césaire and his *Cahier d'un retour au pays natal*, another work with a long genesis, and one on which James would explicitly comment at length in the 1963 added appendix to his history.

For all genetic criticism's supposedly empirical focus and archive-driven preoccupation with materially concrete manuscript evidence and solid documentation, the reality sought here is an archival one: that of the manuscripts themselves. Manuscripts are usually considered separately from the finished published text. Genetic criticism often bypasses and eliminates political contexts, folding back instead on the materiality of the manuscripts themselves, and not on what is taking place in the world at large. Left out of this genetic criticism approach is the all-important relay binding together the work of a politically driven Marxist like James and the genesis of *The Black Jacobins* play drafts: political matters.

New perspectives from genetic criticism devoted specifically to theatrical genesis have been most usable for my purposes.[28] When applied to the theater, genetic criticism provides antidotes to that old cliché that a play's text is a dead corpse, while its performance is a living, vital body. Performance studies focuses almost exclusively on the finished play as performed to audiences, neglecting creative preparatory work leading up to that moment. While theater genetics claims to focus on the interplay between page and stage, what is indisputable is that the textual pole remains dominant despite claims to the contrary. But genetic criticism's textual focus usefully highlights the crucial role played in theatrical productions by written materials of all kinds, and this has helped me to make the most of all the written vestiges directly connected to the genesis of the play texts and performances.

Drafts of James's Haitian Revolution writings are scattered throughout the world in archives, libraries, and private collections, with the most important holdings at the University of the West Indies, Trinidad, and at Columbia University in New York. Clearly, this scattering of scripts is a result of James's usual collaborative working methods, whereby he would have copies typed, annotate them, and then send them to comrades around the world for political discussion and feedback. This was particularly the case after James's deportation from the United States in 1953. Around that time, his political organization regrouped in Detroit and became known as the Correspondence publishing group, with correspondence being the main method of their political collaborations.

The French-Francophone genetic criticism model needs to be decolonized, broadened, and politicized in order to confront works like *The Black Jacobins*. This is a work that does not revel in the pleasures of the pre-text or aesthetics for their own sake. Instead, James's Haitian Revolution–related writings are written from a strongly Marxist point of view and guided by clear political ideas regarding the Caribbean region, the United States, Europe, and Africa, and by James's own political struggles and responses to the twentieth century's most significant events across the Caribbean and Africa.

James himself had definite plans for publication of these changes. As revealed in a commentary to an alternative scene of *The Black Jacobins* play, he intended to publish an edition of the play text that would provide a story of the making of the play, including the multiplication of alternative scenes and his own commentaries upon their significance.[29] Dexter Lyndersay, first director of *The Black Jacobins* play in 1967, gave James a concrete example of a similar venture as a possible model for the published edition of the play: William Gibson's *The Seesaw Log*.[30] Of course, neither of the two published versions of this play did demonstrate the crucial degree to which the play was reworked. But the fact that James wanted to preserve all these intermediate stages and their accompanying commentaries to the point where the various drafts of *The Black Jacobins* play would constitute a veritable palimpsest also bears witness to a large part of the work that is therefore deserving of more attention.

Theatrical genetic criticism sheds invaluable light on some of the multilayered activities that make up the creative process of writing the play while still in that transitional phase when it has not yet crystallized into final form. This theater subgenre of genetic criticism stresses most strongly the status of play drafts as perpetually unfinished and incomplete works. Nowhere, however, does this geneticist accent on the dynamism and openness of the theatrical work stress any properly political interpretations of such open characteristics. Genetic criticism—even in its theatrical guise—remains strikingly apolitical.

On the unique relationship between radical politics and unfinished or incomplete dramatic works, Augusto Boal's *Theater of the Oppressed* is instructive.[31] If bourgeois theater can be thought of, after Boal, as finished theater, only presenting complacent images of the complete finished bourgeois world, then radical political theater of the left would by contrast reject any closed spectacles and always seek to enter into dialogue and ask for explanations. This idea provides a useful conceptual framework for reading James's sprawling and anarchic perpetual rewrites of material related to *The Black Jacobins*. The unfinished and open nature of the multiple drafts could be read as a type of handmaiden form for revolutionary theatrical and real-world processes of dynamic action, transformation, and re-creation where "theater is change and not simple presentation of what exists: it is becoming not being."[32] As a Marxist, playwright-activist James does theatrical work that can never be finished, nor ever end neatly and complacently in a state of serene repose. Instead, the open and unfinished form and contents of *The Black Jacobins* play drafts combine to reinforce the importance of hastening actual political and societal transformations, changes, transitions, political actions, and successful struggles for liberation. What is incomplete and unfinished here is political action and transformation.

Interviews: Rewriting the Death of the Author

To prepare for the writing of this book, I interviewed a number of people who were closely connected with James and *The Black Jacobins*, or with later incarnations of his 1967 play, including Selma James, C. L. R.'s widow; Robert A. Hill, C. L. R.'s literary executor; and directors of James's *Black Jacobins* play, including Yvonne Brewster, Rawle Gibbons, Eugene Williams, and Harclyde Walcott. Collaborators who were involved in various *Black Jacobins* translation projects have also been consulted, including Ferruccio Gambino, James's closest Italian comrade at the time of the 1968 Italian publication of *I Giacobini neri*, and Raffaele Petrillo, the actual translator, as well as Rosa López Oceguera, the Cuban translator of the eventual 2010 Casa de las Américas translation, about which James had been in talks since 1961. Also very useful have been interviews and records left by others, including James's great-nephew Darcus Howe and his widow and fellow Race Today Collective collaborator Leila Hassan, about a projected C. L. R. James Foundation in London, for which the plans are among Darcus Howe's papers at Columbia University.

On the South African and Haitian contexts of the trajectory of *The Black Jacobins* throughout South Africa and Haiti, I have been privileged to speak to Sean Jacobs, Grant Farred, Lukanyo Mnyanda, Michel Hector, Michel Acacia, Jhon Picard Byron, and Claudy Delné. This has been very useful as it was impossible to give a prominent place to the explicit reception history because of a lack of reliable data for sales of *The Black Jacobins* in places like Haiti and apartheid South Africa. These interviews have helped me to approach the question of reception from a much broader perspective, similar to the approaches of Terence Cave and Ann Rigney in their studies of the afterlives of Mignon and Walter Scott.[33]

I also draw on James's own statements given during interviews and lectures, especially the series of lectures on *The Black Jacobins* that James delivered at the Institute of the Black World in Atlanta in 1971, but which have only recently been made widely available since their 2001 publication in the journal *Small Axe*.[34] One of these lectures, intriguingly titled "How I Would Rewrite *The Black Jacobins*" and delivered at the institute on June 18, 1971, is especially useful for my purposes. In this lecture, James reveals that he would only give Toussaint a walk-on part were he to rewrite *The Black Jacobins* again from scratch. But beyond the conditional of this snapshot of a hypothetical rewriting, it is important to recognize that James actually did reply to this key challenge of how to rewrite *The Black Jacobins* and that his stories of the Haitian Revolution responded with several different answers over a period of many decades. This type of source, as well as James's own autobiographical or programmatic statements, contained in the drafts of his unpublished autobiography or in author interviews during his lifetime, have given me extra authorial insights into the processes of making and remaking *The Black Jacobins*, which would not be available from any other kind of source.

Literary studies have generally followed Roland Barthes's famous declaration of the "death of the author" and his thorough discrediting of biographical-type criticism, where the author's general biography is linked to the meanings of the text.[35] This, according to Barthes, closed down the textual openness and meaning. The goal of this book is not to produce an excessively biographical account of *The Black Jacobins*. However, James as an author powerfully asserts and reasserts his ownership many times over the long genesis of his most famous work. With a political thinker and organizer like James, his own words and those of others close to his *Black Jacobins* projects need to be taken into account. I therefore want to make a special case against the death of the author and for considering the extratextual nature of James's real political life and declarations. Many studies of James have been based, quite rightly, on questions of his political biography. Attention turns here to the detail of James's writing, and it is necessary to tell a different story than the death of the author because, especially in the case of such a political person as James, his authorial voice simply cannot be banished from his own writing: we need the extratextual authorial voice to make sense of the work.

James writes the past of the Haitian Revolution as drama twice. Drama is a special literary category that offers a politics-ready representing machine for a fundamentally political person like James.[36] Theater is a showing form of historical representation where the audience is brought to witness the past and the future in the present, and where characters are given a voice of their own, with the drama acting as a sort of megaphone for James's political views.[37] Various reflections contained within drafts of the play also have James offering commentaries on his authorial choices as playwright.[38] James also revisions the past as history for the two 1938 and 1963 editions of his history. Where the story of the past of the Haitian Revolution is concerned, James turns to actual drama writing in addition to history writing. Especially when telling the past as history, James is an overt, controlling voice who self-consciously expresses his views on the action. Not taking his controlling historical voice into account is not an option, and this is why interviews and authorial statements and lectures form an important part of this book's methodology.

Relations between form and content and the varying generic forms in play are at the fore of this book's main concerns. In this respect, Hayden White offers a well-known paradigm concerning the history/literature debate. His narrativist approach to history stresses connections between history and fiction writing and similarities between fictive structuring processes of emplotment produced by both historians and fiction writers. David Scott's Hayden White–inspired reading of James's history revisions contrasts two modes of historical emplotment: the romance of the 1938 first edition of the history versus the emplotment of tragedy in the 1963 second edition. *The Black Jacobins* is always written and rewritten by James from an explicitly Marxist historical perspective. White's famous phrase "the content of the form" reflects on the formal characteristics of history and, above all, on its narrative quality.[39]

Genre is an important issue, and *The Black Jacobins* is notable for its distinctive crossover generic qualities.[40] This book tries to go beyond the distinctive literary feel of *The Black Jacobins* and to analyze its trajectory as actual drama and work of literature.[41] James himself spoke of a clear-cut distinction whereby between 1932 and 1938, "Fiction-writing drained out of me and was replaced by politics. I became a Marxist, a Trotskyist," and that "literature was vanishing from my consciousness and politics was substituting itself."[42] Fiction implies, however, a strong tendency to untruth, to make up something. This book pays attention to the special literary category that is drama, and to the particular crossover generic qualities it offers to a fundamentally political person like James.

So close is the relationship between theater and politics that they are often presented as going together hand in hand as second cousins. Theater has been described as the "most public of the arts," and as one of the arts of presentation/representation that, like photography, has a privileged access to truth.[43] This intrinsically political role of theater as a representing machine also strongly connects it with action, as long-dead characters and historical events from long ago can be brought to life by flesh-and-blood actors who perform these deeds in the present tense of theater's liveness, as if they were happening now. With pieces of political theater like *Toussaint Louverture* (1936) and *The Black Jacobins* (1967), the purpose is both to enact politics and revolution (depicting as it does the plight of the slaves/oppressed who fuel the capitalist economy and their revolution for changing the world) and to provoke the audience to do politics and revolution in their turn by resisting a state of affairs similar to the one resisted in the play. Turning the past back into drama again allows James to go further in showing peoples of African descent "taking action on a grand scale"—a key motivation behind his writing of *The Black Jacobins*, as stated clearly in his 1980 foreword to the history.[44]

Historiography of the Haitian Revolution

My reading of James's use of sources chimes with that of Bernard Moitt, who argues that James managed to reconstruct the world of the Haitian slaves, and in so doing "transcended linguistic and cultural frontiers in the historiography of the Caribbean."[45] This is certainly true, and *The Black Jacobins* itself is the result of James's extensive use and interpretation of French-language sources, including those of the earliest Haitian historians and those of his Haitian contemporaries in the early twentieth century.

James refers to the two early pillars of Haitian Revolution historiography: Thomas Madiou (1814–84) and Alexis Beaubrun Ardouin (1796–1865).[46] On Madiou, James indicates that this Haitian historian has given an outline of Moïse's alternative to his adoptive uncle Toussaint's program, although James also notes that its authenticity has been questioned. As for Ardouin, he poured his criticism on all dark-skinned leaders of the Haitian Revolution, including Toussaint, Dessalines, and Christophe, and attacked Madiou for being their apologist.[47] On Ardouin's six-volume study of Haitian history, James notes:

> Ardouin has written a very curious book. He is a Mulatto and hates Toussaint, hates the French (Roume, Sonthonax and all), and twists his evidence to suit his purpose. A Haitian scholar has informed the writer that he has detected Ardouin suppressing portions of letters which would prejudice the particular point he was proving. There is no reason to doubt this. Yet Ardouin has covered a great deal of ground. His hatred sharpens a remarkable acuteness and his book is one of the most valuable sources for any serious work on the San Domingo revolution.[48]

There are four references in total to Ardouin's history. James observes that these savage attacks are at the heart of Caribbean and Haitian historiography, and we will see that James's dialogic interventions on the Haitian Revolution also engage with these polemics.

For *The Black Jacobins*, there is one Haitian history that remains its most important source, and that is Horace Pauléus Sannon's three-volume *Histoire de Toussaint Louverture*, which is a homage to this Haitian revolutionary. Sannon (1870–1938) was the first president of the Haitian Société d'Histoire et de Géographie, which was founded by prominent intellectuals during the American occupation of Haiti in 1924. The histories of the society's founding president Sannon would be the strongest influence on James in the 1930s. In 2009, the president of that same Haitian Société d'Histoire et de Géographie called *The Black Jacobins* a "beacon of a book" for "a new approach to the revolution which emerges from the nation-state."[49] Back then in the 1920s, as first president of the society under the American occupation he vehemently opposed, Sannon explicitly set out the goals of the society's patriotic duty as to conjure up the past for reassurance, pride, and explanation of the present.[50] Most of all, James shares with Sannon his fundamental approach to the study of the revolution through the historical biography of Toussaint Louverture.

Introduction | 15

Sannon receives a grand total of fifteen references throughout *The Black Jacobins*, including a substantial in-text reference to his views on mixed-race mulattoes "as a typical intermediate class with all the political instability of that class" (230).[51] In this regard, James says, "No one has written more wisely and profoundly on the San Domingo revolution and Toussaint Louverture" than Sannon. A surprisingly short but decidedly positive reference is then made to Sannon in the annotated bibliography: "The best biography yet written of Toussaint" (383). James would follow Sannon by quite often letting Toussaint speak through his correspondence. Toussaint's letters as retranscribed by Sannon and Schœlcher thus occupy an important position in the *Black Jacobins* overall.

When looking at James's use of sources throughout *The Black Jacobins*, it is clear that, although he has consulted letters, reports, and other documents in the Paris archives, most of his sources are secondary ones.[52] He relies on the likes of nineteenth-century French abolitionist Victor Schœlcher's (1804–93) biography *La Vie de Toussaint-Louverture*, a work featuring extensive retranscriptions of Toussaint's letters.[53] James's history is heavily indebted to Schœlcher, more so than is acknowledged anywhere in the text, footnotes, and bibliography. One striking characteristic of James's Toussaint is that he is forever speaking in the first person directly out of the pages of his correspondence as mediated by Schœlcher. Such extensive first-person addresses already give James's history a distinctly dramaturgical feel, as if James is letting Toussaint speak for himself. There are nine references to Schœlcher in total, although the entry for him in James's annotated bibliography is decidedly wary: "Schœlcher is a French radical of the nineteenth century. He hates slavery, hates Bonaparte, and though his heart is in the right place, despite many shrewd comments, he is too uncritical to be trustworthy. But he has digested an enormous amount of original material of which he prints many extracts. All modern writers on the San Domingo revolution are indebted to him and his book should be read, although with extreme caution" (383).

On James's sources, Chris Bongie, Kirsten Silva Gruesz, and Susan Gillman have all pointed out that Pamphile de Lacroix's *Mémoires pour servir à l'histoire de la Révolution de Saint-Domingue* (1819) is of vital importance to the biographical portrait of Toussaint that James paints throughout *The Black Jacobins*.[54] If James's use of sources can be thought of as unsilencing the past by writing back to pernicious accounts and misrepresentations of the Haitian Revolution, James himself has been accused of silencing one source in particular: early Haitian historian Joseph Saint-Rémy (1815–58).

Marlene Daut has accused James of the "utterly myopic conclusion that Saint-Rémy hated Louverture 'like poison.'"[55] James can be thought of as silencing "a great deal of what Saint-Rémy actually wrote." Nick Nesbitt has argued that James should have followed French historian Albert Mathiez, who rehabilitated French revolutionary hero Robespierre. This would have stopped James from continuing to caricature Robespierre as some kind of "sinister dictator."[56]

An extremely important Haitian French-language source for James were the histories of Alfred Auguste Nemours (1883–1955), who was a Haitian general, diplomat, and military historian.[57] James and Nemours had actually met in Paris while James was doing research for *The Black Jacobins*. It was Nemours who opened his eyes to the military skills of revolutionary Haitians, as James would later recall in his 1980 foreword to the history (vi). Nemours receives fourteen references. Most of these references are, unsurprisingly, to be found in the two chapters—chapter 11, "The Black Consul," and chapter 13, "The War of Independence"—which deal most explicitly with Toussaint's military skills. Nemours was convinced that Haitians' military skills had been neglected by other historians, and that they were "additional proof of their humanity."[58] Nemours's blind admiration for Louverture has been criticized and was apparently such that Nemours sought to trace Toussaint's French descendants.[59] On Nemours, James's comments have been described as "very generous" when James describes Nemours as "an enthusiastic admirer of Toussaint but exceptionally fair" (382), and as "a great admirer of Toussaint" (308n15).[60] What James highlights as valuable is the fact that Nemours has "worked over the terrain" so carefully, with "extensive research among the archives in France," and his attentive studies of Toussaint's campaigns are commended. General Nemours is cited as the source who "has listed a mass of evidence on French military opinion of the great strength of the blacks at the time of submission" (327n26), underlining that Toussaint's strategy of submission was not because of imminent defeat by the French army. Nemours is credited with making several important documents linked to the Haitian Revolution more widely available; for example, James notes that Toussaint's "Constitution is printed in full in Nemours, *Histoire militaire...*, Vol. I, pp. 95–112" (263n20). Likewise, a note accompanying a long string of quotations from Leclerc's correspondence to Napoleon observes that Nemours has performed the task of retranscription on which *The Black Jacobins* is based: "Leclerc to the First Consul, February 9th, 1802. The letters retranscribed from the Archives of the Minister for War, by General Nemours.

See *Histoire Militaire de la Guerre d'Indépendance...*, Vol II, p. 53–120." Not always does James agree with Nemours on all points, but James weighs up all the issues from volume to volume of Nemours's multivolume work:

> General Nemours, a Haitian, a great admirer of Toussaint, and one who has made a careful study of this campaign, contradicts traditional Haitian history. He describes this battle as a defeat for Toussaint. But he bases his conclusions on, among other points, the supposed treachery of Maurepas. In Volume II of his work, however, he disproves the treachery of Maurepas, on evidence acquired after he had published Volume I. The result of the battle must for the time being remain undecided. See Nemours, *Histoire Militaire...*, Vol. I, pp. 210–211 and Vol. II, pp. 250–252. (308n15)

Apart from the many references to Nemours and Haitian Revolution military strategy as conveyed by Nemours's *Histoire Militaire*, James also singles out the importance of Nemours's *Histoire de la captivité et de la mort de Toussaint-L'Ouverture* (1929), although this book is not cited in his bibliography. The usefulness of this work of Nemours's is referenced in the footnotes as follows: "The definitive account of Toussaint's captivity with many of the most important documents printed in full" (363n78). From this note, it transpires that all the information on Toussaint's death in *The Black Jacobins* history, but particularly in the 1936 play *Toussaint Louverture* where it is a climactic scene, has come via Nemours.

Later, another new Haitian historian of importance for James would be Jean Fouchard, who established the Maroons—runaway slaves—as an important theme of Haitian historiography, making links between *marronage* and revolution.[61] James would later prove an important mentor to Fouchard's work, to which he would often make reference, as in his 1980 foreword to *The Black Jacobins* and drafts of his autobiography. James would also later present Fouchard's work to English readers when he was asked to write the preface to the 1981 English translation of Fouchard's book.[62]

What marks *The Black Jacobins* out from many previous non-Haitian histories of the revolution is the fact that it tells the story of the Haitian Revolution as a success—in fact, *The Story of the Only Successful Slave Revolt in History*, as the subtitle to James's first play, *Toussaint Louverture*, sums it up. As will be seen, at all points of their evolution—from article to play to history and back to play again—James's Haitian Revolution writings are profoundly dialogic. By uncovering the dialogic structure at the very heart of James's *Black Jacobins* project, we will see in the chapters that follow that James constructs his writing about the Haitian Revolution as a response to the denigrating representations of Toussaint and the revolution found in the likes of Sidney Harland, J. A. Froude, and T. Lothrop Stoddard. James will be seen to explicitly write back to these denigrating tales with his Haitian success story.

As an explicitly Marxist interpretation of the Haitian Revolution, it must also be acknowledged that James's 1938 history *The Black Jacobins* helped to alter standard Marxist historical explanations. Notably, James's 1938 work goes some way toward shifting the north-south Eurocentric view that revolution would occur first of all in Europe/advanced capitalist countries, and only subsequently thereafter would spread to the underdeveloped world.[63] And while it is true that the 1938 edition of *The Black Jacobins* ends with "let the blacks but hear from Europe the slogans of Revolution and the Internationale" (315), James does also indicate that revolution can be, and indeed already has been, initiated in colonized, underdeveloped parts of the world deemed backward according to the Marxist orthodoxy of the day, which expected backward colonial-type countries to follow the lead of the working classes in the most advanced countries. This idea is reworked in the 1938 history incarnation and is also developed later in the work's history, particularly in the light of James's elaboration, as part of the Johnson-Forest Tendency in the United States of the 1940s and early '50s, of his defining Marxist political positions. But already, from the very start of James's writings on this subject in the 1930s, the Haitian Revolution is held up as an alternative historical model for those in the colonized world, as a precursor to decolonization.

The Haitian Revolution (1791–1804) was the only successful slave-led revolt, one which inaugurated the first black republic and fundamentally reshaped the world historical map of the time. What links the subject of the revolution itself with James's pioneering *The Black Jacobins*, a work that revolutionized historiography, particularly that of the colonial world, is that both rewrite history from their very beginnings.[64] This is a rewriting project that then intensifies as it continues when James returns to his Haitian Revolution writings to rewrite them as history and as drama.

James and his historian descendants, including David Geggus and Laurent Dubois, have made much of the self-renaming and linguistic reshaping of the new world of Haitian independence.[65] Like the world of the French Revolution examined by Ronald Paulson, the Haitian Revolution renames a new revolutionary reality into being by imagining a radical break with the old contaminated lexicon of the colonial past, capable of resettling new beginnings from a ground zero of history.⁶⁶ Accordingly, James and his scions have examined how autonomous new words and names are invented, through which to reshape linguistically the new world of independence. Greatest among these renamings, as analyzed by James and subsequent historians following his lead, is the choice by the former slaves of the new name of Haiti for the country—the indigenous name for the island—with which the old colonial European-bestowed relic "Saint Domingue" was replaced.⁶⁷ This revolutionary onomastic process of self-renaming has also been read by James and others as changing words and their meanings, as is also evident in the very language used in the Act of Haitian Independence.⁶⁸ Declared on a symbolic date for new beginnings—January 1, 1804—this key proclamation has been read by Laurent Dubois, after James, as even rewriting and overhauling the French language bequeathed to Haitians by their former colonial masters through the coining of new verbs including *lugubrer*—"to gloom"—from the French adjective *lugubre* (gloomy): "le nom français *lugubre* encore nos contrées" (The French name still glooms our lands).⁶⁹ There have been several interpretations of this verbal neologism of independence in the context of a document that its author, Haitian revolutionary Jean-Jacques Dessalines's secretary Louis Boisrond-Tonnerre, declared should be written on parchment made from the skin of a white man, with his skull as an inkwell, his blood as the ink, and a bayonet for a pen, with this symbolic dissection of the colonizer's body being read as the fiercest symbolic rejection of all things French.⁷⁰

Marlene Daut has also examined how early Haitian memorialists, including Baron de Vastey and Boisrond-Tonnerre, used the colonizer's language to curse at the French, like Caliban in *The Tempest*, as they produced their own narratives of the Haitian Revolution as alternatives to those produced by the French.⁷¹ Her work has uncovered how these early Haitian authors prevented the Haitian past from being silenced, rewriting the Haitian Revolution in their turn. Like Vastey and Boisrond-Tonnerre, James combats negative representations of Haiti and its revolution in accounts from Europe and the United States.

After James, several historians have pointed to the Haitian Revolution as the most radical statement of the overlapping ages of revolution and enlightenment, arguing that it should rightfully be seen at the center of both ages, and not silenced on their margins, as has often been the case.⁷² During the Haitian Revolution, as James shows at length in his history and especially in his plays, former slaves reworked for themselves the banner words of the

Enlightenment/French Revolution idiom—words like freedom, equality, fraternity, and independence—reinterpreting such ideals within the framework of their own situation. Even the most enlightened of the Enlightenment thinkers advocated only a gradualist approach where slaves would gradually be prepared for abolition, with freedom something to be earned by deserving slaves, but also, most importantly, something to be granted benevolently by the colonial power of white abolitionists.[73] Instead, the Haitian Revolution is presented as a revolution of the slaves' own making; a self-emancipation. This is not, in other words, abolition as scripted by Europeans or Enlightenment thinkers. Rather, the radical antislavery of the Haitian Revolution is a story of major historical transformation of world importance where slaves vindicate themselves as active actors and as subjects of history in their own right; a vehement rejection of their condition as slaves—things, objects, and even "pieces of furniture" according to the *Code Noir*.[74] This inaugural self-fashioning that is the Haitian Revolution, whereby Haiti writes its own revolutionary agency, making its own history, thus already constitutes a radical rewriting of world history.

Central to the present study are the multiple layers of rewriting that intersect through the linchpin of these two bastions of historical significance: the Haitian Revolution and C. L. R. James's *Black Jacobins*. Rewriting is fundamentally linked with the practice of history in the Caribbean. From its first appearance, *The Black Jacobins* itself revolutionized the formation, scope, and perspective of historiography through its bold reinterpretation of events that themselves radically rewrote revolution and the world of Atlantic slaves. Where these rewriting layers—historical reshaping by the events of the Haitian Revolution and historiographical transformations inaugurated by *The Black Jacobins* and its rethinking of the history of the colonized world—come together most forcefully is in James's own extensive remaking of *The Black Jacobins* and in his reflections upon that long process of reconstruction itself. Chapter 2, "Making History," also probes James's collaboration with former protégé Eric Williams on ideas about capitalism and slavery.[75]

The 1949 French edition of *Les Jacobins noirs* gave a major historical boost to Haiti's celebrations of the *tricinquantenaire*—the 150th anniversary of the Haitian Revolution in 1954, only five years after this landmark publication. James had also hoped for his play *Toussaint Louverture* to be published by the same major French publisher, Gallimard, and he approached them about this in 1954, but to no avail. Around the time of the 1954 tricinquantenaire celebrations, James was also seriously planning to undertake a trip to Haiti in 1957–58. Chapter 5, on the afterlives of *The Black Jacobins*, examines James's correspondence at the time with a number of key Haitian intellectuals, including writer Félix Morisseau-Leroy and historian Étienne Charlier, as well as senior Haitian government and embassy figures, dating from the beginning of the rule of François "Papa Doc" Duvalier. Historiographically, James's *Black Jacobins* had a real impact in its land of inspiration. As Michel-Rolph Trouillot has suggested, it opened up to Haitians new vistas in both analysis and writing style.[76] The most prominent history book during the tricinquantenaire celebrations was Étienne Charlier's *Aperçu sur la formation historique de la nation haïtienne* (1954).[77] This book drew most on Charlier's main inspiration: *The Black Jacobins*, espousing an explicitly Marxist viewpoint—a first in local Haitian historiography.[78]

Only shortly after the 1954 tricinquantenaire celebrations, Duvalier, who claimed to be Dessalines's political heir, became Haiti's head of state. François "Papa Doc" Duvalier's dictatorial regime (1957–71), followed by that of his son Jean-Claude "Baby Doc" Duvalier (1971–86), had a determining impact on Haitian historiography. Papa Doc Duvalier used propaganda to manipulate history writing; a negative type of rewriting, portraying Duvalier as Dessalines's ideological son through the repetition of the phrase "François Duvalier, the Renovator," ending the list of Haitian historical heroes. Many historians were silenced, and some of Duvalier's left-wing opponents were killed while others left for exile, and those at home were only rarely published. Propaganda also promoted Duvalier's history book *Le Problème des classes à travers l'histoire d'Haïti* (1959), with its *noiriste* racialist interpretation of "classes" in Haiti, diametrically contrasting with the Marxist approach of James's history.[79]

This book argues that James should be seen as an early contributor to a deconstructionist type of postcolonial historiography, which has become most associated in the context of the Haitian Revolution with Michel-Rolph Trouillot's *Silencing the Past*. In his compelling account of the silencing of the Haitian Revolution, Trouillot draws attention to the uneven power in the production of sources, archives, and narratives, highlighting the silences that enter the process of historical production at four crucial moments: moments of fact creation (making sources), moments of fact assembly (making archives), moments of fact retrieval (making narratives), and the moment of retrospective significance (making history in the final instance).[80] This unequal access to source making continues to this day, Trouillot argues, with unequal access to archives and hence to history making; so much so that

Trouillot refers to archives as "products/symbols of neo-colonial domination."[81] This book argues that James writes back to such silencing, disavowing, and misrepresenting of Haitian history.[82]

When faced with such silencing, misrepresentation, gaps, and blanks vis-à-vis Caribbean slavery and anticolonial slave resistance in the official historical and cultural records, one response could be to throw up one's hands like V. S. Naipaul, merely lamenting the void of Caribbean nonhistory.[83] Confronted with Caribbean history, the question James and others after him invariably grapple with is: How to unsilence the past? How to represent the unrepresentable: the horrors of the forced migration of the slave trade/Middle Passage, and plantation slavery? On the advantages of specifically literary resources for the rewriting of Caribbean history, the model proposed by Martiniquan writer Édouard Glissant's notion of *une vision prophétique du passé* (a prophetic vision of the past) is extremely useful, and this is elaborated around his sole historical play, Monsieur Toussaint, based on the Haitian Revolution after James and his *Black Jacobins*, which Glissant cites as his main inspiration.[84] Central to this future-oriented vision for rewriting the past is Glissant's idea that the historian must be seconded by the poet in the Caribbean in order to fill the considerable gaps specific to Caribbean history—the slave trade, Middle Passage, plantation slavery, anticolonial rebellion, and so on. Faced with the gaps of Caribbean history, and to link pasts, presents, and futures, James, like Glissant, turns to the resources of a specifically literary form: those of drama. One of drama's main features is its particular stress on the present. Drama's performance aspect will be seen to be a crucial tool for the long process of making *The Black Jacobins*, and for the active and transitive process of unsilencing the Caribbean past.

Rewriting history is a practice that is central to new ways of doing history pioneered by James in *The Black Jacobins*, such as the history-from-below perspective, many of which are deliberate reactions against the traditional paradigm of historical objectivity: Rankean history and Ranke's oft-quoted summary of the historian's task to tell the past "wie es eigentlich gewesen" (as it actually was).[85] "History from above" is an alternative applicable label for this approach that is distinct from history from below. This book argues that James, throughout his lifelong elaboration of his *Black Jacobins* project, becomes a key player in the move to reorient Caribbean, and particularly Haitian, revolution historiography toward history from below. Already in the 1930s, James envisioned black ex-slaves functioning as a Greek chorus in his 1936 *Toussaint Louverture* play, and his 1938 history already constitutes a pioneering Marxist history from below *avant la lettre* of 1960s work by Albert Soboul, George Rudé, E. P. Thompson, Eric Hobsbawm, and others. Ideas previously pioneered by James in his 1930s work are crystallized, inspiring him to combine new from-below historical and political perspectives from the intervening period between the moments of his 1936 play and the 1967 play *The Black Jacobins*, applying them to new contexts. These include the influential history-from-below approaches of French and English Marxist historiography of the French Revolution and James's most important political theories, developed during his consequential political years in the United States (1940s–early 1950s), as part of the Johnson-Forest Tendency.

James's own role in pioneering historiographical approaches to history writing from below needs to be acknowledged. Most of all, the close family ties between his study and his mentee Carolyn Fick's groundbreaking history of Haiti from below need to be identified. Fick herself has revisited the 1973 origins of her 1990 study of the Haitian Revolution from below, and has outlined that her work bears the indelible stamp of James's "overpowering influence."[86] The story she tells of the making of her history illuminates the major roles played by her influential mentor James and his *Black Jacobins*. James it was, along with George Rudé, who first planted the seeds for her subsequent study on the Haitian Revolution. James and Rudé encouraged Fick from above to follow the lines of a more popular history of the Haitian Revolution. As Fick puts it, James had "left an indelible mark on the original conception and the eventual evolution."[87]

Fick admits that in 1973 she was "totally unaware" that James himself was "already thinking beyond the biographical analysis of Toussaint Louverture" toward an analysis focusing on "the revolutionary and creative power of untaught slaves," as indicated in his 1955 letter to Haitian historian Charlier.[88] Moreover, Fick reveals that had she known that James could have done the project himself, she would have been "terrified," and perhaps would never have agreed to undertake the new history from the bottom up. It is also informative to learn that James put his two mentees working toward an alternative historiography of the Haitian Revolution—Fick and Jean Fouchard—in touch with each other, leading Fouchard to direct Fick to her richest source for her research. Fick's study of the Haitian Revolution from below and Fouchard's focus on the Haitian maroons can be thought of as, at once, profoundly inspired by James's earlier *Black Jacobins* history, and as rewriting and correcting it in their turn in line with new historiographical approaches from below.

On the question of leaders and masses in James's famous work, Fick's own assessment in the pages of her *The Making of Haiti* was:

> Although he was chiefly concerned in 1938 with the role of the leadership of the revolution, i.e. the black Jacobins and particularly Toussaint Louverture, the inarticulate masses are never lost from view, and though their activities are not always explicitly documented in the book, it is they, nonetheless, who provide the initiative and impetus, if not the driving force of any insurrectionary movement. So for the first time, the revolutionary potential of the masses is treated as an integral part of the revolutionary process, but again these masses, though vitally important, are not in themselves the direct subject of the book, chiefly concerned as it is with the problem of leadership and colonial struggle. And like Sannon's book, it is a study of the revolution through the historical biography of its greatest leader, Toussaint Louverture.[89]

Today, when James's *Black Jacobins* is discussed in conjunction with Fick's study, there remains a tendency to present these two works as almost diametrically opposed, as in Alyssa Goldstein Sepinwall's 2013 comment: "Yet where James suggested that the Revolution 'was almost entirely the work of a single man—Toussaint Louverture,' recent work has looked at the revolution more from below, tracing the efforts of multiple kinds of actors."[90]

What I am suggesting instead is that James's approach is less diametrically opposed to that of his mentees than previously assumed, including Carolyn Fick, Jean Fouchard, and their from-below historiographical approaches. From the beginning of the 1930s and through the 1950s–80s, James's retelling of the story of the Haitian Revolution should be recognized as the crucial precursor to historical approaches from below. It will be shown that James preempts pioneering studies of European crowds from below by Soboul, Rudé, Thompson, Hobsbawm, and others, taking them in new directions by widening the focus to Haitian revolutionary crowds, and from sansculottes, *bras-nus*, and *enragés* to the *menu peuple* mass of ordinary black ex-slaves.

Especially in the 1967 play *The Black Jacobins*, this crowd, representing the great mass of slaves, will be seen to function as a chorus, operating as an organizing tool for theater from below, as in the type of radical Marxist theater theorized by Augusto Boal.[91] And while it is certainly true that

The Black Jacobins history in both its 1938 and 1963 editions does continue to tell the story of the Haitian Revolution through the historical biography of its greatest leader, Toussaint Louverture, it will be demonstrated that as *The Black Jacobins* evolves, James increasingly points the way toward a type of history writing that would break the mold of political biography of great leaders. Instead, as he writes out the initial hero Toussaint Louverture, James will also be seen to write in more popular leaders, including Moïse and Samedi Smith. Yet James's *Black Jacobins* in all its forms is more than a history from below. Like other Marxist histories, it also illuminates the importance of crises in the ruling class and high politics, or history from above, and is best seen as a total history.

Chapter Outline

Chapter 1, "Toussaint Louverture Takes Center Stage: The 1930s," charts James's evolving interest in Toussaint Louverture and the Haitian Revolution from his earliest writings in a 1931 article on this subject up to the 1936 staging of his play *Toussaint Louverture*. Here the dialogic aspect of James's first 1931 Haitian Revolution–related intervention—"The Intelligence of the Negro: A Few Words with Dr. Harland"—is uncovered: a dialogic quality that will be shown to be boosted by James's turn to the theater in his first full-length Haitian Revolution–based work. Connections are found between James's vindicatory action-centered approach of making theater and doing politics. This chapter reflects on James's uses of drama as a different type of representing machine than fiction in order to bring protagonist Toussaint's biography to life. A relative chronology is proposed for all the *Toussaint Louverture* play scripts consulted, including one interesting set of shaky handwritten changes that begin to write in the character of Toussaint's adoptive nephew, Moïse. Analyzed here is the politicization of James's deployment of Toussaint with the past of the Haitian Revolution used for vindication purposes as a great success story and as a vehicle for propaganda. Collaboration with lead actor Paul Robeson is then explored as a crucial building block for the final shaping of the two 1936 *Toussaint Louverture* performances.

In chapter 2, "Making History: *The Black Jacobins* (1938)," the focus is entirely on the first edition of *The Black Jacobins* history to allow comparison with its predecessor, the 1936 *Toussaint Louverture* play, and to explore the advantages that telling the past as history brings to James the historian as he shapes his historical narrative line. Genealogies of *The Black Jacobins* history are surveyed with special attention to French connections and collaborations with James's former protégé Eric Williams. An important section considers James's representation of Toussaint as icon and symbol in the 1938 history, and that of a larger cast of black Jacobins. The configuration of Toussaint's dialogic epistolary exchanges is demonstrated to be an important part of James's method. Challenging David Scott's interpretation that the 1938 history is not a tragic text, that text is shown to be already full of Toussaint's tragic flaws as contributing factors to his downfall. Finally, the first 1938 history edition's closing symbolism of defiant upright rebellious images is explored.

Chapter 3, "Rewriting History: *The Black Jacobins* (1963)," tracks the impact of changes made throughout the revised 1963 history. Revisions include fundamental changes to Marxist language and terminology, and the refiguring of leader Toussaint Louverture in the progressive metamorphosis of the text. On tragedy and *The Black Jacobins*, more is made of the fact that tragedy is a genre that pertains to the theater, and that the reader is encouraged to watch the protagonist's blunders and final catastrophe as they would watch a tragedy on stage or screen. The chapter assesses James's rethinking of sources, bibliography, and positioning of the mass of ex-slaves as a chorus. Additionally, the function of the most prominent 1963 change of all is analyzed: the addition of an appendix titled "From Toussaint Louverture to Fidel Castro." Important new directions sketched out in the 1963 changes are shown to reflect James's political evolution in the intervening years, especially his elaboration during his involvement with the Johnson-Forest Tendency (1940s–early 1950s) of his most significant political ideas, history-from-below perspectives, and the results of intensive study of dialectics, leaps, and speculative thought.

Chapter 4, "Reshaping the Past as Drama (1967)," turns to the remaking of *The Black Jacobins* as a second play. After establishing the relative chronology of all available play scripts for this 1967 version, using methodologies from genetic criticism and book history, this chapter considers the special resources of drama that are exploited by James to show the past of the Haitian Revolution. The main objective here is to give James his proper due for the important role he played in writing the play. How does James's rewriting of *The Black Jacobins* as a play in 1967 incorporate changes to the protagonists and alternative ways of doing history, Marxism, and drama? How is the relationship of the Haitian revolutionary leadership to the popular masses rethought? My reading of the play focuses on the epilogue, arguing that it constitutes a unique crossover document between play and political speech, pamphlet, or interview. Ultimately, the epilogue is seen to change completely the key and register of the play's ending.

Chapter 5 is titled "Future Directions: Afterlives of *The Black Jacobins*" and maps out some of the work's impacts and afterlives after and beyond James's own rewriting of his Haitian Revolution–inspired material. My closing section addresses key translations, subsequent performances of the play, the impact of *The Black Jacobins* in Haiti itself, and monuments to James and his work, including the setting up of archives, libraries, institutes, and centers, all bearing his name.

A Note on Transcription Conventions

In terms of transcription conventions as applied in this book—especially in chapter 3—I use bold type to indicate James's own subsequent **additions** in a later draft or printed edition. Crossing out with strikethrough is used to signal his ~~deletions~~ of material. Otherwise, I follow James and his correspondents in their use of underline, italics, and all caps for emphasis.

1 | Toussaint Louverture Takes Center Stage:
The 1930s

This chapter charts James's evolving interest in Toussaint Louverture and the Haitian Revolution from his earliest writings in a 1931 article on this subject up to the 1936 staging of his first play, *Toussaint Louverture*. It uncovers the dialogic quarrel of James's first Haitian Revolution–related intervention in 1931—his article "The Intelligence of the Negro: A Few Words with Dr. Harland."[1] When James turned to theater in his first full-length Haitian Revolution–based work, *Toussaint Louverture*, this dialogic quality increased. Exploring the dramatic origins of the *Black Jacobins* project, this chapter argues that the first play is almost a one-man show. Other characters do feature, but Louverture is the unifying character who features in almost every scene, bar the final one following the climactic death-in-prison scene. Even at the end of the play, Toussaint is invoked at length, and news of his death spurs the remaining revolutionaries on to unify and avenge him. This focus on Toussaint is, however, offset by the chorus of ex-slaves who undergo a radical transformation from being mostly "naked, wearing either a loin-cloth or a shirt ... dirty and unkempt" to the ending, where they form a "solid mass" who "In dress and bearing [...] are a civilised people."[2]

Until recently, one little-known fact about James's *Black Jacobins* project was that it began and ended life as a play. This chapter connects James's vindicatory action-centered approach with his making of theater, history, and politics. This account of the genesis and evolution of James's first play charts its transformations from script to script. A relative chronology is proposed for all the *Toussaint Louverture* play scripts consulted. James increasingly politicizes his deployment of Toussaint using the Haitian Revolution for vindication purposes as a great success story and as a vehicle for propaganda. Collaboration with lead actor Paul Robeson is then explored as crucial for shaping the two March 1936 *Toussaint Louverture* performances.

Toussaint Louverture versus Harlandacity

"I would have preferred to write about Toussaint Louverture," wrote an exasperated C. L. R. James in a 1931 article refuting the pseudoscientific racism of a certain Dr. Sidney C. Harland, an English scientist based at the Imperial College of Tropical Agriculture in Trinidad, and his article "Race Admixture."[3] It is in this riposte to Harland that James makes his first published use of Toussaint Louverture, and the biographical portrait of Toussaint he sketches in 1931 prefigures his later work on the Haitian Revolution.

James's dialogic history writing will be analyzed from the viewpoint of the Caribbean quarrel with history, as theorized by Edward Baugh.[4] James writes back to misrepresentations of the Caribbean by the likes of Harland, Stoddard, Froude, and others.[5] A key source of inspiration for James in the 1931 article, it can be assumed, would have been the famous book-length rebuttal by black Trinidadian schoolmaster John Jacob Thomas in *Froudacity: West Indian Fables Explained* (1889) of English historian James Anthony Froude's notorious travelogue *The English in the West Indies; or, The Bow of Ulysses* (1888).[6] Indeed, from the later vantage point of 1969, James himself would pen an introduction to Thomas's *Froudacity*, correcting at length "Froudacious" Froude.[7] In 1969, James would rewrite every single Froudian racist sentence about Haiti on a single page, transforming each one from passive to active voice where the actions of the Haitian people were concerned. This active and transitive process of unsilencing, this chapter argues, counters the general silencing of the Haitian Revolution by Western historiography, as theorized by Michel-Rolph Trouillot.

James's rewriting of imperialist Froude-type history turns the focus instead to achievement and vindication. Robert Hill has identified James's heavy investment in "men of action," including Toussaint Louverture, who are all linked by achievement.[8] James's positive vindication of the symbolic currency of the Haitian Revolution and Toussaint Louverture is rooted in a Caribbean intellectual tradition, including Anténor Firmin (1885), Hannibal Price (1900), and Louis Joseph Janvier (1884), which counteracts racist tirades belittling and demonizing Haiti's revolution and independence.[9]

Using history and the biography of Toussaint Louverture, James's 1931 quarrel with Dr. Harland provides a prototype for James's later writings on the Haitian Revolution, delivering hammer blows to Harland's attempts to "prove" the dangers of "race admixture" and black inferiority. Toussaint Louverture constitutes in James's early article the main prong of his point-by-point rebuttal, and is the main weapon in his arsenal against Harland. Invoking Gobineau, James underscores that Harland's ideas are built on arbitrary and "unscientific" opinions, which are so "antiquated" that it is as if Harland's mind were moving in a previous decade.[10] James redeploys the same statistics as Harland to make a mockery of them.[11]

What I want to pinpoint is the intensely dialogic quality of James's first published article featuring Toussaint Louverture—a dialogism subsequently used as a primary tool in his plays and history versions on the Haitian Revolution, despite these texts being less explicitly framed as an address to an interlocutor. The dialogic driving James's retelling of the story of the Haitian Revolution is put in motion by James's quarrel with Harland. As James dismantles Harland's dubious racialism, the framework James uses to shape his "few words with Dr. Harland" is that of the quarrel, and the quarrel motif is here a vital means of contesting assumptions about racial inferiority.

This idea of the quarrel with history is a productive framework for analyzing the intensely dialogic qualities of James's 1931 riposte. Harland's case for "negro inferiority" rests squarely upon ahistoricity and presenting this phenomenon as incontrovertible fact. In order to counter Eurocentric colonial history and ahistoricity, James must therefore write of history. This is where we see the broad outlines of the future play *Toussaint Louverture* and *The Black Jacobins* history taking shape before our eyes: James's quarrel with history itself constitutes these works.

In "The West Indian Writer and His Quarrel with History," Baugh paints a picture of Caribbean quarreling where history is written about in negative, adversarial terms as nightmare, bogeyman, blight, nothingness, historylessness, absence, void, negation, pain, wound, catastrophe, powerlessness, denial, invisibility, shame, problem, gap, silence, alien. A line from Derek Walcott's "The Schooner Flight"—"I met History Once, but he ain't recognize me"—personifies the difficult relationship between the Caribbean and history as an opposition between antagonists: the unrecognized Caribbean versus supercilious History embodied as a white colonial "Sir," in plantertype attire "in cream linen and cream hat," and with plenty of superiority besides.[12] When James has "A Few Words with Dr. Harland," we already see a version of *The Black Jacobins* in microcosm that is specifically framed as an answering back to racialist perspectives on black inferiority. Instead, Louverture is the prototype for actively making history.

When the bare bones of Toussaint's biography are sketched out in James's 1931 article, Toussaint is portrayed as a quintessential man of action when his achievements are listed. As straightforward as this listing of actions and achievements might seem, James's response piece itself constitutes that relationship between action and history as it goes along. In stylistic terms, this passage is almost breathless in its exposition of Toussaint's actions. In the simplest language and shortest sentences possible, actions are piled high, one on top of the other, through quick-fire parataxis. This accumulation of actions is further reinforced by strings of active verbs as Toussaint springs from one action to the next at a breakneck pace. Action is therefore not only the subject of the biographical passage, it is also a key constitutive feature of the means of representation. At this early stage of James's writing about the Haitian Revolution, we already see him making important decisions about how to represent the past and how to rethink the proper subject of history.

Action is central to how we perceive any history, but especially in Caribbean contexts: history can be seen either as events that befall us, always from elsewhere, or as things we actively do, use, make ourselves.[13] Active versus passive thus signals a crucial dividing line at the heart of debates about Caribbean history. What is significant about James's early biographical sketch is that Toussaint is the active subject of nearly every single active verb. Action is the focal point of this biography, and action is personified in Toussaint Louverture; it makes him the emblematic hero of Caribbean past achievements.

In the foreword to the 1980 edition of *The Black Jacobins* history, James would reveal his motivations for engaging with the Haitian Revolution in the first place. Having been "tired of reading and hearing about Africans being persecuted and oppressed in Africa, in the Middle Passage, in the USA and all over the Caribbean," he made the conscious decision to represent the Caribbean past through the prism of "people of African descent [. . .] taking action on a grand scale and shaping other people to their own needs."[14] What James outlines in this statement is a decision to shift the dominant voice of Caribbean history telling from passive to active. Already prefigured in the 1931 article, we see in microcosm James's action-centered approach to making Caribbean history and his contribution to rewriting previous colonial history of the region by shifting all verb forms from passive to active voice, and by transforming the inferior object of other people's history into the protagonist, hero, and active subject of the Caribbean's own history.

When James began to teach and write, there was little sense of West Indian history or literature to support him. As he put it, "I don't know much about West Indian literature in the 1930s—there wasn't much to know."[15] History is the primary tool James employs to rebut the likes of Harland, Froude, and

Crown Colony misgovernment in the British West Indies when strongly making the case for West Indian self-government in 1932–33 publications.[16]

Shortly after arriving in Britain, James had his book *The Life of Captain Cipriani* privately printed by a small press in Nelson, Lancashire, in 1932. Captain Cipriani was a white Creole Trinidadian labor and political leader. The 1932 political biography of Cipriani and the invocation of Toussaint's biography in the 1931 Harland response piece provide the biographical model of historical and political analysis on which James subsequently builds his dramatization of Louverture's life story in the 1936 play, and the history of the Haitian Revolution as an account of Louverture's life in his 1938 history.

In 1933, James was asked to shorten the book drastically for publication by Virginia and Leonard Woolf's Hogarth Press, London. The resulting abridged pamphlet was retitled *The Case for West-Indian Self-Government*. These early works are important milestones along the road toward James's Haitian Revolution–related writings. Properly speaking, these related early works in 1932–33 constitute James's first rewriting. In this case, changes were instigated by Leonard Woolf and Hogarth Press, who asked James to slash almost all of the biographical detail about Cipriani's life. These changes prefigure James's 1960s reworking of *The Black Jacobins* history, which would remove some of Toussaint's biography to focus on anticolonial struggle more generally. The 1933 title tells its contents: it makes the case that the West Indies are already fit for self-government or dominion status instead of alien Crown Colony misgovernment.

Going to history and biography to show that there is nothing innately inferior about West Indians, James answers the charge, made notably by Froude, that the West Indies have no history of their own. No history of one's own would mean no viable representation of history, hence the importance of historical representations to counterbalance flagrant misrepresentation. James, as sections of his unpublished autobiography and *Beyond a Boundary* reveal, would first explore the relationship with history in pedagogical settings. This experience of teaching history influenced his making representations of Caribbean history—an active, transitive process—whereby Harland and Froude's "inferior" West Indian object would instead become the protagonist and hero and subject of the Caribbean's own history. James started to make theatrical representations. Before coming to England in 1932, James had already been involved in theater, staging plays including Molière's *Le bourgeois gentilhomme* and Shakespeare's *Othello* in colonial Trinidad. It was also there that he had gone on to write "a now-vanished drama about local life," producing it with his students for the public.[17] In terms of politics, he had supported Cipriani's Trinidad Workingmen's Association before leaving Trinidad. Once in England, from 1932 on, he would continue to make theater and do politics. It was in Nelson, Lancashire, that James discovered Trotsky's *History of the Russian Revolution* and Marxism. London was also an important place for his political activities, as he became a Marxist, a Trotskyist, joining and later chairing the Marxist Group inside the Independent Labour Party.[18]

Recovering the Play *Toussaint Louverture*: The Story of the Only Successful Slave Revolt in History

Not until 2013 and the publication of the Hull manuscript was there ready access to the long-lost 1936 play script itself. Before this twenty-first-century discovery, *Toussaint Louverture* was often briefly mentioned in passing as a stepping stone in James's 1930s career to the more famous 1938 history. A handful of commentators including Reinhard Sander, Nicole King, and Frank Rosengarten have cross-read the 1936 playbill and contemporary reviews of the two March 1936 performances against the published script of James's later 1967 play *The Black Jacobins*.[19] One crucial piece of evidence from the two *Toussaint Louverture* performances is the original playbill. Even after discovery of the play scripts, this program continues to be an important piece of substantiating evidence for the running order of the actual performances on March 15 and 16, 1936.

The program gives the breakdown of the acts, scenes, characters, and actors in the play as performed. Such clues enable us to project what the actual performance script would have contained. The play as performed was clearly a streamlined version compared to longer play scripts including the Hull script, on which the 2013 critical edition of the play is based. As for the playwright's own author's note in the 1936 program, signed "C. L. R. J.," this offers useful information for dating the play's genesis: "The play was conceived four years ago [1932] and was completely finished by the autumn of 1934."[20]

New pieces in the puzzle of the 1936 *Toussaint Louverture* play's genesis are being discovered all the time, and no doubt still more play script versions are out there. Scripts have been found in locations dotted around the world in various states of genesis. This is surely both testament to, and remnant of, James's collaborative working and political methods, through which James would send documents at different stages to political comrades and other correspondents, located both near and far. One reason why all new finds of long-lost *Toussaint Louverture* play scripts are exciting is that the playwright himself did not even possess a copy of the play for many years—until the 1950s—according to Selma James, C. L. R.'s widow, and his literary executor, Robert A. Hill.[21]

James's own correspondence among his papers refers to copies of the play being sent out to, and acknowledged by, several correspondents, including the publisher Gallimard in France and the Haitian embassy in London in August–September 1953, after James's deportation from the United States and return to Britain. This was on the eve of the 150th anniversary of Haitian independence (1954), and James underlined the timeliness of the 1936 *Toussaint Louverture* play for marking the anniversary celebrations, as he sought to have the play translated into French and performed in the land of its inspiration.[22]

It appears therefore that James had the play script of *Toussaint Louverture* back in his possession from the 1950s onward, after his return to England. This information is helpful in charting the milestones in *Toussaint Louverture*'s genesis. In particular, it suggests that handwritten additions in two copies of the script stored at University of the West Indies (UWI Box 9, Folder 227) represent intermediate staging posts on the road from *Toussaint Louverture* in 1936 and *The Black Jacobins* history in 1938 to the 1963 revised edition of the history and the play *The Black Jacobins* in 1967.

Previous scholarship on *Toussaint Louverture* has tended to focus on a single script: Christian Høgsbjerg bases his 2013 Duke University Press critical edition on the Hull script, which is consequently now the most readily available version of the play; and Fionnghuala Sweeney bases her work on the Moorland-Spingarn script.[23] Further points of reference will be Mary Lou Emery's comments on the Yale Beinecke Library script, among the Richard Wright papers, and one of the University of the West Indies scripts.[24] My analysis contributes to the project of recovering *Toussaint Louverture* by adding a comparative dimension to the mix. Ten scripts of the 1936 play are compared, along with the published act 2, scene 1, which appeared in *Life and Letters Today* in spring 1936, around the same time as the March performances.[25] Also analyzed here for the first time is the script from the National Library and Information System Authority of Trinidad and Tobago (NALIS) discovered only in autumn 2014 by Høgsbjerg, and not processed and digitalized by NALIS until 2016. This chapter proposes that the NALIS play script is the closest one to the actual full-length performance script of *Toussaint Louverture*.

The ten scripts analyzed are:

1. THE HULL PLAY SCRIPT was catalogued (DJH/21), formerly among the Jock Haston papers at the University of Hull, and now located in the Hull History Centre at U DJH/21/1.[26]

2. THE MOORLAND-SPINGARN SCRIPT is housed in the Alain Locke Papers (Box 164–68, Folder 8), Manuscript Divisions, Moorland-Spingarn Research Center, Howard University, Washington, DC. Alain LeRoy Locke (1885–1954), a distinguished African American writer and philosopher, was proclaimed Father of the Harlem Renaissance.[27] As the cover sheet of the Moorland-Spingarn script gives names and addresses—"C. L. R. James, 9 Heathcote Street, London W.C.1" and "Return to Mrs. Paul Robeson, 19 Buckingham Street, Adelphi, W.C.2"—Fionnghuala Sweeney has suggested that this copy would have "circulated between James and Eslanda Robeson in the lead-up to the period of rehearsal, and that circulation may have been an important part of the evolution of the eventual staging."[28]

3. THE DARTMOUTH SCRIPT is in the Errol Hill Papers (ML-77, Box 70), Rauner Special Collections Library, Dartmouth College. Hill tells how this script came into his possession in a 1998 letter to Michelle A. Stephens: he was presented with the typewritten copy by James, who was under house arrest in Trinidad in March 1965 on the orders of Prime Minister Dr. Eric Williams.[29]

4. THE YALE SCRIPT can be found in the Beinecke Rare Book and Manuscript Library among the Richard Wright Papers at JWJ MSS 3. Richard Wright was a close friend of James and the latter's second wife, Constance Webb, who would later write Richard Wright's biography (1968), and share memories of the writer in her own memoirs.[30]

5. THE COLUMBIA SCRIPT of *Toussaint Louverture* is housed among the C. L. R. James Papers, MS#1529 in the Rare Book and Manuscript Library, Columbia University Library, New York (Box 5, Folder 18). These papers were previously located at the C. L. R. James Institute in New York.

6–9. At UWI, there is one copy of *Toussaint Louverture* in Box 12, Folder 275. There are also three copies in Box 9, Folder 227 (marked copies 1, 2, and 3). These **UWI SCRIPTS** are located in the C. L. R. James Collection, Sc 82,

West Indiana and Special Collections, the Alma Jordan Library, University of the West Indies, St. Augustine, Trinidad and Tobago. These papers were previously housed at James's home in London.

10. THE NALIS SCRIPT is located in Series 14, Box 6, master file number 14837 in the Sir Learie Constantine Collection, National Library and Information System Authority of Trinidad and Tobago, Port-of-Spain, Trinidad. This script was processed in summer 2016, and was donated by Lord Constantine's daughter, Gloria Valère. This script has been signed and dated by the playwright. Beside the title, James has added in pen "by C. L. R. James." In the top left-hand corner is written, also in James's hand:

> *Sept 5, 1935.*
> *Scarborough.*
> *From Nello.*
> *For Harry.*
> *With best wishes and many*
> *thanks for lots of things.*

The dedicatee here is James's great friend Harry Spencer from Nelson, Lancashire, to whom *The Black Jacobins* history is also prominently dedicated in 1938. Harry Spencer had raised the sum required for James's first research trip to Paris.[31] Out of this raw research material was born both the 1936 play and the 1938 history. When James lived with the Constantines in Nelson, Spencer lived nearby.

Toward a Relative Chronology of the *Toussaint Louverture* Play Scripts

What emerges when all ten scripts are compared are five basic generations of scripts with a sixth additional layer of rewriting:

1. Hull/Moorland-Spingarn
2. Dartmouth/Yale
3. Columbia/UWI Box 12, Folder 275
4. NALIS script
5. UWI Box 9, Folder 227, copies 1, 2, and 3
6. Handwritten annotations in James's own hand from a later date on copies 1 and 2, housed at UWI, Box 9, Folder 227

Among the ten play scripts I have consulted, some are exact carbon copies, as in the case of the Hull and Moorland-Spingarn scripts; the Columbia and UWI Box 12, Folder 275 scripts; and the three scripts housed at UWI in Box 9, Folder 227, of which copy 3 is incomplete.

Emerging as the earliest versions are the identical Hull and Moorland-Spingarn scripts. Both share the same typographical errors, letter-type pressure variations, alignment, and overtyping, among other features. The Hull script appears to be the sharper of the two copies, suggesting that it comes from higher up the pile of carbon copies. They seem to be the earliest scripts because many of the handwritten corrections and deletions are then subsequently made throughout the other play scripts. At 109 pages each, these two scripts are also the longest, which suggests that they are the furthest removed from a streamlined performance script. Both scripts are also corrected in the same hand, which does not seem to match samples of James's own handwriting and signature on the cover sheets of the NALIS and Moorland-Spingarn scripts. Even though the actual corrections are not written in his hand, they still likely constitute authorial revisions via dictation during the typing and emendation processes.[32] James is not identified anywhere on the Hull script as the author, whereas the playwright's name was handwritten twice (once crossed out) on the messy cover page of the Moorland-Spingarn script. One difference between the scripts is that the Moorland-Spingarn script does have a cover page. This features information about rehearsals suggesting that it was already circulating between playwright and lead actor in the lead-up to rehearsals.[33] Not much time therefore appears to separate the earliest scripts from the rehearsal period.

Next in the sequence come the Dartmouth and Yale scripts. Both scripts are cleaner than the Hull/Moorland-Spingarn scripts, containing no handwritten additions or deletions. Furthermore, they incorporate the handwritten additions from the earlier Hull/Moorland-Spingarn generation of scripts. Despite not being identical carbon copies—Dartmouth has 95 pages, while Yale has 99—they belong together in the same generation of scripts because they contain many of the same misspellings. Visually and materially, the Dartmouth and Yale scripts look alike, sharing many similar features, such as spacing, page layout, and pagination. They also share virtually identical cover sheets. The additional designation *A Play in 3 Acts* of both the earlier Hull and Moorland-Spingarn versions is missing. Unlike those scripts, the Dartmouth and Yale scripts do clearly feature the playwright's typewritten name.

Then comes the third generation: the Columbia and UWI Box 12, Folder 275 scripts. Exact carbon copies, they are corrected in the same hand. These drafts do not have a typed cover sheet, a feature they share only with the Hull and Moorland-Spingarn manuscripts, although the latter does have a unique handwritten cover sheet. Without any cover sheet, James's actual name does not figure on either script. These two particular scripts contain a number of quite wordy asides that do not feature in any other script:

> Toussaint: [...] Trumpeter! Sound the attention. **The attention only, mind you. Last time you sounded the order fire before all our men had jumped down the ditch, and some were killed by our own shots.**
> **Trumpeter: General—I—I**
> Toussaint: I know. Wait for me to give the command.[34]

Toussaint's surname is written without an apostrophe as Louverture all throughout five of the play scripts: the Hull, Moorland-Spingarn, Dartmouth, Yale, and NALIS scripts. However, "L'Ouverture" is spelled with an apostrophe in four copies of the script: the Columbia and UWI scripts (Box 12, Folder 275, and the three copies in Box 9, Folder 227). Another difference is the addition of a single word to the play's designation, *A Chronicle Play in 3 Acts*, in the Columbia and UWI scripts. "Chronicle" underlines that the gravitational center of this drama is biographical, centering on the career of a single exceptional historical character—Toussaint Louverture—with the entire play used to illustrate the life, character, and political development of the hero.[35]

As for the three UWI copies housed in Box 9, Folder 227, my impression is that these copies were typed out again, using one of the earlier scripts as the basis. It is likely that this retyping took place after, possibly quite a long time after, the two 1936 performances. Copies 1 and 2 of the UWI Box 9, Folder 227 scripts contain handwritten additions made in James's own hand, probably in the 1950s while reworking his Haitian play for publication in France by Gallimard (rejected) and prospective performances in Haiti itself.[36] Their content resembles the earlier generations of scripts (Hull/Moorland-Spingarn, Dartmouth/Yale), and it is as if these three copies act as a bridge from the four earlier scripts of *Toussaint Louverture* to James's second play, titled *The Black Jacobins*, completely bypassing changes made as the play approached performance in the NALIS script and the 1936 scene published in *Life and Letters Today*.

So, while the content of these UWI scripts in Folder 227 resembles that of earlier generations, visually the three scripts look different from earlier ones. What I am proposing is that the three UWI copies in Folder 227 were typed not long before James made the handwritten changes on these pages. These three copies designate the play a chronicle play, as is the case for the Columbia and UWI Box 12, Folder 275 scripts, but here all three contain a cover sheet listing the author and the play as well as the chronicle genre. Visually, these three copies are given the look of a dramatic page setup. Running heads indicate the act, scene, and page numbers for each individual page.[37] These typographic configurations of the play's pagination immediately identify these scripts visually with the dramatic genre. The use of a theatrical notation system gives these scripts the look of prompt notes for a performance script. However, it is far from certain that this was ever their actual status or function. Instead, the more distinctively dramatic page setting suggests a later, renewed attempt to take the play to the stage and to expand the textual information into performance.

Toward the Staging of *Toussaint Louverture*: Changes to the NALIS Script

Considered together, these nine play scripts examined thus far are much of a muchness, with some small and significant variations, enabling the reconstruction of the scripts' chronology, and which suggest that they were produced in relatively close succession. One play script is, however, markedly different from the other nine consulted: the NALIS script, which was only processed in summer 2016. This NALIS script, usefully the only script to be dated (September 1935), offers a vantage point from which to survey the evolution of *Toussaint Louverture*. In terms of chronology, this chapter proposes that the NALIS script is currently the closest to the performance script when compared with the structure of the play according to the 1936 program accompanying the two actual performances. The other nine scripts all contain a total of eleven scenes, across three acts. As per the 1936 program, the NALIS script now contains only eight scenes in its three acts, with three scenes completely cut from the play. Act 1 originally contained four scenes, which became two scenes; act 2 still contains two scenes, while act 3 has five scenes reduced to four. Overall, the play has evolved as shown in table 1.1. The NALIS script and the program give us the streamlined version of the play with eight scenes instead of eleven. What are the three deleted scenes? And

Table 1.1 From Page to Stage: Evolution of *Toussaint Louverture* (1936)

Note: Bold font indicates added text. An arrow indicates progression from an earlier play script to a later one, and from one earlier variant to a later one. My editorial comments appear in square brackets.

HULL SCRIPT	NALIS SCRIPT	SCENE PUBLISHED IN *LIFE AND LETTERS TO-DAY* 14, NO. 1 (1936)	PLAY AS PERFORMED (1936 PROGRAM)
Act 1, scene 1. A moonlit evening. The verandah of M. Bullet's villa on the outskirts of Cap François.	[Scene cut.]		[Scene cut.]
Act 1, scene 2. August 6th, 1791. The depths of a forest.	→ Act 1, scene 1. The depths of a forest in the French portion of the West Indian island of San Domingo. August 6th, 1791. **An hour before midnight.** [New time specified.]		Act 1, scene 1. The depths of a forest in the French portion of the West Indian island of San Domingo, August 6th, 1791.
Act 1, scene 3. The slave encampment at La Grande Rivière. April 1793.	→ Act 1, scene **2**. The slave encampment at La Grande Rivière. April, 1793.		Act 1, scene 2. The slave encampment at La Grande Rivière, April, 1793.
Act 1, scene 4. Early 1794. The mountain retreat of Toussaint's wife and two sons.	[Scene cut.]		[Scene cut.]
Act 2, scene 1. Five years later. A room in the Government buildings in Port-au-Prince.	Act 2, scene 1. **Eight** years later. A room in the Government **B**uildings in Port-au-Prince. [Three years added.]	Act 2, scene 1. [Added paragraph contextualizing scene and imperialist rivalry among great powers.] A room in the Government Buildings in Port-au-Prince.	Act 2, scene 1. **Eight years later.** A room in the Government Buildings in Port-au-Prince. [Time reinserted.]

Table 1.1 (cont'd)

Note: Bold font indicates added text. An arrow indicates progression from an earlier play script to a later one, and from one earlier variant to a later one. My editorial comments appear in square brackets.

HULL SCRIPT	NALIS SCRIPT	SCENE PUBLISHED IN *LIFE AND LETTERS TO-DAY* 14, NO. 1 (1936)	PLAY AS PERFORMED (1936 PROGRAM)
Act 2, scene 2. Nearly two years later. Bonaparte's apartment in the Tuileries. [Handwritten time indication in Hull, but typed in UWI275; UWI227.]	Act 2, scene 2. Bonaparte's apartment in the Tuileries [No time indicated.]		Act 2, scene 2. Bonaparte's apartment in the Tuileries. [No time indicated.]
Act 3, Scene 1. Toussaint's hut in the mountains. Early 1802.	[Scene cut.]		[Scene cut.]
Act 3, scene 2. March 24th, 1802. About six o'clock in the evening. The fortress of Crête-à-Pierrot in San Domingo. On a rampart running diagonally. [Features Toussaint.]	→ Act 3, scene **1**. March 24th, 1802. About six o'clock in the evening. The fortress of Crête-à-Pierrot in San Domingo. [Features Dessalines.]		Act 3, scene 1. The Fortress of Crête-à-Pierrot in San Domingo, March 24th, **1801**, about six o'clock in the evening. [Change of date by one year, location first instead of time. Toussaint is again the revolutionary featured.]
Act 3, scene 3. Late in 1801, Leclerc's villa on the outskirts of Cap François. [Year remains 1801 despite previous Hull script scene dated March 24th, 1802.]	→ Act 3, scene **2**. Late in 1801. Leclerc's villa on the outskirts of Cap François. **There is a balcony with steps leading down to the courtyard below.** [Scene elaborated.]		Act 3, scene 2. Leclerc's villa on the outskirts of Cap François, late 1801. [Location comes first and date second, unlike other versions.]

Table 1.1 (*cont'd*)

Note: Bold font indicates added text. An arrow indicates progression from an earlier play script to a later one, and from one earlier variant to a later one. My editorial comments appear in square brackets.

HULL SCRIPT	NALIS SCRIPT	SCENE PUBLISHED IN *LIFE AND LETTERS TO-DAY* 14, NO. 1 (1936)	PLAY AS PERFORMED (1936 PROGRAM)
Act 3, scene 4. Late in 1801 → **Late in 1802.** Toussaint's cell in a prison in the Alps. [Date handcorrected in Hull, corrected in UWI275, but omitted in Dartmouth and Yale, which both just read, "Act 3, Scene 4."]	→ Act 3, scene **3. Late in 1801.** Toussaint's cell in a prison in the Alps.		Act 3, scene 3. Toussaint's cell in a prison in the Alps, late 1801. [Location comes first and date second, unlike other versions.]
Act 3, scene 5. May 1802. The large dining hall in the semiofficial Hotel de la République, Cap François. [In UWI275 date reads May **1803**; Dartmouth and Yale just read **1803**.]	→ Act 3, scene **4. May 1802.** The large dining hall in the semiofficial Hotel de la République, Cap François.		Act 3, scene 4. May 1802. **Leclerc's villa on the outskirts of Cap François.**

how does their loss reconfigure the play? From the nine other play scripts, the opening and closing scenes of act 1, scenes 1 and 4, are cut, and so too is the opening scene from the final act 3.

Scene Changes in *Toussaint Louverture*

Originally, act 1, scene 1 was undated and set on "a moonlit evening" on "the verandah of M. Bullet's villa on the outskirts of Cap François." The play would have begun with Colonel Vincent, visiting representative of the French revolutionary government, being welcomed by Monsieur Bullet, white planter and president of the Colonial Assembly. This scene had cast Vincent as the freshly arrived colonial ingénue. Colonial San Domingo initially strikes him as an earthly paradise, beautiful in name and characterized with its stunning scenery and fertile soil. Soon, any paradisiacal first impressions are shattered when Vincent hears about the deadly punishments to be meted out to slaves and to a white campaigner for mulatto rights, M. Ferrand de Baudière. These literally render Vincent speechless, as he can only splutter "M. Bullet, I—I—" (2013, 52), and later on, "I have seen active service in many parts of the world M. Bullet, but—" (2013, 54).[38]

In response, archetypal planter M. Bullet would have spouted Harland-type pseudoscience about craniometry and the inferiority of the black race: "[The Negro] is a sub-human type. In fact, scientists have proved that their sloping forehead prevents the full development of the brain" (2013, 53). The original opening scene contrasted civilization with barbarity. Against the backdrop of barbaric slave treatment, there are strains of Mozart playing, as the planter and French representative drink to liberty, equality, fraternity, and the motto of the new French Republic after Bullet has tried to convince his guest that such notions do not apply to the slaves because of their supposed subhumanity.

In its original formation, then, the first scene would have ended with the Colonial Association president and French representative drinking to one interpretation of the French revolutionary motto "Liberty, Equality, Fraternity," one which denies that black slaves are even human beings. Thereafter, scene 2 would have opened with early Haitian leader Boukman also proclaiming "Liberty—Equality—Fraternity." This mirroring of the French revolutionary motto at the end of scene 1 and the beginning of scene 2 would have underlined the importance of such notions to the slaves and their own understanding of the French Revolution and its motto.

The NALIS script gives the best indication of what changed in the play as performed. Now, we start with the slaves themselves and a brief depiction of the Bois Caïman ceremony, during which the first major slave revolt of the Haitian Revolution was planned. Both versions outline differences between Toussaint and Dessalines's leadership styles, lingering on what we could call, after Paul B. Miller, Toussaint's "enlightened hesitations" to drink the blood of the sacrificial animal as Dessalines and the others encourage him to partake symbolically of the revolution.[39] Toussaint's enlightened hesitations mean that he literally "remains motionless" and "still hesitates" until he at last responds to the crowd's incitement: "He takes the vessel into his hands and drinks" (NALIS, 4). Such "enlightened hesitations" contrast greatly with what could be called Dessalines's unenlightened certainties, as that leader decisively galvanizes the crowd to fight for the key notion of liberty or death.

Interestingly, the historical Ferrand de Baudière who campaigned for mulatto rights and was hanged is now split into two characters: Ferrand and Baudière.[40] Previously, Jeannot had told this tale of a singular "white man, old man, with a white beard" (2013, 55). But henceforth Toussaint recounts, "They killed Ferrand and Baudière to-day[. . . .] Ferrand petitioned on behalf of the mulattoes for civic rights, and the planters hanged him on a lamp-post[. . . .] Baudière went with Ferrand to support the petition. They tied him to the tail of a horse and dragged him until he died" (NALIS, 2–3). From the 1936 program, no Ferrand de Baudière appeared as a character in the play as performed, and it is not known whether he was discussed as one or two characters.

The two other omitted scenes were both set in Toussaint's household. The closing scene of act 1 was set in "the mountain retreat of Toussaint's wife and sons" in early 1794, while the original opening scene of act 3 was set in the same location, but in early 1802. One consequence of these scenes being removed is that neither Toussaint's wife, nor his two sons Isaac and Placide, feature in the play any longer. Originally, the first of these scenes had highlighted treachery of imperialist machinations, with Bullet and General Maitland of the British army asking Toussaint to help them restore slavery on the island and bribing him with an offer a million francs.

Most of the remainder of the scene is then taken up with a play within the play: a reenactment of the French Convention passing a decree to abolish colonial slavery in Paris in February 1794. According to the stage directions, an inner curtain would have risen behind Louverture, showing the audience the president in his chair and the convention in session. This dramatization would have been "an almost verbatim report of the sittings of the [French

Assembly on] 3rd and 4th February, 1794." At the news, Madame Louverture would have fainted with the words: "The boys—to grow up free—never to be slaves. I used to dream of it at nights," with Toussaint catching her as she falls (2013, 80). Cutting this scene would have avoided costly extra roles for actors needed to act out brief cameos set in a metropolitan Paris location within a scene otherwise set in a mountain hut in Haiti. In the NALIS script, the reworked following scene, act 2, scene 1, now has Roume sum up this development for Toussaint in a single sentence: "Luckily for us the French Government abolished slavery completely." Originally, act 1, scene 4 would have closed with Toussaint entrusting his sons to France to be educated. Deletion of this scene means that even fewer female characters now appear on stage.

After their initial appearance in the original act 1, scene 4, Toussaint's sons would also have made brief appearances elsewhere in the earlier scripts. In the first versions of act 2, scene 2, set more than six or seven years later, Isaac and Placide were to have had an audience with Bonaparte, along with their tutor Coignon, during which the French first consul would have put on a show of fatherly concern and deep admiration for Toussaint, while gifting them with special uniforms to take home. Immediately beforehand and afterward, Bonaparte's false flattery and racist treachery would have been writ large, when he reveals the real intentions of the French expedition: to overthrow Toussaint and restore slavery. In the NALIS script, this part is summed up in only three added lines, making it clear that the sons will be used as bait so that Toussaint accepts the arrival of the French expedition force and does not believe rumors that the expedition is directed against him (NALIS, 54). Elsewhere what is added makes it obvious that economic greed—the slave trade in numbers, and the worth of San Domingo—motivates Bonaparte: "**Lose the slave trade—20,000 slaves a year!**" (NALIS, 55). The third scene to be cut from *Toussaint Louverture* as performed is act 3, scene 1, which would have featured Madame Louverture again, alongside the two sons, Isaac and Placide, and their tutor, Father Coignon. This would have been the reunion scene between Toussaint and sons. Immediately after their homecoming, the two sons attempt to convince their father of the French expedition leader Leclerc's peaceful intentions, with Isaac ultimately siding with France and Placide with his father's forces.

This scene would also have been instrumental in presenting challenges to Toussaint's power, not only from his son Isaac, but also from his own officers, namely Christophe (2013, 110–11). Originally, Placide and Isaac would also have been present in act 3, scene 3 in earlier script versions of Toussaint's capture by the French. Significantly, they would have been the ones to witness the absolute treachery of the French leaders, with Placide crying out, "You French traitors!" (2013, 122). In the NALIS script, this has been replaced with Toussaint's own exclamation "**Ah, treachery!**" when he suddenly catches sight of the soldiers (NALIS, 76). Overall, these three omitted scenes mean a shorter play with fewer roles and actors, thus simplifying storylines and streamlining the play for production while further concentrating attention on Toussaint.

The 1936 program scene summaries and the NALIS script contents indicate further significant changes made during the evolution toward performance. One significantly changed scene, which would change again according to the 1936 performance program, is act 3, scene 2, which becomes act 3, scene 1 in the NALIS script and the performance program. Previously Toussaint had been the main character watching the battlefield, but this instead becomes Dessalines in the NALIS script. However, the character then seems to have reverted to Toussaint in the play as actually performed, according to the 1936 program. Reading and writing are central to the action in this scene, taking on even more importance when it is the illiterate leader Dessalines who needs to have Christophe's letter about his surrender to the French read out for him. When the messenger delivers Christophe's letters, Dessalines opens the letter, examining the signature.

At first, there is good humor, with Dessalines taking one of the letters and proclaiming, "Ah, give me one. I will read it" (NALIS, 60). After that, the stage directions say, "*The letters are handed up to him and he pretends to read,*" with Dessalines next "*[turning] the letter over, and [reading] near the end.*" This part of the NALIS script is not really worked out because it is unclear whether Verny continues to read or whether it is the illiterate Dessalines, which would make less sense. Next Dessalines jokes, "See how well I can read." But after the laughter, Dessalines is described as "leaping up" when Verny takes over reading the letter again, with Dessalines forcing him to read and reread. Repeated reading of the letter makes Dessalines accuse Verny, "You read it wrong," but when he orders the letter to be handed over to him, Dessalines "*Handles the letter impotently,*" encouraging Verny to "Say it is a trick." With disbelief, Dessalines examines Christophe's seal and his secretary's handwriting. New details in the stage directions of the NALIS script emphasize Dessalines's inability to read: "**He looks at the letter all ways**" (NALIS, 62). Dessalines declares, "**You have education Verny. Tell me. What is it**[? ...] **You can read books, Verny. What is it? Tell me. I** listen" (64). In earlier versions of this scene, Toussaint, who can read, grabs the dispatches and reads them himself. Replacing Toussaint with Dessalines in the NALIS script foregrounds illiteracy and the problem of access to the written word.

Significantly, this scene has a different ending in Dessalines's mouth in the NALIS script. Dessalines speaks only "After a long pause," waiting for Verny to interpret the other leader Christophe's words to him. Originally, Toussaint had ended the scene with the exclamation "Surrender!—and have others decide our fate," but now Dessalines declares after the pause, "Summon the men in marching order. We shall never haul down our flag. We shall cut our way out to-night. Afterwards we shall see" (NALIS, 65). Dessalines is more defiant, but indicates here that his men will surrender. Changing the protagonist from Toussaint to Dessalines is an interesting move that clearly raises questions of leadership and access to reading and writing. As these changes lengthen and complicate the scene considerably, it is not surprising that the 1936 performance version of the play seems to have reverted to Toussaint occupying the central role.

Staging Imperialist Antics

This section examines James's use of the Haitian revolutionary past in the 1936 *Toussaint Louverture* play as a vehicle for responding to particular sets of contemporary circumstances, which form the backdrop for immediate or recent contexts, including: the U.S. occupation of Haiti, 1915–34, and fascist Italy's conquest of Ethiopia in October 1935, after a protracted buildup.[41] In terms of critical context, I am building on work by Christian Høgsbjerg and Raphael Dalleo, who have highlighted the importance of one or both contexts for James in the 1930s.[42] Dalleo has noted a silence about the occupation in James's Haitian Revolution–inspired work. The present chapter seeks to interrogate this supposed silence further, following Høgsbjerg, by arguing that James is, in fact, less silent on these topics in the 1936 play, and that *Toussaint Louverture* speaks increasingly loudly about these events by developing themes and characters related to interimperialist rivalry throughout the drafts.

Dalleo rightly points out that the 1936 author's note in the *Toussaint Louverture* play program makes "a strange set of assumptions," but, as is the case throughout James's work overall—only a fraction of which has been published—topics revolve, in the same manner noted by Santiago Colás regarding "silence and dialectics" regarding James's (non)discussion of Latin

America.⁴³ There is also a constant dialectical tension regarding the U.S. occupation and present-day Haiti throughout James's writings, where it is a more prominent topic in some places than in others.⁴⁴ The key sentence in James's 1936 playbill note is, "the independence so hardly won has been maintained." What does James's tautological statement have to say about the U.S. occupation of Haiti? Significantly, it is in the same program statement that James outlines the timing of the play's completion by the autumn of 1934—in other words, just after the last U.S. marines left Haiti on August 15, 1934. This endpoint also has *Toussaint Louverture* "completely finished" before the November 1934 Walwal incident, which would prompt Ethiopia's appeal to the League of Nations in protest against military aggression, and before fascist Italy's 1935–36 conquest of Ethiopia.

Timing-wise, however, the 1934 endpoint of the play's writing has James penning *Toussaint Louverture* in 1932–34 when the end of the occupation was already in sight. Martial law ended in 1931, and negotiations of U.S. withdrawal from Haiti were already underway, with the end of the occupation set in 1932 for the end of 1934.⁴⁵ This section argues that these recent contexts both impact the forceful anti-imperialist message of *Toussaint Louverture* and influence the play's representations of archimperialist representations of the great powers.

It was against the backdrop of James's involvement in efforts to raise the Ethiopian question in Britain that his play was moving from the page to the stage and addressing the great imperialist powers of the time. Thus, the play also needs to be read against a 1936 backdrop too, and not only a 1934 one. For Dalleo, James's "strange set of assumptions" from the 1936 author's note "emphasizes Haiti's uninterrupted freedom as well as its current status as equal member in the world of nations."⁴⁶ James's author's note is paradoxical, according to Dalleo, because Haiti was admitted to the League of Nations at the height of the U.S. occupation in 1920.⁴⁷ James's brief reference in the program to the contemporary situation in Haiti, while avoiding naming the occupation, "surely speaks to an underlying anxiety," according to Dalleo, in an author's note that presents "an overstated performance of how fully Haitian independence has been preserved."⁴⁸

What is particularly overstated by James here is the assumption that Haiti is, in fact, "entirely French" and that "Haitians look on France as their spiritual home." This emphasis on Haiti's Francophilia seems completely out of place in a statement prefacing a 1936 play all about driving the French colonizers out of Haiti for good. For Dalleo, James's note is "unusually Europhilic," placing the emphasis on the Caribbean as an extension of Europe, which could be read as an attempt to deflect attention from what by the 1930s had become "the obvious rise of U.S.'s power in the region."[49] It is, however, not the case that James is downplaying the threat of U.S. power in the Caribbean region. Instead, James's overstatement of Haiti's Francophilia in the 1936 note dramatically spotlights Haitian culture's attachment to French culture and the French language in the face of the U.S. occupation; an overstatement of Haiti's Frenchness that cuts the U.S.'s neocolonial antics down to size.

It is only against this neocolonial background that James's affirmations of Haiti's profound attachment to France can begin to be understood. Direct reference is also made in the program statement to Haitian Colonel Nemours, who at that time occupied a prestigious position as permanent delegate for Haiti to the League of Nations. Nemours was a Haitian general and military historian whom James met in Paris during research for *The Black Jacobins*, out of which *Toussaint Louverture* was also born. It was Nemours who actually reenacted in a Parisian café the maneuvers of Toussaint's military victories "using books and coffee cups upon a large table to show how the different campaigns had been fought," as James would later recall in the 1980 foreword to the history.[50]

For Dalleo, Nemours is a compromised figure because he even testified in favor of continuation of the U.S. military presence in the aftermath of the December 29 massacre at Les Cayes, which is "hardly incontrovertible proof of Haiti's independence, and if anything suggests that his career advancement owed to his acceptance of the non-sovereign status quo."[51] However, Høgsbjerg convincingly makes the point that Nemours is a complex figure who had spoken out against Italy's invasion of Ethiopia, and that Haiti was "one of the only countries to stand in solidarity with Ethiopia."[52] In fact, the reference to Nemours in the program's preface to the 1936 play indirectly links the Haitian and Ethiopian contexts because Nemours made a famous speech on October 10, 1935: "Craignons d'être, un jour, l'Éthiopie de quelqu'un" (Let us fear to be, one day, someone's Ethiopia!). This solemn warning to the European powers of the day was published as a booklet with the same title, which collected all of Nemours's most famous speeches.[53]

One of James's main collaborators during the 1930s in London was fellow Trinidadian George Padmore, who had published a pamphlet on the U.S. occupation of Haiti at its height in 1931.[54] Like Padmore, James's concerns with the lessons of Haiti for the present are refracted through both the U.S. occupation of Haiti and the Italian invasion of Ethiopia. Even if James barely mentions them in the 1936 program, he uses the Haitian example to stage contemporary resistance in Haiti of the U.S. occupation and in Ethiopia, linking both to anti-imperialist struggles more broadly.

The Ethiopian struggle had an immense impact on James's political work and thought. His campaigning for the Ethiopian cause included a speaking tour across Britain and the writing of impassioned pages in newspapers, opinion pieces, and political pamphlets, all devoted to raising solidarity over the Ethiopian crisis. It was the Ethiopian cause that formed the backbone of James and his London colleagues' Pan-Africanist activities: James would go on to chair the International African Friends of Abyssinia (IAFA) in 1935, and was also very involved in the organization's later incarnation as the International African Service Bureau from May 1937 onward, as editorial director of its journal *International African Opinion*.[55]

James and his IAFA colleagues wanted to form an international brigade and to fight in Ethiopia. James felt that he could have been useful from a strategy and tactics perspective, and at an August 1935 meeting public meeting of the IAFA he gave a speech outlining a Haitian Revolution–inspired scorched-earth strategy to be pursued in Ethiopia if all else failed in the face of Italian invaders. In the face of defeat, the Ethiopians should "destroy their country rather than hand it over to the invader. Let them burn down Addis Ababa, let them poison their wells/water holes, let them destroy every blade of vegetation."[56] James was unequivocal in advocating this military strategy of destroying anything that might be useful to the enemy. His scorched-earth comments were no doubt inspired by his research on the Haitian Revolution. This strategy would subsequently feature prominently in both the 1936 play and 1938 history. Political campaigning about the Ethiopian cause was then broken off in 1936 to continue politics by other means: as a play.

Through its subject matter, themes, and characterization, the play is used to critique foreign powers. Turning to drama gives James an effective weapon for showing in action the "incredible savagery and duplicity of European Imperialism in its quest for markets and raw materials," a key point made discursively throughout James's early 1936 article for the League of Coloured Peoples journal *The Keys*, titled "Abyssinia and the Imperialists."[57]

Diplomatic intrigues are writ largest throughout the pivotal act 2, scene 1, where the interimperialistic rivalry, hypocrisy, and lies of all foreign powers are omnipresent. Representatives of the great powers—France, Britain, and America—meet in secret to discuss their positions and shared interests, as they cross and double-cross one another. Arguing among themselves, along the lines James outlines in "Abyssinia and the Imperialists," they try to carve up the island among themselves, seeking to profit from a renewed scramble for colonial power.[58]

Scandalous hypocrisy characterizes all the two-faced imperialists throughout the play. Representatives of the great powers agree on only one aim: to counter the rise of Toussaint. Special condemnation is reserved for U.S. Consul Tobias Lear and British General Maitland. The way that the real historical figure Lear is portrayed brings the U.S. occupation of Haiti to mind.[59] Lear always makes a show of prefacing all his comments with assurances of complete neutrality in such colonial matters, but what is said exposes naked greed for a share of the loot (2013, 83–84). Ultimately, what unites these interimperialist rivals is their shared colonial interests: preservation at all costs of the "dominance of the white race," as Lear puts it. On this single issue alone, they are all agreed. When Toussaint unexpectedly arrives in this scene, fresh from victory on the battlefield, these hypocritical representatives of the great powers immediately launch into showering Toussaint with false praise, flattery, and accolades (85–86).

Changes to act 2, scene 1 made in the NALIS script and in the published scene in *Life and Letters Today* (spring 1936, cited as LLT) further spotlight the imperialist antics and treachery of the great powers. One substantial difference between these versions and the earlier scripts is the postponement of the arrival of the other revolutionary leaders Christophe and Dessalines. Originally, earlier scripts, such as the Hull script, had Toussaint, Dessalines, and Christophe all arriving at the same time (NALIS, 32; LLT, 12).[60] Now the late arrival of Dessalines and Christophe serves to get Toussaint out of the way while waiting for them, with Maitland proposing, "If I may suggest it Commander-in-Chief, you certainly need a few minutes to refresh yourself. Pray take them. The Consul and I will chat pleasantly together until you and your officers are ready." At this, Toussaint bows and exits.

Removing Toussaint from this part of the scene means that the audience is privy to an extra secret exchange between Maitland and Lear. The function of the "pleasant" chat is to underline the duplicity of imperialist representatives by allowing their racism to emerge even more strongly. Now their added backstairs negotiations contain racist comments from Lear, "**That darkie has more brains than you gave him credit for,**" and from Maitland in the NALIS script, "**This is the fault of the early Commissioners who promoted him. He should have been kept in his place from the beginning**" (NALIS, 33), and in the *Life and Letters Today* scene: "You know, Consul, in dealing with Orientals and men of colour, white men can never have that full confidence that we can have in one another, for instance" (LLT, 12–13). Such racist exchanges serve to expose the layers of hypocrisy and treachery in the great powers' imperialist maneuvering.

These new layers can become quite complicated. Act 2, scene 1, as it appears in the NALIS script and *Life and Letters Today*, almost gives the impression of being three scenes in one, with all the comings, goings, and separate conversations taking place among different sets of characters and as speeches become considerably longer. Both the NALIS and *Life and Letters Today* versions work out more fully the treachery of imperialist machinations by extending dialogues among the representatives of the great powers, especially those of Britain and the United States, that speak to and condemn the recent U.S. occupation and the Ethiopian crisis.

Another scene further lengthened and complicated as it moves toward performance in the NALIS script is Toussaint's death scene in prison, act 3, scene 3 (act 3, scene 4 in the nine earlier scripts preceding the NALIS script). Complicated subscenes within scenes are added here. As in the earlier scripts, the scene still opens with Toussaint and his servant Mars Plaisir, but three extra pages are inserted (NALIS, 80–82). The added detail underlines the humiliation and disempowerment of the former Haitian commander in chief, Toussaint, as he is forced to wear a convict's uniform instead of a private's uniform.

What complicates this scene is this completely added stage direction:

> **They** [Mars Plaisir and gaolers] **go. Toussaint bows his head down on the table. The stage grows gradually dark, stays dark for a few moments and then gradually becomes light again. <u>It is now four months later</u>. The scene is the same, except the time is winter. Streaks of water glisten down the walls. Toussaint, greyer and otherwise visibly nearer death, sits huddled and shivering by a small fire. He stares straight in front of him like a man in his dotage.** (NALIS, 83)

What was previously one scene is now broken up in complicated fashion with an elaborate stage direction to denote the passing of four months. In the NALIS script, General Caffarelli, the first consul's aide-de-camp, enters, but this time accompanied by a "new Governor." As Baille had previously been the only named jailer with a speaking role, announcement of his death adds another layer to the scene (NALIS, 86–87). The 1936 program descriptors and cast list for this scene in order of appearance list both "Governor Baille" and a "gaoler," but it is unclear whether the play as performed presented the death of Baille the prison governor.

All ten versions of the death scene end with Toussaint's dying words, pronounced defiantly, "(*Loudly and clearly*) Oh, Dessalines! Dessalines! You were right after all," as he falls to the floor. However, an expanded NALIS script stage direction would have had Toussaint travel in his dying mind's eye back in time to the pivotal scene staging imperialist antics: act 2, scene 1, back to Dessalines calling on Toussaint not to trust any white imperialists, and to declare independence:

> [. . .] The clock strikes three. The stage goes **slowly** dark, **then** ~~and~~ gradually **becomes light** ~~lightens~~ again. **Toussaint is seen fallen forward in his chair. The grate is empty.** After a few minutes **of silence** the clock strikes three again. At the first stroke, he holds his head up. By the third he has risen to his feet. **Out of the blackness of the rest of the stage emerges the scene which is filling the mind of the dying Toussaint. Christophe and Dessalines are to one side, Maitland and Tobias Lear on the other. Dessalines has just finished appealing to Toussaint to accept the support of England and America as King of San Domingo. The crowd outside is shouting for Toussaint. He walks back and throws the window open. He waves to the crowd. As he returns slowly to the group waiting for him the scene fades.** (NALIS, 88)

Quite how this complicated time-hopping scene within a scene would have been acted out by the same actor playing the dying Toussaint is unclear. Replaying this segment and traveling back in time to combine two scenes into one would have driven home the main anti-imperialist lesson of the play: that blacks must organize and fight for themselves and must not trust any imperialist power. However, given the complexity of such a restaging, it is likely that Toussaint's dying words alone—"Dessalines! Dessalines! You were right after all"—would have recalled the anti-imperialist message in the actual 1936 performances of *Toussaint Louverture*. For the play as performed, the 1936 program does not note the reappearance of the characters necessary to reenact the earlier scene segment: Christophe, Dessalines, Maitland, Tobias Lear, and, of course, the crowd. None of the contemporary reviews make any reference to such a tangled scene within a scene either.

Paradoxically, such changes lengthen the script, taking it further from a streamlined performance version precisely as the dialogue and characterization are worked out fully. At one point in the death scene, Toussaint delivers a single speech of eighteen lines alone with no interjections. The NALIS and *Life and Letters Today* versions of these scenes are the closest thing we have to the performance script of the *Toussaint Louverture* play in terms of content changes and dates, but these word-heavy script versions still belong to the page as they make their way toward the stage and performance. Several reviews of the 1936 performances criticized the play for being too long and unwieldy, which suggests that lengthening changes came at a cost to the play itself.[61] Had the play been staged in its original and shorter 1934 format, it is likely that it would have received less criticism for its length.

Despite the play's overall length, James's anticolonialist activism certainly sharpened his revisions to his play. *Toussaint Louverture* draws particularly on the parallel symbolism of Haiti and Ethiopia. At the time of fascist Italy's invasion of Ethiopia, there were only three independent black states in the world: Ethiopia, Haiti, and Liberia. However, Haiti's status as inspirational Pan-Africanist independence symbol was sometimes downplayed, especially in the 1930s, with more focus on Haiti's failures as a postcolonial state.[62] But James, one of the leading Pan-Africanists at that time, tells a different success story in this play and chooses this subtitle: *The Only Successful Slave Revolt in History*.

As the playwright builds on the play's scaffolding, all the major imperialist powers and their betrayals of independent countries such as Haiti and Ethiopia are attacked further. In his article "Abyssinia and the Imperialists," James begins with the idea of lessons to be learned from the crisis. Indeed, the whole play should be read as an anti-imperialist lesson. As these scenes evolve, they generate outrage, disgust, and condemnation at such imperialist duplicity. At the end of the play, Dessalines's words echo James's lessons on Ethiopia. Amid wild cheering from a militant crowd, Dessalines proudly proclaims, "Haiti no colony but free and independent. Haiti the first free and independent Negro State in the new world" (act 3, scene 5, 132).

Calls for unity come as the symbols of independence—the new name of Haiti and the Haitian flag—are being created. When Dessalines pulls Christophe and Pétion onto the tabletop where they grip arms, and when the blue and red portions of the French tricolor are united in the new Haitian bicolor, with the white being trampled underfoot, this scene offers a closing image of symbolic Pan-African unity where, in this case, mulattoes and blacks "get much closer together," for this and other fights, as James called on workers and peasants of Britain, Africa, Europe, and India, and all "sufferers from imperialism all over the world" to "break our own chains."[63] Victory is the focus of *The Only Successful Slave Revolt in History* as the play closes with this picture of victorious slaves liberating themselves from, and winning against, one of the most powerful armies of their day.

Using the success story of the Haitian Revolution, James depicts peoples of African descent as fully capable of fighting for self-emancipation now in the 1930s and in the near future because, already 130 years previously, this was successfully achieved in Haiti. Prefigured by the ending of this play is a vision of successful anticolonial revolution where the oppressed take on the oppressors and win. Driving home the main anti-imperialist lessons of the play—that blacks must organize, fight for themselves, and not trust any imperialist power—the play ends on an optimistic note of Pan-African unity and successful anticolonial revolt.

Paul Robeson and *Toussaint Louverture*: "The Whole Damn Thing Changed"

Success and vindication were also behind James's decision to write a play in the first place, as he revealed in a 1980 interview: "I wrote a play called *Toussaint Louverture*. I was busy working on the historical account of the Haitian Revolution and being very much involved in politics and seeing there was a story in which Blacks had done splendid things, I thought it would be nice—not nice, but effective to produce it, because there weren't many plays that said Black people had created any distinguished events of the time. So I wrote the play."[64] Once the playwright had written the script, the prestigious and progressive Stage Society agreed to put it on at the Westminster Theatre in London's West End, but only on the condition that Paul Robeson would perform in the title role.[65] All the extraordinary lengths James had to go when tracking down Robeson are detailed in James's memoir "Paul Robeson: Black Star."[66] This offer came at the right moment for Robeson, after two disturbing experiences that altered the future direction of his work: an encounter with fascist brutality in Berlin in December 1934 while en route to Moscow to meet Soviet filmmaker Sergei Eisenstein, and the unwitting role he was forced to play in a pro-imperialist film, *Sanders of the River*.[67]

Immediately following Robeson's life-changing exposure to fascism in Berlin was his exposure to communism—a "strongly affirmative" experience.[68] In the USSR, Robeson met Eisenstein to discuss making a film based on the Haitian Revolution with Robeson in the lead as another Haitian revolutionary: Henri-Christophe.⁶⁹ Like James, Robeson was championing at this time the antifascist Ethiopian cause.

James suggests that ideological differences prevented him and Robeson from taking the play any further as a film or a commercial venture: "But at that time Paul was headed towards Moscow and I, as a Trotskyist, was most definitely anti-Moscow."⁷⁰ However, there were also considerable overlaps between their political outlooks and values at this time, as James indicates in his 1970 memoir dedicated to Paul Robeson.⁷¹ In addition to sharing commitments to antifascism, black liberation, and working-class causes, Robeson and James also had a strong common interest in fighting reductive Harlandesque/Froudacious stereotypes of black inferiority.

During this period in the 1930s, film roles for black actors were still very limited in scope and tended to be servile, menial, and restricted to "Uncle Tom roles of every description," "faithful dog-like devotion," or "hate-filled barbarians, savages, cannibalism only one degree removed from the wild animals of the jungle," according to Peter Noble.⁷² The lead role in *Toussaint Louverture* therefore gave Robeson a rare opportunity to break this stereotype.⁷³ Robeson was actively seeking out alternative roles against the "continually-grinning old school of stereotype," for, he said, "we must express ourselves/we must show ourselves to the best advantage."⁷⁴ Efforts to break down prejudices and stereotypes led Robeson to experiment with "test pieces"—ventures that would be less financially lucrative, but which would do more to fulfill the actor's political needs.⁷⁵ *Toussaint Louverture* was one such test piece. Aspects of the play chiming most with Robeson's own active search for appropriate roles included the play's subject matter and significance, the anti-imperialist thrust, and the antidotes it provided to demeaning roles, turning the tables on the old stereotypes of white civilization versus black barbarity.

By all accounts, Robeson's crucial lead role was instrumental in making the play a success. Without Robeson and his vital presence in the play, *The Black Jacobins'* history would subsequently have been "significantly different in quality," as Robert Hill has convincingly suggested.⁷⁶ Playwright James himself also vividly recalled in 1983 Robeson's contributions to *Toussaint Louverture*: "The moment he came onto the stage, the whole damn thing changed."⁷⁷ In fact, collaboration with Robeson changed the play so much that James was even led to make revisions that were initiated either by Robeson or with him firmly in mind. Of the rehearsals, James recalls one particularly memorable moment when Robeson cut short a long speech at its climax: "A courageous chief only is wanted." As James recalled, "When so quiet a man made a definite decision, you automatically agreed."[78] In other words, Robeson rewrote the play too, and his input was decisive in changing the drama. This anecdote is helpful for working out the chronology of the play scripts and projecting the version of the play performed in March 1936. All scripts consulted would appear to predate this big change instigated by the play's lead actor. The line Robeson chose to make his last is the first line of the passage in the scripts.[79]

What is glimpsed from this account of the usually obliging Robeson's uncharacteristic intervention is a vision of the collaborative nature of James's work, even if, as the playwright wryly observes from the later vantage point of 1970, he was then generally less open to collaboration on the play.[80] In this early collaboration, Robeson clearly considered the interpretation and significance of this particular passage. His magnificent singing voice also found an opening and was written into the play, as James recollected.[81] Interestingly, these two Robeson-added play features are the ones usually singled out for praise in many reviews.[82] James succinctly summed up Robeson's success: "When the play was performed he, if not it, was a great success."[83] All contemporary reviews singled out the lead actor for fulsome praise, with most reviews featuring his name prominently in the title.

Certainly, Robeson added star quality to the production, and thanks to him *Toussaint Louverture* had a far greater impact than it would have had without him. Many reviews of the play attest to his popularity.[84] Superlative praise permeates all the reviews, and adjectives used to describe Robeson's playing of Louverture include "magnificent," "great," "earnest," "fine," "powerful," "passionate," "magnanimous," "moving." Many times he is called a "genius."

Reviews presenting Robeson as a magnificent actor are usually more negative about other members of the cast.[85] Condescension is palpable in the backhanded compliments and bizarre comments with racist or exoticist inflections, concerning black players "enjoying themselves" with great "naturalness," or respected film critic Ivor Brown's odd statement in *The Sketch* (March 25, 1936) that "Toussaint's negro generals liked dressing up, and the coloured actors seemed to like dressing up as generals. I liked them too."[86] Frequently, only white actors were singled out by name by reviewers unable to see individual black actors, with almost all reviews "permeated with colonial and racial ambivalence," as Emery has noted.[87]

References also abound to the black characters and actors as "hordes," a collective designation that does not seek to differentiate among individuals.

Often reviewers describe these black "hordes" as too willing, gullible, or simplistic, interpretations at odds with the play's vindicationist message.[88] From such reviews, one might think that this play was even the story of an unsuccessful slave revolt, given the emphasis on the slaves' collective "flaws" and references to their "inadequacy," "weakness," "flightiness," "simplicity," "littleness," "ignorance," "savagery," and their "child-like" nature. Anyone reading these reviews would receive a completely skewed impression of the play's narrative—one where revolution is not successful because the slaves are far too simplistic, gullible, passive, and weak, leading to them being easily outmaneuvered, tricked, and overcome by white imperialist troops. Such a play would be the complete antithesis of the actual play and its story of successful revolution by black slaves who fight and win their freedom for themselves.

Other reviewers did, however, understand what the play was all about. The main lesson of *Toussaint Louverture* is, for instance, summed up well by one reviewer who describes feeling: "'How can one listen to Robeson, and still think in terms of white superiority?'"[89] Nearly every single review, including negative ones, draws attention to the dignity and nobility brought to the role by Robeson. Frequently, his performance as Toussaint is described with words such as "dignified," "noble," "dignity," "nobility," "integrity," "earnest," "earnestness." Reviews comment positively on Robeson's "quiet dignity," "fine, dignified performance," "His dignity, eloquence and the quick play of his wit," and his "tremendously sincere acting," which build a portrait of "The hero [as] the noble Negro." One review is even subtitled "A Dignified Study." Such components united James and Robeson in their search for a play about the Haitian Revolution, one that would represent black characters and their historical achievements in a heroic light and go beyond presenting black actors in entertainment or adjunct-type roles.[90]

Later in 1965, James would stress the need for "straight plays bursting out of our [West Indian] history."[91] Surely, in 1936, this search for serious, straight plays bursting out of history would have been even more urgent still. Collaboration with Robeson during rehearsals therefore had a major impact on the trajectory of the play as it moved toward performance. Robeson had a major impact on James, the play, the future trajectory of *The Black Jacobins* history, and James's pursuit of vindication of black historical achievements. James's drama places the great revolutionary Toussaint Louverture in history and at center stage. In James's memoirs, his task was also to place Robeson—"one of the most remarkable men of the twentieth century."[92] Robeson, like Toussaint

Louverture, represents the prototype for James's conception of great black men of history and action.⁹³

One or two critics commented that Robeson's towering physique was quite incongruous and at odds with that of Toussaint Louverture, whose frail-seeming outward appearance gained him the nickname *fatras bâton* (thin or throwaway stick in Haitian Kreyòl).⁹⁴ One criticism of the play made the following objection in the *Liverpool Post* (March 17, 1936): "Physically, he was hardly suited to the role of the forty-seven-year-old ex-coachman, worn out with years of slavery, and, it is said, a man of small stature." James would recall observing Robeson's imposing, magnificent physique at close quarters during rehearsals, where he got a "good look at Paul" and got "to know him well."⁹⁵ Robert Hill has made the valuable point that Robeson "*shattered* James's colonial conception of the Black Physique."⁹⁶ Shattering encapsulates Robeson's monumental contribution not only to this serious "straight" play "bursting out of our history," but also to *The Black Jacobins* history in the process of being written at this point in the 1930s.⁹⁷

In short, Paul Robeson came along and "[changed] the whole damn thing" where the actual work of representation of the Haitian Revolution was concerned, shattering in the process any conceivable notions of black inferiority. Instead, throughout James's recollections, Robeson comes to represent something much more positive: "a truly heroic figure," a monumental "black star," and an immense giant. Robeson is James's prototype of the great man of action who is used as the vehicle for the great Haitian Revolution, but also for tapping into "*our* history" and "*our* potential bursting at every seam."⁹⁸

This production of the Haitian play and plans for a Haitian film brought Robeson and James together, with the lead actor Robeson playing a critical role in actually rewriting the script, injecting singing during the death scene in prison, and cutting Enlightenment philosopher Abbé Raynal's famous passage about a courageous Black Spartacus being needed.⁹⁹ James would later say that he was not a "theater person," and surely the fact that Robeson was fully a theater person helped to transform the play for performance. According to James's own recollections, since Peter Godfrey, the director of the play, was sometimes absent from rehearsals, it fell to James the playwright to rehearse the cast himself.¹⁰⁰ James has described the level of control that he attempted to exert over delivery of every line, as an inexperienced playwright and director. All of this meant that both James and Robeson played very hands-on roles with significant input and collaboration from Robeson when the play was in rehearsals. For one of the play's two performances, James would even be forced on stage to act, playing the role of the absent actor Macoya.[101] Through their shared Haitian project, James's and Robeson's understanding of the Haitian Revolution and its significance developed through the 1936 play's production. As for James, after the March 1936 performances of *Toussaint Louverture*, he would deploy the same research on the Haitian Revolution that informed the play to write his history *The Black Jacobins* for publication in 1938.

On the Road between *Toussaint Louverture* (1936) and *The Black Jacobins* (1967)

In terms of chronology, the three copies of *Toussaint Louverture* scripts housed in UWI Box 9, Folder 227 appear to have been typed up using one of the earlier scripts of the play as their basis. Changes made, for example, to the NALIS script and the *Life and Letters Today* scene from spring 1936 have not been made here. These scripts are carbon copies from the same typing and feature the use of a more distinctly theatrical notation system. Running heads appear throughout the scripts to indicate the act and scene numbers and pagination, with numbering beginning again with each new act. I follow this precise notation system when referring to these three scripts.

These handwritten corrections made in James's own distinctively shaky hand constitute major revisions and are, this section argues, of great consequence in terms of both scope and content. What is also proposed here is that these handwritten insertions were not added in the run-up to the 1936 performance of *Toussaint Louverture* but instead belong to a later period. It is difficult to date these additions precisely, but both C. L. R.'s widow, Selma James, and Robert A. Hill, literary executor to the C. L. R. James estate, believe that these handwritten lines probably date from the 1950s. It was also after James's return to England from the United States in 1953 that he started to send out copies of the play to the French publisher Gallimard and the Haitian embassy in London during the historical fever of the approaching 150th anniversary of Haitian independence.[102]

These handwritten additions constitute an intermediate staging post on the road from James's first play in 1936 to his second in 1967. Repeatedly, changes made throughout copy 1 insert the character of Toussaint's adopted nephew Moïse, who did not even feature at all in the first play, and whose name is nowhere to be found in the 1936 program. These handwritten changes all bear witness to James's profound rethinking of his story at a crucial juncture in the intervening period between his first and second plays. From being completely absent in the 1936 play as performed, Moïse will become the alternative central character around whom *The Black Jacobins* will revolve, as well as a contrasting foil to rival his adoptive Uncle Toussaint. Only copies 1 and 2 contain any handwriting, whereas copy 3 contains no handwriting at all and is only a partial copy, going up to 2.1.14.[103] Where handwritten insertions are concerned, what is added is different in copies 1 and 2. Additions made to the first copy are more far-reaching in terms of both scope and content, while copy 2 boasts different changes, which tend to be relatively minor, serving mainly to correct typos and add accents.

New focus on Moïse is added throughout copy 1, with Moïse written in toward the end of act 1, scene 1, where he is clearly introduced and given a speaking role (1.1.13–1.1.14 and 1.1.29–1.1.31). In the two pages of his first appearance, Moïse's name replaces that of Captain Antoine, described as "one of the men in the ranks." In James's scrawling handwriting, a heated exchange is created between Dessalines and newly introduced Moïse, and these additions clearly prefigure the rivalry between this pair over leadership styles and the figuration of Moïse as champion of the ordinary rank and file in *The Black Jacobins* in 1967. Here, Dessalines's authoritarian barking out of orders at a minor and anonymous rank-and-file soldier, Antoine, becomes more personal and insulting as the attack is redirected toward Moïse:

> <u>DESSALINES</u>: Captain **Moïse** A̶n̶t̶o̶i̶n̶e̶!
>
> One of the men in the ranks comes up and salutes.
>
> <u>DESSALINES</u>: You son of a slave, fit only to be a slave! One blast—march; two blasts—about turn; three blasts—halt. Blast you! **Don't think because Toussaint is your uncle that you will get any favours here.**
>
> <u>MOÏSE</u>: **I don't ask for any favours.**
>
> [<u>DESSALINES</u>] Y̶o̶u̶ ̶c̶a̶n̶'̶t̶ ̶l̶e̶a̶r̶n̶—̶h̶o̶w̶ ̶y̶o̶u̶'̶l̶l̶ ̶t̶e̶a̶c̶h̶?̶ ̶I̶'̶l̶l̶ ̶r̶e̶d̶u̶c̶e̶ ̶t̶o̶ ̶t̶h̶e̶ ̶r̶a̶n̶k̶s̶.̶ (**Dessalines raises his hand as if to strike him, but Moïse** A̶n̶t̶o̶i̶n̶e̶ **stands firm**). Go and call **your uncle, quick** T̶o̶u̶s̶s̶a̶i̶n̶t̶ ̶B̶r̶e̶d̶a̶. Quick. Don't answer me back. I'll reduce you to the ranks.
>
> <u>MOÏSE</u> A̶n̶t̶o̶i̶n̶e̶ **steps backwards and hurries off. Dessalines roars at him** Salute, you swine, salute!
>
> <u>MOÏSE</u> A̶n̶t̶o̶i̶n̶e̶ salutes smartly and goes off.

Roughly sketched out here are the beginnings of Moïse's principled and steadfast stand in his rivalry with Dessalines.

Moïse is also inserted at the end of act 1, scene 3 as silent witness to all the hypocrisy and treachery among the Haitian leaders. Toussaint's previously monologic despair now has a new interlocutor:

> TOUSSAINT (his head in his hands) ~~Oh~~ **To Moïse: Did you hear?**
> **Moïse ~~shakes~~ nods.** Oh God! These are the men on whom the fate of the black race depends. What future is there for us!

Now Moïse is also present for the Raynal reading. To close this scene, insertions have Moïse sharing Toussaint's reading of the famous Raynal passage: "A courageous chief only is wanted...." A number of lines are reattributed to Moïse:

> **MOÏSE:** White men see Negroes as slaves. If the Negro is to be free, he must free himself. We have courage, we have endurance, we have numbers. (1.3.31)

Then added stage directions have them reciting the rousing climax of that passage in unison:

> **Toussaint reading, while Moïse who knows the words by heart, repeats them with him:**
> Where is he? That great man whom Nature owes to her vexed, oppressed and tormented children?
> ~~MOÏSE:~~ Thou hast shown me the light, oh God! I shall be that leader.

From the crossed-out speech attribution of the final two lines of the passage, we can see that James was toying at one point with allocating the final rousing lines to Moïse. Instead, they symbolically both recite these Enlightenment antislavery lines together in unison. According to Nicole King, Moïse and Dessalines "do not 'read' anything other than the will of the people."[104] But already when he is sketched here into the first play, Moïse reads a great deal, and this is the case in the second play too, where, for example, he reads and translates for the masses the news about the French abolition of slavery. Significantly, Moïse is here given the Raynal lines that equate with his unequivocal views about true independence, freedom, and self-activity of the masses—the popular leadership style attributed to Moïse in the 1967 *Black Jacobins* play.

Close ties are stressed whenever Moïse is inserted (1.3.29–30). Additions here include confusing instructions with several arrows pointing in various directions with asterisks, and instructions along the lines of "Remove to next page," "Add over the next page," "Insert ***." Another scene where Moïse is similarly introduced by hand and given an even more extensive and pivotal role is act 2, scene 1. Close familial bonds linking Moïse to Toussaint are always stressed throughout this scene. Whenever they address each other, attention is drawn firmly to the closeness of their uncle-nephew relationship:

> Moïse DESSALINES: Uncle Toussaint. (2.1.14)
>
> TOUSSAINT: [. . .] King of San Domingo! Well, **Moïse** Christophe. **You as my nephew will be a prince** (2.1.16)
>
> Moïse DESSALINES: **Uncle** Toussaint, you are too soft with these people. You will pay for it one day. What are you going to do now? (2.1.16)
>
> Moïse DESSALINES: **An expedition** It is coming in any case. **Uncle, you say** Toussaint says be loyal to France (2.1.17)
>
> TOUSSAINT: **My boy,** I know. (2.1.17)
>
> Moïse DESSALINES: [. . .] Finish with all this loyalty, **Uncle** Toussaint. (2.1.17)
>
> Moïse DESSALINES: **What is this Consul business Uncle?** Confidence in a white man. Take the offer Toussaint. (2.1.19)[105]

Familial ties linking Toussaint and his adopted nephew Moïse are repeatedly stressed, to the point that their closeness is depicted as being tantamount to a father-and-son relationship. Drama has a way of tightly compressing relationships, as Lindenberger has argued.[106] Moïse is here presented as Toussaint's proxy son, compressing father-son-type family bonds as tightly as possible. Intimacy of these close-knit bonds is compressed further in other ways, too. Gesture, and the fact that they address each other by name so often, also indicate the intimacy they share:

> TOUSSAINT: [. . .] **Good-night, Moïse** [. . .] **Gentlemen, and Moïse, (putting his hand on his shoulder) among other uses the night is for sleep. Moïse, wait outside.**

From being completely absent, Moïse is suddenly propelled by all these additions into becoming Toussaint's closest and most trusted ally, as attested to by Toussaint's added closing discussion with Dessalines over promoting Moïse as rapidly as possible through all the ranks:

> **Dessalines: I shall promote him to Brigadier General (OVER) and make him governor of the Limbé district.**

> ~~Dessalines~~ [. . .]
> **Toussaint: He has influence. He must have responsibility.** (2.1.19–
> extra page)

Sometimes handwritten insertions are only partial in nature, and do not always make it clear how everything fits together. Above, for example, there are two successive speech attributions to the same character Dessalines, which could be a mistake. It seems strange to have the idea of this promotion coming from Moïse's rival, Dessalines, instead of Toussaint.

Generally, the rewriting of this script is incomplete. Moïse is inserted into these two scenes only, and nowhere is mentioned his execution on Toussaint's orders. In *The Black Jacobins* in 1967, this sentencing to death of Moïse forms the centerpiece of the entire play. Handwritten annotations in this script of *Toussaint Louverture* are, however, clearly working toward this dénouement because the narrative thread is left hanging unresolved precisely at that point where family-type bonds could not be any tighter, strongly prefiguring the 1967 play, where compression of the father-son uncle-nephew close-knit relationship between this pair builds up to Toussaint's sentencing to death of his adopted son/nephew as the most outrageous violation of this, the closest of relationships, which occupies a position at the very epicenter of the second play.

This rewriting has an incomplete status, and we see James toying with various options. In the process of rewriting this scene, James introduces Moïse and pushes him conspicuously to the forefront in what becomes a two-way dialogue between Toussaint and Moïse. Moïse usurps Dessalines by taking over many of the latter's original lines, plus some entirely new lines designed specifically for Moïse. Meanwhile, Dessalines is relegated from his former pole position to the third position previously occupied by Christophe, while Christophe is written out and removed from this particular scene entirely.

Moïse's most distinctive character traits in *The Black Jacobins* are already clearly on display in these additions:

> **Moïse ~~DESSALINES~~**: Don't trust France don't trust any of those whites. Take their ships, take their guns, whoever offers take; and then let the French come and the British (<u>he glares at Maitland</u>) and even the Americans (<u>he glares at Lear</u>) (2.1.15)

Moïse is most articulate in his devastating critique of imperialist treachery and hypocrisy. As in the 1967 play, Moïse is unequivocal that France and the other foreign powers cannot be trusted, and that true freedom—independence—must instead be sought.

There are some incongruities, such as the image of Moïse as prince-in-waiting of San Domingo, which does not square up with the staunch advocate of true independence and freedom from any shackles to colonial powers. As for Dessalines, instead of Christophe, now being offered and accepting the present from the British king, this is also slightly off-key because in both the original and the later plays, it is Christophe, Haiti's future king, who aspires the most to be like foreign monarchs with their luxurious lifestyles, including such dinner services.[107] In *The Black Jacobins* play, Dessalines would be clearly portrayed as being in favor of Toussaint's acceptance of the British offer of kingship in addition to his position of favoring independence, not seeing, unlike the ever clear-sighted Moïse, that such dishonest bribes are designed only for the British to get their hands on the colony and restore slavery.

These handwritten annotations only partially rewrite this and the other scene. What is clear is that this represents an intermediate stage between the moments of the two plays (1936 and 1967), and also between the two editions of *The Black Jacobins* history (1938 and 1963). This rewriting, particularly the highly significant writing-in of Moïse, clearly constitutes a step toward the subsequent reorientations of the 1967 *Black Jacobins* play. It is, however, also worth noting that the second play barely contains a single line that is the same as any from *Toussaint Louverture*. When rewriting his play in the 1950s, James seems to have decided to go beyond changing that play only here and there, as he was constrained to do in the footnotes and other relatively interstitial sites of his revised later edition of *The Black Jacobins* history. Instead, he decided to rewrite from scratch a new play based on the Haitian Revolution.

Why did James need to revise his play? Importantly, such textual changes strongly reflect what was going on in the outside world as James rewrote his play, especially in the context of decolonization. James carefully introduces Moïse, allowing him to act as a foil to the other Haitian Revolution leaders, making them appear worse or better as leader types. These insertions of Moïse also start to indicate a shift in James's own explanation of the Haitian Revolution, away from vindicationism and toward criticism of new postcolonial rulers, as James's disillusionment with leaders including Eric Williams and Kwame Nkrumah grew throughout the era of decolonization, when James was beginning to rewrite his play for those times. In the 1950s, colonial countries were gaining their independence, as James himself had forecast already in the 1930s, but, as will be discussed, a gulf was already starting to widen between James's predictions for future decolonization and his growing disappointment with the leaders emerging from former colonies. Repeated insertion of Moïse shows compelling evidence of James's subsequent rethinking of his first play.

Other handwritten changes swap lines attributed to Toussaint's sons, Isaac and Placide, in two scenes. This underlines the French expedition's duplicity by having the son who swore allegiance to France call the French "traitors" when Toussaint is captured:

> ISAAC: Father!
> P̶L̶A̶C̶I̶D̶E̶: You French traitors—(3.3.23, copy 2)

Here, having these words come out of Isaac's mouth effectively highlights the perfidy of this betrayal because in an earlier scene it was Isaac who had sworn loyalty to the French over his own father, whereas his brother Placide declared himself for Toussaint and San Domingo. Likewise, in copy 1, Isaac takes over Placide's lines when responding to the two-faced Bonaparte:

> [Isaac] P̶L̶A̶C̶I̶D̶E̶: yes, sir. We have been away for over six years.
> I̶S̶A̶A̶C̶: But we are sorry to leave France where everyone has been so kind to us (copy 1, 2.2.29)

This change of lines makes it clearer that Isaac has been completely taken in by French hypocrisy, in keeping with his decision in the opening scene of act 3 to go over to the French side, setting Isaac up for the sudden realization of French treachery when Toussaint is arrested. As discussed, according to the program list of characters, it seems that Isaac and Placide were cut from the actual performance version, but it seems that James was toying with including both again while reshaping the first play.

Another minor change is the name given to the maid to Mme. Leclerc, wife of the French expedition leader. Previously called Suzanne, the maid is now renamed Kikite. There seems to have been some rethinking as the original name "S̶u̶z̶a̶n̶n̶e̶" and an alternative "L̶o̶u̶i̶s̶e̶" are both struck through and replaced with "Kikite."

Toward the end of copy 1, further small but significant changes are made:

> Leclerc's villa on the outskirts of Cap François. Sitting on the balcony are Madame Leclerc and S̶u̶z̶a̶n̶n̶e̶ L̶o̶u̶i̶s̶e̶ Kikite, her mulatto companion. Pauline, like S̶u̶z̶a̶n̶n̶e̶ Kikite, is dressed in the local costume [. . .]
> Kikite S̶U̶Z̶A̶N̶N̶E̶: Let us have another Creole ball, Madame (3.3.15)

Even though these changes are not in James's own hand, it does not necessarily mean that he is not behind them through dictation or other means. This renaming has clearly been the subject of much rethinking, as evidenced by the fact that the original name "~~Suzanne~~" is first struck through, but then so too is the next alternative "~~Louise~~" before "Kikite" is finally settled upon as the replacement name. "Kikite" is a more obviously Kreyòl-sounding name.[108] One factor behind this name change is probably the fact that Suzanne is also the first name of Madame Louverture, Toussaint's wife, in the longer versions of the play. It is likely that a new name was sought to differentiate that other Suzanne, who is referred to only three times toward the end of copy 1 as Kikite. As with the Placide/Isaac changes, this is an incomplete rewrite, with the Kikite changes left half-finished in UWI Folder 227. As for copy 3, it contains no handwritten annotations at all, and is only a partial copy, ending abruptly at page 2.1.14. Such incompleteness and disorder is testament to the amount of rethinking and reworking of the play when these significant changes were being made.

Overall, it is Toussaint who takes center stage in the almost one-man show *Toussaint Louverture*, but subsequent changes begin to write in an alternative protagonist. From Moïse's complete absence in *Toussaint Louverture*, he would lead a larger cast of secondary characters in the 1938 edition of the history, as will be seen in chapter 2. The handwritten changes to the first play in the 1950s allow Moïse to be written into the play from which he had been previously absent. These changes in copy 1 guide us along the road of the genesis of the first play, past the first edition of the 1938 *Black Jacobins* history, which is the subject of chapter 2, and then back to the drama and James's complete rethinking of his first play, which is dealt with in chapter 4. From the 1950s vantage point of the handwritten additions to his first play, James returned to theater as a useful tool for rethinking the past of the Haitian Revolution. When James began to rework that play, this rewriting was driven especially by the Johnson-Forest ideas of the early 1940s through early 1950s and beyond, which James had worked on in collaboration with comrades in the United States. But before that, *The Black Jacobins* 1938 history would grow out of the same contexts as *Toussaint Louverture* in 1936.

2 | Making History: *The Black Jacobins* (1938)

As James himself made clear already in 1938, history and drama are profoundly interconnected. In the pages of the first version of his own distinctively "theatrical" history, he declared, "There is no drama like the drama of history."[1] Beyond this clear statement, which is the present book's epigraph, James's narrative history has a distinctive theatrical dimension throughout, with repeated references to drama. This theatrical dimension would then become even stronger in the revised edition of the history in 1963, as explored in chapter 3. In the 1938 edition, James's famous use of the image of history as theater prefaces the announcement of Toussaint's death in the final chapter. James, like Trotsky before him, makes striking use of the theatrical metaphor by choosing a theatrical form through which to present his narrative history.[2] There is page after page of theater-like "curious dramatic dialogue" throughout, featuring chief "actors" including Louverture (155). Following *Toussaint Louverture* in 1936, then, James again brings the San Domingo masses and their leaders onto the political stage by turning his play into a historical narrative.

What happens, this chapter asks, when James re-visions the past as history? In chapter 1, we saw that already his 1931 article invoking Toussaint Louverture anticipated the political road he would later travel. When James came to England, and while he was coming to Marxist politics, he represented the past of the Haitian Revolution as drama, using the play as a megaphone for his political commitments to loudly denounce imperialism and the rise of fascism. The 1938 *Black Jacobins* history comes out of the same raw research and can be considered as a rewriting of *Toussaint Louverture*. This chapter focuses entirely on the first edition of *The Black Jacobins* because its publication in 1938 was itself a historical event, which inspired African independence movements.[3] Treating the 1938 history on its own first also enables differences between James's telling of the past as history and showing of the past as drama to be identified.[4]

The chapter starts by examining the journey of James's Haitian Revolution–related writing back from the stage to the page. Next, I consider how James's twin 1938 histories—*A History of Negro Revolt* and *The Black Jacobins*—are already an early case of James rewriting his own work. In addition, the chapter looks at how James builds on Marxist and Trotskyist models of history writing, permanent revolution, combined and uneven development, and total history. Analysis of James's narrative will spotlight the history's double beginnings as key sites of communication. Following this, the French and Francophone origins of the 1938 history are explored, as Paris was a place of intense collaboration between James and others and a key site for the interlinked geneses of *The Black Jacobins* and Eric Williams's *Capitalism and Slavery* (1944). After this, the chapter looks at how dialogic aspects of the history counter historical misrepresentations of the Haitian Revolution. The chapter also explores tragic overtones throughout the first history edition, engaging with Scott's masterful narrativist argument about the 1938 history being emplotted as romance, and the 1963 revised edition being emplotted as tragedy. Romance, it is argued, is here filtered through Marxist lenses, and tragic overtones are also already clearly present in the 1938 original. Attention is paid to the initial representation of leaders and masses. Finally, the chapter closes by exploring the history's closing focus on Africa and its sense of anticipation of the coming African revolution.

From Stage Back to Page

James reworks his story from *Toussaint Louverture* when elaborating the first edition of *The Black Jacobins* history. This rebuilding of the past of the Haitian Revolution as a history narrative means that the 1938 history already constitutes a rewriting of James's Haitian material.[5] When James reconfigures the past as history, he re-creates the play's meaning. The earlier play employs a showing form of representing the past, where spectators witness the past, and actors imitate the past. In *The Black Jacobins* (1938), we see James in the process of telling history. Now James the historian acts as narrator with a more overt, controlling voice, clearly presenting actions in certain ways and expressing views about these actions. When writing history, James can refer to and exemplify meaning more clearly. Refashioning his research material and changing his mode of expression from play to history also allows James to spell out the political dimension of his play, explicitly cutting a Marxist path through his story.

In this more clearly Marxist-inspired history, there is a strong sense of chronology and change over time. James the historian makes the past reconnect by changing the beginning, middle, and ending of the story. Tense and time shift as James re-presents the history, repositioning the history's present- and future-oriented dimensions. As in the play, events in the past are told in chronological order, although James re-creates meaning by rewinding and fast-forwarding, more explicitly than in the play, to the Russian Revolution and to the present day of the late 1930s.

Telling the past as history enables James to recapitulate, to add commentary in the text and footnotes, to intervene more overtly, to foreground his shaping of the historical narrative line, and to engage in dialogue with other sources as he deploys the apparatuses of footnotes and the new annotated bibliography. This whole (re)telling process contrasts with the play, which does not come with sources and footnotes scrolling below the stage during performance.[6] In the history, we become more aware of the intertextual nature of James's story, of how *The Black Jacobins* communicates with other histories.

As for the change of title from play, *Toussaint Louverture*, to history, *The Black Jacobins: Toussaint Louverture and the San Domingo Revolution*, this indicates a change in focus where the characters of this story are concerned. Toussaint Louverture is still the hero of the story, as the subtitle shows, but the history is populated by a wider cast of multiple black Jacobins. Louverture still plays the central role, and the story of the Haitian Revolution is still mostly retold from his point of view. The history also features many long extracts quoting directly from his correspondence. In this way, Louverture still speaks to us directly from the pages of his letters in a manner that recalls the dramatic monologues and dialogues of a play. Now the perspective changes, and it is almost as if we are projected into Toussaint's head. We see what he is thinking, as James gives explanations bringing out the complexities of his main character's actions, motivations, and strategy through commentary on the incorporated letters.

This retelling of the past of the Haitian Revolution as history presents a more multilayered historical canvas, filled with more complex characters and subplots as James lengthens and adds new chapters to the story, according to the conventions of history writing. One example of James literally rewriting the play by introducing new characters and historical episodes is the reference added to the 1938 history about British agent Cathcart. In response to a review of the play, James had invoked Cathcart, personifying him as the one who refused any British trade until all whites on the island had been killed.[7] This crucial supplement to the play about the abominable role played by representatives of colonial powers in their internecine interimperialist fighting is written into the first edition of the history. Now Cathcart and his ilk are described as "civilised cannibals" who "in their greed for trade wanted to drive a wedge between Hayti and France to break all possibilities of unity" (307).

Layers of complexity are also added to the 1938 history, for example, when tragic overtones are added to Toussaint's character. As David Scott has argued in his illuminating reading of the two editions of the history, Toussaint's tragic flaw is made more prominent by some of the changes of the revised 1963 edition. Below, the chapter nuances Scott's interpretation by arguing that tragedy and tragic elements are already embedded in the original 1938 history. Here, the chapter follows Scott and others like Hayden White and Alun Munslow who encourage readers to pay attention to the narrative construction of textual history itself. Drama—the subject of chapter 1—is more obviously narrative construction than a textual history. However, Scott's and White's notion of historians like James being storytellers who emplot the past as drama is useful for this chapter.

Visions of History: *A History of Negro Revolt* (1938) and Trotsky's *History of the Russian Revolution* (1930)

Already in its original 1938 edition, *The Black Jacobins* first appears under the sign of rewriting. Even if not announced as such, rewriting constitutes an important component of the first iteration of *The Black Jacobins* history. Not only does the history rework *Toussaint Louverture*, it also relates strongly to James's other main 1938 publication *A History of Negro Revolt*, later revised in 1969 with the new title *A History of Pan-African Revolt*. Both 1938 histories were born out of the same moment and emerged from the same research material. Both works focus on slave resistance, but *A History of Negro Revolt* sweeps wider as it chronicles different black revolts throughout the world across the Caribbean, Africa, and America. The major landmark along this road of black revolts is the Haitian Revolution, and the opening chapter of *A History of Negro Revolt*, which outlines the Haitian Revolution in a more compact twenty-page format, is appropriately titled "San Domingo." In this way, the first chapter of *A History of Negro Revolt* rewrites *The Black Jacobins* before the second title was even published in October 1938.

Originally, *A History of Negro Revolt* was published in the left-wing monthly review FACT. Manning Marable has noted that James finished the work quickly by April 1938.[8] Some have criticized this volume. Worcester, for example, described it as "marred by a distracting degree of sloppiness both at the level of presentation and theory."[9] Bill Schwarz has described the history as "slight."[10] Beyond its shortcomings, however, Christian Høgsbjerg, Michael O. West, and William G. Martin have called the work a "pioneering and exceptional" contribution to the historiography of revolutionary "black internationalism."[11] When the Race Today Collective republished it in 1985, they underlined that *A History of Negro Revolt* "represented a major political intervention aimed [. . .] at smashing the prevailing ideas on slavery and capitalism."[12] Certainly, *A History of Negro Revolt* is less well-known than its more famous 1938 twin history *The Black Jacobins*, yet they contain many of the same statistics and much of the same narrative. This includes the famous lines about how the plantations were "huge sugar-factories" with proto-proletariat slaves "closer to a modern proletariat than any group of workers in existence at the time and the rising was, therefore, a thoroughly prepared and organized mass movement."[13] Throughout *A History of Negro Revolt*, slaves and colonized blacks are themselves presented as the motive force actively shaping the history and development of Caribbean, African, and American society.

A History of Negro Revolt also represents an important milestone along the road of *The Black Jacobins* because some lines even prefigure the later 1963 history appendix's outline of a strong pattern of Caribbean identity, including: "The Negroes in the West Indies have developed in a manner peculiar to themselves" (1963, 73). Dialectical tensions of James's work also emerge in *A History of Negro Revolt* as he focuses on the Caribbean labor revolts of 1937 at greater length than elsewhere. Schwarz has noted an extraordinary silence in *The Black Jacobins* about these labor rebellions.[14] Here becomes apparent again the dialectical tension running throughout James's work, which means that he mentions certain subjects in some places more than others, including the U.S. occupation of Haiti from 1915 to 1934.[15]

If *The Black Jacobins* in its first edition is in an important sense about Africa, already in *A History of Negro Revolt* James turns to the Caribbean, and what he writes is already self-reflexive, prefiguring the 1963 revised *Black Jacobins* appendix on Caribbean identity. What is key to both works is the idea of blacks actively organizing themselves, governing themselves, and representing themselves in historical and literary narratives instead of being passively misgoverned and represented by aliens from the second-rate echelons of the old colonial system. Both 1938 histories also connect with James's earlier 1932–33 works in powerfully making the case for West Indian self-government with dominion status for the British West Indies.[16] In works like *The Life of Captain Cipriani* (1932) and its abridged version *The Case for West-Indian Self-Government* (1933), as well as in *A History of Negro Revolt* and *The Black Jacobins*, the reflexive is important, and these works constitute self-translations of one another. Self-representation is both the purpose and the means of James's historical writing fighting for self-government—political representation in the colonial world—which is reinforced by the history book's representation of anticolonial black struggle. Turning inward to the self is important here, as James always insisted that "Africans must win their own freedom. No-one can win it for them."[17]

Politically and culturally, the bonds that link *A History of Negro Revolt* and *The Black Jacobins* are of great significance, even more so because both 1938 histories would be rewritten in 1969 and 1963 respectively. Like the famous 1963 appendix, the 1969 epilogue to *A History of Pan-African Revolt* brings the work right up to date by reviewing the thirty years since 1938, widening its focus to new revolts across the Pan-African world, fast-forwarding through two decades, and continuing to reshape the all-important reflexive relation between representation and self-representation. Earlier works by James are all landmarks along the road of the making of *The Black Jacobins*, and are already inscribed with rewriting from the outset during the productive 1930s period of James's writing.

In *The Black Jacobins* 1938 history, James adopts a biographical method, following in the footsteps of his 1932 political biography telling of Captain Cipriani's life. When rewritten in condensed form as *The Case for West-Indian Self-Government* in 1933, the shorter pamphlet cut out nearly all biographical material on Cipriani, refocusing attention on the anticolonial struggle for self-government.[18] Like James's 1932 biography of Cipriani, his 1938 *Black Jacobins* history tells the story of the Haitian Revolution mainly through the lens of a single figure—Toussaint Louverture—using biography as the mode of historical and political analysis, whereas *A History of Negro Revolt* stripped out most biographical content, like *The Case for West-Indian Self-Government*. James's study of politics and history that is *The Black Jacobins* (1938) also builds on searing attacks on colonialism from the earlier works, developing the clear Marxist perspective of *A History of Negro Revolt*, and hammering home the point that the ex-slaves are a revolutionary force because they move on their own, and they draw on their own capabilities in their struggles.

These earlier works can be thought of as stepping stones through James's politicization, including *World Revolution 1917–1936: The Rise and Fall of the Communist International* (1937). This work was summed up by publisher Frederic Warburg as "a kind of Bible of Trotskyism."[19] It was one of the first accounts of the Comintern ever written, and one of the first to be "written in English from a revolutionary socialist point of view."[20] In it, James exposed Stalinist distortions and accumulating crimes precisely when Stalin was consolidating his power.[21] This early work influenced G. Selvarajatnan, who later led the Madras textile mill strike, and formed the basis of Sri Lankan Trotskyist Leslie Goonewardene's *Rise and Fall of the Comintern*, which was published ten years afterward, with an introduction by Ajit Roy, James's comrade.[22]

These previous works overlap and intersect with *The Black Jacobins*, where their political and historical insights are further developed. Both *A History of Negro Revolt* and *The Black Jacobins* develop in tandem, with the opening "San Domingo" chapter of the first 1938 volume constituting a compressed, but simultaneously wider, spinoff of the full-length history of the Haitian Revolution. The genesis and formation of this outgrowth are completely intertwined with those of *The Black Jacobins*, with *A History of Negro Revolt* covering a wider range of black struggles across the world. Cross-reading James's 1938 pair of histories reaffirms that both represent important historical documents, advancing far ahead of their time. Both histories would be revised during that other active moment of *The Black Jacobins*: the 1960s. At that point, James would declare that both histories had stood the test of time, and needed little updating. Chapter 3 examines how even though the actual changes were few in number, they add substantially to the framework of *The Black Jacobins*.

The Black Jacobins also needs to be considered in the light of Trotsky's monumental *History of the Russian Revolution* (1930), from which James derives much of his method and style.[23] Following Trotsky's historical analysis of the Russian Revolution, James's history is an inquiry into the dynamics of another great revolution: the Haitian Revolution.[24] In addition, *The Black Jacobins* must also be viewed within the context of other Marxist writings on history, including those by Marx himself.[25] In *Beyond a Boundary* and his unpublished autobiography, James recalls his hard reading and rereading of Trotsky, Marx, and Lenin during his political awakening in Red Nelson, Lancashire, England.[26]

In a 1940 article on Trotsky, James equates rewriting with Trotsky's own Marxist method of writing history: "Let us look at his style, for words were his greatest weapons as a man of action. He expressed himself always amply, completely, and with care, writing and rewriting and rewriting. Man of action though he was, the whole of him is contained in his books."[27] Of Trotsky's *History*, James wrote, "Too much material can swamp. But to Trotsky, who since 1905 had the main lines of the map clear, it defined, clarified, enriched, illustrated."[28] James's history writing builds particularly on Trotsky's and Marx's models, echoing Trotsky's and Marx's famous prefaces, and rewriting them in his turn.[29]

Beginnings: Making the Past Connect

The first *Black Jacobins* history edition has a double beginning: both a preface and a prologue. Both hammer home James's fundamental point about slavery and the slave trade being the economic basis for the rise of capitalism. The prologue—the history's second beginning—has a memorable first sentence: "Christopher Columbus landed first in the New World at the island of San Salvador, and after praising God enquired urgently for gold" (xv). This sums up in twenty-odd words that the colonial enterprise from Columbus onward was all about money. If the 1963 appendix is a "remarkable model of economy," according to David Scott, this is even truer of the prologue. At only one and a half pages in length, it covers a centuries-long time span from 1492 and the moment of Columbus's discovery of Hispaniola up to 1734 and beyond to the explosion of the slave trade. Next, by the end of page 1 of chapter 1, "The Property," we seem to be on the eve of 1789. In terms of page span to time span, therefore, we initially have 250 years compressed into only a page and a half, followed by 308 pages devoted to the sixteen years from 1789 until the massacre of the whites at the beginning of 1805, followed by fewer than four pages toward the end devoted to postindependence Haitian developments, roughly the period of 1805 through the early 1930s, some 126 years. Thus, the vast bulk of the entire work concentrates on the main years of the Haitian revolutionary struggles from 1791 to January 1, 1804. James's history follows his Marxist models by stressing interconnections between long-run and short-run developments, and also asserts the combined rise of capitalism, colonialism, and slavery.

How a text opens or closes is always important. Always a self-conscious reflector on beginnings and endings, James is a writer who frequently makes full use of multiple paratexts in his work, multiplying new prefaces, appendices, epilogues, and postfaces, particularly from one edition to the next. With the two beginnings—preface and prologue—James doubly draws attention to the prefatorial site of his history.[30] James's sentences often double back on themselves, as Scott notes, echoing the introduction to Karl Marx's *Eighteenth Brumaire of Louis Bonaparte* about individuals making history, but only in certain circumstances. James begins his biography of Louverture by rewriting Marx: "Yet Toussaint did not make the revolution. It was the revolution that made Toussaint. And even that is not the whole truth"; "Great men make history, but only such history as it is possible for them to make" (viii).

By taking the correlation of the individual and the circumstances to his biographical model, however, James shows that history cannot be understood through the personality of one great man alone, even if he draws vivid pen portraits of Toussaint.[31] But, while James's preface signals that the history will mainly be a portrait of the revolution through Toussaint's personality, the evolving circumstances are also crucial to the historical developments James outlines.

Chapter 2, "The Owners," reads early travel and natural history accounts by planters, colonists, and travelers against the grain.[32] The chapter begins with images of nature working in harmony, providing exotic and aesthetically pleasing vistas as far as the eye can see in every direction. Abundant ripe fruit promises juicy sustenance, and lush vegetation provides sensory stimulation that will welcome, cocoon, and soothe the newly arrived traveler from Europe. Such descriptions would not be at all out of place in any of the travel and natural history accounts outlining first impressions of the colony of Saint-Domingue. Such first impressions also tally with those of newly arrived Colonel Vincent at the start of the 1936 play as written, but not performed, who views his unfamiliar surroundings with wonder as if he were in a paradisiacal Garden of Eden. As James notes in the history, "The traveller from Europe was enchanted at his first glimpse of this paradise, in which the ordered beauty of agriculture and the prodigality of Nature competed equally for his surprise and admiration" (18).

However, James's history narrative quickly serves to shatter any paradisiacal illusions because he immediately zeroes in on what is missing from the typical idyllic description, namely the slaves who power the whole plantation system. To destroy any illusions about natural features, James brings into view not only the degeneration and corruption of the white settlers—even a "relation of the de Vaudreils, a Châteauneuf, or Boucicaut, last descendant of the marshal of France, passing his life between a bowl of rum and a Negro concubine" (20)—but particularly the cruel treatment meted out to the human bodies of slaves powering the generation of immense wealth.[33] Tableaux of inhuman punishments inflicted upon the slave population are the meat of this chapter about the owners, and it is tellingly from these pages that Dexter Lyndersay, director of the *Black Jacobins* play in 1967, would select scenes to dramatize for that play's prologue. France's role in destroying colonial Saint-Domingue is made clear by such miniscenes, and James extracted many of these descriptions from French and Haitian sources.

French Connections: Genealogies of the 1938 *Black Jacobins* History in Paris

Much of the preparatory reading and archival work for the 1938 history was carried out in France. It was in Paris that leading Anglophone Trotskyist and Pan-Africanist James came into direct contact with his prominent Francophone counterparts. France and especially Paris began to assume a new importance for James. This was especially the case from 1934 onward when James became a committed Trotskyist, attending meetings of the European section of Trotskyists "[e]very three or four months," usually representing the British section.[34]

Interwar Paris was the formative site for James's *Black Jacobins* research. There it was that James followed and laid out his own archival traces in the Paris archives.[35] These trips to Paris in the 1930s enabled James to conduct the research for *The Black Jacobins*. According to his own accounts of the work's genesis, one important six-month research trip lasted from winter 1933 through spring 1934.[36] In Paris, James consulted the holdings of the French National Archives, the War Office, and the Colonial Office. Beyond Paris, James also spent some days in Bordeaux and Nantes, where he searched for documents on the slave trade and the Caribbean.[37] Another trip made by James in 1935 was vividly documented by his former comrade and lover, Louise Cripps, whose memoirs paint a picture of Paris buzzing with excitement around the Trotskyist movement, but also fraught with danger.[38]

It was also in Paris that James met Pierre Naville, leading French Trotskyist, early surrealist, sociologist, and the future translator of *The Black Jacobins* in 1949. In James's unpublished memoirs of this period, Naville's impact on the future trajectory of *The Black Jacobins* is underlined, as is James's active taking part in Trotskyist activities centered in Paris: "Naville [...] who was one of the leaders of the Trotskyite movement in France in 1936 and I used to go regularly to France to take part, and used to take part with Naville, and Naville took it upon himself to translate *The Black Jacobins* into French, put it to Gallimard, they published it and he wrote an introduction, that was a notable piece of work."[39] The situation of massive unrest in France opened up vistas of revolutionary possibilities, according to James, who saw the activities of the French working class as continuing the tradition inherited from their French revolutionary forebears: "the French workers have a revolutionary tradition. Their spirit is high. This May Day [1937] there will be tremendous demonstrations. Before another May Day arrives, there are likely to be barricades in the streets."[40]

Paris was also the site of James's first encounters with radical groups of the leading Francophone Caribbean and African intellectuals. James was one of the leading figures of the Pan-African movement in England, and France's capital city was the central hub of all the political, social, and cultural Pan-African networks spanning metropolitan France and its colonies.[41] It was also Paris that was the birthplace of Negritude.[42] In Paris, James came tantalizingly close to the forefather of Negritude, Martiniquan Aimé Césaire, who was based in Paris at this time, but the pair would not actually meet until early 1968 in Cuba.[43] However, it is more important to emphasize that their most famous works, *The Black Jacobins* (1938) and *Cahier d'un retour au pays natal* (1939), were contemporaries, both sharing Parisian origins and long intertwined trajectories of repeated rewriting. In chapter 3, I cross-read James and Césaire with reference to James's own extended translation and analysis of Césaire's *Cahier* in the new appendix of the revised 1963 history.

Instead of fantasizing about the what-ifs of James and Césaire meeting earlier, we can focus more concretely instead on James's actual meetings with another central figure, known as the enfant terrible of Negritude: French Guianese poet Léon-Gontran Damas.[44] Of the Negritude poets, Damas was the first to publish a collection of poetry (*Pigments*, 1937), which would be viewed by many as "a manifesto of Negritude."[45] In winter 1933, Damas put Paris and its sources of material at James's disposal, guiding him through the maze of relevant bookshops, libraries, and archives, and helping him to find French-language material by the most rapid means.[46] Consequently, James would claim that his knowledge of Damas was unique. If Negritude consisted

Making History (1938) | 79

at this time mostly of "interminable discussions" among the founders, then James engaged directly with one prominent figure in this lively Negritude conversation.⁴⁷ These dense networks of political meetings, cafés, restaurants, bookshops, poetry readings, dance halls, and "the spirit of Paris" collectively created the discursive field that nourished *The Black Jacobins*.⁴⁸

Interwar Pan-African Paris was also the site where James encountered, through the intermediary of George Padmore, Tiemoko Garan Kouyaté, the Paris-based West African anticolonial leader who led the Ligue de défense de la race nègre and the Union des travailleurs nègres.⁴⁹ Kouyaté seems to have made a great impression on James, as he did on Padmore.⁵⁰ James recalls discussing the Trotskyist movement with Kouyaté, commenting, "he could agree with me about everything except that one thing would be needed. I asked what that was. 'That Trotsky was a Black man, that's all.'"⁵¹ On Kouyaté and Padmore, James noted, "George kept up that acquaintance with Kouyaté although Kouyaté remained in the CP and George left and would have nothing to do with them."⁵² James seems to have been unaware of Kouyaté's own break with, and expulsion from, the Communist Party in 1933, but James's recollections give insight into the special links joining him and Padmore to Francophone counterparts such as Kouyaté.

An important living Francophone Haitian source for *The Black Jacobins* was Alfred Auguste Nemours (1883–1955)—a Haitian army general, diplomat, and military historian. In drafts of James's autobiography, Nemours is remembered for introducing James to useful contacts in 1930s Paris, including the Haitian ambassador, who gave James "great insights into the mulatto side of the Haitian people."⁵³ Nemours's importance for the genesis of the 1936 play was such that he is explicitly named in the author's note in the program for *Toussaint Louverture*. James's invocation of Nemours there recalls his protests against the Italian invasion of Ethiopia before his appointment in 1937 as Haiti's minister plenipotentiary. As discussed, James's 1980 foreword to the Allison and Busby edition of *The Black Jacobins* would recall how in the 1930s Nemours instructed James on tactics, bringing his military skills to life for James with large coffee cups and books in a Paris café.⁵⁴ Although Nemours and James came from very different backgrounds—Nemours was born into a wealthy Haitian family and schooled in Paris, while James was from the emerging black middle class of Trinidad—James's foreword underlines their shared Caribbean culture.⁵⁵

Representations of Toussaint Louverture have always tended to make this figure act as an icon and symbol.⁵⁶ Variously, Toussaint has been vilified, racialized, ideologized, romanticized, or sanctified by Haitian and foreign historians and writers.[57] Haitian sources were important for *The Black Jacobins*, and James drew at length from Nemours's history of Toussaint's captivity and death. Nemours's Toussaint is messianic, and his history of him hagiographic, but James summed this up generously, as Forsdick has noted, when he wrote that Nemours was "an enthusiastic admirer of Toussaint, but exceptionally fair" (319). James also drew at length on Nemours's history of Toussaint's captivity and death, an invaluable source for both James's 1938 history and especially his 1936 *Toussaint Louverture* play, which lingered on Toussaint's death scene and Paul Robeson's solo in it.

If Nemours's approach toward Toussaint is messianic, then, in contrast, James already in his 1938 history presents Toussaint as admirable but flawed. Unsurprisingly, James's references to Nemours abound in chapter 11, "The Black Consul," and chapter 13, "The War of Independence," which concentrate on the military strategies and main battles of the Haitian Revolution. Nemours's history of Toussaint's captivity and death is summed up by James as the "definitive account of Toussaint's captivity with many of the most important documents printed in full" (300n1), and in James's annotated bibliography to *The Black Jacobins*, he calls this "A thorough and well-documented study" (322). Nemours is singled out repeatedly as a source whose archival research and "mass of evidence" (271n1) are of great value. Above all, *The Black Jacobins* bases itself upon the foundations of Nemours's careful transcribing of the letters from Leclerc, leader of the French expedition, to First Consul Bonaparte, and of other invaluable nineteenth-century documents, such as Toussaint's constitution, which Nemours prints in full (220n1).

In France, James followed in the footsteps of Haiti's first historians, Thomas Madiou and Beaubrun Ardouin, consulting many of the same documents. The backbone of James's 1938 history is Haitian historian Horace Pauléus Sannon's three-volume *Histoire de Toussaint Louverture* (1920–33).[58] Like Sannon, James often lets Toussaint speak for himself in the present tense through his acts and his correspondence.[59] Superlative praise is always given to Sannon's history of Toussaint Louverture, which is proclaimed in the bibliography of *The Black Jacobins* to be "the best biography yet written of Toussaint" (319). James's use of Sannon as a source helps him to make the point that race is subsidiary to the class question.

James's archival work in France formed the basis of *The Black Jacobins* history, but like most Haitian historians, James mainly reworked secondary literature on the Haitian Revolution into a new narrative in *The Black Jacobins*.[60] Primary sources consulted are listed at the start of the bibliography, but James concedes, "The writer does not claim to have examined these archives exhaustively. Those at *Les Archives Nationales* alone would take many years. But much of the ground has been covered by other writers which makes independent research easier" (317). In the 1938 bibliography, James also makes a prominent reference to the collection of Dr. Jean Price Mars, whose key work *Ainsi parla l'oncle* (Thus spoke the uncle, 1928) led to the revalorization of Haitian culture and the birth of indigenism in Haiti (317).[61] A footnote giving the address of Price Mars as "Pétionville, Hayti" (317n1), indicates that James had been in correspondence during the writing of the history.[62] Price Mars's work would become a pillar of the added appendix in the 1963 edition of *The Black Jacobins*. Based on his French and Haitian authorities, his Paris research, and Karl Marx's *Capital*, James would develop an important foundational argument about capitalism and slavery.

Capitalism, Slavery, and Eric Williams

James's understanding of the relation of slavery to capitalism can be charted throughout *The Black Jacobins*, where James builds his capitalism-slavery argument on Marx's own exploration of the capitalist mode of production and class struggle. In *The Black Jacobins*, slave-based plantation labor is presented by James as a savage capitalist system against which the "mass"—the word used repeatedly throughout the history—struggles and wins.[63] Savagely violent plantation slavery is presented by James as an important form of primitive accumulation of surplus capital.

Debates about the precise relationship between capitalism and slavery have been waged since Marx's *Capital*, through Eric Williams's doctoral thesis, James's *The Black Jacobins* (1938), the 1944 publication of Williams's *Capitalism and Slavery*, and beyond to the New Historians of Capitalism (NHC) group, who from the 2010s have revived Williams's basic argument about the relationship between capitalism and slavery, as well as its critics.[64]

The Black Jacobins shares many common features with *Capital*, including a complex textual history.[65] *The Black Jacobins* too is made up of a palimpsest of different drafts, and these can all be seen collectively as the "original(s)," following Robert Young and Emily Apter's readings of Marx's *Capital* as a palimpsestic "messy editorial object."[66] Marx's key work was rewritten and stitched back together by Marx himself and his collaborator

Friedrich Engels, as well as by influential readings by the likes of Louis Althusser. Likewise, James's *The Black Jacobins* has been reworked and stitched back together in its turn by its author and others, allowing us to find new narratives within it and to see the whole work in new lights across all its moments of reconfiguration (1931, 1934, 1936, 1938, the 1950s, 1963, 1967, and beyond).

On the topic of capitalism and slavery, especially relating to Caribbean slavery, there are strong links between James's history project and the research that would become his protégé Eric Williams's *Capitalism and Slavery* (1944).[67] On his trips to Paris, James would sometimes be accompanied by Williams, his fellow Trinidadian and former pupil who would become the future first prime minister of independent Trinidad and Tobago from 1962.[68] While Williams was pursuing his undergraduate and postgraduate studies at the University of Oxford, James acted as unofficial mentor, and his autobiographical notes recall one particular "history lesson" that finally enabled Williams to grasp the full Marxist historical method with reference to the French Revolution.[69] In his unfinished memoirs, James sharply outlines his own generative role in shaping the thesis of Williams's *Capitalism and Slavery* in reminiscences colored by their subsequent acrimonious split, almost thirty years later.

According to James, his research for *The Black Jacobins* directly spawned the central thesis of Williams's subsequent history *Capitalism and Slavery* (1944): that the basis of the abolition of slavery was economic. James presents himself "[writing] with [his] hands," and "[writing] down in 2/3 pages" the subject of Williams's doctoral thesis based on his "French authorities and some research on the history of abolition in Britain."[70] Williams is presented as a faithful scribe who copies out word for word the thesis plan formulated by his mentor. Such memoirs present James instigating and formulating the central thesis to be investigated, but James also claims responsibility for actually writing certain lines of *Capitalism and Slavery*. According to James, "there are certain places where I wrote into Williams' book and I am going to say what they are, because anybody who reads those passages will know at once that they were not written by Williams, they were written by somebody like me," and "There are certain passages in it which I either wrote or dictated to him, and anyone who knows us both would be easily able to detect them." James would also stress his own role in getting *Capitalism and Slavery* published in 1944 with his suggestion that Williams pay the publication costs himself.[71]

James's 1938 history already makes the link between the rise of European capitalism and Caribbean slavery, which would later be popularized by Williams and come to be known as "the Williams thesis" or "the Williams Effect."[72] Already in 1938, *The Black Jacobins* history also anticipates what has become widely known as the Williams decline thesis. James memorably points out that had slavery still been profitable, William Wilberforce or Thomas Clarkson or any other abolitionist would have "preached themselves as black in the face as any Negro" (312). *The Black Jacobins* and *Capitalism and Slavery* fit together. In a bibliographic note, Williams would even note that his work followed the same central thesis about the slaves as *The Black Jacobins*: "On pages 38–41 [of *The Black Jacobins*] the thesis advanced in this book is stated and concisely and, as far as I know, for the first time in English."[73] Here Williams acknowledges *The Black Jacobins* as an important model for *Capitalism and Slavery*.

However, we could also talk about a case of James versus Williams, and of *The Black Jacobins* versus *Capitalism and Slavery*. At the root of the differences between the two histories, according to Oxaal, is that, unlike Williams, James sought to demolish the historical lie of "Negro passivity" under slavery.[74] The focus on slave resistance is the main story in James's history, but more of a companion theme in that of Williams. Where *Capitalism and Slavery* overlaps the most with *The Black Jacobins* is in chapter 12, "The Slaves and Slavery," which takes us beyond mainland Britain to the colonies and the slaves themselves. Questions have been raised about whether chapter 12 even fits into the rest of *Capitalism and Slavery*, notably by Michael Craton.[75] Indeed, on the genesis of this chapter 12, Selwyn Ryan notes that after being sent the proofs of *Capitalism and Slavery*, James told Williams that he had left out the slaves completely. Then Eric Williams went away and had to write this new chapter 12 right at the end.[76] What is clear is that Williams owes a considerable debt to James for the formulation of his central thesis.[77] His endnotes do highlight that "special mention" must be made of James's *The Black Jacobins* (1938), but James receives only brief acknowledgment in the first endnote reference to chapter 12: "See C.L.R. James, *The Black Jacobins* (London, 1938) for the slave revolution in Saint Domingue."[78]

In his unpublished autobiography, James recalls that Williams also played a considerable role in looking up references, preparing, and even writing certain lines in *The Black Jacobins*.[79] His recollections of Williams's role as collaborator on archival research in Paris, and his writing of a number of footnotes and passages are filtered through their later sharp split. Williams is damned with faint praise—"I don't think there is much more to him than that"—and presented as some kind of superhuman pen-pushing administrator and fact-checker, capable of collecting and storing prodigious amounts of information in the archives.[80] James's autobiographical notes do, however, stress crucial reciprocal influences on the genesis of both famous histories—*The Black Jacobins* (1938) and *Capitalism and Slavery* (1944).

Repeatedly, James uses his 1938 history to probe the interrelationship between the rise of early capitalism and slavery before such links were popularized through Williams's 1944 history *Capitalism and Slavery*. Slavery, race, and the rise of capitalism also feature in Marx's writings, but only at the margins, whereas in James's 1938 history these become the central issues. However, links between slavery and the rise of capitalism, and between economic decline and abolition, are subordinate theses throughout *The Black Jacobins*, albeit important ones because they reinforce the vindication theme that there is nothing inherently inferior about the slaves racially.

One way in which *The Black Jacobins* breaks new historical ground is by laying bare how the rise of capitalism was powered on the backs of slave labor. Marx had already made the link between primitive accumulation and slavery of Africans, but James's original contribution to Marxist and colonial historiography was to make this argument central to *The Black Jacobins*. As James puts it unequivocally in the chapter "The Owners," their vast accumulation of capital was based squarely on the exploitation of unwaged labor: "The slave-trade and slavery were the economic basis of the French Revolution"; "The capital from the slave-trade fertilized them [the industries developed in 18th century France]"; "[on] the success or failure of the [slave] traffic everything else depended"; "slavery and the colonial trade were the fount and origin and sustenance of this thriving industry and far-flung commerce[....] By 1789 San Domingo was the market of the new world" (35–37). Repeatedly, James presents the "new world" of the nascent capitalist system as bound up from the start with New World colonialism and plantation slavery in the Caribbean, with its "huge sugar-factories," proto-proletariat slaves described as "closer to a modern proletariat than any group of workers in existence at the time," "revolutionary labourers," and "luddite wreckers" (68).

Combined and Uneven Development, Permanent Revolution, and Total History

The Black Jacobins history is also built on the foundations of Trotsky's twin theories—uneven and combined development and permanent revolution—

which become important parts of the "theoretical bedrock" of James's 1938 history as well as *World Revolution* (1937), as noted by Paul Le Blanc.[81] These related ideas are fundamental for James's 1938 history.[82] Trotsky's theories have at their source the paradox of backward Russia. Trotsky outlines how backward conditions in the countryside were mixed with areas of advanced and highly concentrated industry.[83] According to the Marxist schema of history, human society advances from lower to higher stages of development; a theory of stages from feudalism to capitalism and beyond to socialism, conceived of as the highest level. According to traditional Marxist theory, then, the capitalist mode of production would develop uniformly across the world starting in already advanced northwestern Europe, with backward countries having to go through all the same stages as the advanced capitalist nations. According to Trotsky, however, backward countries like Russia could make leaps over certain stages of development.

These linked ideas—permanent revolution and uneven and combined development—are pivotal to James's 1938 history, where they travel to the colonial contexts of San Domingo plantation slave society and anticolonial revolution in Africa and the Caribbean, beyond the Russia and China of Trotsky's examples.[84] Permanent revolution is used in *The Black Jacobins* as a model for explaining the development of the Haitian Revolution as the only successful slave revolt in history. In the more distant past of the Haitian Revolution, these slaves suffered, according to James, from the "concentrated oppressions of slavery" and responded as "[r]evolutionaries through and through [...] brothers of the cordeliers in Paris and the Vyborg workers in Petrograd" (231).[85]

If Trotsky's 1930 *History* already contains the germs of history from below, then surely this is even more the case in James's 1938 history, where the direct interference of the enslaved masses in the revolution is clearly foregrounded.[86] *The Black Jacobins* certainly subjects ordinary people—ex-slaves—and their struggles against their colonial masters and plantation slavery to historical scrutiny. Although not often seen as an example of history from below, *The Black Jacobins* arguably pioneers and prefigures attempts to practice history from such perspectives already in the 1930s.[87] In James's 1938 history, there is already a focus on the two thousand other popular leaders who would also need to be taken away in order for the French to win (286), and there is a firm interest in the actions and thoughts of the enslaved.

There is a strong focus on tensions between the black Jacobin leaders Toussaint and Dessalines and the great mass of the population, the ex-slaves, that shines the spotlight on the masses down below and the differences between their material class interests and those of the top leadership, who are also brought into view in this pioneering history from below, or, more accurately, this visionary total history of both top and bottom.[88] James's total history shares the panoramic perspectives of his Marxist model—Trotsky's history writing.[89] *The Black Jacobins* is more than a history from below, and it appeared long before the late 1950s and early 1960s work on bottom-up perspectives by French and English Marxist historians: Soboul, Rudé, Thompson, Hobsbawm, and others.[90]

Writing Back to Misrepresentation and Falsification

James's emphasis on class as well as race comes in sharp contrast to some histories of the Haitian Revolution before James, such as T. Lothrop Stoddard's presentation of the events simply as a race war. James uses history in 1938 as a tool for rewriting and challenging misrepresentations of the revolution by Stoddard and others. James writes back to the type of history writing that has served to deprecate, objectify, and dehumanize black colonial people on the basis of race. *The Black Jacobins* should be seen, at least in part, as James's polemical reply to one particular history: T. Lothrop Stoddard's *The French Revolution in San Domingo*. While James's full-length *The Black Jacobins* history is not framed as clearly as a point-by-point rebuttal of Stoddard's arguments—like James's earlier 1931 article response to Harland or his 1969 introduction to *Froudacity*—James deploys multiple footnotes and his annotated bibliography to dismantle Stoddard's racialist arguments. Unlike James, Stoddard is unashamedly pro-white and always at pains to stress the exclusively racial character of this "struggle" and the "color line" in San Domingo. James's *Black Jacobins* history corrects the likes of Stoddard and Froude by always referring to the Haitian Revolution and its revolutionaries as such.

The keynote to Stoddard's history is tragedy. Repeatedly, he refers to the situation as "a great tragedy," "a grim tragedy," "the downfall of white supremacy," "the great disaster," or a "grim tragi-comedy." Portraying the events as a tragedy, Stoddard follows the well-trodden narrative line of many of his racialist counterparts—the Froudes, Harlands, and Spenser St. Johns. It is this constant manipulation of the tragedy storyline in such racist accounts that leads me to nuance David Scott's sophisticated arguments about James reimagining the Haitian Revolution as tragedy for his second history edition. Even when revised in 1963, *The Black Jacobins* continues to respond to, and counteract, the gloom and negativity of histories told through decidedly racist lenses. For Stoddard, this was exclusively "a war of colors," in which "race hatred was very intense."[91] Stoddard shares Harland and Froude's obsession with typologies of upper versus lower races, painting a sensationalist picture of the black race, with whom such attributes as cannibalism, horrible smells, laziness, and indolence are endlessly associated.[92] In the bibliography, James takes Stoddard to task for his prejudices: "With industry and ingenuity, Lothrop Stoddard pursues his vendetta against the Negro race. His thesis is that the white race destroyed itself in San Domingo through its determination to preserve its racial purity, and with the aid of extracts from the correspondence of irresponsible private persons and by ignoring whatever does not fit into his case he builds up a mirage of proof. In various footnotes we give examples of his methods" (321). Countering such historical misrepresentations is a major aim of James's history writing in *The Black Jacobins*, where James directly counters the "professional white-washers" (7) of history and "Tory historians, regius professors and sentimentalists" (11) like Stoddard, Froude, and Harland.

Exploring how *The Black Jacobins* history is constituted, this book builds on the issue raised by Michel-Rolph Trouillot of the active and transitive process of silencing the Haitian Revolution at all stages of the production of history. Exposing "the brazenness of these imperialist historians" (319) and their "dishonest misrepresentation" is an important part of James's task of history writing. Misrepresentation or silencing by the likes of Stoddard and others is clearly revealed throughout *The Black Jacobins* as a deliberately active and transitive process in its turn, although those precise terms are never used. From this perspective, James's writing back to the likes of Stoddard and their misrepresentations, silences, and skewed misuse of evidence can also be read as an active and transitive process, whereby James reads these sources back against the grain, rewriting them to expose these misrepresentations as loudly and visibly as possible. Active and transitive too is James's own process of making history whereby he repositions evidence previously manipulated by the likes of Stoddard to generate a new alternative narrative. This is the process of the constitution of historical representation, from which *The Black Jacobins* history is made.

References throughout *The Black Jacobins* make it explicit that James's history is written to counter deliberate acts of manipulation, suppression, and falsification in some historical narratives of the Haitian Revolution: "Unfortunately *suppressio veri* and *suggestio falsi* are not the only devils to be contended with. Hard experience has taught the lesson that it is unwise to take anything on trust and an examination of even apparently *bona fide* quotations with reference duly attached has unearthed some painful mistakes of unscrupulousness" (317) A case in point of such deliberately misleading, untrustworthy, and manipulative *suppressio veri* and *suggestio falsi*–type silencing is highlighted through reference to Stoddard's highly selective use of sources and reorientations of their viewpoints:

> When the French captured Port-au-Prince in 1802, Lacroix who was left in command found among Toussaint's effects, "locks of hair of all colours, rings, golden hearts crossed by arrows, latchkeys" [...] and an infinity of love-letters[....] This does not suit Mr. Lothrop Stoddard's racial theories. On p. 388 of his book, *The French Revolution in San Domingo*, he writes as follows about the relations of white women with the black generals: "The negro generals had greatly abused their power in this respect. For Toussaint's gross misconduct in this regard, see Lacroix II, 104–5." How many will look up Lacroix? Naturally they believe after reading Stoddard that Toussaint and his generals raped white women or forced them to sleep with them through fear. Thiers, in his famous *History of the Consulate and the Empire*, actually says so. (217)

Performing such cross-readings of deliberately skewed historical interpretations against their original sources enables James to uncover processes of silencing built upon other narratives, often repeating inaccuracies until they sediment and come to be accepted as fact.[93] Through his exposé of Stoddard, James demolishes the foundations on which are built all such typical examples "of the cloud of lies which obscure the true history of imperialism in colonial countries" (217n1). James foreshadows Edward Said's implicit call for the colonized to represent themselves and purge all misrepresentations.

To counter Stoddard-type lies, James predicates the foundations of his storyline on vindication of extraordinary achievements and slave resistance. As in James's 1931 reply to Harland, active slave resistance is repeatedly highlighted throughout *The Black Jacobins* and reflected by active strings of verbs: "They *undertook* vast hunger strikes; *undid* their chains and *hurled themselves* on the crew in futile attempts at insurrection[....] Some *took the opportunity* to *jump* overboard, *uttering* cries of *triumph* as they *cleared* the vessel and disappeared below the surface" (3, emphasis added). References abound to the brave revolutionaries choosing to show by example how to die with bravery. Like Stoddard, James devotes considerable space to infant mortality, but whereas Stoddard uses this and slave infertility as "evidence" of racial inferiority and of slaves being "half-human" and "fit for nothing else but slavery," James focuses on slave resistance, including use of poison and manipulation of newborn babies' jaws (9).[94]

Against racialist depictions of slaves as inferior and only half-human, James makes it clear that the slaves remained "despite their black skins and curly hair, quite invincibly human beings; with the intelligence and resentments of human beings" (5). Throughout *The Black Jacobins*, James clearly underlines the ex-slaves' superiority and feats of achievement in the face of the greatest adversities. Later, James would indicate in a 1971 lecture that one way he would rewrite *The Black Jacobins* history afresh would be to rely far less on the perspectives of even the most sympathetic foreign white observers. Instead, he would try to find perspectives from the ex-slaves themselves or people very close to them. As it is, use of such sympathetic descriptions in the 1938 edition already marks a significant departure from the likes of Stoddard, whose perspective focuses instead on accounts of hostile observers, writing out any agency of the slaves themselves.

Singled out above all others is Toussaint Louverture for his "sheer ability and natural strength of character," "formidable mastery over himself, both mind and body" (71), "his character and personality," "immense prestige," "superiority" (72), "exceptional intelligence" (73), and "extraordinary abilities." Vindication of Toussaint's exceptionalism leads to him being explicitly referred to as a "great man of action" (118, 170). As in the 1931 article and 1936 play, there is nothing neutral about this vindication in colonial contexts, which becomes "a cultural and ideological necessity," as Robert Hill has eloquently pointed out.[95] Here again, James's superlative building up of the heroic protagonist must be seen as actively countering denigrating presentations of Toussaint from histories by the likes of Stoddard.[96]

Contrasts between Stoddard's disparaging remarks about, and James's superlative vindications of, Toussaint become clear when they discuss his letters. Both acknowledge that Toussaint's written French was full of orthographical errors, and both make much of the process of constant rewriting through which secretaries would reshape his letters, until they finally said what Toussaint wanted them to say. But whereas Stoddard's tone is only condescending, James uses the many layers of Toussaint's letter writing and self-representation to vindicate his superlative achievements (162–63).[97] Just as slogans of freedom and equality were recast for the black slaves in their context of recent slavery, so too does James present the rewriting process through his secretaries as Toussaint's method of shaping letters by hammering his will into them, and turning them into "a masterpiece of prose excelled by no other writer of the revolution" and some of the greatest political documents of those revolutionary times.

Louverture is presented in the 1938 edition of the history as exemplifying the qualities of the black masses as a whole, spotlighting their strength, vigor, fearlessness, vision, courage, determination, collective irresistible élan, and their intelligence, which soared particularly high because liberty and equality meant far more to them than to the French soldiers when they went into battle.[98] James emphasizes the mass strengths of their revolutionary organization and fighting capabilities, into which is turned their dream of freedom. This transformation is facilitated, for example, through the "Eh! Eh! Bomba! Heu! Heu!" freedom chant translated by James (11), a transition song of revolutionary transformation, which acts as an epigraph to chapter 4, "The San Domingo Masses Begin," describing the rise of the organized mass movement.

The effectiveness of the slave revolutionaries' scorched-earth policy is explained from James's class perspective via the words of an unknown ordinary prisoner as inscribed in the sources:

> It was the people [who won the victory]. They burned San Domingo flat so that at the end of the war it was a charred desert. Why do you burn everything? asked a French officer of a prisoner. *We have a right to burn what we cultivate because a man has a right to dispose of his own labour*, was the reply of this unknown anarchist. And far from being intimidated, the civil population met the terror with such courage and firmness as frightened the terrorists. (298)[99]

From James's footnote, this looks as if the prisoner's reported speech comes from a source in the Paris Archives Nationales, a memorandum by Lacroix translated by James. Beyond literal French-English translation, however, James is instrumentalizing these reported words in order to foreground a class-based analysis. This unnamed anarchist, precisely because he is so unknown, is identified by James with the great mass of the population; a representative of those types of "bands, hundreds of thousands of them," "masses of Abyssinians and other Africans," with whom James had wanted to join when he declared himself willing to travel to Ethiopia to join the antifascist fight there against Mussolini's troops.[100]

The Black Jacobins history grew out of the same context as *Toussaint Louverture*, and in both places James's focus is firmly on vindicating the achievements of "splendid fighters," which was how James referred to Ethiopians. Ultimately, the theme of *The Black Jacobins* is the history of a tremendous revolutionary process, leading to extraordinary transformations on the very first page of the original preface: "The revolt is the only successful slave revolt in history, and the odds it had to overcome is evidence of the magnitude of the interests that were involved. The transformation of slaves, trembling in hundreds before a single white man, into a people able to organise themselves and defeat the most powerful European nations of their day, is one of the great epics of revolutionary struggle and achievement" (ix). This extraordinary transformation is also echoed at the end of chapter 13, "The War of Independence": "That night Rochambeau held a council of war and decided to evacuate the island. Toussaint had been dead only seven months, but his work was done. *Of men who had cowered trembling before any white ruffian, he had made in ten years an army which could hold its own with the finest soldiers Europe had yet seen*" (305, emphasis added). In this way, both the beginning and ending of *The Black Jacobins* history are framed by this incredible success story of both the one (Toussaint) and the many (the masses), including the likes of the unknown prisoner cited above.

Vindication of "the only successful slave revolt in history," the exact same formulation as in the first play's subtitle, is presented as the organizing theme of the whole history book from its very first pages. Through this vindicatory stance, James's history book is again diametrically opposed to the outlook of the grim tragedy, as recounted in the racialist account of a Stoddard, which explains away the loss and fall of this colony as the result of yellow fever, thereby undermining any agency of the freedom-fighter slaves themselves. Tongue firmly in cheek, James sarcastically demolishes attempts to deny that any revolutionary process of transformation into a well-organized fighting force had taken place (229). He also dismantles Stoddard-type accounts that artificially inflate the role of yellow fever in order to justify the loss of such a profitable colony toward the end of his 1938 history (268). James hits all such active and transitive processes of silencing, banalizing, and trivializing firmly on the head. By reading these yellow fever arguments against the grain and rewriting them, James completely debunks them.

On the subject of *Toussaint Louverture*, James retaliated against a *New Statesman* review of his 1936 play by invoking the British agent Cathcart and his role in instigating the massacre of all whites. In James's reply, he wrote that the proper place for such clarification of the great political issues at stake would be in history or biography. Hence, James's 1938 biographical history gives the Cathcart episode a prominent position, right at the end of the historical narrative. Adding Cathcart here enables James to write back to misleading falsifications of the Haitian events by Stoddard-type historians who portray the Haitian Revolution as nothing more than a race war. In this way, James explicitly unsilences the abominable role played by the imperialists—British and American agents like Cathcart—in the massacre.

This dialogic quarreling principle running throughout the whole *Black Jacobins* 1938 history also involves writing back to a negative type of revisionism: Stalin's notorious rewriting and falsification of history, which involved writing out and silencing his opponent Trotsky before assassinating him, as well as building up Stalinist mythologies, with the Stalinist regime using "the past as raw material to be shaped and reshaped to meet the present political requirements."[101] James directs his rewriting so that it is as far removed as possible from the Stalinist regime's type of revisionism.[102]

Following Trotsky's *History*, the coordinates of James's *The Black Jacobins* include the Russian Revolution, as well as the French and Haitian revolutions. Stalin is explicitly mentioned only once in James's 1938 history—the reference to "Stalin's firing squads," in addition to "Franco's heavy artillery" (viii). *The Black Jacobins* needs to be considered a positive creative rewriting of Stalinist falsifications. James's Haitian Revolution actors vie for the analogical parts of Lenin and Trotsky. As James writes of Louverture sentencing to death his nephew Moïse: "It was almost as if Lenin had had Trotsky shot for taking the side of the proletariat against the bourgeoisie" (238). Here, Dessalines-Stalin forms the last point of this Haitian Revolution–Russian Revolution triangle, although that parallel is made less explicitly. James builds on Trotsky's *History* creatively throughout *The Black Jacobins*, making explicit comparisons with the Russian Revolution at a number of crucial junctures. James actualizes these insights in his own application of Marx and Trotsky's methods and theories to historical analysis of a different revolution—the Haitian one.

Tragic Overtones and Leadership Models

The chief actors of the 1917 Russian Revolution, with parallels between Toussaint-Lenin, Moïse-Trotsky, and Dessalines-Stalin, are an essential aspect of Toussaint's tragic flaw. Parallels and contrasts between Lenin and Toussaint in particular are drawn to stress similar crises and problems faced by these two leaders, the class character of the events, and the profound consequences of their dilemmas, treachery, decisions, actions, and hesitations (236–39).

Written just after *World Revolution* (1937), *The Black Jacobins* is infused with the legacy of the Russian Revolution of October 1917, and one which, as we have seen, targets Stalinist degeneration of that revolution, as well as Stalinist falsifications and negative rewriting of history. One event—Toussaint's sentencing to death of Moïse—particularly recalls the great purges involving the sentencing to death of once high-ranking communists. All the comparing and contrasting of Lenin and Toussaint thus serve to point out Toussaint's error even more strongly. These Lenin-Toussaint analogies occur amid past conditional tense–heavy passages about what Toussaint should have done, and then what would have happened. From the Toussaint-Lenin connections, both leaders are shown trying to find some good reason for collaborating with the former enemy and for seeming to betray the mass of the people, but Lenin comes off more favorably in James's comparisons. Toussaint should have mitigated the consequences of his actions, like Lenin.

Although Toussaint remains recognizable across all of James's different representations of him, he is nevertheless portrayed significantly differently between *Toussaint Louverture* in 1936 and *The Black Jacobins* in 1938. David Scott has brilliantly applied Hayden White's narrativist approach to history to *The Black Jacobins*, arguing that the main shift between the 1938 and 1963 history editions involves changing the dominant story form of *The Black Jacobins* from "anticolonial Romance" to "postcolonial tragedy."[103] According to Scott, the 1938 history edition is a "reverential anticolonial story of [. . .] revolutionary heroism," "the Romantic portrait of the revolutionary hero," and a tale of romanticist anticolonial overcoming.[104] Scott has shown that more attention needs to be paid to the form as well as the content of this history.

Romance prevails in the 1938 edition, but through Marxist lenses because *The Black Jacobins* is a Marxist grand narrative.[105] It is not situated in the "thin air of 'meanings, attitudes and values'" of postmodernist narrativism, but is instead located within literature and history's "proper material abode" and "social relation" and is "more concrete and usable" for Marxist historians.[106] To privilege only the formal characteristics, or, to use Hayden White's memorable phrase, "the content of the form," in connection with James's refashioning of his historical narrative actually makes little sense because the rewriting also belongs to James's materialist Marxist conceptions and methods of history.[107]

As for tragedy, according to Scott, it is only in the 1963 edition that James introduces tragic elements and meditations on tragedy, changing the overall shape of the story James tells. This section develops Jeremy Glick's argument that tragedy is there all along already in 1938 by analyzing more closely the detail of tragic elements already present in the 1938 history.[108] To counter the idea that the 1938 edition is not a tragic text, this section argues that the 1938 version of *The Black Jacobins* already contains significant discussions of tragedy and foregrounds Toussaint's specific error, total miscalculation, and vacillating character. While it is true that tragedy is further emphasized and more prominently embedded in the 1963 edition, it is already, this chapter argues, a dominant mode of representing Toussaint Louverture and the Haitian Revolution all along, right from the first 1936 and 1938 incarnations of *Toussaint Louverture* and *The Black Jacobins*.

In many ways, James's 1936 play seems to fit better the romanticist vindicationist mold of which Scott speaks, because Toussaint's character in that first play is presented as virtually pure, unflawed, unwarped, and there is little representation there of any problematic tensions between leaders and masses. Nevertheless, James's 1936 play is, overall, a classic Shakespearean tragedy, along the lines of *Othello*, with protagonist Toussaint alone and dying in prison at the end, while mourning, "Oh, Dessalines! Dessalines! You were right after all!"[109] Tragedy is already there and highly visible throughout the play, which challenges Scott's thesis. Then, when compared to *Toussaint Louverture*, tragic overtones are even more clearly introduced throughout the 1938 edition of *The Black Jacobins*.

While Toussaint's rise forms a key part of *The Black Jacobins* story, and the history—like the play—is still constructed around the major milestones of his career, the 1938 history already describes in considerable detail the flaw responsible for Toussaint's downfall. It is true that James only incorporates the famous explicit paragraphs about hamartia and tragedy into the revised 1963 history.[110] Already, however, *The Black Jacobins* (1938) contains prominently embedded within it the framework of tragedy and the superlative but flawed tragic hero.[111]

Throughout the 1938 history, commentary added by James the historian explicitly condemns Toussaint as well as the other leaders for committing an "abominable betrayal" where the great mass of slaves was concerned: "In the long and cruel list of leaders betraying brave but ignorant masses this stands high, and Toussaint was in it up to the neck. Though working in a subordinate position he took the leading part in the negotiations" in a "masterpiece of diplomatic correspondence" (82) presented to the French Assembly. Singled out for particular condemnation during the "telling" of this episode in the 1938 history is the readiness of Toussaint, chief diplomat in these negotiations, to help with restoring the status quo of slavery for the average slave, and with actually leading the blacks back to slavery in return for the freedom of a small number of leaders.

Such is the scale of this "abominable betrayal" that James concludes that "Political treachery is not a monopoly of the white race" (83). Here, Toussaint is roundly denounced for doing "Judas work." Such "political vices" (74) are, James's history tells us, the usual accompaniments to superior knowledge and exceptional characteristics. Overall, this is a very different presentation of the protagonist's character from the play, in which Toussaint has virtually no flaws.

Already, Toussaint's flaws are cataloged discursively throughout the 1938 history, where he is forbiddingly aloof and stern. Above all, the 1938 history emphasizes his increasing failure to communicate clearly with his followers, or to clarify his strategy.[112] In *Toussaint Louverture*, leaders and masses always seem united by wild cheering, while leaders embrace, with hardly any attention paid to Toussaint's betrayal by his own generals. In contrast, throughout the 1938 history, Toussaint is portrayed as more shut up within himself with his diplomatic intrigues and as increasingly confusing his own masses, particularly as he appears to favor rich planters over them.

Repeatedly, we are told of Toussaint's grievous or grave error, weakness, specific mistake, failure, crime, dilemmas, and vacillations, which are already firmly inscribed into the fabric of the first version of this history:[113]

> Toussaint had burnt his boats[....] But, too confident in his own powers, he was making one *dreadful mistake*[....] His *error* was his neglect of his own people. They did not understand what he was doing or where he was going. He took no trouble to explain. It was dangerous to explain, but still more dangerous not to explain. His temperament, close and self-contained, was one that kept its own counsel. (200)

> If he had a *weakness* it was in keeping people mystified. (210)

> Toussaint recognised his *error*. (233)

> In allowing himself to be looked upon as taking the side of the whites against the blacks, Toussaint committed the *unpardonable crime* in the eyes of a community where the whites stood for so much evil. And to

shoot Moïse, the black, for the sake of the whites was *more than an error, it was a crime.* (237–38)

But Toussaint, like Robespierre, destroyed his own Left wing, and with it sealed *his own doom.* The *tragedy* was that there was no need for it. (237–38)

[...] a miserable and tell-tale indication of *vacillation.* (247)

Grievous had been his *error* [....] His desire to avoid distraction was the very thing that caused it. It is the *recurring error* of moderates in face of a revolutionary struggle. (248)

In every revolution there are many who hesitate and though decisive action may not be immediately effective, *vacillation* is certain to lose them all[....] The *vacillation* of the leaders was killing the revolutionary ardour of the people at every turn. (258)

It was a terrific blow to the revolution [Christophe submitting to Leclerc and the French] [....] *The fault was entirely Toussaint's.* His combination of fierce offensives with secret negotiations was too tortuous a method for Christophe[....] Christophe was an ex-slave, a man of the revolution, one of Toussaint's staunchest supporters. If he surrendered to the French, why should the black labourers go on fighting? Once more the masses had received a shattering blow—not from the bullets of the enemy, but from where the masses most often receive it, from their own trembling leaders. (270–71)

It was his [Toussaint's] ultimate confidence in the army and the people that led him to make his *mistake.* (273)

On the other hand, it was unlikely that Leclerc would dare to arrest him while Dessalines, Belair, and the others still had command of their troops. It was here that he was *wrong.* (277)

Throughout the 1938 history, tragedy is in the tension and gap between the individual and the mass base. Toussaint's failure to communicate as he loses touch with the Haitian masses marks a revolutionary degeneration.[114]

What constitutes the tragedy is nowhere clearer than during the narration of Toussaint's decision to have his adopted nephew and presumed successor Moïse shot for treason (233). From complete absence in *Toussaint Louverture*, where he was not even a character, Moïse here in James's 1938 history is Toussaint's most trusted officer and near-son, becoming pivotal to

Toussaint's downfall. However, Moïse's characterization is not very fully developed. Instead, the history presents us with a sketchy pen portrait roughly outlining Moïse's function as different leader type, one more in touch with the masses of the people, who acts as a foil to Toussaint's leadership style at this decisive juncture in the history narrative. Moïse is introduced relatively late in the history—his first proper entrance is on page 180—and thereafter he appears on only several other brief occasions.

Moïse's function is to give glimpses into Toussaint's strategies, dilemmas, and also tensions with the mass of his own people. Almost every appearance of Moïse throughout the history is accompanied by references to his famous bravery and conspicuous ability (213), and yet, these references are brief because, as James acknowledges, his source material regarding Moïse was not very substantial: "What exactly did Moïse stand for? We shall never know. Forty years after his death, Madiou, the Haytian historian, gave an outline of Moïse's programme, whose authenticity, however, has been questioned. We have very little to go on, but he seems to have been a singularly attractive and possibly profound person" (232). This near-absence of useful source material on Moïse means that James's Moïse-related comments are often speculative and prefaced by hypothetical words, such as "possibly." This reflects James's later comments in a key 1955 letter to Haitian historian Étienne Charlier that Moïse was one of the "minor" characters who interested him the most, remarking that very little substantial evidence was available about him.[115] Nevertheless, James sketches a clear Moïse-versus-Toussaint dynamic, where Moïse stands steadfastly for the common man—the ordinary black ex-slave laborers—from whom Toussaint is dangerously distancing himself. No longer does Toussaint stand for the black laborers' complete emancipation from their former degradation of slavery—hence, the widespread insurrection during which revolutionaries would call out, "Long live Moïse."

After Moïse's death, James continues to deploy him as a counterexample to Toussaint's lack of support for the masses. Following the shooting of Moïse, the past conditional is used everywhere in abundance to point out what Toussaint should have done in sharp contradistinction to what he actually did:

What *should* Toussaint *have done*? (236)

He *should have* declared that a powerful expedition could have no other aim than the restoration of slavery, summoned the population to resist, declared independence[....] With Dessalines, Belair, Moïse and the

> hundreds of other officers, ex-slave and formerly free, it *would have been easy* for Toussaint to get the mass of the population behind him[....] With the issue unobscure and his power clear, many who might otherwise have hesitated *would have* come down on the side that was taking decisive action. (238)

And yet, Toussaint is not the only flawed character already in the 1938 history. Compared to *Toussaint Louverture*, Dessalines's character is also more negatively portrayed in the 1938 history. Tensions between Dessalines and the rank and file are revealed in the 1938 narrative: "And Dessalines travelled over the island reorganising the local troops. Many of the petty chiefs and the rank-and-file viewed him, as was natural, with distrust. He and Pétion won them over or hunted them down, and destroyed them" (295). It is made clearer than in the 1936 play that Toussaint's arrest and deportment to prison in mainland France are the direct result of plotting by Dessalines and other leaders.

Beyond the Russian Revolution parallels, there are also future-oriented analogues. In this way, the end of *The Black Jacobins* sums up and points out the implications for the future.[116] As is usual in Marxist historiography, the historical narrative is concerned with connections between the past, the present, and the future.[117] And particularly toward the end of his history, James stresses the greatest present-day relevance of the story he has told about the Haitian Revolution. From the overall pattern of historical developments that James outlines throughout his narrative, he repeatedly stresses their special significance for the coming emancipation of, and anticolonial revolution in, Africa in the today of the late 1930s, and in the future projected by James from that standpoint. Repeatedly, through this pattern of historical developments, attention was drawn to the Haitian revolutionaries' counterparts in Africa of the 1930s as they prepared for their own revolution against all the "prowling tigers" (225) of imperialism with a constant focus on "Africa to-day."

Ending: The Coming African Revolution

Continually, the today of 1938 is presented as a moment even more clearly and impatiently ready for anticolonial struggle and emancipation across Africa than the slaves of San Domingo had ever been 150 years before. A keen sense of anticipation permeates the 1938 history ending:

> The forces of emancipation are at work, far more clearly to-day than in 1789. In Europe and Asia the forces of revolution, though damped down,

> smoulder in every country[. . . .] The African revolution will be as merciless as that of Dessalines. (314)
>
> [...] these instinctive strivings of 150 years ago are clear-cut political policy to-day (316)

There is always a keen sense of anticipation that millions of Africans are about to rise up. The book closes on a hopeful note, with the Haitian Revolution as a beacon lighting the way to liberation. *The Black Jacobins* presents the range of the revolution's achievements, dramatic events, and striking personalities, as James looks from the standpoint of all his activities with the International African Service Bureau across the Pan-African world, indicating a new road for Africa and looking to a mass movement of Africans and colonials. Particularly in the concluding pages, there is a strong sense that the great imperialists of the day are mediocre, mistakenly assuming their own greater worth compared to that of the Africans they govern—similar to a complaint made by James when making the case for West Indian self-government in 1932–33.[118]

In his summing up and pointing out the implications for the future at the end of the 1938 history, James particularly stresses the possibilities of Marxism for the coming African revolution:

> Let the blacks but hear from Europe the slogans of Revolution and the *Internationale*, in the same concrete manner that the slaves of San Domingo heard Liberty and Equality and the *Marseillaise*, and from the mass uprising will emerge the Toussaints, the Christophes and the Dessalines. They will hear [. . .] the quiet recruits in a black police force, the sergeant in the French native army or British police, familiarising himself with military tactics and strategy, reading a stray pamphlet of Lenin or Trotsky, as Toussaint read the Abbé Raynal. (315)

Marxism is presented as key to the anticipated anticolonial revolutionary transformation of Africa. This idea of using models from European Marxism to provide guidance elsewhere in new African contexts is also reiterated in the last sentences of the whole 1938 history: "The African faces a long and difficult road and he will need guidance. But he will tread it fast because he will walk upright" (316).[119]

As a projection of the coming African revolution, the emphasis on the defiant, ready-for-action, "upright" stance of the African presents an almost phallic, virile, transcendental closing image of uprising, which foreshadows

Césaire's image of Negritude as uprising.[120] "Upright" is the very last word of James's entire 1938 narrative, and it heralds in historical discourse the crescendoing repetition of the word "debout" (upright/standing up) that can be found in Aimé Césaire's famous poem *Cahier d'un retour au pays natal* (1939), where the example of the Haitian Revolution is also presented as a decisive act of blacks standing up for the first time.[121] At this point in 1938, James did not yet know Césaire, whose *Cahier* would not be published until the following year. By the time of the publication of the revised edition of *The Black Jacobins* in 1963, however, James would translate substantial portions of Césaire's poem for commentary in the most famous 1963 history addition, the appendix titled "From Toussaint Louverture to Fidel Castro." Already here, driving the ending of *The Black Jacobins* in 1938 is a rebellious image of the colonized African in action finding a defiant upright revolutionary stance.

3 | Rewriting History: *The Black Jacobins* (1963)

This chapter follows the revision trail of the 1963 Vintage edition of *The Black Jacobins*. That revised edition and those changes are integral to the text as it is known today. Through the new edition, James's history became an "active" text in the 1960s, as Stuart Hall has called it.[1] As much a text of the 1960s as the 1930s, the history acted as a catalyst fueling and a road map guiding radicals emerging during the civil rights and Black Power movements of the 1960s and beyond.[2] David Scott has called the 1963 publication "an event."[3] This chapter examines how changes made by James in the early 1960s directly reactivated and updated the history to renew it for those times. As its coordinates shift, it is also striking, however, how little changes: much of the 1938 history was left standing as it traveled from heralding anticolonial revolution for Africa in the 1930s, fast-forwarding to the West Indies in the 1960s and the very strong pattern of unique West Indian historical development and identity that James paints in the new appendix.

There have been many significant readings of *The Black Jacobins*. Two are especially relevant to this chapter. David Scott's *Conscripts of Modernity* (2004) makes an incisive argument about how James changes the shape of the history he writes from one narrative form (romance) to another (tragedy) by offering a meditation on tragedy in a set of added paragraphs at the beginning of the final chapter 13.[4] My analysis of the revised history builds on Scott's study by focusing on other prominent and significant changes made elsewhere by James when revising. Another valuable source is Susan Gillman's essay "Black Jacobins and New World Mediterraneans" (2013). This usefully conceives of James's history as a text-network, with Gillman mathematically expressing *The Black Jacobins* (1963) and its new appendix as "from Columbus to Toussaint + from Toussaint to Castro = from Columbus to Castro."[5]

This chapter identifies the changes that shifted the text-network collectively constituting *The Black Jacobins*. Composition of the revised text-network was multilayered: James signals in the footnotes that they were changed in 1961, and he dates the new preface January 4, 1962. Last to be inserted into this reworked text-network puzzle was the appendix, as we know from James's correspondence with his editor. As the revised history was actually published in 1963, I refer to the 1963 edition and changes, even if their (re)creation was staggered time-wise in the early 1960s.

In the new preface, James draws attention to the history of his history and how it has become "part of the history of our time."[6] Upholding its own historical achievements, the revised history confirms that only James and a few others had correctly forecast what was coming: "I have retained the concluding pages which envisage and were intended to stimulate the coming emancipation of Africa. They are a part of the history of our time. In 1938 only the writer and a handful of close associates thought, wrote and spoke as if the African events of the last quarter of a century were imminent" (vii). Later in 1971, James would give a series of lectures about how he wrote, and might rewrite again, *The Black Jacobins*. In particular, he drew attention to what he calls, after Hegel, "speculative thought," which he describes as "thinking about what is going to happen as a result of what you see around you," adding that "unless in the words of Hegel, you are doing speculative thought, you are not doing any thought at all."[7]

Scott, Gillman, and Gary Wilder have underscored the relevance of Reinhart Koselleck's notion of "futures past."[8] Additionally, James's speculative thought can be seen more positively as a cross between Koselleck's "futures past" and Wilder's idea of "untimely vision," with "not yet realized but ever-available emancipatory potentialities."[9] Untimely visions, where the moving target of *The Black Jacobins* is out of sync with the corresponding historical period, emerge strongly from the revised edition.

The positive untimeliness of *The Black Jacobins* is such that James would signal to his editor Morris Philipson in November 1961 that both the history and *Toussaint Louverture* had been "too early for [their] time."[10] In that letter, James discusses how he was proposing to revise his 1936 play for publication. In effect, this also summed up how he was rewriting the history: by updating it "in method and style and with the greater understanding which the years and the tremendous impact of colonial events have made on the modern world." This chapter tracks the history's changing coordinates as it is recalibrated, arguing that in its original and revised iterations, as in the original edition, the history remains forward-facing and less pessimistic than is suggested by Scott's reading of some of the changes. Indeed, the tone of the revised edition is decidedly celebratory in places, although references to tragedy are reinforced by the changes.

Attention is also paid to the changing paratexts of the revised history—the new preface, footnotes, updated bibliography, and appendix—because these high-visibility textual outsides are where rewriting is concentrated.[11] Although these textual sites are in some cases technically the margins, they occupy important and visible positions in the revised edition—at the beginning, ending, and around the edges of the original text. As the sidelines or margins expand in revisions, there is a tug of war between the text's insides and outsides, as the margins expand, sometimes encroaching on the text proper.

Rewriting is a highly visible process, as James contrapuntally points out in the 1960s footnotes what he still maintains and what was previously successfully forecast in 1938. This chapter argues that *The Black Jacobins* history in its revised version, especially the new appendix, is part autobiographical memoir and part political record, overlapping with other projects James was working on around this point in the early 1960s. These include the projected memoir *My Own, My Native Land: Warning to the West Indies* and his actual memoir *Beyond a Boundary* about his life, the West Indies, and cricket, published in 1963 like the revised history. *Beyond a Boundary* also went through several drafts, and its title went through numerous incarnations: *Who Only Cricket Know*; *WG, A West Indian Grace*; *West Indian Progeny of WG*; and *The Cricket Crusaders*.[12]

Analysis of the changes is supplemented with information drawn from James's correspondence with Philipson about the projected rewriting as he was carrying it out. Changes will be shown to go some way toward those suggested later by James in his 1971 lecture "How I Would Rewrite *The Black Jacobins*," including his undertaking to base the history on different types of sources. Ultimately, however, the chapter argues that while revisions show the extent of James's rethinking of the history, the actual changes made throughout the revised edition are relatively minor and tend to be made in the interstices and margins of the textual outsides—the prefaces, appendix, beginnings or ends of chapters, footnotes, and the expanded bibliography.

One important point, then, is that the history remains substantially the same, treating the same slice of history as the 1938 edition. Apart from the appendix fast-forwarding to the early 1960s, it is still based mostly on James's

1930s research, with almost all his sources and references remaining the same. Making far-reaching changes would have meant completely changing most of the 1938 history. This chapter argues that the history revisions constitute a staging post toward James's fuller rewriting of *The Black Jacobins* as a play in 1967, unrestricted by the scholarly apparatus of history writing: footnotes and bibliography.

To analyze the rewriting process and 1963 changes, James's discussions with his editor about the rewriting are explored. Changes then investigated include the new Vintage preface, the updating of contemporary references, and the removal of some Marxist language. Next, the focus shifts to James's refiguring of Louverture and new emphasis on leaders versus masses. Following on from this, James's rethinking of his sources in the revised bibliography is assessed. Finally, the most conspicuous addition—the appendix titled "From Toussaint Louverture to Fidel Castro"—is studied in detail. How does James relate the West Indies to its own history for the first time, and rewrite his speculative history from this perspective?

Correspondence about the Rewriting

September 1960 was the moment when James started to contact publishers in New York about republishing his history. Initially, James played down the extent of any revision needed: "There are a few contemporary references which I would like to delete, that's all."[13] Initially, his plans were to add an introduction of not more than ten pages, and to photo-offset the plates and text with no changes.[14] Morris Philipson at Random House proposed to bring out a copy in the Vintage Books Series, and wrote to the author, "[You could] make any changes, omissions or alterations that you would wish to make for such a new edition."[15] Changes were high on James's agenda, and he indicated that "[t]here are numbers of political references in themselves very slight, but nevertheless obtrusive," which he wanted to take out.[16] Later in March 1961, James announced that he was "already cutting out as many of the Marxian terms as possible."[17] Early on, he wanted to add a new introduction of a few pages linking "what took place in the Caribbean in the eighteenth century with what is taking place there today, what is known in general as the passing of colonialism."[18] He sketches out here an embryonic version of what would eventually become the appendix titled "From Toussaint Louverture to Fidel Castro."[19]

In this connection, James also outlined in early letters to Philipson his plans to write a memoir titled *My Own, My Native Land: Warning to the West*

Indies to coincide with West Indian independence: "I am deep in preparation for the book *My Own, My Native Land*. The conference to settle the details of independence is due in the summer of 1961. The actual date is tentatively suggested to be early 1962. We shall be in very good time for this." In the end, the appendix mixed his projected memoir with his actual memoir *Beyond a Boundary*, as well as perspectives from *Party Politics in the West Indies* (1962), *Facing Reality* (1958), and *Nkrumah and the Ghana Revolution* (1977, but mostly written in the late 1950s).[20]

Discussion of changes continued, with Philipson instructing James not to "skimp" on any changes and giving him the "liberty to write as extensive an introduction" as he wished to reflect on contemporary colonial problems drawing from the Haitian experience.[21] Some publisher pressure to make changes was nevertheless applied, with Philipson asking James to "consider possibly cutting some of the detailed material describing the military encounters. Perhaps thirty to forty pages of the book might be eliminated in this way, helping you to make more room for whatever length introduction you may wish to add." James, however, resisted cutting the military material described as extraneous, while making other changes instead: "I am glad that there is some time for me to work on the book. I shall do what I can to cut down some of the detailed material, but the military material in the War of Independence closely reflect and affect the political developments."[22]

As James writes these letters, the appendix begins to take shape as if before our eyes: "In addition to what has happened in Haiti the revolution in Cuba throws the historical evolution of the Caribbean into a very strong pattern. At any rate, there is time to work on it."[23] A serious car accident injured James while he was in Jamaica on April 28, 1961. Selma James had to write to Philipson to inform him about her husband's injuries. It would not be until June 23, 1961, that James would write to give his publisher an account of his health since the accident and an update about the new edition of *The Black Jacobins*: "There is a lot of excitement in the West Indies here about it, especially in view of the approaching independence, the emergence of Castro, and the recent death of Trujillo in the Dominican Republic."[24]

James outlined that what he was writing was the ultimate insider account of the "birth-throes of a nation," with excitement building up to independence in 1962. As James wrote, the preparations for independence were "stimulating and exciting, but also a rather terrifying spectacle. Especially if you happen to belong to it. What is happening in Cuba and the Dominican Republic, the rising undercurrents in Haiti, are all part of the same pattern."²⁵ This letter anticipates imminent independence of the West Indies but also expresses a strong sense of foreboding and disappointment over the breakup of the West Indies Federation and the big countries going independent alone. The "very strong pattern" of West Indian historical evolution and identity, on which the appendix is based, is here already taking shape. Even when James was too ill to work, he continued to rethink and plan what would eventually morph into the appendix.

On November 29, 1961, James sent by airmail from the Caribbean a corrected text of *The Black Jacobins*.²⁶ The next day James sent a letter emphasizing that "the book itself remains fundamentally sound" and had not changed much, although James did usefully give an indication of the revisions' scope: "For the time being I can only say that the revisions I have made have borne in mind [these] criticisms and suggestions from a widely varied set of people." When sending the corrected text, James summed up what the appendix would contain and emphasized that it would be an appendix, not an introduction:

> The West Indies are today in turmoil. From our correspondence I believe you are ready to consider a rather full appendix, which, however, you seem to think should be an introduction. I call it "From Toussaint Louverture to Fidel Castro." The territories are of two kinds, the colonial territories of Britain and France, Santo Domingo, Haiti and Cuba and Puerto Rico, and some smaller islands. While most of my information will be in the shape of analysis of the colonial territories, I intend to show what all previous commentators have ignored, that the past and future of the islands can only be seriously studied in the light of the Haitian development during the revolution and after. The recent history of Cuba with all its pluses and minuses, has in my opinion demonstrated more than ever that the West Indies are a territory that cannot be considered merely as to what extent they approximate or depart from Western patterns. They are territories with a unique history of their own, a West Indian history. In preparing this appendix I have, of course, used a certain discretion in my references to Cuba. But what I propose to do is contemporary and new, and flows naturally from a history of the Haitian Revolution. Before I put it into final shape I would like to know that you are interested in the project.²⁷

Here all the main lines of the appendix are clearly sketched out, emphasizing the overarching subject and theme of the appendix: West Indian history. In a subsequent letter, dated January 18, 1962, James refers to the appendix as "That last chapter" and reports to his publisher: "That last chapter I am working on now. I have in my head all that I want to write, and within a short time I shall have it all down."²⁸ The new preface to the Vintage Edition signed C. L. R. James is dated January 4, 1962, and the appendix would have been the final piece of the revised whole to be sent to Philipson.

The New Preface: Framing Rewriting

The 1963 edition of *The Black Jacobins* was now framed by two prefaces, including the original 1938 one.²⁹ The new preface shifts the coordinates of *The Black Jacobins* history, as James goes back to the erstwhile future of 1938 and changes the focus from coming revolution in Africa in 1938 to independence for the West Indies in 1962. James uses the new preface as a framing device for presenting the nature and scope of the revisions. He starts by stressing that the book is fundamentally sound, underlining how little has been changed for historical accuracy.

Another function of the preface is vindication of the first edition's visionary forecasting of "the coming emancipation of Africa." James highlights that only he and a handful of close associates had correctly envisaged and stimulated anticolonial struggles back in the 1930s as if they were imminent. Proudly, he proclaims that these foundations and concluding pages about the coming emancipation of Africa are left standing now in 1962–63, despite the shift in tense, as "a part of the history of our time."

The preface draws attention to the significance and purpose of the history's most prominent addition—the appendix. The appendix summary outlines how new it is to study the West Indies in relation to their own history instead of that of former colonial powers Britain, France, Spain, or America. As discussed in chapter 2, the original preface to the first edition remains unchanged, apart from two small changes: "Such elementary conceptions lend themselves willingly to narrative treatment and from **Tacitus** ~~Herodotus~~ to **Macaulay** ~~Michelet~~, from Thucydides to Green, the traditionally famous historians have been more artist than scientist" (x/viii).³⁰ Here James changes the foundational figures of the Western tradition of historical writing to figureheads more recognizable to English-speaking readers of history in the 1960s, superimposing new coordinates over the history-writing process. These changes indicate that James has been rethinking just who are the leading Western historians, in addition to reconsidering key aspects of their legacies.

Updating and Changing without Altering "the Whole Movement of the Thing"

Retrospectively, James provides insights into the rewriting of his history in a 1971 set of lectures on *The Black Jacobins*, especially "How I Would Rewrite *The Black Jacobins*." These lectures are invaluable because they indicate what *The Black Jacobins* could have looked like had James been able to rewrite it completely. They also provide the author's own later commentary on the partial rewriting that he did complete for the 1963 revised edition. Repeatedly referring to himself as "poor James, condemned to footnotes," he signals that he "didn't want to change the book too much, because when you change a book, you change not only pages here and there but you alter the whole movement of the thing. So what I did was to put footnotes in the 1963 edition. And those who have eyes to see let them see."[31] James estimated that he had made no more than eight pages of changes in total for the revised 1963 edition.[32] Certainly, the actual revisions, few in number and size, constitute small changes that do not "alter the whole movement of the thing." While James's rewriting is relatively minimal, my own estimates would be that approximately fifteen pages have been deleted, with about thirty-seven pages added, including the new appendix. James is downplaying the extent of his rewriting of the revised history overall.

Many changes are small factual or spelling changes. Spellings consistently changed throughout the volume are "Hayti" and "Haytian," which are modernized to become "Haiti" and "Haitian." References to Port-au-Prince are changed to give the historically accurate name of Port-Républicain of the city during the French Revolution. Haphazard 1938 accents are corrected. Some factual details are altered, including reducing the estimates of the native population: "from an estimated **half-a-million, perhaps a million** from between one and three million to 60,000 in 15 years" (ix/vii).[33] Other minor changes alter probability, such as the origins of Louverture's name: "It is **not improbable** more probable that the slaves called him L'Ouverture from the gap in his teeth. Later he dropped the apostrophe" (126/100); "But it is **not impossible** highly probable that, sick and tired of the reaction and fearing for the future, he had proposed to Toussaint that they should seize the colony, purge it of the white slave-owners, and make it independent" (193/159). In both cases, the degree of probability lessens a quarter of a century after the original.

Previous predictions often stand to show how the book is part of the history of its time. When corresponding with publishers about republishing the history, however, James underlined one type of change that he wanted to make when revising: the deletion of obtrusive contemporary and political references.[34] Changes made to contemporary references are most prominent. There are eight footnotes or in-text references reminding us that a remark had originally been made in 1938, or that it was still true in 1961 when James was correcting the text.[35] This trail of additional footnotes underlines the visionary original forecasts of 1938, while retaining, reinforcing, and updating the temporal markers.[36] This updating of the contemporary references also confirms what is still unfulfilled and bound to happen. He renews the previous edition's "speculative thought" about what is now going to happen based on the intervening period between the 1930s and 1960s.[37]

Examples rewind to the anticipation of anticolonial revolt and decolonization, to when many talented Africans were waiting in Africa to usurp the positions of mediocre European officials and governors, underlining retrospectively James's successful forecasting of the coming upheavals in Africa. Reference points all change, and repeated references to Hitler after the 1938–61 gap between the moments of re/writing make us think of all that has intervened in between. Footnote references historicize some remarks as pre–World War II, on the eve of which *The Black Jacobins* was previously published.

One conspicuous reference has James directly interject in a 1961 footnote regarding the surprising moderation of the slaves in their treatment of their former masters, "**This statement has been criticised. I stand by it. C.L.R.J.**" (88n1/68). In a letter sent to his editor the day after he sent the corrected text, James wrote, "One day soon I shall send you my experience with the book in England, in the US, in France, in Africa and now in the West Indies. For the time being I can only say that the revisions I have made have borne in mind these criticisms and suggestions from a widely varied set of people."[38] In the changes, we see James revising, or taking a stand and choosing not to revise, in response to criticisms and suggestions made by others from around the world as he shifts contemporary reference points.

Omission is another of James's 1961 responses to the original text. In several cases he simply deletes obtrusive 1930s political references. One anomalous pre–World War II comment is, "Yet Bonaparte was no colonist, and his anti-Negro bias was ~~as~~ far from influencing his major **policies** ~~policy as Hitler's anti-Jewishness would influence his~~" (270/226). Other outdated 1938 references also cut include original references to Franco's Moors—North African soldiers used by Spanish dictator Franco during and after the Spanish Civil War (124/98–99).[39] References to Kenya in 1938 are also deleted because in the early 1960s Kenya was on the cusp of independence.[40] Other deleted references describe organizations calling for African emancipation and Indian independence, some of which had happened in the interim between 1938 and 1963, including Indian independence in 1947.[41] One reference to San Domingo being "worth more to eighteenth century France than India to the Britain of to-day" (1938, 43) is replaced with a more general hyperbole when San Domingo is called "**the most profitable colony the world had ever known**" (1963, 57). Finally, a statement is turned into a rhetorical question: "But without Pitt and the interests he represented **how effective would they have been?** ~~they would have been as effective as those who to-day propose the abolition of racial discrimination in Africa~~" (73/56). Here, James reinforces his distinctive initial argument of *The Black Jacobins* about abolition, slavery, and capitalism: that abolitionists would not have stood a chance had slavery and colonization always remained so economically lucrative.

De-Marxifying the Language of *The Black Jacobins* (1963)

Another important set of revisions was his "cutting out as many of the Marxian terms as possible"—his attempts to "de-Marxify" the language of *The Black Jacobins*.[42] When the two history editions are compared, some degree of de-Marxification of the language used does emerge:

> ~~We of this generation, with our experience of revolution and counter-revolution can appreciate the combination of sternness and wisdom which Toussaint showed.~~ (235/196)

> ~~Workers of the world, unite! Mankind was still half a century from that slogan. But a~~ A regiment of Poles [...] (318/263)

> It is a recurrent tale this. ~~Lenin, almost single-handed, had to drive his Central Committee to insurrection with boots and fists~~ (338/280)

Some explicit quotations from Marx and Engels and the 1848 *Communist Manifesto*, as well as some direct references to the Russian Revolution and Lenin's seizing of power, are deleted. Despite this noticeable de-Marxifying of the language, it must be emphasized that *The Black Jacobins* remains a Marxist analysis still shaped by historical materialism in its revised version as in 1938. James might not use the Marxist terms as frequently as before, but *The Black Jacobins* is imbued with the thing itself: Marxism and a Marxist sense of historical development. These changes echo James's 1967 statement that when he is in the Caribbean, he never explicitly speaks about Marx/Marxism, but nevertheless he applies Marxism in practice to his analysis.[43] This can be extrapolated to the apparent de-Marxification of *The Black Jacobins*: now the text says "Marx" less frequently and explicitly, but the history remains fundamentally Marxist in its inspiration, analysis, and content.

Marxist references still feature throughout the revised history, where there are no fewer than eight direct mentions, including the index entry for Karl Marx. References also include Marx's *Eighteenth Brumaire* and *Communist Manifesto*. In addition, James's commentary in the new appendix on Césaire's poem *Cahier d'un retour au pays natal* (Notebook of a return to my native Land) reads that poem as "a poetic incarnation of Marx's famous sentence, 'The real history of humanity will begin'" (44n11, 197, 401). Marx's quotation "Revolution is the locomotive of history" is part of the fabric of the two history editions, and both state that it is the scientific study of revolution begun by Marx and Engels, and amplified by Lenin and Trotsky, which justifies the history's pointing to an alternative course that Toussaint should have taken (282/109). The foundations of the work remain strongly Marxist, even if Marxist terms appear less frequently in the 1963 edition.

Despite Marx and Marxism being named less frequently and explicitly, the commentary added throughout *The Black Jacobins* reflects James's own contributions to Marxism in theory and practice, worked out during the intervening decades between editions, which he dedicated to political organizing in the United States and beyond as part of the Johnson-Forest Tendency (1940s–early 1950s) and later Correspondence and Facing Reality. Together, they had broken with the orthodox Trotskyist concept of the vanguard party, focusing instead on the self-activity of the masses in making revolution. As James rewrites his history between the lines in the early 1960s, he points to these new historical perspectives and political positions he and his comrades worked out in the interim.

Refiguring Toussaint Louverture

What is changed also reorients the text's presentation of Toussaint Louverture as leader and the masses. Increasingly, it almost becomes a case of Louverture versus the revolutionary masses and their popular leaders. The reader is no longer called upon as frequently to admire Toussaint's special attributes: that exceptional "combination of sternness and wisdom which

Toussaint showed" (235/196). Toussaint is less explicitly portrayed as single-handedly driving the revolution (338/280). Indeed, in the revised 1963 edition, James shows the Haitian Revolution being won in spite of, and not because of, Toussaint's revolutionary leadership.

In the 1971 lecture "How I Would Rewrite *The Black Jacobins*," James said that he would give Toussaint only a walk-on part were he to rewrite the history again. Although Toussaint does remain central throughout, his presentation is refigured by the revisions.[44] Deletions work toward writing Toussaint out of the narrative. Between the 1938 and 1963 editions some fifteen pages are deleted, of which at least ten concern Toussaint himself. Many deletions make Toussaint sound less unwavering, more vacillating, with fewer explanations about his motivations and strategy, and with fewer positive superlatives.[45] There is also less of Toussaint speaking to us directly in the first person from the pages of his correspondence, and his strategy is no longer explained away to the same extent (148/119). Originally, James had drawn on Louverture's correspondence to show how "ready for action" was "a recurrent phrase with him" (161/132). Now, there is less praise for "action" man Toussaint than in the original. Omissions in 1963 include 1938 praise of Toussaint's nobility and moderation, which when telescoped becomes "**Combining military superiority with propaganda, Toussaint won seven victories in seven days**" (201/165–66).

Toussaint's actions are also less clearly explained away throughout chapter 10, "Toussaint Seizes the Power," where there is generally less justification of Toussaint's motivations and actions. Cuts also make Toussaint sound less noble and impervious to flattery (226/187, 235/196).[46] Besides numerous deletions, the revised edition of the history contains notable additions too, which also reorient the 1963 version's presentation of Toussaint. Attention is mostly drawn to Toussaint's flaw, for example: "**Once only in his political life did he ever fail to meet an emergency with action bold and correct**" (108/85). Major additions also include the following:

> **Toussaint in his twelve years of politics, national and international, made only one serious mistake, the one which ended his career. Strategic necessities he always saw early, and never hesitated in carrying out whatever policies they demanded. Now that he had dismissed Hédouville, the official representative of the French Government, and his acknowledged superior, he saw that he had now to crush the Mulatto state of Rigaud. The great danger now was a French expedition**

and it was suicidal to allow Rigaud and his Mulattoes to remain in control of the south and West. They would most certainly welcome a French force and ensure the ruin of the black state (224–25/185)

What is added highlights the seriousness of Toussaint's flaw and focuses on his closely guarded strategy, characterizing him as a more authoritarian leader.

Most additions make Toussaint's flaw plain, and strings of past conditionals spell out what he should have done regarding the mass of the people: "Instead of reprisals, Toussaint should have covered the country, and in the homely way that he understood so well, mobilised the masses, **talked to the people, explained the situation to them and told them what he wanted them to do**" (285–86/239). Louverture is portrayed as not paying enough attention to what the crowds of Saint-Domingue's masses are actually doing. What is added indicates how James would have liked to further elucidate the activities and mentality of the masses—a daunting task since most slaves and leaders left no written records of their own.[47]

Apart from the appendix, the next-longest additions are the new interpolated paragraphs at the beginning of chapter 13, "The War of Independence," which have been brilliantly analyzed already by David Scott. He is right to call these additions on tragedy (289–92) the most important in the revised edition. What remains to be emphasized is that tragedy is a genre that pertains to the theater, and the additions not only emphasize Toussaint's flaw but encourage the reader to watch his blunders and the inevitable catastrophe play out as they would watch a play or a tragedy on stage or screen. In these new paragraphs, Toussaint's flaw becomes crystallized with what is added, emphasizing that his defeat, imprisonment, and death "**are universally looked upon as a tragedy**," containing "**authentic elements of the tragic.**"

Attention is also drawn to Toussaint's "**tergiversations, his inability to take the firm and realistic decisions which so distinguished his career**" as he "**became the embodiment of vacillation**," "**misjudging events and people**," "**vacillating in principle and losing both the fear of his enemies and the confidence of his own supporters.**" James reminds us that nothing should be allowed "**to obscure or minimise the truly tragic character of his dilemma, one of the most remarkable of which there is an authentic historical record,**" and calls on the reader to see Toussaint as being in a lesser category than dramatic creations Hamlet, Lear, Phèdre, and Ahab: "**His splendid powers do not rise but decline**" while the "**hamartia, the** tragic flaw, which we have constructed from Aristotle was in Toussaint not a moral weakness" but "**a specific error, a total miscalculation of the constituent events**." Even if this tragedy loses something of the "**imaginative freedom and creative logic**" of the great tragedies of drama, the emphasis is instead placed on "**the historical actuality**" of Toussaint's dilemma. This is such that his story "**far exceeds the social significance and human appeal**" of Napoleon's last days at Saint Helena, and Hitler and Eva Braun's suicide in the Wilhelmstrasse during the years between 1938 and 1963.

These revisions reveal the 1963 edition's meditation on tragedy and the unfolding of Toussaint's tragic dilemma.[48] Scott's astute argument about narrative emplotment via Hayden White centers on the two different storytelling modes of the two history editions: romance and tragedy. As discussed in previous chapters, according to Scott, the 1938 history is emplotted as romance, whereas the 1963 history is emplotted as tragedy. From the 1963 insertions highlighted in bold above, such changes do explicitly embed tragedy in the revised history edition. The 1963 interpolations outlined in bold above lay major new emphasis on the story form of tragedy, and what is added by James points to a tragic refiguration of the dominant mode of emplotment throughout the 1963 revised history edition.

As Scott himself makes clear, he is "only interested in the career of a single idea of James's in this period."[49] Beyond this single track—tragedy—it is also interesting to see how else the history develops. The story Scott tells about *The Black Jacobins* also reads through James and his 1963 moment to our times of the twenty-first century, reconfigured from the perspective of "the bleak ruins of our postcolonial present" and a "time of postcolonial crisis in which old horizons have collapsed or evaporated and new ones have not taken shape."[50]

It is possible to read more tragedy into the 1963 revised history than perhaps is actually added there, and to "conscript" *The Black Jacobins* into the political pessimism and despair of postmodernist historians, including White. Narrativism has been criticized by Marxist commentators including Alex Callinicos, who attacks narrativism's presentation of history writing as nothing but a series of narrative choices, and he its reduction of historical writing to its formal characteristics alone.[51]

Certainly, James's own prominent additions in 1963 do reframe the story as one of tragedy. Nevertheless, as previously argued, tragedy and the tragic already feature prominently in the 1938 edition. Equally, the romantic vindicationist anticolonial story told by James in the 1938 version remains in the

Rewriting History (1963) | 115

1963 edition. Like a palimpsest, some of the original romance story about the figuration of Toussaint's biography has been partially erased to make room for another story—that of tragedy. But elements of romance and tragedy combine in the 1963 iteration, which continues to employ Toussaint's story and that of the Haitian Revolution as vindication. Indeed, the vindicating thread of the 1963 edition remains highly significant. Furthermore, tragedy never completely eclipses anticolonial romance and overcoming, and the story James retells in 1963 for his own times remains less bleakly pessimistic than Scott's own extrapolation of this story to our own tragic times.

There is also a pronounced vindicatory tone added throughout revisions about the original 1938 edition's visionary forecasting. Unlike postmodernist and post-Marxist narrativists, James does not criticize the Marxist theory of history. Instead, he builds on his serious contributions to Marxist theory and practice, which come together through the new Marxist historical perspectives further elaborated throughout the 1963 revisions, which help James to develop the theme of leaders versus masses.

Leaders versus Masses

Already in the original 1938 history, James had presented the ex-slave masses as pitted against leaders like Toussaint and Dessalines, following Pamphile de Lacroix's observation that it was "not the avowed chiefs who gave the signal for revolt, but obscure creatures, for the greater part personal enemies of the coloured generals" (338/280), and French commander Leclerc's observation, "It is not enough to have taken away Toussaint, there are 2,000 leaders to be taken away" (346/286). New reflections in 1963 gesture toward what the anonymous masses of the population and popular movements actually did and thought. In his 1971 reflections about rewriting the history again, and in two extensive footnotes added to the 1963 edition (276n6, 338n39), James spells out that the obscure creatures are always the ones who attack constituted authority in all insurrections, and he lets the reader know that he is concerned with the two thousand more popular leaders.[52]

Two mammoth footnotes are prominent in the revised history because of their length. Both footnotes consist of three substantial paragraphs, taking up almost two-thirds of the pages on which they appear. James's 1971 lecture indicates that these footnotes would form a substantial part of the history were he to rewrite it again. There is almost a tug of war between the text proper and the footnotes. Both added footnotes anticipate Marxist historiographical tendencies from below and the civil rights and Black Power popular movements emerging in the 1960s and '70s. James contributed to refashioning Marxism during this period, and the changes reflect this by emphasizing the mass of the ordinary rank and file as opposed to the top leadership. As argued in chapter 2, James himself was an early pioneer of history from below and total history, plotting out his 1938 story about the enslaved Haitian masses—the ultimate subalterns—and their leaders leading world revolution. The revised edition was published in 1963 when the defining histories from below were starting to be published by E. P. Thompson, Albert Soboul, and George Rudé, among others.[53]

In the new footnotes, James roughly sketches out what a history of the slave revolution from below might look like, building on work by Lefebvre—forefather and pioneer of this approach—and shifting the focus from the French to the Haitian revolutions, and to other obscure popular leaders.[54] Both footnotes refer to Lefebvre's mimeographed lectures, which James purchased in Paris in 1956. Most of the first footnote is taken up with Lefebvre's analysis of the sansculottes, the rank and file, "the extreme democrats" who wanted "the direct government of the people by the people." This significant footnote, this chapter argues, reorients *The Black Jacobins* by turning attention away from the black Jacobin authoritarian leaders and toward the black sansculottes instead. It is also significant, I would argue, that James updates his 1938/1963 statement about Haiti that is *The Black Jacobins* with his 1964 essay "Black Sansculottes": "This is now," James writes in 1964.[55] Indeed, this intervention on Haiti and the black sansculottes dating from approximately one year after publication of the revised history is so important that it should be seen as itself constituting a rewriting of James's previous Haitian Revolution writings, including the history in both its 1938 and 1963 incarnations. Together, James's new Lefebvre footnotes, his 1964 "Black Sansculottes" essay, and his 1971 lectures all suggest that were he to rewrite the history more radically from a later perspective, the title and subtitle of that rewritten book would no longer speak of black Jacobins and Toussaint Louverture. Perhaps a more fitting title for a more completely rewritten history could be *The Black Sansculottes*.[56]

Both added footnotes of the revised 1963 history briefly indicate how extreme democrats organized themselves and shaped the revolution. The first footnote (276) is located where the revolutionaries choose insurrection against Toussaint, whom they no longer support once he no longer represents "that complete emancipation from their former degradation which was their chief goal." James extrapolates Lefebvre's analysis to his arguments about Toussaint making the greatest mistake of his career by not listening to the masses.

The second footnote (338) is added just after Leclerc's remarks about the obscure creatures and not the avowed chiefs being the ones to give the signal for revolt. Here James mainly quotes Lefebvre, but in the "How I Would Rewrite" lecture of 1971, James puts together Lefebvre's talk of "unknown leaders" with the French commander Leclerc's remark about it not being enough to take away Toussaint because there are two thousand other leaders to be taken away. In the lecture, he extrapolates from the 1963 footnote, claiming that he "will go even further than Lefebvre." If Lefebvre is concerned with the obscure leaders, not the prominent ones, in 1971 James asserts, "*I am not*. I am concerned with the two thousand leaders who were there."[57] The Lefebvre footnote is inserted immediately after the original 1938 references to popular leaders including Derance, Samedi Smith, Jean Panier, "and other nameless petty chieftains," who were constantly being hunted down as "brigands" (337–38).[58] In the 1971 lecture, James indicates that these alternative popular leaders and the masses they represent would now be his starting point for the book: "If I were writing this book again, I would have something to say about those two thousand leaders. I have mentioned a few here and there, but I didn't do it with that in mind."[59]

James indicates how much time and space he would spend elaborating points briefly sketched out in the actual 1963 changes, were he to rewrite the book entirely from scratch in 1971. He indicates that he would spend four or five whole pages on descriptions of the little local leaders from different types of archival sources closer to the majority of the ex-slaves, instead of outsider sources, with most of his research aimed from the start at getting this information, and with page after page of this hypothetical rewritten history using the ex-slaves' actual statements telling what they were doing.[60] Based on the actual changes in 1963, we can see how James himself started to shift the coordinates further toward history from below, connecting more explicitly with the focus of Fick's future 1990 study.[61]

Another key passage on which James indicates he would spend at least two pages of his hypothetical rewritten history is about the Paris masses and the Paris Commune during the French Revolution. In both the 1938 and 1963 versions, one sentence is dedicated to this, even if the sense of that sentence is completely overhauled to mean almost the exact opposite when rewritten in 1963. Originally, the sentence read in 1938:

> The Paris Commune, the real revolutionary centre of Paris was at the height of its influence, and on May 31st and June 2nd with firmness but great moderation, it made the Girondin leaders retire from the Convention, placing them only under house arrest, and offering hostages out of their own ranks as guarantees for their safety (111)

This becomes in 1963:

> **The Paris masses deserting** the Paris Commune, **hitherto** the real revolutionary centre of Paris, **organised an independent centre of their own, the famous Evêché;** and on May 31st and June 2nd, with firmness but great moderation, made the Girondin leaders retire from the Convention, placing them only under house arrest, and offering hostages out of their own ranks as guarantees for their safety (138)

No longer is the Paris Commune doing this at the height of its influence. Instead, the Paris masses are all deserting the Commune, now portrayed as the former, no longer the current, real revolutionary center of Paris. What is added shows these Paris masses organizing themselves "an independent centre of their own, the famous Evêché," whereas no mention was made of the Evêché in 1938. In the 1971 lecture, James spends more than two pages spelling out the significance of what the Evêché militants did, saying that, even when rewritten, the sentence does not tell what really happened.[62] James's attention begins to shift downward, focusing not so much on the Jacobins as instead on the enragés as the more radical rank-and-file revolutionaries and spokesmen for the common people in the French Revolution. Instead of the black Jacobins, James indicates that he would like to focus on the black sansculottes and enragés and on their activities and motivations.[63] Were he rewriting the history again in 1971, James says that he would see to it that two pages were spent so that the people could understand what the Evêché represented, how they left the Commune and had to form a new body of leaders to be able to carry out the Days of May insurrection of May 31–June 2, 1793, with James spelling out that the independent actions of the Evêché militants almost opposed those of the Jacobin leadership.[64] By extension, this analysis can be linked to added emphasis in new footnotes about the extreme left wing of the Haitian Revolution revolting against Toussaint, masses versus the top leader. The relationship between the revolutionary leadership and the popular mass movements is clearly being problematized.

This added focus on the popular movements within the Haitian Revolution is perhaps best summed up by the excision of one lengthy passage from the 1938 history regarding the Kina family (1938, 203–4). The story about the Kinas as told by James was rather vague on details, following his source Nemours.[65] We are told that Jean and Zamor Kina were father-and-son carpenters, and the 1938 edition quickly glosses over the Kinas fighting on the British side against Louverture. Most of the anecdote focuses on the fact that the Kinas were imprisoned in the Alpine fortress the Fort de Joux (ironically, the same prison as Louverture). The story recounts that the two Kina men were eventually pardoned and set off to join a battalion garrisoned in Italy. Their story in the original is made to encapsulate the exceptional boldness of spirit of all Haitians, with the Kinas representing what the people in San Domingo were like, but subsequently, there is no mention of the Kinas in the 1963 edition.

As David Geggus points out, Jean Kina's career was a strange one.[66] He started out, like Toussaint, in the slave elite, but then followed a very different path when he fought to defend slavery and white supremacy. Whether James changed his account because of new research or knowledge about the Kinas is uncertain, but these exceptional Haitian leaders no longer serve as representatives of ordinary Haitians. In the revised 1963 edition, the reference is replaced with this: "**At bottom the popular movement had acquired an immense self-confidence**" (244/204). This sweeping new sentence indicates that James wanted to shine light on the bottom of the popular movements within the Haitian Revolution beyond the fine examples of history from above that *The Black Jacobins* total history also contains. These changes bring out the chorus of the ex-slaves themselves. According to the 1971 lecture, "the chorus was often decisive in the solution of the problem."[67] Through the 1963 changes, the chorus of ex-slaves takes shape as a decisive force pitted against the main leaders, even if only the broad lines of this approach begin to be sketched out through scattered interpolations.[68]

The marginal history revisions act as signposts to the contributions to Marxism made by James and his Johnson-Forest Tendency, Correspondence, and Facing Reality political organizations in the intervening quarter century between the two history editions. This includes the turn away from the vanguard and toward the self-activity of the masses reflecting developments in Marxist theory and practice made by James and his Johnson-Forest Tendency comrades.[69] Changes to the history reflect the American Jamesians' emphasis on what common people can contribute directly themselves, often working almost against their top leaders, including top union representatives. One of the main activities associated with the publications of the Johnson-Forest Tendency's later incarnations as the Correspondence and Facing Reality groups was known as the "full fountain pen" and the "third-layer school." These actions would involve intellectuals acting as mere scribes so that ordinary American workers, including women and young people, could tell their own working experiences and stories of factory life from the inside.[70] Their organizations moved the center of their operations from New York to Detroit.[71] As previously discussed, biography is an important part of James's Marxist history writing, as seen from his elaborations of *The Black Jacobins*. Life writing of ordinary American factory workers recounting their everyday lives from the inside would be central to firsthand accounts, including Paul Romano (Phil Singer) and Ria Stone (Grace Lee Boggs) in *The American Worker* (1947), and Martin Glaberman in *Punching Out* (1971), as well as numerous such accounts in the newsletters and papers run by the American Jamesians.[72] These full fountain pen and third-layer school activities could be interpreted as a rewriting technique used frequently by the American Jamesians. While in the United States during the intervening years, James and his comrades worked out perspectives and proposals about the need to Americanize Marxism.[73] This translation or Americanization of Marxism, then, involved translating Marxism into American terms ordinary people could understand.

As for *The Black Jacobins*, it is translated and rewritten by James to speak to situations in parts of the world that had been colonized, including Africa and the West Indies. James insists on the importance of people speaking out for themselves in their own voices, not passively but actively expressing themselves. Such work links closely with the Correspondence and Facing Reality groups' publications, including *The People of Kenya Speak for Themselves* (1955).[74] How do the (formerly) colonized speak and act for themselves actively in the first person? This becomes one theme driving the elaboration of James's work in general, including his Haiti-related writings, where James shows that ex-slaves are capable of leading revolution and of writing new pages into the history books.

Rethinking Sources and Bibliography

Some of the most conspicuous changes in the 1963 revised history are in the bibliography. Yet few have commented on these differences between the 1938 and 1963 editions apart from Robert A. Hill. His "Literary Executor's Afterword" to James's *American Civilization* (1993) makes an incisive appraisal of the second edition's expanded bibliography, noting the importance of the sansculottes, enragés, and *sociétés populaires*.[75] Examining James's revised bibliography gives a snapshot preview of what the history book rewritten for the 1960s and '70s would look like.

James's own self-criticism of his source use is enlightening. In the 1971 lecture about how he would hypothetically rewrite *The Black Jacobins* again, James takes himself to task for going to the archives and history books of the colonizer and selecting their external descriptions of slave life. Instead, James says in 1971, he would now find alternative sources from the slaves' own point of view.[76] To add insider and further-below perspectives on alternative popular leaders and the chorus of ex-slaves would mean writing a different book. In liminal yet highly visible places in the *Black Jacobins* text-network—the footnotes, revised bibliography, and the 1971 lectures on (re)writing—a picture emerges of James inflecting *The Black Jacobins* along the lines of one of the most important contributions to history since World War II: history from below.

"The French Revolution" section of the revised 1963 bibliography is the most changed, retaining only the single initial sentence from the original bibliography. Michelet now heads the line of development traced by James through French Revolution historiography. Pointing out that Michelet has "very little to say on the colonial question," James also adds that "many pages in Michelet are the best preparation for understanding what actually happened in San Domingo."[77] This same line of development is also traced verbally in James's "How I Wrote *The Black Jacobins*" lecture of 1971, where Michelet heads the line: "The greatest of them all is Jules Michelet. I don't know of any greater history book than his today. People have discovered a lot, but Michelet remains the great master. Michelet wrote in the 1850s and people learn a great deal."[78]

On Jaurès, the 1938 and 1963 versions of *The Black Jacobins* bibliography are quite different. Originally James had condemned Jaurès as "very weak on the actual intervention on the masses" and the situation in the colonies (1938, 319–20). In 1963, Jaurès bookends the modern period of French Revolution historiography, with James underlining how he established "once and for all the economic basis of the Revolution" (1963, 384). Now James describes Jaurès as "a great parliamentarian" and "one of the early labour leaders" who "shows a sympathetic understanding of the great mass movements."

In 1963, there is less about the extent of James's indebtedness to Jaurès, who had been acknowledged back in 1938 as the basis for a whole section of *The Black Jacobins* on the rise of the French bourgeoisie (1938, 35n1).

Pride of place in this revised timeline of French Revolution historiography is now given to Georges Lefebvre. From not appearing in the 1938 bibliography, Lefebvre is now mentioned twice in different places in the 1963 revised bibliography:

> **The crown of this work of over a century has been attained by M. Georges Lefebvre, whose one-volume history of the Revolution, and his mimeographed series of lectures to students at the Sorbonne, are a fitting climax to a lifetime of indefatigable scholarship, sympathetic understanding and a balanced judgement of all parties, groups and individuals in the Revolution, which it would be difficult to parallel** (384)

To this is also added a cross-reference to one of the 1963 added footnotes, showing how James wants to reorient his source material by following Lefebvre in paying more attention to obscure leaders and ordinary people in the Haitian and French revolutions.

Next James adds an important bibliographic reference to Daniel Guérin. This work is highly praised as "**a brilliant, original and well-documented iconoclastic study, which centres around the conflict between Robespierre and the various mass movements**" (1963, 384). In between James's 1938 and 1963 history editions, one new account of the enragés was published by his fellow independent Marxist and friend Daniel Guérin, whose 1946 book presented the enragés as the spokesmen for the incipient proletarian revolution of the bras nus.[79] This is another all-important source, which reorients James's 1963 history toward the roles played by mass movements and left-wing counterparts of the sansculottes and enragés and their conflicts with the top revolutionary leaderships. In the oral presentation of this revised bibliography in the 1971 lecture, James referred to Guérin as "a friend of mine" who had written "a special book."[80] Guérin had also helped James arrange the French translation *Les Jacobins noirs* by Pierre Naville, published in 1949 by the prestigious French publishing house Gallimard. In 1958, James would refer to Guérin's book as "the finest study of the activities of the working class during the French Revolution."[81]

Guérin's *La Lutte des classes* was a work James knew well, as James had been commissioned to translate it. Unfortunately, James would only complete three chapters, and the translation itself was ultimately abandoned.[82] Nevertheless, such intimate knowledge of Guérin's book provided James with the impetus to highlight the roles played by popular movements and alternative popular leaders in the course of the Haitian Revolution.

One entry shared by both the 1938 and 1963 bibliographies is Kropotkin's history of the French Revolution. In 1963, he is used as the counterpoint to U.S., and especially British, studies of the French Revolution, which try to be "fair to both sides" (384–85). In his lecture "How I Wrote *The Black Jacobins*," James would expand orally on how futile attempts to be fair to both sides always are, especially with reference to revolution. Taking sides and not being afraid of the excesses and explosions of revolution is central to James's re/writing of *The Black Jacobins*.[83]

By ending his revised bibliography with the cross-reference to Lefebvre, James indicates the reorientation of his sources to spotlight ordinary people and alternative popular leaders.[84] Subsequently, in the 1971 lectures, James would repeat and go beyond the 1963 revised bibliography's line of development, verbally adding Albert Soboul—leading historian of the sansculottes—further indicating the downward shift of James's own attention toward the black sansculottes.[85]

James's revised bibliography gives the reader an altered whistle-stop tour through his French Revolution sources. Elsewhere, other minor bibliographic and footnote references have also been reworked. Under the listings for "San Domingo Archives," the bibliographic footnote giving Jean Price Mars's address is now omitted (379/317). Although Price Mars would live until 1969, this information would have risked quickly becoming out of date. Also, the celebrated work of this Haitian forefather of indigenism and Negritude became one of the key signposts along the road to West Indian identity plotted by the new appendix.[86]

Under the bibliography heading "BIOGRAPHIES OF TOUSSAINT L'OUVERTURE" is a new reference to Aimé Césaire's 1961 biography *Toussaint L'Ouverture*, bringing the bibliography up to date.[87] There, James announces his French West Indian counterpart by his fame. Compared to the enthusiastic praise in James's appendix for Césaire's famous poem *Cahier*—analyzed in the next section—the slant on Césaire's Toussaint biography is more grudging: "The book, as could have been expected, is extremely competent and gives a good picture of Toussaint and the San Domingo Revolution. I find, however, that it lacks the fire and constant illumination which distinguish most of the other works of Césaire" (389). Although, as the appendix shows, James was a great admirer of Césaire, this criticism stands out. I agree with Madison Smartt Bell's assessment that this was the only biography that could have rivaled James's own and given it "a run for its money."[88] Despite his profound reflections on source types, the actual sources of the 1938 edition of *The Black Jacobins* change little in the 1963 edition. As James never did begin the whole project from scratch again, these interstitial 1963 changes demonstrate the general direction in which he was trying to shift *The Black Jacobins*.

Appendix: "From Toussaint Louverture to Fidel Castro"

As the most conspicuous and well-known addition, the appendix has been the most commented upon of all the 1963 revisions to *The Black Jacobins*. For David Scott, it is "James's historiographical gift to the then emerging postcolonial Caribbean nation-states."[89] I agree with Scott's reading that there is a striking discontinuity between the main history and the appendix, instead of an organic, seamless connection between the two parts.[90] Scott has pointed out that, at scarcely thirty pages, the appendix is a "model of narrative economy."[91] Another influential reading of the appendix is that of Susan Gillman, who expresses the text-network of *The Black Jacobins* as an equation: "from Columbus to Toussaint + from Toussaint to Castro = from Columbus to Castro."[92] To this, I would add that through the addition of the appendix, *The Black Jacobins* text-network becomes more than the sum of all its parts.

Certainly, the appendix is the key addition, which contributes more to the history than thirty pages and the new connection between Toussaint and Castro. This famous extended essay also lays out the history of the book itself since the 1930s in conjunction with a snapshot of West Indian history from 1804 up to the 1960s. My own reading of this concluding essay insists on its telescopic, doubled vision and on the hybridity of the appendix as a document that straddles the style of James's political pamphlets, composite social commentary and journalism style, literary criticism of West Indian literature, and an account of West Indian political developments, including the breakup of the West Indies Federation and independence movements. For Scott, the appendix emphasizes tragedy, the breakup of the West Indies Federation, and James's split with Eric Williams. These are indeed markers that signpost the road of the appendix. However, this document is still forward-facing and optimistic, traveling back to the future to celebrate the speculative thought of what was foreseen previously in 1938, and praising the extraordinary achievements of

West Indians in many spheres. James's work of the 1960s is still marked by revolutionary optimism.[93]

The title of the appendix also tells its contents, as James always pointed out in his 1961–64 correspondence. It presents a long line of West Indian development from Louverture and the Haitian Revolution right up to Castro and the Cuban Revolution, and then to the early 1960s when James was penning his appendix as the Federation failed and emerging West Indian nations announced their independence. From the outset, James makes it clear that what links Louverture with Castro is not the most obvious reason that both led revolutions in the West Indies. Instead, James uses these bookends to chart the quest for a national identity through the appendix's timeline of West Indian development through (1) the nineteenth century, (2) between the wars, and (3) after World War II. As discussed, James was not so silent about the U.S. occupation in 1938 as claimed by Dalleo.[94] In 1963, the appendix deals with the U.S. occupation and Haiti at quite some length (394). The occupation dates are wrong, as in the 1938 edition, but the target is Haitian resistance.

The same quotation from a Haitian minister's speech is used for different purposes in the two editions.[95] Originally, in 1938 the quotation was used to show how Haitians have turned back to France following recognition of Haitian independence because what is known as the race question is really based on economic exploitation. However, the same quotation is redeployed in the appendix, where it is now framed critically to ridicule the "hollow pretensions" of the Haitian elite's aping of French civilization.[96] James shows how Haitians turned instead toward Africa and the idea of Negritude.

Negritude is the fundamental concept that is shown by the appendix to link historically the long line of prominent West Indians concerned with Africa. Negritude is presented as a complete rejection of European civilization and the old colonial system in the West Indies. James makes this point clearly in his translation and analysis of Aimé Césaire's famous poem of Negritude, *Cahier d'un retour au pays natal* (1939).[97] Always James would argue that Negritude is essentially of West Indian origin and the work of West Indian Césaire, not Senghor, and that *Cahier* is the finest poem ever written about Africa.[98]

My commentary on James's own translation of Césaire's poem shows that this translation is extremely free. For James, the main point is not to provide an equivalent word-for-word rendering of Césaire's French original. Instead, James's creative translation possessively makes the famous poem his own. This principle of proprietary free translation is clearly at work, even in James's inventive rephrasing of Césaire's title: *Cahier d'un retour au pays natal* (literally, notebook/jotter/exercise book of a return to the native land), which becomes in James's translation "Statement of a Return to the Country Where I Was Born," with "Statement" evoking a communication setting forth a political position. Similarly free is James's translation of the title of Haitian Jean Price Mars's 1928 *Ainsi parla l'oncle* (Thus [or so] spoke the uncle) as "This Is What the Uncle Said." James's strong translations give both titles the air of clear political communications, such as political speeches or pamphlets.

These strong translations can also be interpreted as "strong readings" in Harold Bloom's sense from *A Map of Misreading*.[99] Bloom theorizes "strong" (mis)readings as what happens when one brilliant writer appropriates work by another equally accomplished writer.[100] This involves, according to Bloom, a misreading or strong reading of the original work, serving to bring out new qualities that were previously obscured or latent in weaker readings. It is in this context of strong Bloomian misreadings that James's strong reading of the poetry of his contemporary, Césaire, can be mapped out, illuminating *Cahier*'s complex relations with *The Black Jacobins*. In the appendix, the poem is incorporated into James's revised work, literally becoming part of *The Black Jacobins*. This strong reading constitutes, in fact, James's strong rewriting of Césaire's poem as it is transformed anew. When James's version of *Cahier* is set against Césaire's own, the strength of James's creative mis/reading and mis/translation emerges. James transforms the sense of the original poem, creating new meaning. The creative dialectical development of *The Black Jacobins* as a whole—the total changing process of its rewriting—is enacted in the appendix when James makes Césaire's poem move by amalgamating it there with his own writing.

A substantial part of the appendix is taken up with Césaire's famous poem. Through creative selection and analysis of excerpts, James makes the poem his own. First of all, he begins about two-thirds of the way into the poem with the "definition" of Negritude through what it is not—"my negritude is not a stone." Certain French conventions are not translated, for example "ni . . . ni" (neither . . . nor), which instead becomes in James's phrase, "my Negritude is *no* tower, *no* cathedral," making the double "no" reverberate. One line of the original poem is left out altogether.[101] Instead, James jumps in his translation to the next lines: "Hoorah for those who never invented anything / for those who never explored anything / for those who never mastered anything."

At one point in his translation of Césaire, James again strays far from the original with his unique version: "for in order to *project myself* [quite different

Rewriting History (1963) | 127

from the original *me cantonner*, "to confine/billet me"] into this unique race you [the original *pourtant*—meaning "still" or "though"—is not translated] know the *extent* of my *boundless* love" (400).[102] Some significant differences are added here, with the substitution of the very different "boundless" for *tyrannique* (most literally "tyrannical"). With all this focus on projecting himself and boundless experiences, James projects his own boundless vision onto Césaire's poem, making it his own.

James's creative translation of Césaire's *Cahier* animates the principle of dialogue that is at work on so many different levels of James's writings on the Haitian Revolution. Changes to the speaker pronouns start to constitute a dialogue in James's version of the poem. Here, it is as if James is showing the process of a "rendezvous of victory" being made by all the active participants in this dialogue process.[103] Changes to the speaker pronouns show a desire to represent everybody, as in making a place for all at the "rendezvous of victory," as James puts it in the climax to his creative translation of Césaire's poem. Rewriting the poem formally, James breaks up several long lines in free verse from Césaire's prose original into more traditional poetic verse, reframing the new shorter verse-like lines as a poem, and making them stand out more against the prose narrative of the rest of the appendix. By rewriting the form and content of Césaire's poem, James presents it as *the* Caribbean identity poem, formally summing up the very strong pattern of that identity James is trying to get at throughout the appendix.

I would like to conclude this analysis of James's translation of Césaire by drawing attention to what James identifies as the center of the poem. In fact, the entire poem is recentered by James, who chooses to conclude his translation right in the middle of a line in the middle of a stanza, when he ends by translating "et il est place pour tous au rendez-vous de la conquête." Most literally, this is "and there is room for all at the rendezvous of *conquest*," but James instead renders it "and there is a place for all at the rendezvous of *victory*." In French, as in English, there are equivalent words: *conquête* = conquest, and *victoire* = victory. James could have translated this passage more closely as "at the rendezvous of conquest," but his changing of one word is highly significant. "Conquest" has more negative connotations, while "victory" is more positive: the perspective of winning—to borrow the subtitle of his wife and collaborator Selma James's *Race, Sex, and Class*.[104] Victory suggests triumphant winning, whereas conquest suggests the act of being passively conquered or vanquished. Victory is what takes place after the initial conquest, and victory refers to the winners, while conquest refers to the losers. James changes his ending of Césaire's poem, which is not its actual ending in *Cahier* at all, by rewriting it. This—James's own rewriting of Césaire—would later become the title of a whole volume of James's selected writings published in 1984 by Allison and Busby, *At the Rendezvous of Victory*, including his 1964 "Black Sansculottes" article with its references to the Haiti of 1964.[105]

James's own creative translation of the poem in the pages of *The Black Jacobins* particularly stresses what James would always say about *Cahier*: that it is one of the most drastic attacks ever made in the twentieth century on Western civilization.[106] James concentrates on the lines at the center of *Cahier* where Césaire repudiates Western civilization as strongly as he can. In the appendix, James presents himself and *The Black Jacobins* as Césaire and *Cahier*'s exact contemporaries who can express the same rejection of standards and values because of their parallel educational experiences at Queen's Royal College in Trinidad and Lycée Schœlcher in Martinique (402).[107]

The essence of the old colonial system is presented by the appendix as remaining unchanged right up to 1963: "In 1963, the old colonial system is not what it was in 1863; in 1863 it was not what it had been in 1763 or 1663. The fundamentals outlined above, however, have not changed" (406). Much of the appendix is about the need to strike serious blows at the old colonial system and the growing gulf between the old colonial system and modern twentieth-century civilization.[108] The perseverance of the old type of colonial system is ascribed to the nature of power in the Caribbean: "Power here is more naked than in any other part of the world. Hence, the brutality, savagery, even personal cruelties of the régimes of Trujillo and Duvalier, and the power of the Cuban Revolution" (408). The United States is shown to be a major player in this battle between the old colonial system and democracy, keeping Duvalier in power (409). In this section, "After World War II," the brutality of François "Papa Doc" Duvalier's dictatorship is attributed to U.S. influence and contrasted with the "tremendous" Cuban Revolution.[109]

A special place in the appendix is reserved for the widespread protest in Trinidad against the American occupation of Chaguaramas, a U.S. naval base, between 1940 and 1963. On this issue of the return of the naval base at Chaguaramas, James writes as if buoyed by all the mass protest. Here, Eric Williams, political leader of the Trinidad People's National Movement (PNM) Party who would go on to become premier of Trinidad and Tobago in 1959 and first prime minister in 1962, is never specifically named in the appendix; he is referred to throughout this episode only as "the political leader" (411–13).[110] Again, the telescopic appendix merges with autobiography as James writes of the tremendous mass meetings and mass demonstrations. Overall, the tone at this point is celebratory, and James writes that the people demonstrating were "free, freer than they might be for a long time." With these words, James leaves the Chaguaramas issue hanging on a positive note of unsurpassed popular support.

Elsewhere James has summed up Williams's address, "From Slavery to Chaguaramas," thus: "But the Doctor say they [the Americans] must go and therefore they must go. Williams used a tremendous phrase. He said 'I will break this Chaguaramas issue or it will break me.' And the average Trinidadian said 'We can't allow Chaguaramas to break the Doctor. We must break it.' He had it in his hands. I was there at the time."[111] Despite the celebratory tone, the way that this episode is left hanging as if in midair has ominous overtones, because what is not recounted is the next step in the story, that Williams did go back on his word, allowing the Americans to stay in Chaguaramas after all, ultimately extending the lease for the naval base, although the United States would abandon Chaguaramas in 1967.[112] These ominous overtones do suggest an inflection of postcolonial tragedy in the appendix, as argued by Scott, but the main thrust of the story of West Indian development as told in the appendix remains celebratory—although with some significant silences.

The appendix is also a record of the five years that James spent in national politics in the West Indies, and noticeably words such as "nation" and "national" dominate the appendix, referring to a single West Indian nation.[113] So bitterly disappointed was James by the failure of the West Indies Federation that he described it as the West Indies going to independence "as to a funeral," although here the tone is not uniformly pessimistic.[114]

The purpose of the appendix is to outline the development of the West Indian quest for a national identity, which James approaches through a long commentary on West Indian literature. Here James writes, "The West Indian national identity is more easily to be glimpsed in the published writings of West Indian writers" (413). According to James, it is important to look at West Indian literature because the West Indian nation is right in the process of finding itself.[115] Following the earlier commentary on Aimé Césaire seeking a road out of the West Indies via Africa, James now offers short commentaries on the West Indian writers Vic Reid, George Lamming, V. S. Naipaul, and Wilson Harris. A quotation from Derek Walcott toward the appendix's end is also given. As James put it elsewhere, "Something is going on among us. Otherwise the good writers are making it up. And good writers don't simply 'make up.' They are working from something[....] But in order to know what they are doing and how they are getting on, you have to be aware of the movement of literature on the whole and its influence on society."[116] James shows how these West Indian literary voices encapsulate the idea of a West Indian identity, which is the main theme of the appendix.

Like the mass of the population, the West Indian writers are presented as not simply seeking a national identity, but as expressing one already (417). Repeatedly, James concludes that West Indian writers, like West Indians in general, have brought something new. In the appendix, James parades before the reader the signposts that have guided him toward the conception of West Indian identity—Toussaint Louverture, Fernando Ortiz, Jean Price Mars, Captain Cipriani, Fidel Castro, Vic Reid, George Lamming, V. S. Naipaul, and Wilson Harris—an all-male lineup of personalities and writers.[117]

To conclude this chapter, I end with some reflections on the hybridity of the form and content of the composite final document that is the appendix. It is appropriately in this hybrid finale to *The Black Jacobins* that James presents his ideal amalgamated vision of Caribbean federation—one that would be far more inclusive than the short-lived political union of the actual Federation of the British West Indies, which lasted from January 3, 1958, to May 31, 1962. James's ideal Caribbean federation would encompass Césaire's Martinique, Guadeloupe, Jean Price Mars's Haiti itself, Fernando Ortiz's Cuba, and the former Dutch Caribbean territories, in addition to the Anglophone islands of the region.[118] In the hybrid appendix, it is also fitting that James turns from history writing to literary criticism in the quest for a West Indian identity, sounding West Indian literary voices including Césaire, Ortiz, and Price Mars, in addition to commentaries on Anglophone writers Vic Reid, George Lamming, V. S. Naipaul, and Wilson Harris.

James ends the appendix with an image of the line of development from Toussaint to Castro turning inward in the process of discovering itself: "Passion not spent but turned inward. Toussaint tried and paid for it with his life. Torn, twisted, stretched to the limits of agony, injected with poisonous patent medicines, it lives in the state which Fidel started. It is of the West Indies West Indian. For it Toussaint, the first and greatest of West Indians, paid with his life" (418). This process of turning inward is presented as the key to West Indian identity throughout the semiautobiographical self-translation constituted by the 1963 history revisions, especially the self-reflexive appendix. The essential features of West Indian identity here do sound pessimistic because they are associated with negative actions almost to the point of being broken—"torn," "twisted," "stretched," and even "injected" with poisonous substances. However, there are positive overtones too. Repeatedly, James identifies the West Indian characteristic he is chasing by turning inward as "peculiar."

Changes in this high-visibility text-network shift the space-time coordinates as *The Black Jacobins* moves from the Africa of the 1930s toward the West Indies of the 1960s in search of an identity. James rewrites his speculative history from the perspective of relating the West Indies to its own history in order for him to grasp and magnify what characterizes the uniqueness of the West Indies "with no parallel anywhere else." West Indian identity, like *The Black Jacobins* history project itself, has an unfinished and provisional quality.

4 | Reshaping the Past as Drama (1967)

James's second play, *The Black Jacobins* of 1967, is radically different from his first play in 1936. Although they enact the main events of the Haitian Revolution, both plays barely share a single word in common. They also diverge in terms of characterization and plot, but both feature similar imperialist figureheads of the great powers while also showcasing Toussaint, Dessalines, and Christophe. In the second play, however, more popular leaders and their actions are foregrounded. As can be seen from table 4.1, which compares and contrasts elements of the two dramas, some scenes roughly correlate in terms of characters featured and events narrated. However, there are many stark differences. Notably, the *Black Jacobins* play does not include Toussaint's death scene in captivity in France. New characters who did not appear at all in *Toussaint Louverture* are prominent in the 1960s play, especially Moïse, Toussaint's adopted nephew; Marie-Jeanne, a prominent female character; and Samedi Smith, a popular leader. At the epicenter of the new play is the showdown between uncle and adopted nephew, Toussaint and Moïse.

The remaking of *The Black Jacobins* as James's second play came more than four years after the 1963 revision of the history by the same title. While its predecessor of more than thirty years, *Toussaint Louverture*, was only recently published in 2013, surprisingly, less seems to be known about *The Black Jacobins* play than would be expected, despite the script appearing twice in print (1976 and 1992) and being performed across a number of countries over the decades since its 1967 Nigerian premiere.[1] Changes made by James throughout the second play's evolution start to dramatize the activity of the ordinary rank-and-file black sansculottes, whereby the masses mobilize themselves as they act against the vanguard of the top Haitian revolutionary leaders.[2]

Charting the remaking of *The Black Jacobins* as it premiered at the University of Ibadan, Nigeria, in 1967, this chapter examines James's role in writing the

Table 4.1 Comparing the Plays: From *Toussaint Louverture* ("TL," 1936) to *The Black Jacobins* ("BJ," 1967)

TOUSSAINT LOUVERTURE, EARLY DRAFTS INCLUDING HULL SCRIPT	TOUSSAINT LOUVERTURE AS PERFORMED IN 1936 (FROM PROGRAM)	TOUSSAINT LOUVERTURE UW1227, COPY 1, TRANSITIONAL CHANGES	THE BLACK JACOBINS EARLY DRAFTS, INCLUDING UW1230, UW1228, UW1229	THE BLACK JACOBINS AS PERFORMED IN 1967 AND PUBLISHED
Act 1, scene 1. A moonlit evening. The verandah outside M. Bullet's villa. Music: the minuet to *Don Giovanni* playing against insistent beating of drums. Newly arrived French representative Colonel Vincent witnesses cruel deadly punishments decreed for Ferrand de Baudière.	Deleted.	As in Hull script.	Act 1, scene 1. 1791. Living room of M. Bullet, a plantation owner. Mme. Bullet and Marie-Jeanne, mulatto house slave, sing *Vendetta* aria from Mozart's *Don Giovanni*. Moise added to early drafts by hand.	Act 1, scene 1. 1791. Inside living room of M. Bullet, a plantation owner. Features Moise as Toussaint's trusted officer versus wild Dessalines. Marie-Jeanne pursued by M. Bullet and Dessalines. Amazement when Toussaint kisses Mme. Bullet's hand.
Act 1, scene 2. August 6, 1791. The depths of a forest. Representation of ceremony (Bois Caïman).	Act 1, scene 1. The depths of a forest in the French portion of the West Indian island of San Domingo. August 6th, 1791. [Similar to Hull, but reference made to Ferrand and Baudière as two people in NALIS script.]	As in Hull script.	Act 1, scene 2. Military headquarters of General Toussaint Louverture, 1794. Early drafts build up presentation of three soldiers: Marat, Max, Orléans. Moise announces French abolition of slavery. Arrest of Spanish general.	As in early drafts. No corresponding representation in 1967 play of Bois Caïman ceremony.

Act 1, scene 3. The slave encampment at La Grande Rivière, April 1793. Features slave leaders.	Act 1, scene 2. The slave encampment at La Grande Rivière, April 1793.	Act 1, scene 3. Moïse written into scene by hand, calls Toussaint "Uncle," 1.3.13–14 and 1.3.29–31. Toussaint appoints Moïse aide-de-camp. Moïse witness to leaders' squabbles, then shares Toussaint's reading of Raynal.	Act 1, scene 3. Living room of Tobias Lear, American consul and Governor Louverture's/General Maitland's headquarters, 1798. British offer of kingship. Moïse takes principled stand, calling for independence. We see interimperialistic alliances, rivalries, and racism. [Scene 4 not indicated.]	Picture of Moïse built up through drafts. From being absent in *TL*, Moïse is added and his role elaborated in UWI227 additions, through the drafts of *BJ*.
Act 1, scene 4. Early 1794. The mountain retreat of Toussaint's wife and sons. General Maitland makes Toussaint British offer of kingship, corresponds to *BJ* act 1, scene 3. M. Bullet represents planters turning traitor to France to uphold slavery status quo. Roume announces French abolition of slavery via scene-within-scene of Convention declaration, corresponds to *BJ*, act 1, scene 2.	Deleted. Not sure from NALIS script how news of French abolition of slavery announced.	As in Hull script, but James's hand changes word "Negro" to "black." M. Bullet: "You damned **black** Negro! You dismiss us—. You think." (1.4.38)	Act 1, scene 4. 1800. Bedroom of Marie-Jeanne. Strong female character who extracts information from French representative Hédouville, which she communicates to Toussaint variously through Mars Plaisir, Célestine, and Dessalines. No corresponding strong female characters in *TL*.	Act 2, scene 1. When worked out portrays Marie-Jeanne as a determined revolutionary in her own right, much more than Dessalines's love interest.

Table 4.1 (cont'd)

TOUSSAINT LOUVERTURE, EARLY DRAFTS INCLUDING HULL SCRIPT	TOUSSAINT LOUVERTURE AS PERFORMED IN 1936 (FROM PROGRAM)	TOUSSAINT LOUVERTURE UW1227, COPY 1, TRANSITIONAL CHANGES	THE BLACK JACOBINS EARLY DRAFTS, INCLUDING UW1230, UW1228, UW1229	THE BLACK JACOBINS AS PERFORMED IN 1967 AND PUBLISHED
Act 2, scene 1. Five years later. A room in the government buildings in Port-au-Prince. Features representatives of major imperialist powers. Toussaint's victory surprises them. This corresponds to the similar staging of imperialist antics in BJ, act 1, scene 3.	Act 2, scene 1. Becomes eight years later. Same location. Scene elaborated further in Life and Letters and NALIS scripts. Partly like BJ play, act 1, scene 3 is British offer of kingship, imperialist antics, and act 1, scene 5/act 2, scene 2 mentions sending Vincent to France with constitution.	As in Hull script.	Act 1, scene 5. Headquarters of Toussaint Louverture: 1800. Toussaint gives constitution to Vincent and dispatches him to Bonaparte in France. Early drafts of this intermediary scene in UW1229.	Act 2, scene 2. Headquarters of Toussaint Louverture: 1800. As in early drafts.
Act 2, scene 2. Nearly two years later. Bonaparte's apartment in the Tuileries. Bonaparte's angry, racist response to constitution, punishment of Vincent, instructions to brother-in-law Leclerc about French expedition. Feigns fatherly concern for Toussaint's sons.	Act 2, scene 2. Bonaparte's apartment in the Tuileries. Toussaint's sons deleted. [No time given.]	As in Hull script, but some lines are swapped for Toussaint's sons, Isaac and Placide, 2.2.29 in copy 1.	Act 1, scene 6. Office of General Bonaparte, Les Tuileries, Paris, France; 1800. Vincent presents constitution to Bonaparte. Alternative version of scene also introduces French expedition leader Leclerc. Lyndersay objected.	Act 2, scene 3. As in earlier drafts. Does not contain Leclerc's cameo appearance as in later draft.

Act 3, scene 1. Toussaint's hut in the mountains. Early 1802. Toussaint and his wife's reunion with sons and tutor. Sons asked to choose between father and San Domingo or France.	Scene cut.	As in Hull script.	Alternative scene with Toussaint and wife's reunion with sons shows that James toyed with including them in *BJ*, too, in a scene "merely" suggested "for future reference." Tutor's name misspelled. UWI229.	Scene cut from later drafts and published/performance scripts.
Act 3, scene 2. March 24, 1802, about six o'clock in the evening. The fortress of Crête-à-Pierrot in San Domingo. On a rampart running diagonally. Battle scene featuring Toussaint in early drafts, and Dessalines in NALIS script. Learn of Christophe's surrender to French. There is no Moïse in *TL*, and no equivalent for *BJ* scene.	Act 3, scene 1. The fortress of Crête-à-Pierrot in San Domingo. March 24, **1801**, about six o'clock in the evening. Reverts back to Toussaint, according to 1936 program.	As in Hull script.	Act 1, scene 7. Headquarters of Toussaint Louverture: 1802. Mme. Bullet/Toussaint affair, Toussaint's depths speech, showdown with Moïse, French troops arrive. Alternative act 1, scene 7 commentary about degree of rewriting. Some versions both Mme. Bullet and Toussaint read Raynal. Some feature Mme. Lespinasse, additional white woman seeking Toussaint as godfather for son.	Becomes act 2, scene 4. According to Errol Hill and Yvonne Brewster, James wanted to cut details of Toussaint's affair with Mme. Bullet. Lyndersay elaborates by hand Moïse's final exit below prologue in Columbia script. In *BJ* we do not witness a battle scene, only the revolutionaries coming from battle.

Table 4.1 (cont'd)

TOUSSAINT LOUVERTURE, EARLY DRAFTS INCLUDING HULL SCRIPT	TOUSSAINT LOUVERTURE AS PERFORMED IN 1936 (FROM PROGRAM)	TOUSSAINT LOUVERTURE UW1227, COPY 1, TRANSITIONAL CHANGES	THE BLACK JACOBINS EARLY DRAFTS, INCLUDING UW1230, UW1228, UW1229	THE BLACK JACOBINS AS PERFORMED IN 1967 AND PUBLISHED
Act 3, scene 3. Late in 1801. Leclerc's villa. Toussaint comes to sign peace, betrayed and captured by French traitors. Witnessed by sons. Scene features Pauline Leclerc's frivolous plans for a ball, and news of yellow fever toll on French troops. [Set late in 1801 despite previous scene being set in 1802.]	Act 3, scene 2. Leclerc's villa, late 1801. Like earlier versions, but maid called Suzanne as before. Toussaint's sons do not feature here.	Act 3, scene 3. Pauline Leclerc's mulatto maid's name changed from Suzanne to **Kikite**, UW1227, copy 1, 3-3-15, perhaps to avoid confusion with Suzanne Louverture, Toussaint's wife, who ultimately did not appear in TL as performed.	Act 2, scene 1. Headquarters of Dessalines: 1802. Features peasant soldier Samedi Smith and soldiers Orléans and Marat. Toussaint discusses plans for retirement. Dessalines and Christophe arrange to have Toussaint captured by French. Marie-Jeanne overhears.	Act 3, scene 1. Headquarters of Dessalines: 1802. As in earlier drafts. More focus on Toussaint's own officers betraying him than in TL. BJ does not present Toussaint's arrest by French.
Act 3, scene 4. Late in 1801. Toussaint's cell in a prison in the Alps. Features Toussaint's death.	Act 3, scene 3. Late in 1801. Toussaint's cell in a prison in the Alps. NALIS script has complicated scenes with Toussaint traveling back in time in his mind's eye, and jailer Baille's death/replacement.	As in earlier scripts.	No Toussaint prison/death scene in BJ.	No Toussaint prison/death scene in BJ.

Act 3, scene 5. May 1802. Inside Hôtel de la République. News arrives about slavery being restored. Dessalines and Pétion break with French. Leclerc has yellow fever. Leaders hear of Toussaint's death and French restoration of slavery. Leaders unite linking arms and standing on table. [Some versions read 1803: UWI275, Dartmouth, Yale scripts.]	Act 3, scene 4. May 1802. Leclerc's Villa. [NALIS script contains some additions and more lines for Christophe. Not clear from program what exactly was performed in 1936.]	As in earlier scripts.		Act 2, scene 2. 1802. Headquarters of Dessalines. We see Dessalines proclaiming independence and new name for Haiti. He proclaims himself emperor. News of Toussaint's death arrives. Instead of dashing tears from his eyes as in *TL*, Dessalines observes that Moïse was right. He forces Marie-Jeanne to dance with him and orders minuet to drown out the Samedi Smith anthem.	Act 3, scene 2. 1803. Headquarters of Dessalines. Scene built up to contain more of a musical standoff between the minuet and the Samedi Smith song. Bleaker, less triumphant ending than corresponding scene in *TL*.
				Epilogue: Scene that would have traveled to present day. Three versions, one set in West Indies after breakup of federation in UWI230, 37–40. One has theme that fighting means taking risks, and alternative final page asks true meaning of independence. Lyndersay worked out a prologue instead based on *BJ* history. Some scripts have one page of prologue and epilogue.	Version of prologue that Lyndersay worked out fully is in Columbia script, along with lines for Moïse's final exit, inspired by the epilogue, and presented to the playwright as a substitute for the epilogue to which James was so attached.

play through a study of his fascinating correspondence with its first director, Dexter Lyndersay. The chapter gives a relative chronology for all available 1967 play scripts, using methodologies from genetic criticism and book history. Special consideration is given to James's exploitation of the resources of drama in the 1967 play to show the past of the Haitian Revolution. This chapter explores how James's rewriting of *The Black Jacobins* as a play incorporates changes to the protagonists as the relationship of the Haitian revolutionary leadership to the popular masses is rethought. The chapter argues that the play's epilogue should be read as a political speech or pamphlet. Ultimately, the epilogue will be seen to change completely the key and register of the play's ending.

For want of the text of *Toussaint Louverture* until 2013, *The Black Jacobins* had understandably sometimes been read as the 1936 play, and was even wrongly billed as belonging to the 1930s period of James's life and work when published in Anna Grimshaw's *C. L. R. James Reader* (1992).[3] James's own role in the 1967 play has sometimes been seen as minimal to the point of nonexistent.[4] According to Cudjoe, too much space in the 1992 *Reader* is devoted to this play because "James's involvement was minimal if not absent" and "the revised version [was] written by Lyndersay." In 1994, Scott McLemee suggested that the play was not, in fact, written by James at all, but was instead adapted for the stage from his history of the same title by some unnamed person.[5] Mary-Lou Emery cites email correspondence dated November 28, 2002, from Jim Murray, director of the C. L. R. James Institute in New York, claiming that James had merely "authorized" the 1967 play with his signature.[6] In turn, these viewpoints have then been cited by others.[7] However, James's own contributions were far from negligible, although collaboration was here as elsewhere a crucial part of James's method.

This chapter starts by examining James's collaborative working methods on the play. Collaborators seem to have included James's own Facing Reality comrades, including William Gorman and Priscilla (Prisca) Allen, from James's February 1967 correspondence. Next, the correspondence between playwright James and director Lyndersay is analyzed to pinpoint James's own contributions. As previously discussed, Scott's influential narrativism-inspired reading of some of the 1963 history revisions follows Hayden White's foregrounding of the "content of the form" and the storytelling qualities of history writing. Important relationships between form, content, and the varying generic forms in play—history, narrative, and drama—are right at the fore of this chapter's main concerns. Often, history is thought of in terms of theater with such clichés as the "drama of history," a revolution described as a great drama, or historical characters described as tragic protagonists on the stage of world history.⁸ James also always saw the game of cricket as a dramatic spectacle, such as one would find in theater.⁹

Reconfiguring the past as drama, the chapter argues, is liberating because it frees James from the need for referential apparatuses of history writing proper, including footnotes and bibliographies to gloss existing historiography and refer to sources. A further advantage of drama as a means for representing the past is that its multivoicedness enables alternative characters of whom there is little archival trace, such as Moïse, to speak more audibly, an active process of unsilencing gaps in official historical records of the Caribbean.¹⁰

Making drama out of history, it is argued, enables James to go furthest in rewriting the Haitian Revolution from below. Reshaped, *The Black Jacobins* play will be shown to bear strong imprints of Marxist history from below and ideas developed during James's intensive political collaboration and theorization in the United States in the 1940s as part of the Johnson-Forest Tendency concerning self-activity, self-organization, mobilization of the masses from below, and rejection of the orthodox Marxist-Leninist concept of the vanguard party.¹¹ Turning to drama again, I argue, enables James to tell a different story of the Haitian Revolution and change the protagonists by shifting the spotlight downward during the rewriting of *The Black Jacobins* as a play in 1966–67. Explored as a corrective to the history of leaders, and as a version of the Haitian Revolution seen from below, the play is analyzed particularly from the viewpoint of its demythologization of revolutionary leaders Toussaint, Dessalines, and Christophe, simultaneously bringing into view crowds, peasants, ordinary soldiers, and popular alternative leaders, of whom there is little archival trace.

Genre has rightly been viewed as an important issue for *The Black Jacobins*. Described as "genre-challenging" by Kara M. Rabbitt, and as an "analytic *tour de force* of literary distinction" by David Geggus, *The Black Jacobins* history has been noted for its distinctive crossover generic qualities.¹² Beyond this distinctive literary feel of *The Black Jacobins* history, however, few have analyzed its trajectory as an actual drama or work of literature. Based on *The Black Jacobins* play, Nicole King connects James's fiction and nonfiction, seeing fiction as the "foundation of James the writer and thinker" and usefully going against James's own clear-cut distinction whereby he claims that between 1932 and 1938, "fiction-writing drained out of me and was replaced by politics. I became a Marxist, a Trotskyist."¹³ Such generic and literary crossovers are fundamental to both the histories and the plays, but the emphasis on fiction is perhaps slightly misplaced. Fiction implies a strong tendency to untruth, to make up something. Drama, this chapter argues, is a special literary category with particular qualities that would appeal to a fundamentally political person like James.

Theater has been described as the most public of the arts and as second cousin to politics, as having a special politics-ready quality, and as one of the arts of presentation and representation that, like photography, has a privileged access to truth.[14] This intrinsically political role of theater as a representing machine also strongly connects it with action, as characters and historical events from long ago can be brought to life now by flesh-and-blood actors who perform these deeds in the present tense of theater's liveness, as if they were happening now. Conventionally, performance is thought of as ephemeral, a process of vanishing or disappearing, the very antithesis of James's saving and unsilencing of material traces of alternative histories. However, this rather neat equation of performance = disappearance has been challenged by several scholars, including Diana Taylor, Rebecca Schneider, and Joseph Roach, who argue that theater performance as representational practice offers different ways of accessing and telling history.[15]

Indeed, the extant play scripts in themselves are, as leading Caribbean theorist and practitioner of drama Errol Hill reminds us, only ever incomplete pieces of the puzzle, and nothing but the dead corpses that remain of performances.[16] Play scripts can be extremely valuable for research purposes because they often constitute the only permanent records we have of a play's existence, and they can reveal much about the playwright's intentions, although a play script can never be a substitute for the actual performance of the play, for which the script is only the vehicle. The word "fiction" is therefore somewhat misplaced in critical discussion of the play, because drama is a very peculiar form of literature, fundamentally different from any other.

A play is also the only literary form that remains unfinished when the playwright completes his script, whereas the author would be the one wholly responsible for the creation of a poem, novel, short story, or essay.[17] In contrast, the play script is not a discrete art object in its own right, and it is certainly not the end product. Theater making is always fundamentally collaborative, and even more so with a political person like James. To bring a play to life requires collaboration with the play's director and actors and can only be realized in performance. Above all, drama needs to be action; hence the appeal of this literary form for James, who makes it clear in his preface to the

1980 edition of *The Black Jacobins* history that he wanted to write an account in which peoples of African descent were not passively being acted upon or having emancipation bestowed upon them as a gift by white abolitionists.[18] Instead, James wanted to show them directly "taking action on a large scale." Drama thus has the special characteristic that it endows historical events with liveness, as if they were ongoing present actions, while simultaneously being an important communal activity and social act that contrasts with the normally private acts of reading and writing.[19]

Records of Remaking in Collaboration

James's closest collaborators were always his political allies. In a February 4, 1967, letter, James asked William Gorman and Priscilla Allen for their feedback on the play, and to look up certain references in *The Black Jacobins* history.[20] The possibility of James re/writing the play in collaboration with Allen is especially thought provoking because she was herself a playwright then and also published articles on Herman Melville, with many of her interests intersecting with those of James.[21] Politically, she was an active member of Facing Reality, a significant contributor to the radical feminist activities of the group, and a main author, alongside Selma James, of the *Wages for Housework Notebook No. 1* in a pamphlet published in 1975.[22] The potential role played by Allen in elaborating *The Black Jacobins* play perhaps helps to explain the creation of strong female roles in the play, most notably that of Marie-Jeanne, the mulatto courtesan who becomes Dessalines's wife, actively fighting alongside her husband in the revolution, and who can be thought of as the female equivalent of Moïse.[23]

Another active collaborator in the radical Caribbean and feminist circles surrounding C. L. R. James and Selma James was Clem Maharaj (1939–95), a former jazz drummer from Trinidad.[24] He was the son of Stephen Maharaj, a pharmacist and politician with whom James had organized the Workers' and Farmers' Party (WFP) in Trinidad in October 1965 ahead of the 1966 general election there.[25] The result of that election was total defeat for the WFP candidates, all of whom lost their deposits with less than 12.5 percent of the vote. The younger Maharaj would become an activist and writer in his own right.[26] Again, as with Priscilla Allen, it would be good to know how much creative input Clem was able to contribute to the (re)writing of the play and to what extent he was acting as James's amanuensis and following his orders. Apart from James's own shaky scrawl, many of the revisions on the various scripts dotted around the world are in the handwriting of Clem Maharaj.[27]

The story of *The Black Jacobins* play's genesis also bears witness to a lively interactive process of rewriting and collaboration between playwright and stage director. When leafing through its multiple annotated drafts in various states of genesis, one has the physical sensation that the play text has been thoroughly reworked by James from first page to last with annotations, multitudes of alternative scenes, reworked stage directions, modifications taped over previous suggestions, insertions of new lines of dialogue, insightful commentaries regarding how the author arrived at this particular version, and crossed-out lines and deletions. Scattered throughout libraries and archives across North America, the Caribbean, and the United Kingdom are a number of scripts of this particular play, alongside a wide range of documents that bear witness to the extent of James's own involvement, especially in the run-up to the December 14–16, 1967, world premiere of *The Black Jacobins* by the Arts Theatre Group at the University of Ibadan. It is important to consider the unique palimpsest-like multiple versions of these annotated manuscripts and typescripts with all their layers of modifications, corrections, cuts, and adaptations.

James's own shaky handwriting features throughout some of these versions as he corrects early drafts directly or via dictation. What emerges strongly from the commentaries that James appends to the play is that the author was already thinking, while writing these multiple drafts, about the need to preserve them. Notes about alternative scenes show James asserting his right to return to his work and to preserve what he can in the face of the director's cuts. Such is the case for the alternative act 1, scene 7, which eventually becomes act 2, scene 4. This scene represents the "showdown with Moïse," as James himself called it, and becomes the centerpiece of the whole play at its midpoint. James makes clear that he wants to publish the records of remaking the play:

> This scene has been subjected to a serious analysis and interpretation. The result is that I have decided to rewrite it entirely. I am not for one moment suggesting that the present Act 1, scene 7 should be rejected and this one substituted. That will depend upon the producer and to some degree upon the actor; and I have discovered that there is a definite difference of response to particular scenes according to the country in which this play is being read. I will not disguise, however, the fact that I believe this ver-

sion is infinitely superior to the previous. As far as publication in Britain, the United States and France is concerned, I shall certainly print the version now submitted. I also propose to print as appendices all alternative versions with an Afterword in which I will discuss how the play has been arrived at.[28]

One of the earliest drafts of this introductory note can be found in UWI Box 9, Folder 229, in a copy marked "SELMA" in James's shakily capitalized script. This seems to be a rough first stab at this alternative scene and accompanying introductory commentary because different scraps of paper are taped or paper-clipped together, with overtyping of initial mistakes, as the scene begins to take shape, all corrected in James's own hand. The multilayered nature of James's own rewriting process is made clear here, as well as his definite plans for publication of an edition of the play text, which would show the successive states of development, including alternative scenes.

Director Lyndersay gave James a concrete model for showcasing the alternatives in a published edition of the play: "Your idea of keeping a sort of journal of changes is good—it has been done with William Gibson's play *Two for the Seesaw* called THE SEESAW LOG."[29] *The Seesaw Log: A Chronicle of the Stage Production* gives a day-by-day account of the making of the Broadway play *Two for the Seesaw*. In the end, neither of the two published versions of this play—in Errol Hill's collection *A Time and a Season* (1976) or Anna Grimshaw's *C. L. R. James Reader* (1992)—demonstrates the degree to which the text of the play was modified. But the fact that James wanted to preserve all these intermediate stages and their accompanying commentaries, to the point where the various drafts of *The Black Jacobins* play constitute a veritable palimpsest, also bears witness to a large part of the work that is therefore deserving of more attention.

For giving James his due for (re)writing *The Black Jacobins* play, director Lyndersay's statements are instructive. On the occasion of the 1993 UWI restaging of this play in his native Trinidad, Lyndersay corrected his copy of the program's production note regarding the making of the play: "**C. L. R. James** Written and **wrote a play that was** performed in London as 'Toussaint L'Ouverture' in 1936. The **material** play was later edited **rewritten by James** by Dexter Lyndersay, and produced **directed in Nigeria by Dexter Lyndersay.**"[30] Correcting wrong information, Lyndersay makes clear that it was James, and not the director, who was responsible for the rewriting of the play. Likewise, Lyndersay clarified in a review he wrote of the 1993 Trinidad production that he had never actually laid eyes on a script of the original

1936 play.[31] Instead, it was James who rewrote the play in 1966 and then gave a copy of it to Lyndersay in London in 1966. Lyndersay thus corrects rumors that the director did all the adapting. This chapter focuses on James's own multiple authorial interventions in unpublished drafts to rewrite—and to reflect on the process of rewriting—the play.

While underlining the author's central role, this chapter also brings to light the strongly collaborative nature of this rewriting process. I want to examine the role of collaboration in the theatrical genesis of *The Black Jacobins* between playwright James and stage director Dexter Lyndersay.[32] This analysis is based on the correspondence that shuttled backward and forward from Lyndersay in Nigeria to James in London. This was an intense collaboration in the two months leading up to the performances, beginning with Lyndersay's October 8, 1967, letter to inform James that *The Black Jacobins* would open the new season for the Arts Theatre Group at the University of Ibadan, Nigeria.[33] Two months later, this play would be performed for the first time in a run lasting from December 14 to 16, 1967, against the backdrop of the Nigerian Civil War raging in the south.

From the letters Lyndersay sent to the playwright and his program note that accompanied the Nigerian performances, it is clear that many elements were added by the director, including the insertion of a prologue adapted from opening pages of *The Black Jacobins* history, pointing to the cruelty of the treatment meted out by white masters to their slaves and the slaves' growing resentment at receiving such treatment. The first draft of this prologue, also dated October 8, 1967, is typed on letterhead for the School of Drama, University of Ibadan, Nigeria, showing Dexter Lyndersay's responsibility for introducing this feature. Subsequent letters make it clear that Lyndersay was continuing to elaborate the prologue still further: "There is more prologue now," Lyndersay announces in a second letter dated October 31, 1967.[34] Headlining his third letter to James, of November 9, 1967, is Lyndersay's statement "WORKING ON PROLOGUE," indicating the director's contribution to this section of the play, including changes to the stage layout from two levels to four different areas.[35]

Where choreography and music were concerned, the director's influence was again instrumental, and these added elements make the play more Caribbean. Vodou becomes the prominent choreographic dimension of the play, for which Lyndersay was responsible. This choreography was based on the director's own experiences of dancing in Trinidad as part of Trinidadian dance legend Beryl McBurnie's Little Carib Theatre's production of

Shango. From the start, Lyndersay had outlined his vision of dancing Dessalines "into a voodoo state" and was thinking of using Vodou along the lines of McBurnie's pioneering choreography for the Little Carib Theatre.[36] In particular, Lyndersay hoped to make use of a Trinidadian dancer originally from McBurnie's theater company who was in Nigeria, "here and married and hair-dressing," whom he wanted for the part of the servant Célestine. According to Lyndersay's second letter, dated October 31, 1967, "The dance based on Beryl's *Shango* (in which I danced) is simply fantastic, if I do say so myself!"[37] In the director's program statement for the production, Lyndersay highlighted that the "voodoo dance [. . .] created long before the play by Beryl McBurnie has been further brought to life by the added intervention of the drum rhythms and drumming of Tunji Oyelana and his Orisun Theatre Drummers," as Nigerian drumming entered the mix.

One element added to James's play script through collaboration was the music that Tony White composed to accompany the "Slaves' Lament" of the Lyndersay-authored prologue. Lyndersay describes this song to James as the "Samedi Smith Song," following James's own emphasis on alternative popular leaders such as Samedi Smith in the 1967 play. Here Lyndersay proposes to make it the theme song of the entire play, highlighting James's divisions between leaders and masses.[38]

Some crucial Lyndersay-penned changes are even made to James's own program note. To James's original description of the mulatto courtesan Marie-Jeanne as the "sexual target" of all sections of the population in San Domingo, Lyndersay added, "but [she] is much more besides."[39] In a scribbled note to James, now among his papers at Columbia, Lyndersay makes it clear that this change and the addition of Moïse in the listing of characters in the playwright's note followed James's own emphasis. Lyndersay explained, "Hope you don't mind the addition to M[arie] Jeanne's description. You have written into her character so much more than a sexual target."

The fragile blue airmail sheets that would shuttle backward and forward between Ibadan, Nigeria, and Staverton Road, London, NW2, testify to a lively artistic dialogue. Heated debates take place in these pages, particularly concerning the director's reasons for removing certain scenes or the playwright's attempts to intervene by inserting new alternative scenes. One of these was the epilogue to the play that James had designed to be updatable according to contemporary circumstances and political situations. At the first hurdle, this epilogue, which James would rework into at least two different versions, is rejected point-blank. As Lyndersay reports back, "The epilogue—nobody thinks it will work. I tried it as a Prologue on the second and third readers. No go. Comment: 'Moïse's speech somewhat platitudinous, just as bad as the others because it doesn't say anything.' They think [...] that it *may* work if the speech is a real winner—but even then as Prologue, and even better if it were on film."[40]

With the epilogue rejected, Lyndersay initiates the introduction of mimed scenes for a new prologue adapted from *The Black Jacobins* history by the director. As always, the directorial proposals to the playwright are couched deferentially: "And what can we do instead?" Lyndersay asks James. "I thought of a mimed scene [...] pointing [to] the cruelty and the slaves' resentment that led to the 1st scene of the play. What do you think? Will it disturb the rhythm or set a wrong one?" A subsequent letter from Lyndersay regarding this prologue suggests that James did express reservations regarding the introduction of mimed scenes because he felt that there should be much less emphasis on "physical cruelty" as the reason driving the slave revolt.[41]

James's active role in rewriting the play is writ large in the comments lobbed back and forth about the myriad alternative scenes James produced. Dissent between playwright and director emerges regarding these alternatives. From Lyndersay's increasingly fraught responses, James clearly continued to rework the play, proposing alternative scenes, and then alternative alternatives, right up until at least mid-November. To attempt to put a stop to this flurry of authorial rewrites, unsolicited by the director, Lyndersay headlines in block capital letters the message "THE SET IS ¾ BUILT. COSTUMES DESIGNED AND UNDERWAY. THE WHOLE PLAY IS BLOCKED AND LAST CHANGES ARE SET" in his letter of November 9, 1967. Judging from Lyndersay's even more exasperated exclamation in his letter on November 14, "I couldn't possibly use a new scene now," it appears that James continued to send alternative scenes right up until a month before the production opened on December 14, 1967.

Disagreement arises particularly around the alternative for act 1, scene 7, for which James produced at least three different versions. In opposition to James's own judgment, director Lyndersay retorts, "I can't agree that it is superior to the first. It has the same problems that I have tried to solve in the original!" On logistical grounds, Lyndersay objects to the introduction of two new characters: "Mme. Lespinasse doesn't, it seems to me, add anything to the plot or Toussaint's character (at the cost of the costume, and pay for 1 extra actress) just as the introduction of Leclerc seemed irrelevant to the proceedings with Napoleon (with similar costume [£8 or so] and character commitment)." The playwright's contribution of additional pages and textual changes is confronted with the director's objections as he facilitates the evolution from page to stage and from text to performance. There is also consternation when James chooses to rewrite the Vincent-Napoleon scene, which Lyndersay had already deemed "perfect," "snappy," "palatable," and relatively digestible in terms of historical information, unlike James's unsolicited rewrite.[42]

Differences of opinion also concern the characterization of protagonists Toussaint or Dessalines. Regarding the reworked versions of act 1, scene 7, Lyndersay objects that Toussaint there seems to be another character entirely from the rest of the play: "<u>Who</u> is this Toussaint of 'Leave nothing white behind you'??? The character (regardless of the <u>real</u> Toussaint) <u>you</u> have given me for the rest of the play couldn't pronounce the words (for me at any rate)."[43] Disagreement also emerges over the characterization of Dessalines. Rejecting utterly Lyndersay's interpretation of Dessalines, James rejoins, "I cannot accept that Dessalines is the same person as he is at the end," stressing that the key scene in this regard is the "transition of Dessalines from a devoted follower of Toussaint to the determination that Toussaint must be got rid of, and that the task of getting rid of Toussaint is a task that he (Dessalines) must perform."[44]

Traces of the playwright questioning some of the director's contributions are evident from the shaky question marks made by James as he carefully picks his way through Lyndersay's proposals for certain props. Question marks surround the director's characterization of Moïse as "a damp squib." Question marks also adorn Lyndersay's decision to include an orange as a main prop, and to have Dessalines peel it and throw all the orange peel onto the floor. Shaky question marks also show that the playwright was unsure about another action and prop introduced by Lyndersay: "a snuff-box bit of business for Dessalines." Lyndersay underlines that such props provide much-needed action where the director needs it most on stage, explaining that such insertions provide "much needed humour."[45] Another addition instigated by the director for comic effect concerns the illiterate Dessalines ignorantly sitting on a book, which will provide, according to the director "a nice funny bit."[46]

Large question marks circle the director's main criticism, following the play's first read-through, that "the play has no action as such." Lyndersay charges the play with dispensing history to the audience "in fairly indigestible sizes" and issues the directorial decree that "<u>Any speech over 6 lines must go</u>," which was met with a large question mark from the playwright.

Compromise is the order of the day here, as Lyndersay announces extensive cuts to make the play easier to stage.

Such negotiations are always critical to the genesis of any play, as Almuth Grésillon remarks.[47] Lyndersay's 1967 program note underlines that the creative process was here collaborative "in more ways than is ordinary in the Theatre," with James contributing a "working script." Here, collaborative reconfiguration by multiple hands runs throughout the theater-making process and leaps out from the play script drafts, correspondence, and other written documents relating to the evolution of this play. Lyndersay signals his contributions to reshaping the "working script," signing off one letter with, "Hope all my rearrangements and cuts and changes were good ones! P.S. I shall have a script prepared with all the cuts and additions which I am using (some mine, some yours, some adaptations of yours [...] some dictated by costume and set)."[48] Unfortunately, no such script seems to have materialized yet.

Due to the physical distance separating these two Trinidadian rewriters of *The Black Jacobins*, James's role in the theatrical elaboration of his play was more distant and less hands-on than had been the case for *Toussaint Louverture* in 1936.[49] Had James been able to attend rehearsals in Nigeria, he could have been involved in the rehearsal and staging processes. It would be normal for a playwright to attend rehearsals, make suggestions, and meet all the main people involved ahead of a world premiere of a play. On the other hand, the fact that playwright James was physically so distant from the location of the play performance also had advantages: this long-distance correspondence preserved many traces of the making and remaking of the play. The correspondence shuttling between director and playwright shows no indication that James ever planned to attend rehearsals of the play, but he desperately wanted to attend the premiere in Nigeria.

Preparations for staging the play took place against the backdrop of the first few months of the Nigerian Civil War, making it difficult to find enough money to pay the travel fare and accommodation costs of the playwright in time for the play's opening night. Already in the hastily scribbled postscript to the first letter in which Lyndersay announces the staging of the play, he notifies James, "P.S. Also, I was appointed to act as Director of the School of Drama till Soyinka returns." Underlying Lyndersay's own temporary promotion was the arrest, obliquely referred to here, of world-renowned Nigerian playwright Wole Soyinka, who had just been appointed to this post as the first African director of the School of Drama at the University of Ibadan. Arrested in August 1967 during the Nigerian Civil War, Soyinka was imprisoned by federal authorities for two years, accused of pro-Biafran activities.⁵⁰

As opening night approached, James's letters must have become increasingly peeved at the lack of progress in getting him there. This can be inferred from Lyndersay's response: "It is not that there is 'no use' for you, please. It is just that money's tight + the war is getting costlier and costlier. One has to make the biggest and yet cleverest of cases to loosen purse strings which were once fairly slack." Here, explicit reference is made to the war, its discontents, and its direct logistical effects on play production. Right up to the last minute, Lyndersay pursues funding, noting in a November 19, 1967, letter, "All going well except for the return for you and the 'situation in the country.' More in two days' time when I have tracked down my last lead." Lyndersay also reports a "shortage of staff." Behind these remarks lie overtones of a dangerous time—of terror, disappearances, arbitrary arrests, abductions, and assassinations—taking place in crisis-ridden, civil war–torn Nigeria. Written during the escalation and at the height of this civil war, the director-playwright correspondence reveals these tumultuous Nigerian events backstage.

James's letter to Lyndersay dated November 23, 1967, conciliated: "I regret if I showed some impatience at the difficulties which face you in getting me there. I am aware of them. [. . .] I am very much aware of the special difficulties of Nigeria to-day. I would be an uneducated barbarian if I was not aware of the problems that you face." James further acknowledges the logistical "unverbalized and imprecise mountains" that the director must climb and the "foaming rivers" he must cross if he does end up finding the money for James's travel to Nigeria. Only in a letter dated December 8, 1967, less than a week before the play opened, does Lyndersay report that he has been unsuccessful in getting James to Nigeria. Inconsolable, Lyndersay reports his ultimate failure to come up with enough money for the playwright's £90 fare.⁵¹

About these logistical difficulties, James explains that his impatience had different political roots, based on his own recent experiences of Trinidadian politics: his break with Eric Williams and his People's National Movement (PNM) Party. He reveals a personal Trinidad-related sense of being politically ostracized, with invitations drying up for political reasons:

> I want you to know what was at the back of my mind and what unwittingly slipped through into the letter. As long as I was attached to a government (in this case the Trinidad government and the Federal Government of the West Indies), I was besieged by invitations and could go anywhere,

<u>anytime. The moment, however, that I am not attached to a government, and worse still, am known to be directly opposed to a particular government of the underdeveloped territories, you would be astonished to know the number of people who prefer not to know that I exist.</u>[52]

In his return letter, Lyndersay stressed that "there were <u>absolutely no political reasons involved</u>" in the failure to get the playwright to Nigeria in time.[53]

Even if James did not travel to Nigeria until 1968, his play did travel there in 1967. As James's "man in Nigeria," Lyndersay was translating the play in more ways than one. By his own admission, James was not much of a theater man and needed the director to add stagecraft layers, including music, dance, and mime. The Caribbeanness of the play text was reinforced as it traveled to Nigeria, with Lyndersay adding new distinctively Caribbean codes, cultural forms, and signs, while also teasing out more latent Caribbean markers from the play text. Attentiveness to Caribbean-inspired Vodou drumming and dancing was assimilated into more Nigerian terms, undergoing transformative encounters with local Nigerian customs and traditions, as they were translated into new African rhythms by towering Nigerian artists of the time, including Tunji Oyelana and the Orisun Theatre Drummers. The play's Caribbeanness was underlined more strongly but also refracted in the light of the Nigerian Civil War situation. Lyndersay provided the play text with wit, inventive props, movement, dance, folk traditions, and mime, drawing on a diverse pool of Nigerian talents, and he used the play to mark commonalities across different regions of the world—Trinidad and Nigeria.

The immediate context of the play performances in December 1967 was a political moment in Nigeria when differences were being manipulated to divide peoples and communities in order to better dominate them. The playwright's multiple drafts of the play text, especially the epilogue, were designed to be extrapolated to parallel situations happening in far-flung countries in the present day. Such is the point underscored by the playwright in his author's note for the 1967 program.[54] James again shows awareness of what is at stake when dramatic texts travel, aiming his play so that it could be responsive to changing audiences, and to new pasts, presents, and futures.

Relative Chronology of Play Scripts

This section proposes a relative chronology of the scripts for this play, which forms the basis of my analysis. Based on comparisons of the unpublished play scripts consulted, I propose that there are broadly four main generations of draft scripts involved in the evolution of the play:

> 1. THE EARLIEST COMPOSITIONAL PHASES: the script held at Wayne State University in the Martin and Jessie Glaberman Papers, Box 21, Folder 6, henceforth "WSU1"; and the scripts from the University of the West Indies, C. L. R. James Collection (Sc 82) housed in UWI Box 9, Folder 230
>
> 2. THE SECOND GENERATION: scripts from the University of the West Indies, C. L. R. James Collection (Sc 82) found in UWI Box 9, Folders 228 and 229
>
> 3. THE THIRD GENERATION: the script held at the Schomburg Center for Research in Black Culture (SG MG 53), henceforth "Schomburg"; copy 1 from Pennsylvania State Special Collections Library (VF Lit 0581 R), henceforth "Penn State 1"; copy 2 from Pennsylvania State Special Collections (Blockson Collection, unclassified), henceforth "Penn State 2"; the script from the British Library, Andrew Salkey Archive (10310), henceforth "British Library"; the script held by Columbia University Library, C. L. R. James papers, MS#1529 (Box 5, Folder 14), henceforth "Columbia"; and Harold Preston's script for the role of Maitland in the 1967 production (Leeds MS 1748/4)
>
> 4. THE CLEANEST FOURTH-GENERATION VERSIONS OF THE PLAY, CLOSEST TO THEIR PERFORMANCE AND PUBLISHED VERSIONS: the script held by Dartmouth College, Errol G. Hill Papers (ML-77, Box 70), henceforth "Dartmouth"; the script housed at University of the West Indies, C. L. R. James Collection (Sc 82) housed in UWI Box 12, Folder 280; Wayne State University Martin and Jessie Glaberman Collection copy 2 signed "For Facing Reality from Nello," (Box 44, Folder 18), henceforth "WSU2"; and Dexter Lyndersay's own signed script

There are two published texts of the play in Errol Hill, ed., *A Time and a Season: Eight Caribbean Plays* (1976), and Anna Grimshaw, ed., *The C. L. R. James Reader* (1992).

FIRST GENERATION OF PLAY SCRIPTS

There is quite a jumble of scripts housed in UWI Box 9, Folders 228, 229, and 230, making it hard to determine the number of scripts in each folder. There are several different partial copies and multiples. These earliest scripts are still rough drafts—often extra stage directions and lines are taped or paper-clipped to the script, making multilayered corrections. Some typewritten sheets are corrected in several hands, often by James himself, by director Lyndersay, or by different secretaries and collaborators. A single page placed about halfway through the contents of UWI Folder 228 appears to be the earliest version of the beginning of the whole play. This single opening page remains an embryonic sketch with a rudimentary typo-ridden appearance. Repeated crisscrosses (xxxx) cancel out some of the opening scene as it is in the process of being worked out. This version features only Toussaint, Dessalines, Madame Bullet, and M. Bullet, who are usually referred to only by their initials or abbreviated names: T., Toussaint; Des, Dessalines; M. J., Marie-Jeanne. Otherwise, the earliest versions of the play appear to be the script from Wayne State University, Martin Glaberman Collection, Box 21, Folder 6 (henceforth WSU1), and copy 1 of the drafts held in UWI Box 9, Folder 230 (henceforth UWI230.1). The page order of these early scripts is quite haphazard in places, with WSU1 starting not even at the beginning but with one of the earliest drafts of a five-page scene version featuring British General Maitland, American consul Tobias Lear, Christophe, Moïse, and Toussaint. This version is also among the pages of UWI Box 9, Folder 230, copy 2, where they are reworked by Lyndersay.

Early scripts including WSU1 and UWI230.1 retain the opening stage direction, "The stage is split on two levels." As originally conceived, level 1 was to include a living room and office space, with level 2 positioned below as a space for crowds to assemble. There are multiples of certain pages, and the chaotic scripts are in various states of genesis, with some incorporating handwritten corrections from elsewhere. These early drafts often feature the same typos and keystroke pressure, suggesting they are mimeographed copies. In both earliest versions, James elaborates stage directions about the crowd, with his handwritten additions indicated here in bold: "Crowds say little but their presence is felt powerfully at all critical moments. This is the key point of the play and cannot, must not be written. It must be felt dramatically, **and be the main preoccupation of the stage-manager**" (WSU1; UWI230.1).[55]

On the whole, WSU1 appears to be an earlier draft than UWI230.1 because there is only a general attribution in the following stage direction: "Enter a slave. He speaks: Madame, M. Bullet is here" (WSU1, 1), whereas in UWI230.1 Moïse is introduced specifically: "Enter a **YOUTH, MOÏSE** slave. He speaks. **Moïse**: Madame, M. Bullet is here." In this way, Moïse becomes the first of the slaves to speak in the play, appearing on the stage alongside his female counterpart and fellow revolutionary, Marie-Jeanne. This writing-in of Moïse resembles handwritten changes adding this character to the *Toussaint Louverture* play script (UWI Box 9, Folder 227, copy 1). These similarities suggest that James was reworking the first play as a prelude to writing *The Black Jacobins* play in 1966–67. Further additions include Toussaint now demanding that Dessalines hand over his sword to Moïse: "<u>Toussaint continues:</u> Give it to ~~me~~ **Moïse**" (UWI230.1, 2). Another addition of Moïse is made in a different hand to both copies of the UWI230.1 and the WSU1 drafts: "**You will be quite safe. Moïse will go with you and he will have all**" (4).

Likewise, early drafts from WSU1 and UWI230.1 feature early versions of ordinary unnamed rank-and-file soldiers who will later rename themselves symbolically after French revolutionaries as Max, Marat, and Orléans. Initial typewritten references refer to crowds of ordinary people: "A body of officers, soldiers, civilians, officials, etc." Already, the stage directions draw attention to "<u>a few soldiers, barefooted and somewhat ragged</u>" who are by now "<u>noticeably wary of Toussaint's glance</u>" (5A–5B, WSU1; UWI230.1). Already at this stage, top leaders are pitted against ordinary rank-and-file revolutionaries. References are worked in where such ordinary soldiers are called "brigands" and "bandits," for example: **THEY** [those fighting against the Haitian leaders and the French] **STILL ARE BANDITS. IF WE AND THE FRENCH REALLY COMBINED OUR FORCES WE COULD CRUSH THEM AND THEN HAVE SOME LAW AND ORDER** (UWI230.1; not added to WSU1).

References are made to "A black peasant" who is already named by Toussaint as Samedi Smith, an alternative popular leader. Already in the first drafts, Samedi Smith's representation as popular leader is taking shape. A "p.s." is added with arrows where Toussaint and Samedi Smith exchange words, revealing their previously fraught relationship:

> P.S. [Toussaint:] You had been promoted before you took to the hills—
> Smith: God bless you, Governor, God bless you (WSU1; UWI 230.1)

References to music are generally amplified through handwritten additions. In the WSU1 script, additions in James's hand, two pages, 30–30A, draw attention to the chorus being sung by Samedi Smith's men: "**The chorus outside begins again. Marie-Jeanne sings low but clearly, Dessalines accompanying her by humming. Enter Samedi Smith.**" Being built up here is the popular alternative chorus of the ordinary people.

Reshaping the Past as Drama (1967) | **155**

Changes ordered by James often concern Moïse. Added stage directions have Moïse wearing a black patch to recall his brave sacrifice of an eye for liberty. What is added in James's shaky handwriting to the Moïse-Toussaint dialogue makes Moïse more clearly the voice of the popular masses: "**BEFORE THE PEACE COMES WE CAN MAKE OURSELVES INVINCIBLE HERE. YOU ONLY HAVE TO TELL THE PEOPLE. THEY ARE READY**" (11). Talking clearly to the people is Moïse's solution. The same text is added in a scribe's hand to page 11 of WSU1. Ultimately, these lines would not make it into the performance script or either published version, but the overall thrust of the changes emphasizes Toussaint's flaw and Moïse's alternative popular leadership style.

One thoroughly reworked scene concerning Moïse, subjected to many taped-over revisions, is the scene James would rebaptize in these corrections Toussaint's "descent into his depths speech" (19A–19B, WSU1; UWI230.1). James adds in references about Moïse as Toussaint's adopted nephew or son, detailing Moïse's self-education and popularity with ordinary laborers. Changes clearly show Moïse to be Toussaint's leadership foil. Another taped insertion regarding Moïse's execution is added to Dessalines's discussion with Marie-Jeanne about the need to betray Toussaint: "**FROM THE TIME HE HAD TO SHOOT MOÏSE HE HAS NOT BEEN THE SAME MAN. MOÏSE WAS RIGHT. BUT HE HAD TO BE SHOT THEN. HE HAD TO BE. NOW THE WHOLE THING IS CHANGED.**" Like the chorus singing the Samedi Smith song, Moïse's popular alternative leadership style punctuates James's reworking of the play.

Among these earliest scripts are first drafts of the epilogue, one of James's favorite parts of the play. Initial versions of the epilogue in the two earliest scripts are explicitly set in the present-day West Indies. Direct reference is made to the recent breakup of the West Indies Federation (37–38, UWI230.1) and to the region's new political leaders, who are presented as reincarnations of their Caribbean revolutionary forebears, with the same actors playing modern-day Caribbean leaders. These references would later be made less Caribbean-specific and more universal in subsequent versions of the epilogue. This epilogue about the West Indies Federation and the need for unity would have had other resonances in civil war–torn Nigeria in 1967.[56]

In UWI Box 9, Folder 230, there is also a copy of the play that is mainly handwritten by Dexter Lyndersay (henceforth UWI230.2). His additions change the stage layout from two levels to four different areas (UWI230.2, 1). This version writes out the script again, incorporating strings of alphanumeric sequences for reordering pages, such as 13J, 20Aa, 20Ab, and so on. There are exes and strikethroughs, but mostly, new additions rework transition scenes, for example in the elaborate exchanges between ordinary soldiers (5Aa–5H, F126–35, 20Ab, 30D–30F). Lyndersay extrapolates funny bits and name calling by Moïse, who mockingly calls the other two revolutionaries the Duke of Turkey and the Count of Marmalade (11–11A, UWI230.2). As well as humor, director Lyndersay adds stage directions, movements, and set changes. Dancing to "voodoo drums" is elaborated at length (8Ab), as are Maitland, Lear, and Hédouville's imperialist machinations.

James makes interjections, taking back ownership of the script proprietorially. James particularly rewrites Marie-Jeanne and Dessalines's dialogue (12A–12I), especially concerning the extract from Racine's *Iphigénie*. James annotates it: "This scene to be filled in carefully" (30–30C). James also reworks dialogues regarding Toussaint's constitution between Toussaint, Colonel Vincent, and French consul Bonaparte, underlining that Louverture is demanding the equivalent of dominion status (13b). Finally, Lyndersay writes out the epilogue sequence A–H, which is now set "somewhere in an underdeveloped country" (A), and not specifically in the Caribbean. Lyndersay notes that more transition is needed. James was very attached to the epilogue scene, which originated with him. Here we see the director writing it out again in full to try it out. As the director would soon dispense with the epilogue, these must be early drafts.

SECOND GENERATION OF SCRIPTS

Copies of the play in UWI Box 9, Folders 228 and 229 belong mainly to the second generation of scripts. The order is less haphazard although there are also partial copies. Most scripts in these folders contain cover sheets bearing the playwright's name, the title *The Black Jacobins*, and Copyright 1967, with James's address in London and telephone number. Sometimes, the initial cover sheet of each script is marked "Act I, Scenes I–V pp. 1–23." A second dividing sheet is often placed before the second half of the play listing the following details:

2

The Black Jacobins
Act I cont. Scene VII, pp. 24–30
Act II Scenes I + II, pp. 30–43
Epilogue, pp. 44–46

At this stage, scripts still feature the epilogue plus a single page of prologue. At this second stage, the play consists of two acts, with seven scenes in act 1, two more scenes in act 2, and a three-page epilogue. This two-act, nine-scene play then subsequently develops into a play featuring a first act of four scenes and a second act of four scenes, followed by a third act of two scenes, becoming a three-act, ten-scene play. The genesis of the play is also marked by alternative scenes, and even by alternative alternatives. A third dividing sheet also appears among the copies of the script:

The Black Jacobins
Act I cont. Scene VII, pp. 24–30
Act II Scenes I + II, pp. 30–43
Epilogue, pp. 44–46

Alternative version to Act I, Scene 7, pp. 1–12
Alternative version to p. 46 of Epilogue
Alternative version to Act I, Scene VI

Some of these dividing and copyright cover sheets are signed by James.

Correspondence tells us that the alternative scenes originated with the playwright and that director Lyndersay rejected James's rewrites as performances approached. As discussed above, James's alternative to act 1, scene 7 contains an enlightening self-reflexive commentary about the rewriting process itself (UWI228, 24), and James's wish to publish the play text with a record of the changes.[57] The director rejected these unsolicited rewrites, especially the additions of new characters, on logistical grounds, strongly disagreeing that the alternatives for act 1, scenes 6 and 7 were better.[58] James is constantly rethinking this prelude to his showdown with Moïse, leading to Toussaint's signing of the death warrant for his adopted nephew.

In the alternative scene between Vincent and Bonaparte (act 1, scene 6, which eventually became act 2, scene 3 in the play as published and performed), there are numerous misspelled names, as well as other typos and long speeches, suggesting that this is a relatively early rough draft. In this alternative scene, Leclerc is introduced at the same point as in the 1936 play. Whereas Leclerc and his wife Pauline, Bonaparte's sister, play an important role in *Toussaint Louverture*, here Leclerc would have made a brief cameo appearance with one and a half fairly insignificant lines. Lyndersay compared this alternative version unfavorably with the original scene, which he had previously deemed "snappy" and "palatable."

An alternative is also given for the final page of the epilogue. At the end of Speaker D's original speech, the emphasis was loosely on fighting and taking risks concerning "your liberty, your property, even your life." In the alternative epilogue ending, the focus turns to the true meaning of independence for underdeveloped countries, beyond getting a new flag, new national anthem, new prime minister, and new parliament, and on the need for the people to "get the land back"—a cry recalling the platform of James's Workers' and Farmers' Party (WFP), which called for the redistribution of land out of foreign hands.[59]

Copies of the script in UWI229 also contain interesting alternatives to the alternatives, not seen anywhere else. With the alternative to act 1, scene 7, we see James taping and paper-clipping different versions together in a multilayered rewriting of Toussaint's "descent into his depths" speech. One version even has Toussaint and Mme. Bullet conducting an affair while holding aloft their copies of Raynal and reciting the lines together. This shows the degree to which James rethought the play. Ultimately, the famous Raynal passage would appear in the director-penned extended prologue, where a cameo appearance of Louverture's wife was scripted.

Other rough drafts present James trying to rework transition scenes in rudimentary form, such as those which he calls "intermediary" scenes 1 and 2 between Toussaint and Vincent and Vincent and Bonaparte, where he indicates details to be filled in. The rewriting process is also revealed by James when he writes, "Note: this is not to be substituted for the present Act 2, Scene 1, but is merely a suggestion for future reference." This rudimentary scene toyed with having Toussaint's sons and wife appear in a reunion scene, as in act 3, scene 1 from *Toussaint Louverture*, which ultimately was not performed either, according to the 1936 program. This scene emphasizing family ties would be replaced in the 1967 play by Moïse's characterization as Toussaint's adopted nephew/son.

In the architecture of the play, the final partial draft (the first twenty-three pages) of UWI Box 9, Folder 228 and the scripts contained in UWI 229 are of key importance. The cover sheet of the former is signed by James and headed in his handwriting, "C.L.R.J. Proof Copy Part 1, Do Not Remove MASTER COPY A." The latter's cover sheet is headed in James's shaky capitals: "SELMA (DO NOT TAKE AWAY)." These scripts featuring all the alternatives are crucial because they were marked as master copies. At this second stage in the play's genesis, the scripts originated with playwright James. The playwright's commentary on the rewriting process and his presentation of alternative scenes show that James had definite plans for publication and intended to publish an edition of the play text, which would provide each of the text's successive states of development.

THIRD GENERATION OF SCRIPTS

These scripts appear to be mainly exact mimeographed copies. Penn State 2 appears to straddle the second and third generation of scripts because it displays some features of both script generations. Penn State 2 starts with a signed cover sheet, marked "Part I Act Scenes I–VI, pp. 1–23." Later, it also features a part 2 dividing sheet marked "*The Black Jacobins* Act I Cont. Sc. VII pp. 24–30, Act II, Scenes I + II, pp. 30–43, Epilogue, pp. 44–46," and which is also signed "C. L. R. James." Penn State 2, like the British Library copy, still retains a single page of prologue.

In addition, Penn State 2 features some alternative scenes. Immediately after the prologue comes the three-page alternative version of act 1, scene 6, featuring French Colonel Vincent and Bonaparte. Confusingly, another copy of the same alternative scene is placed at the end of the script. Also inserted in the script is the alternative version of the final page of the epilogue about the meaning of true independence. This copy also contains the alternative version of act 1, scene 7 featuring Mme. Lespinasse in new pages numbered 24a–c, here with the spelling of her name corrected. In previous scripts, for example UWI Box 9, Folder 229, James had hand-corrected the typist's misspelling "Lespinaisse." Unlike other copies, the commentary on the rewriting process prefacing act 1, scene 7 has been signed at the top "C. L. R. James," restating the playwright's ownership of the text.

Otherwise, the scripts of this generation are similar, all containing the same number of acts and scenes, as well as the epilogue, with its original page 45 corrected with correction fluid so that the text now reads, "The chairman of the conference is [xx] to [xx] broadcast. I have arranged so that we can hear [xx]," cutting the epilogue text down in size. Next follows the original epilogue ending, "Fighting means taking risks." Although the Schomburg, Penn State 1, and Columbia scripts do not feature any prologue, all five scripts of this generation share many characteristics.

These scripts also feature the same inserted text, often in the distinctive backward-sloping handwriting of Clem Maharaj that corrects on playwright James's instructions. All copies have the same handwritten insert "A knock at the door," featuring the Spanish marquis breaking off negotiations with Toussaint to pay a visit to the beautifully dressed mulatto courtesan Marie-

Jeanne. These drafts work out Marie-Jeanne's deception of Hédouville, communicating his plots with the mulattoes to Toussaint via Dessalines and the letter. The Schomburg script is the only one to feature an older version of this scene without the intermediary of the maid Célestine reading out Marie-Jeanne's letter to the illiterate Dessalines but instead involving Marie-Jeanne speaking directly to Toussaint's man, Mars Plaisir. Stage directions remain rudimentary but are in the process of being worked out.

One element shared by all scripts in this third generation is that two pages of every script have been typed on the back of information leaflets or newspaper articles with information for the London Notting Hill community. The first page of act 1, scene 7 featuring Mme. Bullet and Toussaint (24) is typed in these versions on the back of pink sheets, providing information about the aims of the "Notting Hill Neighbourhood Service" and announcing a Folk Night on September 18, 1967, in aid of the service. The next page of these *Black Jacobins* scripts (p. 25 of the same Toussaint–Mme. Bullet–Moïse scene) is typed on the back of a copy of an article by David McKie of *The Guardian* from April 1967, titled "Ever Widening Area," detailing the launch of a housing trust to deal with housing difficulties faced by large families and the disabled. These traces of community activities in London in 1967 demonstrate that this generation of scripts originated in London with James and not with director Lyndersay in Nigeria.

The Columbia script (C. L. R. James Papers, Box 5, Folder 17) of *The Black Jacobins* stands out because it straddles the third and fourth script generations closest to the performance and published scripts. The script itself shares the same features as the British Library, Schomburg, Penn State 1, and Penn State 2 scripts; is annotated with the same backward-sloping handwritten insertions by Clem Maharaj; and is reproduced on pages about London neighborhood activities. It contains the same cover sheet and divider sheets, with each one signed by James.

The Columbia script resembles a palimpsest because James's revised script is used as the springboard for certain new changes initiated by director Lyndersay. The most significant change is the draft of the extended prologue, which Lyndersay developed from passages of *The Black Jacobins* history, outlining the harsh treatment of slaves by their masters. From the previous single page of prologue, three pages of prologue are now elaborated and corrected by Lyndersay's hand. Here, Lyndersay starts to subdivide the prologue into separate tableaux, giving each mimed sequence a heading: THE BARBER, THE THIEF, THE SLAVE, THE LEADER, with new ones inserted by hand—THE ENTERTAINER—to focus on the cruel treatment of slaves providing entertainment for their owners. Certain headings are crossed out, with new ones put in their place. This is the case for "THE HOTEL," which becomes "THE WAITER," and "THE FOREST," which becomes "THE COURIER." Such changes focus attention on the slaves themselves instead of the settings. Here we see the distinctive prologue of the play as published and performed taking shape before our eyes. On the beginning of the play itself, Lyndersay adds a note to James about the Mozart minuet: "all of this will be on tape. My actors can't play the piano." There is no longer any epilogue in this version.

It is also here that Lyndersay writes up Moïse's parting lines, prefacing his changes: "Re Moïse's final exit, this is what I came up with for him." Lyndersay adds a note to James: "It is not unlikely that Moïse will now be applauded at his exit. He has done the speech so well during rehearsal that I have myself felt like applauding, Dexter." A postscript is added to this note: "This may be balm (salve?) to your wounds over the epilogue's deletion. D." This note is significant because it indicates that the epilogue represented a tug of war between playwright and director. What Lyndersay notes here reveals that Moïse's extra lines were directly epilogue-inspired, with lines focusing on the need to make the country truly independent functioning as an epilogue substitute.

One of the scripts consulted was that of Harold Preston, bursar at the University of Ibadan, who played British General Maitland in 1967.[60] His script contains many nuggets of useful information about the production, including the rehearsal schedule and pronunciation guides for the cast of difficult French words and Haitian place names. What is interesting about Harold Preston's script is that, in terms of the architecture of the play, it still follows the act and scene formation of the first three generations of scripts, in other words, an act 1 of seven scenes and an act 2 of two scenes. Preston's script contains the additions Lyndersay makes in the Columbia script—the longer prologue of mimed tableaux and Moïse's extra lines that replace the epilogue—but Preston's script represents an intermediary stage between the Columbia script and the fourth generation of performance and published scripts.

Some handwritten changes in Preston's script show how Lyndersay worked out by hand Maitland's lines before performance. What is added has Toussaint and Maitland dictate identical top-secret memorandums to the minister of foreign affairs for the Republic of France and to the minister of foreign affairs for Great Britain respectively to reveal the real intentions behind the British offer of kingship: the restoration of plantation slavery. Preston's script shows how Maitland and Toussaint were scripted to start and finish the same sentences, ending together in "one beat" with the words: "Top Secret." This extended version clarifies an anomaly in the published versions: reference is made in the scene synopses to an "Act 1, Scene 4" split between "Governor L'Ouverture's Headquarters" and "General Maitland's Headquarters" in 1798. This scene is not signaled as such in the script as published, which led Errol Hill to edit the synopses of scenes, only going up to "Act 1, Scene 3 (in the Living Room of Tobias Lear, the American Consul)" because in that version the two scenes run together and are not obviously separate. In Preston's script for the role of Maitland, however, this part is elaborated into its own scene. Lyndersay handwrites a note to Preston, accompanying this version of the changes: "This was the orig. breakdown which I lost + just found. It is slightly better than the one I substituted."

FOURTH-GENERATION PLAY AND PERFORMANCE SCRIPTS

In the four copies of the fourth generation, the play's architecture has become a three-act, nine- or ten-scene play: act 1 (7 scenes → 3 or 4 scenes), act 2 (2 scenes → 4 scenes), and act 3 (comprising the same two final scenes as in the original act 2). In the Dartmouth copy only, the scene synopsis for act 1 has scene 4 crossed out, unlike the other three scripts. As in the two published versions of this play, these play scripts have a cast list that is now divided into characters for the prologue and the main play. These play scripts contain no alternative versions and no epilogue. Mainly, director Lyndersay's stage directions are elaborated at greatest length. This is the case with the transition between act 1, scenes 2 and 3, featuring the Vodou drumming and dancing directions where thirteen lines of stage directions become fifty-one lines across two pages.

Stage directions have been worked out furthest in Lyndersay's own director copy of the script, as is clear from additions at the end of act 2, scene 1: "The strains of Madame Bullet's piano cover the change of scenery, i.e. Marie-Jeanne's bedroom is cleared and two areas set up: Toussaint's office stage right and Napoleon's office stage left." Lyndersay thinks through last-minute changes to stage directions in order to make transitions during the rehearsal process. This is the only script where we find this stage direction, which is also absent from the two published versions of the play.

The second Wayne State University script is dedicated in James's handwriting: "For Facing Reality. From Nello." It is significant that James dedicates his play—politics by other means—to his closest political comrades, his American followers based in Detroit.

The published versions start with a list of "CHARACTERS *in order of appearance*" rather than describing them as "Cast" as in the play scripts. M. Bullet's name is added to the published text. In the 1976 *A Time and a Season* printing only, changes follow Lyndersay's Columbia script changes to prologue headings including "THE WAITER" instead of "THE HOTEL," and "THE COURIER" instead of "THE FOREST," emphasizing the slaves themselves rather than the settings of the mimed tableaux. However, the 1992 *Reader* version retains "THE HOTEL" and "THE FOREST."

Changing the Protagonists: Haitian Revolutionary Crowds

Already James's first play had represented crowds of Haitian revolutionary masses, showing a radical transformation from the beginning where "Most of them are nearly naked, wearing either a loin-cloth or a shirt. All are dirty and unkempt" to the ending, where they form "a solid mass" who "In dress and bearing [...] are a civilised people."[61] *The Black Jacobins* uses a different type of chorus to represent masses versus leaders. What emerges clearly is James's attempt to represent the unrepresented by bringing crowds of ordinary slaves more sharply into view, so that they function as a chorus. Here is written in the entry of the classical chorus, as envisaged by James in his 1971 lecture, where the crowd represents the wider population of ex-slaves and further highlights tensions between leaders and masses.[62] Crowds are written in by stage directions that portray these slaves as alternative collective protagonists, bearing heroic characteristics: "Crowds say little but their presence is felt powerfully at all critical moments. This is the key point of the play and comments cannot, must not, be written. It must be felt dramatically, and be projected as essential to action in the downstage areas."[63] Problematically, however, this crowd as protagonist remains largely silent, with limited and unscripted dramatic roles.[64] Tellingly, while reworking representations of such rank-and-file characters, the playwright poses a revealing handwritten question in the margins: "Should they speak?"[65]

Drama is used as a means of giving voice to those who have none, or next to none, in the imperial archive, and of making crowds of slaves more audible and visible. Nevertheless, even in *The Black Jacobins* play where lower-ranking ex-slaves are supposed to become protagonists, decentering top-ranking revolutionary generals, these subalterns still do not speak much. Here James runs into the same difficulties of portraying a crowd positively faced by other radical playwrights who have failed to achieve goals of shining the spotlight sympathetically on the people and making crowds play a significant role in the action.[66] Marxist playwrights may be happy to agree that their true protagonist is the people, yet readers and viewers would be harder pushed to agree with such assessments, given that the crowd's actual role points to the contrary.[67] Despite new emphasis, crowds still remain problematically rather silent and faceless.

James does take pioneering studies of European crowds from below by Albert Soboul, George Rudé, E. P. Thompson, and Eric Hobsbawm in new directions by widening the focus to Haitian revolutionary crowds, and from sansculottes, bras nus, and enragés to the *menu peuple* mass of ordinary black ex-slaves. This crowd, representing the great mass of slaves, functions as a chorus, operating as an organizing tool for theater from below, as in the type of radical Marxist theater theorized by Augusto Boal, where crowds do not meekly toe the line or speak dutifully in unison, but instead function as dissenting choruses that challenge and answer back.[68] Crowd scenes are used increasingly toward the end of the play to highlight fundamental divisions between official generals and the great mass of ex-slaves, showing that they are fighting for different political goals, with leaders actually fighting against the masses. Nowhere is this made clearer than in the scenes where Dessalines in particular, but also Toussaint and Christophe, actually suppress ordinary revolutionaries.

This widespread repression of popular masses by revolutionary leaders emerges when Dessalines barks orders that the singing of their own popular anthem "To the Attack, Grenadier" must be halted forthwith.[69] Their anthem is used to contrast the masses' political goals and capacities with those of the main leaders—a stark contrast writ large when Dessalines contemptuously mocks this song of the rank-and-file revolutionaries, while Christophe professes not even to know it, showing the extent to which out-of-touch leaders are alienated from the masses.[70] Generals are portrayed carrying out (on French orders) widespread repression of popular forces who continue to fight against the French.[71] Increasingly, this crowd voices opposition, expressing discontent and what, according to Boal, are the fundamental principles of the chorus in radical theater: conflict, contradiction, clash, and combat.[72] At the end of the scene, Dessalines flings open the window and shouts down dictatorially to the crowd below what they must chant: "Dessalines, Emperor of Haiti!"[73] First responding as prescribed, this crowd-chorus then begins to express mass protest through their own revolutionary anthem. As the scene ends, there is confrontation between the expression of popular resistance and the minuet that Dessalines orders to drown out the protest song. At news of Toussaint's death, the popular protest becomes a mournful chant, through which the crowd directs resentment at Dessalines. Hard-nosed in his own pursuit of power, Dessalines very forcibly orders his music and dancing to recommence as the crowd flees. This spectacle of black revolutionaries oppressing the black masses would have been especially striking in 1967 Nigeria, a postcolonial nightmare with Fanonian overtones of black elites behaving after revolution like white rulers.[74]

Samedi Smith, Peasants, Brigands, and Barefooted Men

Called the "Samedi Smith" song throughout the play, the revolutionary fighting/protest anthem of the masses takes its name from an alternative popular leader described as "a black peasant" and "barefooted and in rags," but "undoubtedly a man of authority."[75] Singled out of the crowd as peasant leader of an insurrectionary band, Samedi Smith represents one of the many thousands of obscure leaders organizing popular resistance, about whom James says in his 1971 lecture he would like to know more.[76] Disparagingly, generals repeatedly denigrate Samedi Smith and the mass of ordinary soldiers and peasants as brigands, rebels, insurgents, bandits, robbers, gangsters, and, most tellingly, enemies, creating an adversarial situation in which grassroots rebels are pitted against the triumvirate of top generals, who are now working with French colonial troops to crush popular resistance.[77] Divisions between leadership and masses are made clear when Samedi Smith "speaks with a certain restraint looking at Toussaint out of the corner of his eye," distrusting leaders who go back on their word by conceding peace and relinquishing weapons to the French.[78] Samedi Smith presents ever-multiplying bands as nuclei of effective political rebellion, with soldiers drawn from the ordinary peasantry portrayed as leading spontaneous but well-organized forms of guerrilla war against the old French enemy. Capable of autonomous political organization, these bands fight en masse as a well-organized collective of fighting men. They, and not the top leadership, are presented as the true revolutionaries.

Samedi Smith is the only representative of these bands who actually speaks, but Dessalines and Toussaint note popular leaders are everywhere, singling out Macaya, Sylla, Sans Souci, and Jean Panier, who represent a more popular leadership stratum, able to guide the people's own autonomous action simultaneously against French troops and forces of Haitian generals.[79] Throughout Samedi Smith's interventions, the pronoun "we" predominates to indicate a collective function, where exploits depend less on any single leader, belonging instead to "a socially recognized collection of heroes," much like Hobsbawm's bandits.[80] As collective protagonists, the relationship of these "men of the people" is presented as one of total solidarity with the peasantry, as symbolized by the fact that Samedi Smith, this "champion of the barefooted man," is himself a barefooted ordinary peasant.[81]

Representations of Lower-Ranking Soldiers

Parallel writing in of ordinary soldiers means that they open three scenes: act 1, scene 2; act 3, scene 1; and act 3, scene 2. In the first of these scenes, three rank-and-file soldiers choose new names—Max (from Maximilien Robespierre), Marat (from Jean-Paul Marat) and Orléans (from Louis Philippe Joseph d'Orléans, Duke of Orléans, who changed his name to Philippe Égalité [Equality] during the French Revolution). The ordinary Haitian revolutionaries rename themselves after French revolutionaries, symbolically throwing off their slave names, foisted on them by old masters. A main part of these characters' function is to lug heavy furniture, enabling symbolic prop changes: "removing the remaining signs of French colonial gentility from the central area" and replacing them with "severely functional furniture." Slaves express discontent that slave-like labor continues and freedom remains abstract, not appearing to correlate with any substantive change for ex-slaves. All three scenes show ordinary ex-slaves trying to make sense of the latest political developments, translating the French Revolution into their own terms: "The white slaves in France heard that the black slaves in San Domingo had killed their masters and taken over the houses and the property. They heard that we did it and they follow us."[82] Likewise, these soldiers work out their own understandings of key slogans adapted from the French revolutionary idiom— liberty, equality, fraternity—and such talk shows how receptive these former slaves are to revolutionary ideas, which each interprets in his own way.[83]

By act 3, Marat and Orléans are now higher-ranking soldiers, promoted to the ranks of sergeant and corporal, respectively, and correspondingly more elegantly dressed than their previous "semblance of a uniform."[84] Again, soldiers are "doing the work," arranging heavy furniture, trying to make sense of recent developments that look "pretty bad" in the wake of Toussaint's sentencing to death of Moïse and close aides, including their comrade Max.[85] They reflect on the ramifications of these shootings, try to make sense of happenings in France—the terror and parallel killings of their namesakes—and also lament Toussaint's surrender to the French and retirement. Similarly opening the final scene, act 3, scene 2, Orléans and Marat enter with a "huge throne-like chair," a visual symbol that Dessalines is taking over the reins of power.[86] Now Orléans offers a more positive assessment of the current situation as "looking pretty good," while the final push of the war of independence is debated. Sure that Dessalines will be next governor of San Domingo, even his closest aide Marat does not foresee that Dessalines will aim for even higher power still. When Dessalines declares himself emperor from his throne-like chair, Marat plays rabble-rouser, directing the uncertain crowd to join in the chant: "Dessalines! Emperor of Haiti! Emperor!"[87] As the last soldier to abandon Dessalines on stage as the final scene closes, Marat symbolizes Dessalines's alienation of those closest to him.[88]

Certainly, James comes closest in *The Black Jacobins* play to doing what he said he would like to do in 1971: rewriting the history to give Toussaint Louverture only a walk-on part by foregrounding other obscure popular leaders instead. Even in the 1967 play, Toussaint's role remains more important than a walk-on part, but representational shifts have taken place, with the top black Jacobin leadership of Toussaint, Dessalines, and Christophe now being challenged by popular alternative leaders Samedi Smith, Jean Panier, Sylla, and Sans Souci, and the most important challenger: Moïse.

Enter Moïse, Alternative Protagonist, Stage Left

Writing out initial archprotagonist Toussaint Louverture during the making of *The Black Jacobins* play, James progressively writes in an alternative hero of the masses: Moïse. Here, Moïse takes center stage, and his showdown with Toussaint forms the epicenter of the entire play. Moïse had long been on James's mind, as revealed in his 1955 letter to Haitian historian Charlier: "I notice that there is still very little precise to put one's hands upon in the history of Moyse. He is the man of the minor figures who interests me most. I hope that one day something will turn up."[89] Rewriting *The Black Jacobins* as a play specifically enables James to develop this minor figure Moïse as a main protagonist. Three scenes are crucial for understanding his role: act 1, scene 2; act 1, scene 3; and act 2, scene 4 (act 1, scene 7 in early drafts).

Moïse rushes onto the stage in act 1, scene 2 excitedly waving a copy of the French newspaper *Le Moniteur* and shouting "News, citizens! News!"[90] Taking center stage and dramatically reading the story aloud from the newspaper, he conveys to crowds of ordinary soldiers that the French Convention in Paris has officially abolished slavery in every French colony. Translator and interpreter is a major part of Moïse's role of communicating effectively with crowds of ordinary people. Moïse is translating the written word for them because they are illiterate—the reason why telling their history from below is difficult is that these ex-slaves left no written records of their own.[91] Moïse's translations mediate between revolutions in France and San Domingo, between leaders and masses, between written and spoken words, and between elite and common languages in the colony. Through such translation, the people quickly grasp ramifications of political developments, including why Toussaint makes a startling volte-face, suddenly switching sides from the Spanish to the French Republic now that France has abolished slavery. Moïse's deployment of literacy for effective communication with the great mass of the population contrasts with that other great reader Toussaint's aloof and cerebral uncommunicativeness about his strategies.

Conspicuously dabbing a handkerchief to his right eye as he enters the next scene (act 1, scene 3), Moïse declares that he has "lost an eye in the service of liberty" with bravery depicted visually through use of props as well as bold words.[92] Here, the spotlight turns on the contrasting leadership styles of Moïse, Dessalines, Christophe, and Toussaint, pitting them against one another to reveal different attitudes toward freedom and independence in response to the British offer to make Toussaint king. Moïse's clear-sighted vision for San Domingo's future can be summed up in a single word: independence. As James wrote in 1955, "Toussaint was a revolutionary who had gone a long way but could not continue to what the situation actually demanded, the independence of the island."[93] Toussaint cannot continue to independence, whereas, in stark contrast, Moïse stands clearly for independence throughout, a position that also contrasts with those of Dessalines and Christophe. On the British offer to crown Toussaint, Dessalines also declares himself for independence but has no qualms about accepting this offer, not seeing the threat of binding the island to another slave-holding power. As for Christophe, his lines depict him as weak and wavering. Juxtaposing Moïse and Christophe shows just how much the former's decisiveness and clear-sighted vision contrasts with Christophe's lack of any position whatsoever. Moïse also acts as an incorruptible foil by deriding this pair for being duped by high-sounding aristocratic titles.

At the crux of the play is the showdown (act 2, scene 4; act 1, scene 7 in early drafts) where Moïse acts as defiant foil and challenger to Toussaint, directly calling into question his alienating leadership methods.[94] Here, prisoner Moïse has just been court-martialed and sentenced to death for treason, accused of leading rebellions against Toussaint's rule. Upon entering the scene, stage directions indicate that Moïse's black eye patch should be immediately and prominently visible, speaking to the true meaning of words like liberty, freedom, and independence—causes for which he will not only lose an eye but ultimately sacrifice his life. Presented here as a political organizer with mass popular support, Moïse helps translate slaves' political consciousness into an active collective movement against big leaders and acts as an alternative to the increasingly unpopular and isolated Toussaint. Advocating independence, Moïse makes it clear that this is what is needed in order to safeguard the ex-slaves' freedom, demands reinforced by his parting shot that calls for ties to all symbols of colonialism and slavery to be severed, making San Domingo truly independent.[95] As foil, Moïse acts to show up major flaws in "pitiful old" Toussaint's leadership style, especially his uncommunicativeness about strategies and continued allegiance to the French despite the threat that slavery will return.[96] Clear-sighted as ever, Moïse sees through French assurances that slavery will not be restored.

Labor and land reforms are the main bone of contention. Moïse voices the widespread opposition to Toussaint's rural code that forces ex-slaves to work on the plantations and regiments their labor. Such freedom, Moïse points out, is nothing but an abstraction, devoid of any real meaning, as draconian regimentation of labor carries on as before. As chief agricultural inspector, Moïse articulates the people's personal attachment to the land and their perception that slavery is being restored in all but name because generals have been quick to take control of many sequestered plantations, flogging laborers as if they were slaves. While Toussaint preserves old plantations, farming them out to black generals in order to maintain production, Moïse vehemently opposes this alienating policy, advocating instead the parceling off of the large plantations and redistribution of land to ordinary soldiers, not just to the top leadership.[97]

On behalf of the masses, Moïse opposes another Louverturian agrarian policy—inviting émigré white planters back to take charge of plantations—and is particularly contemptuous of Madame Bullet, the white plantation mistress.[98] Stage directions have him cast "a withering sweep of his one good eye" very pointedly in her direction, while challenging Toussaint to cut all "symbols of colonialism and slavery" completely from San Domingo and make the country independent once and for all.[99] Much of the scene opening portrays close relations between Toussaint and his white mistress, Madame Bullet, and her character indicates that Toussaint is courting white émigré planters, enticing them to return, instead of concentrating on his own people. Significantly, Toussaint describes Madame Bullet as the only one on whom he can count, so alienated is he from the black masses.

Familial ties linking Toussaint and his adopted nephew Moïse are stressed, always presenting them as father and son, and Moïse's death sentence as tantamount to Toussaint killing his own son. As argued about the handwritten additions to copies of *Toussaint Louverture* in chapter 1, drama can compress relationships, as Lindenberger shows.[100] Here, Moïse usurps the role of son, which compresses father-son-type family bonds as tightly as possible. Consequently, Toussaint's sentencing to death of his adopted nephew/son, Moïse, is presented as the most outrageous violation possible of their familial bond, magnifying divergences between the worlds they represent—the people and the top brass—previously held together by their closest of relationships.

Moïse's sentencing to death forms the structural and thematic center of the play, but even after death his popular and principled alternative leadership style and ideas continue to loom large, with Dessalines underlining that the killing of Moïse was pivotal in Toussaint's own downfall, but now Moïse's ideas are flourishing in new soil through thousands of Samedi Smiths.[101] The specter of what Moïse represented is again raised when news of Toussaint's death is announced: "DESSALINES: Moïse told [Toussaint] exactly what to do, but he killed Moïse."[102] Right at the end, clear-sighted Moïse is invoked as the one who could have charted the path toward true independence. What hope is there at the end of this final bleak scene? Very little. Ideals of the Haitian Revolution are symbolized above all by Moïse, and Moïse is dead.

Changing the Ending: The Epilogue

In the unperformed and unpublished epilogue, however, Moïse is not dead but instead reincarnated as modern-day political organizer: Speaker D. Clearly bringing the play up to date, this epilogue rapidly fast-forwards in time from the declaration of Haitian independence to the present day—a time travel indicated visibly by costume changes to modern clothes. As for the setting of this scene, it too is clearly in the present day, taking place in "a private room in a hotel somewhere in an underdeveloped country" at the end of a Bandung-type conference. Unlike the rest of the play, epilogue characters have no names, although stage directions stipulate they should be easily recognizable from parts played before, and Speakers A, B, and C display similar characteristics to their opposite numbers: Toussaint, Christophe, and Dessalines respectively. This namelessness also presents Speakers A, B, and C as modern-day political types.[103] Almost two whole pages of this three-page epilogue sketch out a political skit, dramatizing a startling neocolonial situation where "independence" becomes an empty word bandied about by this new political elite. Costume changes also expose the hypocrisy of this independence situation when actors doff the native dress of all previous scenes only to don Western clothes, reminiscent of similar costume changes in Ousmane Sembène's film *Xala*. There, three-piece suits and briefcases filled with wads of cash bankrolled by the returning/departing neo/colonial white masters act as status symbols and shorthand for postindependence aping of foreign power.[104] In James's epilogue, suits donned by the three speakers are symbols of this hollow independence because they metonymically identify their wearers as postindependence bureaucrat-type leaders, vying to prop up their power with foreign capital.

Genre-wise, beyond romance and tragedy, a third genre—farce, a subset of comedy—emerges strongly from the epilogue.[105] As discussed in chapter 2, one important model for James's Marxist historical narrative is *The Eighteenth Brumaire of Louis Bonaparte* (1851–52). Marx begins that work by linking repetition to farce: "Hegel remarks somewhere that all great world-historic facts and personages appear, so to speak twice. He forgot to add: the first time as tragedy, the second time as farce."[106] Marx wrote this text between December 1851 and March 1852, just after Louis Napoleon's coup d'état, and it deals with recent events between 1848 and 1851, including the overthrow of the king in 1848, the failure of the revolution, the dissolution of parliament, and the crowning of Louis Bonaparte as supreme emperor on December 2, 1851.[107]

With the epilogue, James would have brought in this third genre—farce—into the mix, changing the mode to laughter in the face of farcical seriousness. As Mehlman observes, comic laughter splits into farce, and this is a genre that is opposed to tragedy quite differently than to comedy.[108] How does Marx's Bonapartist farce translate in the *Black Jacobins* play epilogue? James portrays postindependence leaders following the breakup of the West Indies Federation discussing issues of the day, including alignment or nonalignment. In the earliest version of the epilogue, they are explicitly West

Indian, but their origins become less specific as the epilogue is reshaped. These leaders in the epilogue become absurdity personified, as James intertwines disaster with farce.[109] As in Marx's *Eighteenth Brumaire*, there are telling parallels between past and present leaders who are deluding themselves and their nation. Marx portrays Louis Bonaparte as a buffoon who puts on his Napoleonic mask. In the epilogue, mediocre offshoots of the former leaders also act as comedians who theatrically, if not physically, put on the masks of their Haitian revolutionary counterparts in order to play their roles. Vigorous parody magnifies James's objects of derision: the present-day leader types who are portrayed as making the Haitian Revolution travel backward.

One present-day leader does not, however, appear to be farcical. Speaker D/Moïse's clear-sighted and principled seriousness contrasts maximally with the other leader types. Speaker D/Moïse represents not Marx's Bonapartist farcical exact repetitions and failures, but instead a model of repetition with variation: the perspective of organizing politically and delivering strong speeches. Reincarnated as the twentieth-century equivalent of Haitian revolutionary forebear Moïse, Speaker D's popular leadership is buoyed up by the masses, unlike that of Speakers A, B, and C whose struggle is against the people. Now that Moïse has morphed into a principled political organizer, Speaker D concludes the epilogue by delivering a rousing speech about revolutionary tactics to an audience offstage. At the outset, suspense is created by positioning him "three-quarters turned away" from the real audience, with most of his face still hidden. Only when the speech ends, and he half-turns toward the audience, is his true identity as Moïse revealed because now can be seen that symbol of revolutionary struggle for independence: the black patch over the sacrificed eye. Turning to face the real audience, Moïse also deliberately wipes his face with a handkerchief, a gesture that recalls mopping blood from the lost eye, and thereby all the sacrifices for true independence.

This closing speech presents Speaker D, like his Haitian revolutionary counterpart Moïse, as a clear and viable political alternative to the hollow age of independence leadership styles represented by Speakers A, B, and C. Words and substance deliver change and, as a prime function of the epilogue is to act as reconfiguration tool, it is also essential to consider James's own reworking of this epilogue in its three different versions. As discussed, the earliest draft from a specifically Caribbean vantage point makes specific reference to the West Indies, Caribbean politics, and especially the failed West Indies Federation project: "Speaker C: [. . .] The Federation is broken up, it is true. But I still believe that we are one people. And I still believe that we must look forward to a Federation of the whole Caribbean, including Spanish, French, and Dutch territories."[110] Originally, the modern-day reincarnation of Moïse turned determined political organizer Speaker D also ended his speech with direct reference to West Indian unity: "When the day should come when we as a whole recognise that liberty and freedom cannot be inherited but must be fought for and won again by every generation. When West Indians will at last ..." at which point he is cut off by tremendous applause.[111]

Had this Caribbean Federation version actually traveled to Nigeria, however, this particular stress on a federation would surely have taken on very different and extremely loaded ideological valences when played out against the backdrop of the ongoing Nigerian Civil War. As this war was raging, the federal cause and the idea of a unitary Nigeria had overtones in contrast with those of the failed West Indies Federation. Federalists were pitched against secessionists, with catchy slogans of the federal military regime—including "to keep the nation one is a task that must be done"—that preached unity, under which lurked the federal authorities' responsibility for the civil war, acts of genocide against 1.5 million Igbos, and deliberate acts of dividing, isolating, and repressing in the name of unity.[112] This is an example of just what can be at stake when dramatic texts travel; even certain words can take on unanticipated and undesired new political meanings when brushed against the grain by local conditions of the contexts to which they are transported, as here in Nigerian terms.

Caribbean references are then removed from the two subsequent versions where the epilogue is rewritten to make it less localized. As James repeatedly reworked the epilogue, however, he purposefully attempted to make it much less intramurally Caribbean specific, billing it thus in his directions that head later epilogue versions: "completely adaptable to the circumstances and environs of the production and may be altered as necessary." In so doing, the epilogue loses its own situatedness and immediate context, particularly at the end of the second version of Speaker D's present-day speech: "Fighting means taking risks. You have to learn to risk your liberty, your property, even your life."[113] Here, Speaker D's closing words appear just as platitudinous as those of Speakers A–C, whose alternative he is supposed to represent. Similar charges were also made by director Lyndersay when he cut the epilogue ahead of the play's Nigerian premiere.[114]

A third alternative version of the epilogue's final page turns attention to the true meaning of independence.[115] Interrogating the current so-called independence, Speaker D asks, "Independence. What is independence? How can you be independent if the very ground on which you walk belongs to people in London, New York, and Paris?" Independence symbols—new flag, new national anthem, new prime minister, and new parliament—are presented by Speaker D as empty status symbols if true power still resides in foreign hands. A refrain punctuating this version repeats like a mantra, "we must get the land back." References to getting the land back recall the platform of James's Trinidad WFP, cofounded by James in 1965.

A confident optimistic note characterizes all three speech versions, ending with the upbeat Samedi Smith resistance anthem, and one constant throughout all the reworkings is the impact of the closing speech on the crowds. Punctuating Speaker D's speech are bursts of euphoric applause, indicating mass support. Is this representational inscription of Speaker D/Moïse as vehicle of such united popular support wishful thinking on James's part? Certainly, the epilogue does end by inscribing an ideal(ized) response from large crowds. This could be read as a rather utopian representation of the ideal mass popular support James would have liked during his own bruising foray into West Indian politics, particularly the WFP's total election failure in November 1966.

Despite this model of active mass participation set up by the epilogue, James still retains a marked preference for exceptionally superlative, larger-than-life, heroic revolutionary figures, singled out for extraordinary capacities and energy.[116] Even with these shortcomings, however, the alternative version of the epilogue ending does give Speaker D/Moïse a positive proposal that is clearest when the focus turns to the true meaning of independence.

Ultimately, without the epilogue the entire play ends very differently.[117] Its whole purpose is to be usable for other situations; ever-changeable or updatable qualities that are further stressed when reworked by James, so that the epilogue can itself be reconfigured and extrapolated as the play travels to different times and places. Indeed, stage directions in most copies of the epilogue stipulate that contemporary parallels should always be stressed, with references made to the circumstances surrounding the production as necessary. These three pages of epilogue in their various states constitute a hybrid document between play, political pamphlet/speech, and paratext, which reconfigures and reframes the whole play.

Paratexts—all the prefaces, appendixes, and epilogues that multiply in new editions—always function as crucial sites and privileged modes of expression in James's work. To conclude, I consider what the epilogue form enables James to do, arguing that epilogues—and by extension other paratextual near-equivalents, prefaces, and appendixes—offer advantages to James over other modes of writing. Generically, this epilogue form compels maximum use of directness and clarity, and yields the strongest ideological and political insights of the whole play. Compressed into only three pages, the epilogue has a strikingly condensed quality within the architecture of the play as a whole. Use of such concise forms enables James to magnify, concentrate, illuminate, reinforce, make more accessible, and bring to new contexts the crucial points of the preceding main play, around which these paratextual elements are positioned. As a mode of expression, the epilogue most resembles a direct political speech, pamphlet, or interview because it consists of clear, understandable messages; an updatable statement for changing times, summing up and pointing out implications for the future.

Speaker D/Moïse's closing speech is where there is a direct call to action, the clearest exposition of political ideas and of how one actually organizes to change society. Designed specifically with a view to being opened up through extrapolation and reconfiguration to new chronotopes, the epilogue is inscribed with the idea of traveling because its function is to allow the dramatic text of *The Black Jacobins* to travel as widely as possible, enabling themes from the play proper to be reframed through reconfigurations of new pasts, presents, and futures.[118]

Ironically, the epilogue never did permit *The Black Jacobins* play to travel anywhere through time or space because it was discarded on director Lyndersay's orders long before the play was first performed or appeared in print. Endings are key sites of plays, as the very last thing an audience sees performed and ultimately takes away with them when leaving the theater.[119] Minus the epilogue, the play as performed and published ends in a fundamentally different key. Unlike the scene of the declaration of Haitian independence, from which Moïse, the embodiment of revolutionary qualities, is absent, the epilogue actually ends with his rousing, optimistic words looking to the future. Without the epilogue, the play ends as a tragedy instead, with Dessalines portrayed in the act of crowning himself emperor of Haiti, hollowing out all new symbols of independence as they are being created, and violently suppressing ordinary people and their popular revolutionary anthem. In his 1958 pamphlet on Federation, James made it very clear that "freedom from colonialism is not merely legal independence; the right to run up a national flag and to compose and sing a national anthem. It is necessary also to break down the economic colonial system under which the colonial areas have been compelled to live for centuries as hinterlands, sources of raw materials, backyards to the industries of the advanced countries."[120]

On interfaces between plays and politics, this is ultimately a play that shows a revolution in practice. How to bring about change, transformation, and revolution are all key questions that run throughout the play. In terms of characterization, we are presented with revolutionary heroes who want to change society and transform their reality. Relevant here is the slogan that is repeated like a mantra throughout the pages of Augusto Boal's important theoretical statement on political commitment in *Theater of the Oppressed*: that theater is perhaps not necessarily revolutionary in itself, but that theater is without a doubt always "a rehearsal of revolution."[121] According to Boal, the key link between theater and revolution is always action. In performance, he argues, actors act out attempts at political organization and revolutionary action, and dramatic action throws light upon, and prepares for, real action.[122] For Boal, theater is action, quite simply. Of course, there is a certain irony here with regard to *The Black Jacobins* play because the second letter Lyndersay sends James even complains that the play contains "no action as such," a statement met with incredulous question marks by James.[123] Be that as it may, even if James's play text privileges dialogue to the detriment of dramatic action, it is certainly a type of dialogue aimed at effective political organizing and inciting political action and focused on potential forces for revolutionary change and beginning action.

Boal's concept of theater as stimulating action is a productive one for exploring the radical political ramifications of James's own rewriting of the play. If bourgeois theater can be thought of, after Boal, as finished theater, presenting only complacent images of the complete, finished bourgeois world, then popular political theater of the oppressed would by contrast reject any closed spectacles and always seek to enter into dialogue and ask for explanations. This idea provides a useful conceptual framework for reading James's sprawling and anarchic perpetual rewrites of *The Black Jacobins* play. The very unfinished and open nature of the multiple drafts could be read as a type of handmaiden form for revolutionary theatrical and real-world processes of dynamic action, transformation, and re-creation where "theater is change and not simple presentation of what exists: it is becoming not being."[124] As a Marxist, the playwright-activist James does theatrical work that can never be finished, nor can it ever end neatly and complacently in a state of serene repose. Instead, the open and unfinished form and contents of *The Black Jacobins* play drafts combine to reinforce the importance of hastening actual political/societal transformations, changes, transitions, political actions, and successful struggles for liberation. Incomplete/unfinished here means political action and transformation.

5 | Afterlives of *The Black Jacobins*

This book has tracked the evolution of James's engagements with the Haitian Revolution over the course of nearly sixty years. To chart these evolving engagements with Haiti, I have focused on James's own progressive transformations, during his lifetime, of the story he tells about the revolution. Previous chapters have tracked the shifting coordinates of James's constantly mobile *Black Jacobins* project as it changed shape to illuminate changing pasts, presents, and futures. By exploring the genesis and evolution of James's Haiti-related work, the main aim has been to reveal an important process of constant rewriting by the author himself. Issues of genre have been at the forefront of the study, which has explored James's use of the tools of history writing and playwriting—telling and showing—to give center stage to alternative narratives and characters. Collaboration in writing and rewriting, with political comrades, theater directors, and actors, among others, has been shown to have a great impact on the evolution of James's Haitian work overall. Indeed, *The Black Jacobins* is the collaborative project par excellence.

As previously discussed, *The Black Jacobins* itself can be thought of as part of what Susan Gillman calls, via Dan Selden, a "text-network."[1] The *Black Jacobins* text-network multiplies when James's own radical transformation of the history editions, plays, and articles about the Haitian Revolution is considered. Already James himself extends the reference points beyond Columbus and Castro to more recent happenings in Haiti, the rest of the Caribbean, Africa, America, and beyond. As noted, a dialectical tension runs throughout James's work, which means he mentions certain places and contexts but not others, including the U.S. occupation of Haiti, 1915–34. This means that, as argued, *The Black Jacobins* is always far more than the sum of all its multiple component parts.

When, however, works inspired by *The Black Jacobins* are taken into account, it becomes apparent that others have in their turn shifted the coordinates even more, taking *The Black Jacobins* to new contexts beyond those envisaged by James, and making the work speak to new political situations and struggles, historical events and personalities. As will be seen, after James, the work is often taken beyond text to other modalities apart from the textual. This book has already examined the protean transformations of the text-network formed by James's own authorial writings and lectures. In this chapter, we turn to the constellation of other people's interventions, which continue to orbit around the work in question.[2] This text-network keeps proliferating to this day. The main concern here is with uncovering the fashioning of an icon and a classic: *The Black Jacobins* as a monumental object of reference and as a story to be rewritten, transformed, appropriated, and challenged in new contexts and for different purposes.

Having analyzed in previous chapters James's own authorial versions of Haiti-related works, this chapter now turns to what can be termed the afterlives of *The Black Jacobins*. "Afterlives" is used here as a metaphorical notion to invoke the relations between the source text and its avatars.[3] *The Black Jacobins* has produced many resonances and has had a seemingly endless capacity for reincarnation and reinvention by others as well as by the author James himself. By speaking in terms of afterlives, this chapter points to some of the shifting impacts of James's most famous work in a range of situations across the world at different moments. As Charles Forsdick and Christian Høgsbjerg have observed, it is difficult to talk about the impact of *The Black Jacobins* in terms of afterlives, not least because the work itself continues to evolve.[4] An assessment of the work's multiple impacts would constitute an entire book and even then, it would be impossible to give a full encyclopedic account, but this chapter maps out some of the most important coordinates.

What this closing section focuses on, however, is work that seeks to bring James and *The Black Jacobins* back to life and make it live on in new versions of the work. Afterlives examined here include exhibitions, translations, performances, impacts of the work across the world (including in Haiti itself), and monumental afterlives. Some of the afterlives also straddle categories, as with the 2018 British Museum Haiti exhibit and the response piece it generated: a performance by Haitian anthropologist-artist Gina Athena Ulysse.

Exhibiting *The Black Jacobins*

One way to think about the work's shifting impact is through Terence Cave's useful exhibition analogy. In this way, the set of *Black Jacobins* afterlives can be visualized as a virtual exhibition—perhaps along the lines of the major *C. L. R. James: Man of the People* exhibition in London in 1986. This exhibition, which itself constitutes one of the afterlives, explicitly sought to exhibit James's impact across the world over his lifetime. Organized by Darcus Howe (James's great-nephew) and Leila Hassan of Creation for Liberation—the Race Today Collective's arts/cultural arm—the exhibition was also timed to promote and coincide with the concurrent 1986 London production of *The Black Jacobins*.[5]

In the twenty-first century, James's work has inspired at least one other exhibition: the 2011 arts festival and five-day symposium titled "Black Jacobins: Negritude in a Post Global 21st Century," a series of events across the Caribbean, from Barbados to Martinique, curated by David A. Bailey and Alissandra Cummins. It focused on the legacy of James's and Aimé Césaire's ideas represented in visual arts and moving images. From the symposium emerged a book, *Curating in the Caribbean* (2012), which discusses the legacies of James and Césaire, reclaiming *The Black Jacobins* as a Negritude work.[6]

Caribbean artworks commissioned and exhibited included Ras Akyem-i Ramsay's *Blakk-Jacobin* (figure 5.1), which is a portrait of Toussaint Louverture, mostly in blazing reds. His Toussaint is a composite figure, incorporating elements of other Haitian revolutionary leaders, including autocratic Christophe, Dessalines, and Vodou priest Boukman. As there is no reliable physical image of what Toussaint actually looked like, Ramsay's art works against most of the portraits he had previously seen of Toussaint, where the artists "were trying to refine him and approximate him to whiteness in order to validate his abilities."[7] Ramsay instead aims for an alternative Caribbean representation of Toussaint, who is fashioned after James's history. Ramsay painted different versions of Toussaint's portrait. Like James, he has produced variations on a theme, and the two portraits resonate differently. Ramsay's visual responses to Toussaint have also spawned new poetry about the Haitian Revolution, namely Barbadian rhythm poet Adisa "Aja" Andwele's December 2014 poem "Brekin' Open the *Blakk-Jacobin*."[8] Both artwork and poem direct attention visually or through words to the Haitian Revolution's outbreak and the unleashing of Vodou gods' revolutionary energies.

What is most visually striking about Ramsay's painting is its depiction of Toussaint's jacket. This jacket is laden with Vodou symbolism and paraphernalia, which conjures up the role of the spirit ancestors as part of the weaponry of Toussaint's warfare. Ramsay's composite *Blakk-Jacobin* is portrayed as a warrior-shaman—quite a different representation than James's own

FIG. 5.1 Ras Akyem-i Ramsay, *Blakk-Jacobin*, 2011. © Ras Akyem-i Ramsay. From the collection of Anderson Toppin. Photo by William St. James Cummins.

black Jacobin, where Vodou does not play such a central role in his representation of Toussaint. Ramsay has spoken of how James's famous work inspired him to get beyond painting Caribbean visual clichés, the traditional images of fishing boats and palm trees.

Visual responses to *The Black Jacobins* run prominently throughout recent artworks by Lubaina Himid, winner of the 2017 Turner Prize. Her win is already bringing her *Black Jacobins*–inspired works from previous decades to wider audiences than ever before. Several of her most significant artworks started out as direct responses to James's history. One 1987 mixed-media artwork titled *Toussaint L'Ouverture*, exhibited in August 2017 at Middlesbrough Institute of Modern Art, portrays a cutout figure of the Haitian revolutionary

Afterlives of *The Black Jacobins* | 181

hero (figure 5.2). His breeches and boots are made up of a visually striking collage from contemporary newspaper articles and photographs, which display the eye-catching block-capital headline words "ABUSE," "TORTURE," and "RACIST." These headlines ring out of the artwork to draw attention to contemporary problems similar to those which the Haitian Revolution combated over two hundred years ago. Written next to the figure are the words "THIS NEWS WOULDN'T BE NEWS IF YOU HAD HEARD OF TOUSSAINT L'OUVERTURE." Below this comes a direct quotation from James, which inscribes *The Black Jacobins* at the very center of Himid's artwork: "BETWEEN 1789 & 1815 WITH THE SINGLE EXCEPTION OF BONAPARTE HIMSELF, NO SINGLE FIGURE APPEARED ON THE HISTORICAL STAGE MORE GREATLY GIFTED THAN THIS MAN, A SLAVE TILL HE WAS 45," with "C. L. R. JAMES" written prominently underneath. Always, the key source for Himid is *The Black Jacobins*.

Lines from James's history form the basis for the handwritten sections of Himid's Haitian Revolution–inspired art. Her series *Scenes from the Life of Toussaint Louverture*, originally created in 1987, consists of fifteen watercolors.⁹ Again, the starting point is *The Black Jacobins*, and the fifteen paintings engage in a sustained dialogue with James's history. Apart from the direct inscriptions from the text itself in the written parts of many of these artworks, the images visualize key scenes, providing the first illustrations for the famous history. Almost all written elements in these pieces come directly from *The Black Jacobins*. Mixing together her watercolors with James's written texts makes them work like a series of visual commentaries. Himid has asserted that she is "not a historian," but that the series tries to illuminate "an artist's view for historians to use and share." Her artworks together show the sort of silenced histories that James was one of the first to make visible through his history writing. But Himid makes it clear that the creative arts and artists' imaginations are needed to supplement historians' accounts of such events. Himid also highlights James's silences by bringing into view the supporting roles of black female characters. She asks, "who cooked the midday meal? Who will do the laundry?" "Did she [Toussaint's wife] help him with strategy?" One Jamesian silence about Vodou is articulated: "C. L. R. James never mentions Voo-doo." Himid asks, "Did his mother teach him everything he knew?" as she fills a gap from James's history.

The Black Jacobins also directly inspired Kimathi Donkor's major series of five large-scale oil paintings collectively titled *Caribbean Passion: Haiti 1804*. As the title suggests, this is a reworking of the Passion of Christ with

FIG. 5.2 Lubaina Himid, *Toussaint L'Ouverture*, paint and collage on wood, 1987. © Lubaina Himid. Photo courtesy of the Middlesbrough Collection, Middlesbrough Institute of Modern Art. Purchased with assistance from the Art Fund and the Arts Council England/Victoria and Albert Museum Purchase Grant Fund.

a Caribbean-centered focus, marking the 2004 bicentenary of Haitian independence. James's history formed the backbone of Donkor's extensive historical research as the source sparking all five paintings in the series. First to be painted in this series was *Sanité and Charles Belair* in 2000. Donkor explains that his portrait of this Haitian revolutionary couple was inspired by James's discussion of them.[10] In keeping with *The Black Jacobins*, the couple is portrayed as dignified and brave during a moment of rest. James uses the example of Sanité to discuss the crucial role of women fighting side by side with men during the Haitian Revolution.[11] Their courageous stance in Donkor's painting also recalls James's depiction of the couple's bravery during their execution, with both facing death without blindfolds.[12]

James was also the inspiration behind the centerpiece of the whole *Caribbean Passion* series, titled *Toussaint L'Ouverture at Bedourete*—the only painting in the series to feature Toussaint (figure 5.3).[13] As its title suggests, this is an imposing portrait of that named Haitian revolutionary. It visualizes one sentence from *The Black Jacobins* recounting Toussaint's bravery: "He launched the first attack on the fort Bedourete, as usual leading the charge with sword drawn" (1963, 319). Not only does this painting create a visual tableau out of the corresponding passage drawn from the history, it is also a visual reworking of Jacques-Louis David's *Napoleon Crossing the Alps* (1801), an early nineteenth-century portrait of Napoleon. Donkor's image of Toussaint is therefore a reworking of both James and the iconic Napoleon portrait dating from slavery times. Like David's Napoleon, Donkor's Toussaint is depicted astride a rearing stallion as if leading the charge in battle. However, while David presents his Napoleon in complete isolation, Donkor also foregrounds another figure who is not Toussaint. Both are smiling and appear victorious. This anonymous soldier appears in a close-up in the bottom left quadrant of the painting, closer to the viewer than Toussaint. Other black figures are depicted on foot alongside their general mounted on horseback. There appears to be one white and one black dead body on the ground, with one black male character reaching out in despair as he is comforted by a black female. In this way, Donkor is following James's lead on the important roles played by the masses as well as the leaders, and by class in addition to race, and the artist's role as a community activist emerges clearly.

Donkor's postcolonial multilayered reworking tendency continues in work from his 2007 *UK Diaspora* series, which was exhibited at Liverpool's International Slavery Museum August 21, 2017–September 2, 2018.[14] Transformations of well-known portraiture of white colonizers responsible for

FIG. 5.3 Kimathi Donkor, *Toussaint L'Ouverture at Bedourete*, oil on canvas, 2004. © Kimathi Donkor.

slavery and the slave trade run throughout the series, and are at the heart of Donkor's reanimation of his own works. Donkor has used his mixed-media assemblages of the 2007 *UK Diaspora* series to remodel and deface well-known white figureheads profiteering from slavery. It is by visually transforming images of rulers Elizabeth I, Elizabeth II, Margaret Thatcher, and Francis Drake that Donkor exposes the traces of transatlantic slavery in works like *Drake-u-liar, Ran Away by George, Elizabeth Rex Lives,* and *Arise Sir John.*[15] Donkor, like James, also continues this reworking and retelling of history, performing it again. At the Tate Britain museum in 2009, Donkor placed his own *Elizabeth Rex Lives* beside Nicholas Hilliard's well-known oil portrait of Elizabeth I as a loud response to the queen's role in financing and profiting from slavery and the slave trade. At the 2009 exhibition, the audience was called on to deface Donkor's painting with safety pins as they chanted "Liberty or Death," Haiti's revolutionary slogan. Reworking operates as a powerful transformative tool for the artist as it does for his main guide James and his *Black Jacobins*. Both create representations of black revolutionary heroes and their nobility while slashing identifiable portraits of colonialist nobility

Afterlives of *The Black Jacobins* | **185**

to expose the silences and gaps in the archives and historical records concerning slaves and slavery, and to make visible traces of invisible slave labor.

From February to April 2018, the British Museum had a display called *A Revolutionary Legacy: Haiti and Toussaint Louverture*.[16] The exhibit, featuring visual and written representations of the Haitian Revolution, described *The Black Jacobins* as "probably the most influential account of the Haitian Revolution and of Louverture's central role," highlighted James's Pan-Africanism calling for solidarity of peoples of African descent, and provided a helpful commentary on the cover artwork for the 1963 Vintage revised edition of *The Black Jacobins*.[17]

The centerpiece of the display was Jacob Lawrence's series of fifteen silk screen prints titled *The Life of Toussaint L'Ouverture*. In response to this British Museum display, Haitian-born artist-anthropologist Gina Athena Ulysse performed "Remixed Ode to Rebel's Spirit: Lyrical Meditations on Haiti and Toussaint Louverture" on the evening of March 16, 2018. In a blog post for the British Museum, Ulysse reflected on the symbolism of Toussaint Bréda's self-renaming as Louverture (the opening).[18] She made clear that she was aiming to create an opening through a creative performance in response to Louverture and his legacies for Haiti. In terms of methods, Ulysse presented remixing, reworking, and rewriting as necessary for her work of *rasanblaj* (the Kreyòl word for gathering)—"Only a remix will do, for performing this revolution will be live"—a live, unfinishable revolution.

C. L. R. James was never mentioned specifically during the performance or question-and-answer session, but after the event, Ulysse told me that she was following the lead of James's *Black Jacobins* by zooming in so explicitly on Louverture instead of Dessalines. Traditionally in Haiti, Dessalines receives the lion's share of historical and political attention and commemoration and is incarnated as Vodou god Papa Desalin/Desalin Ogou.[19] Recent Haitian James-inspired visual reimaginings of the revolutionary Louverture include work by Édouard Duval-Carrié and Ulrick Jean-Pierre.[20]

Making visible "The Many Faces of Toussaint Louverture" was central to a 2014 exhibition by that name featuring works by Duval-Carrié at Brown University's Center for the Study of Slavery and Justice (May 22–June 15, 2014).[21] In his frequent representations of Louverture, Duval-Carrié is "playing off the idea that Toussaint was a 'Black Jacobin,'" as Anthony Bogues has observed.[22] According to Duval-Carrié, it was only when reading *The Black Jacobins* that he finally understood the full complexity of this historical context of the revolution.²³ Building on James, Duval-Carrié makes Toussaint the protean figure of possibility par excellence.²⁴

Duval-Carrié has produced a brightly multicolored portrait series to reimagine and reshape the revolutionary in response to *The Black Jacobins* with the vivid pink and gold of this book's cover image *Le Général Toussaint enfumé* (2001), as well as *Toussaint Fuschia* (2007), and the bright yellow of *Toussaint Citron* (2006). This series also comprises *Toussaint Noir* (2006), *Toussaint Bonbon Or* (2006), *Toussaint Malachite* (2006), and *Toussaint Chintz* (2014). The artist has called Toussaint "a monument" and has described how in the absence of any pictures showing a true likeness, he has instead created "imaginary images" of the revolutionary.²⁵

One reason for Toussaint having so many faces is that no one knows for sure exactly what he looked like. Fritz Daguillard has reported on the great "variety of likenesses," with hardly any similarities among the iconic representations.²⁶ We still do not know what he looked like.²⁷ It is significant that Duval-Carrié models so many of his representations of Toussaint on the main illustration that served as frontispiece to *The Black Jacobins*: the lithograph by Nicolas Maurin, which was published in 1832 by François-Séraphin Delpech.²⁸ This famous Maurin-Delpech version has become the best-known profile portrait of Louverture and the one that has been repeatedly reproduced despite the fact that the original engraving has been called "problematic" and criticized for caricaturing and replicating racial stereotypes. Apparently, Toussaint's surviving son Isaac rejected its likeness to his father.²⁹ Yet, this image became so popular and was passed down through history as the revolutionary's true likeness. It was assumed to be a copy of an older portrait painted from life.³⁰ Furthermore, according to Fritz Daguillard, Maurin's image could, in fact, be like Toussaint: "Those who saw Louverture have often commented on his prognathism, which is especially striking in this portrait. He owed his salient lower jaw to the loss of his teeth and of part of the upper maxillary during a skirmish."³¹ Even if the Maurin rendering is problematic and reductive, the Toussaint pictured maintains a steady gaze and looks every inch the visionary leader. Overall, the original Maurin rendering of Toussaint already "occupies an exalted status," as Bernier has noted.³² In the Maurin version, he is finely dressed with fine, intricate leaf embroidery decorating a grand uniform, complete with epaulettes, plume, and bicorn hat. This image is accompanied by Toussaint's imposing handwritten signature as *The Black Jacobins* frontispiece.

Duval-Carrié directly models most of his Toussaint series via Jacob Lawrence on the famous Maurin portrait with practically the same profile face shape. The colors in this series present a bright and bold pop-art sequence of Toussaints. By adding different layers of bright color to the original colorless engraving, the artist makes each work look like a colorful locket or inverted cameo brooch.[33] These colors emphasize Toussaint's black race, highlight his nobility, and give him a look of distinction, his gray hair contrasting with the ornate decoration of his uniform and background.

The artist frequently deploys the symbolism and forms of Haitian *vèvè*—the transitory and intricate ritual drawings traced in cornflower that summon the Vodou *lwa*, such as Toussaint "Legba" Louverture, master of the crossroads. Each of Duval-Carrié's profile portraits recall *vèvè* themselves, as if they were crossroads between this world and that other world of the *lwa*. Turning to James has helped the artist turn away from distorted and vilified *mis*representations of Louverture, while also helping him to focus on his flaws and contradictions.[34] *The Black Jacobins* is still inspiring exhibitions and visual representations of Toussaint and his many faces that continue to rework the Maurin-Delpech profile of the 1938 edition's frontispiece. The same image, for example, morphed into the cover design for the 1963 Vintage edition by Loren Eutemy that also involves a clearly Jacob Lawrence–inspired Toussaint profile.[35] James's work has also inspired at least two graphic novels: Akala's *The Ruins of Empires* (2014), focusing on Dessalines and the Haitian Revolution, and a forthcoming adaptation from the 1936 *Toussaint Louverture* play by Nic Watts and Sakina Karimjee. *The Black Jacobins* has inspired visual art, too, that is predicated on reworking.

Travels in Translation

Every step along the path of *The Black Jacobins* sees James translating the story of the Haitian Revolution and his sources into English, including, for example, his Anglicization of Haiti's colonial name *Saint-Domingue* as San Domingo—an English name that was popularized after James used it so prominently.[36] Translation is the key process through which *The Black Jacobins* continues to make an impact today on new generations in different places. Indeed, James's own rewriting of his accounts of the Haitian Revolution can productively be thought of as a process of self-translation.[37] Certainly, translation has always been the primary mode of diffusion of the work across physical and linguistic boundaries, and it is an important part of the composite picture making up the afterlives of *The Black Jacobins*. To date the work has been translated into French (1949, 1983, 2008), Italian (1968, 2006), German (1984), Japanese (1991, 2002), Brazilian Portuguese (2000, 2010), and Spanish (Spanish/Mexican edition 2003; Cuban partial appendix 1975, Cuban full text 2010).[38]

One major landmark, always signaled by James himself, is the 1949 French publication with prestigious publisher Gallimard, translated by James's Trotskyist comrade Pierre Naville.[39] As an accurate translation—usually the main objective of any translator—certain aspects of Naville's rendering are execrable. Careless mistakes include wrongly giving the author's initials as "P. I. R.," mistakenly declaring Jamaica to be his birthplace, and giving the original publication date of the work as 1936. Some typos are introduced and certain footnotes and bibliographic entries are omitted altogether. Nevertheless, this French edition is a milestone in the history of the book because Naville's translation and preface update James's prewar 1938 history, reframing it just after the World War II watershed for France's colonies.

The French edition, published in 1949, came just after France marked the centenary of abolition in 1848. The way Naville frames the French edition in his preface recalls Aimé Césaire's 1948 speech to commemorate that centenary.[40] Instead of memorializing the past, Césaire and Naville turn to engaging the present and the legacies of incomplete emancipation left hanging for more than a hundred years. In his 1948 speech, Césaire proclaimed, "Racism is here. It is not dead[. . . .] The colonial problem confronts us, it is waiting to be resolved."[41] Naville makes similar points in his attempt to excavate France's colonial history in the preface written to present James's history to French readers. James and his *Black Jacobins*—crucial precursors for Césaire—showed that emancipation had nothing to do with benevolent granting of freedom by the metropolitan power.

A major difference between the 1949 and second 1983 (Éditions Caribéennes) French editions is that they straddle James's own 1963 revisions. Consequently, James's famous appendix, updated bibliography, prefaces, and most prominent revisions only appear in French after a two-decade time lag; this delay would have implications for the reception of the work in French-speaking countries, including Haiti. Numerous useful translator's notes were also written by additional 1983 translator Claude Fivel-Demoret. Somewhat lost in translation throughout the 1983 text are less prominent revisions to the updated main text. The subsequent 1983 translation can be thought of as a palimpsest over the skeleton of Naville's imperfect original. In 2008, a third

French edition was published by Éditions Amsterdam, adding a preface by historian Laurent Dubois. A new bibliography covers a good range of James's work, but typos abound.

Another landmark translation was the Italian publication of *I Giacobini neri* by Feltrinelli in June 1968, as the events of Il Sessantotto heated up from Italy's so-called Creeping May, culminating in the Hot Autumn of unrest in 1969, when worker-student alliances peaked.[42] The translation directly connected James's closest Italian *operaisti*/workerist and autonomist comrades, such as Ferruccio Gambino, Sergio Bologna, and Antonio Negri, with James in London and American Jamesians based mainly in Detroit.[43] Problematically, James's subtitle was changed to "The first revolt against the white man."[44] According to translator Raffaele Petrillo, this was "a commercial decision to win the book more Italian readers."[45] But it is wrong to suggest that the Haitian Revolution, 1791–1804, was the first-ever slave-led revolt against white men. James eloquently makes the point in the book that slaves were revolting as soon as slavery existed, and so the changed Italian subtitle, foregrounding race, gives a false picture of what the book is about. The 1968 Italian translation marks the first time that the famous appendix was translated into another language, along with other 1963 revisions and the updated footnotes and bibliography. An important added translator's note about Mussolini's *Leggi razziali* (racial laws) draws attention to James's silence about Italian experiences of fascism in the appendix.

A second Italian edition was published in 2006 by Derive Approdi in Rome. A preface by Sandro Chignola, editor of an important Italian edition of Louverture's political writings, reframes *I Giacobini neri* for postcolonial studies, foregrounding Italian debates on migrants and immigration law.[46] Editor Filippo del Lucchese revised and updated the style and language of the original Italian translation, adding many translator's notes. Like the 2008 French edition, this second Italian edition was published around the time of the bicentennial of the Haitian Revolution and reflects the many new titles on that subject. The 2006 *I Giacobini neri* does not contain James's original or updated bibliography, a considerable loss, but does contain an afterword by Madison Smartt Bell, who writes not only of James's rich use of sources but also of the author's "dogmatic" Marxism being antiquated and making the work age badly.[47] According to Bell, James's interpretation was conclusively invalidated by new evidence only discovered in the 1970s that Louverture was not only free by 1776 but also a slave owner and landowner himself.

A Cuban Spanish translation was a long time in the making, actively pursued by James from the early 1960s onward, as testified by his correspondence with Dr. de la Osa, Cuban minister of foreign affairs, and with René Depestre, Haitian writer at Cuba's Imprenta Nacional, who had fled to Cuba from Papa Doc Duvalier's regime in Haiti.[48] Depestre's 1961 letter about publishing *The Black Jacobins* asked James to change "a few political considerations," deemed to be of "a polemical character." There is no evidence to suggest that James made the Cuban changes proposed by Depestre.

Extracts of the appendix featuring Castro traveled to Cuba in 1975, where it was published in the influential literary-cultural journal *Casa de las Américas*.[49] This translation is marked "Selection and translation by A–Z," meaning that this was done by the journal's staff writers, in fact Roberto Fernández Retamar and his wife, Adelaida de Juan.[50] This version mutilates the original appendix, cutting it down from twenty-eight pages to only five. Some changes correct information about the dates of the Cuban Revolution, including a reference to how "five years later the people of Cuba are still struggling with the same toils" (391), and the correction of the start date of the revolution from "July 1958" to "July 1953" (411/69). Any anti-Stalinist references are omitted, including the story of James's close collaborator George Padmore's period as an active Communist heading up the Negro department of propaganda and organization in Moscow, as well as details of his sharp split with the Kremlin (397–99).

Also deleted are most references to race, Pan-Africanism, and Negritude, including James's extended commentary on Césaire's *Cahier*. This expunging of racial references is a legacy of the so-called Cuban black scare—a widespread fear of blackness among Cuban whites ever since the Haitian Revolution. It is also a reflection of how Cuba has tried to eradicate racism by banning by decree all forms of racial discrimination that could threaten Cuban unity.[51] Negritude and Pan-Africanism together form the bedrock of James's original appendix, and removing racial references changes the story told by the appendix overall about the need to break the shackles of the old colonial system, of which racism is shown to be an essential part.

A dual Spanish-Mexican edition came out in 2003 with Turner in Madrid and Fondo de Cultura Económica in Mexico, which draws parallels with the marvelous realism of Cuban writer Alejo Carpentier.

In 2010, Casa de las Américas eventually published *Los Jacobinos negros*, translated by Rosa López Oceguera and with an introduction by John Bracey, professor of Afro-American studies.[52] According to López, *The Black*

Jacobins was known as the most important book about the Haitian Revolution, and so she was urgently asked to translate it.[53] It was imperative to produce a Cuban edition of the book because James elucidates the Cuban Revolution as, like the Haitian Revolution, an essential building block of Caribbean identity. López translated the appendix again.

German publication of *The Black Jacobins* was also actively sought in 1968–69 via Sergio Bologna, Italian workerist comrade, and Jahnheinz Jahn, a German specialist on African literature, but *The Black Jacobins* only appeared in German in 1984.[54] This German publication was a joint venture between Verlag Neues Leben, one of the most important publishers in East Berlin, and Pahl-Rugenstein in Cologne, which was widely known as the "voice of the GDR" in West Germany.[55] Although the actual text of the two editions is identical, they have different titles, with *Die schwarzen Jakobiner: Toussaint L'Ouverture und die San-Domingo-Revolution* (The black Jacobins: Toussaint L'Ouverture and the San Domingo revolution) for Verlag Neues Leben, and *Schwarze Jakobiner: Toussaint L'Ouverture und die Unabhängigkeitsrevolution in Haiti* (Black Jacobins: Toussaint L'Ouverture and the independence revolution in Haiti) for Pahl-Rugenstein. The East German title is calqued more exactly on the original English title and subtitle, using the German form of the Anglicized French name for the colony Saint-Domingue coined by James himself: San Domingo. Its counterpart drops the definite article "The" of *The Black Jacobins*, emphasizing independence and the country's new name, Haiti.

This dual German edition contains none of James's own authorial prefaces, appendix, or bibliography. Instead, the work is mediated by an afterword written by Hans Bach, a historian at the University of Leipzig. Problematically, Bach conscripts James as "an ardent admirer" of Castro and the Cuban Revolution (444), whereas James's positions on both are more ambivalent.[56] Bach also introduces Negritude for German-speaking readers—something discussed directly by James in the missing appendix. He also focused on the need to correct the work's failings, especially certain terms not used in the proper Marxist-Leninist sense, according to him. Bach also dismisses James as a Trotskyist, describing this as an illness to which James temporarily "succumbed." Consequently, James's political formation in 1930s England is underplayed. Bach's afterword removes the text from James to a context more relevant to the 1980s GDR. This German edition is long, packed with forty-four photographic plates of Haitian visual art, from the catalog of a 1979 exhibition of Haitian art at the Berliner Festspiele. These images foreground Vodou and add anthropological and background commentary to the bones of James's history.

From his papers, it is clear that James also pursued a Japanese translation in 1968.[57] A Japanese edition in 1991 was timed by translator Yoshio Aoki to coincide with the bicentenaries of the outbreaks of the French (1789) and Haitian (1791) revolutions, triggered by the relative lack of knowledge throughout Japan about Haiti.[58] Aoki compares James's study to Ralph Ellison's 1952 novel *Invisible Man*, making a point about how colonial powers sought to contain the Haitian Revolution, making it "invisible." In a 2002 reprint, Aoki added an essay about Haitian history, titled "From Toussaint to Aristide." Aoki's essay charts especially the rise to the presidency of popular Haitian priest Jean-Bertrand Aristide, including his practice of liberation theology, the coup that temporarily removed him from 1991 to 1994, right up until the moment of the 2002 reprinting when he was back in power as Haitian president before a further February 2004 coup that would force him to leave Haiti again.

The Brazilian Portuguese edition was published in 2000 and reprinted in 2010. In addition to James's 1938 and 1980 prefaces, the appendix, and the updated bibliography, translator Afonso Teixeira Filho added a two-page biography of James, a four-page timeline from 1215 to 1995, and Wordsworth's sonnet "To Toussaint Louverture" to the appendix. The translator and Jacob Gorender, Brazilian historian of slavery responsible for writing the text on the cover flaps, frequently refer to parallels between Brazil and Haiti.[59] Translator's notes also give historical background information about Haitian Vodou's links to Brazil's syncretic religion Candomblé. Both Gorender and Filho reclaim Haiti as part of Latin America.

Performing *The Black Jacobins* on Radio, Stage, and Elsewhere

As one of the Caribbean's significant and trailblazing historical plays, *The Black Jacobins* has been remade in theatrical form by the region's most innovative contemporary directors like Rawle Gibbons, Yvonne Brewster, Eugene Williams, and Harclyde Walcott. These directors have, in their turn, subjected James's second play to radical forms of creative transformation. Rawle Gibbons was the director of three Caribbean productions of the play across Jamaica and Trinidad. He has also masterminded performances of the "Return of *The Black Jacobins*" *mas*-action—meaning a mass-based activist type of theater built on Trinidadian carnival/masquerade traditions—about slavery reparations and Haiti after the 2010 earthquake. Gibbons pioneered the revolutionary Caribbean theory and practice of "third theater."[60] For Gibbons, Caribbean third theater is a synthesis of first colonial European theater and second African/Amerindian folk rituals, an intervention that seeks to represent Caribbean historical events. One hallmark of Gibbons's theater practice is the location of performances often in unconventional spaces, including steelpan yards and open spaces. Of his 1979 production of *The Black Jacobins*, which traveled across Trinidad and Tobago, Judy Stone declared that "yard theater," as popularized by playwright and critic Marina Maxwell, had come of age and triumphed.[61]

Gibbons's subsequent 1993 production of *The Black Jacobins* was located at the Curepe Scherzando panyard. As a deprived area, Curepe provided its own unique soundtrack to the play. Gunshots and sirens were heard. Characters responded to these noises, incorporating improvisation into the performances. Gibbons also had uniformed militiamen force the audience to leave their seats for the intermission. At the play's end, the audience members were invited to sign a petition calling for a United Nations intervention force to be sent to Haiti. This innovative use of unconventional settings was used to encourage audience participation and call-and-response techniques of collaboration with the audience, calling on spectators to engage with present-day Haiti as part of the Caribbean's collective responsibility.

Adapted as a radio play, *The Black Jacobins* was broadcast on December 13, 1971, on BBC Radio 4 in the ninety-minute *Monday Play* slot.[62] Certain sounds have dramatic impact, such as the scratching of Toussaint's fountain pen as he signs the death warrant of his adopted nephew, Moïse.[63] Also sounded is Dessalines's symbolic creation of the new Haitian bicolor from the old French tricolor: "Christophe, give me a French flag. **See, I tear off the white strip—no white in our flag.**"[64] Toussaint's affair with plantation owner's wife Madame Bullet is also exposed verbally for blind radio by replacing the visual eyepatch prop with extra lines. In the radio play, markers of race and status are always spelled out, for example where Moïse points to "this French woman here," saying that she stands for "all symbols of colonialism."

The Black Jacobins continues to have a special impact on the stage that must be recognized, with theater playing a major role in disseminating the work, particularly across the Caribbean and in London. *Black Jacobins* afterlives must be sought not only on the page, but also on the stage in the fifty years since the 1967 premiere. After 1967 and his extensive collaboration with Lyndersay, James had direct input into the 1986 London staging by Yvonne Brewster three years before his death, and he attended a 1979 Trinidad performance at his Alma Mater, Queen's Royal College. The play has also been staged at least three times since the playwright's death in 1989. Ripples made by the drama can be tracked through interviews with directors, playbills, posters, program notes, and production scripts.

Pivotal in the making of Caribbean theater, the play has been staged at least five times across the Caribbean (1975 and 1982 in Jamaica, 1979 and 1993 in Trinidad, and 2004 in Barbados). For the 1975 Jamaican staging, director Rawle Gibbons recalls that his focus was on staging the first production in the Caribbean region. Revolution was the context of the play's Caribbean debut, as the Black Power movement and student-led protests escalating since 1968 exploded. Out of this context was born a more revolutionary Caribbean theater. Aptly, the play was harnessed for a more experimental theater practice, as evidenced by staging the play not on a formal stage but instead in the rotunda, or round, of an adjoining exhibitions space used for unconventional work.

Gibbons also directed the next 1979 Trinidad production, which rediscovered James for his native Trinidad. According to Judy Stone's review, the opening night "made Trinidad history as much as it celebrated Haiti's."[65] This piece of Trinidad history was also watched by James himself, and it would have been the first time he saw the play performed, since he had missed the Nigerian premiere. Memorialized in Stone's review was the playwright's reaction to the standing ovation at the end: "It was enough that the play was done," and "[h]e had not presumed to hope that it would be done as well," calling Claude Reid's interpretation of Dessalines "a revelation."[66]

The play returned to Jamaica in 1982 for its third Caribbean production, directed by Eugene Williams. This was the first production of the Graduate Theatre Company of the Jamaican School of Drama. Again, the 1982 production was experimental in nature, making novel use of space and avoiding the usual proscenium arch of small theaters. Critics praised the production's spare bare-essentials aesthetics as "Brechtian."[67] Production posters were headlined "A tragedy on the use and misuse of Power." Summing up the play's significance as "one of the historical, iconic cultural markers of Caribbean history and the struggle for nationhood," Williams sees the 1982 play production as an important doorway and "sort of apprenticeship place" for students coming out of the "cultural boil" of the 1960s and '70s—vibrant decades for theater and cultural development across the region.[68] Due to financial constraints, the five members of the School of Drama, along with a couple of members of the schools of music and dance, had to play multiple characters, leading one reviewer to advise a second viewing of the play to help understand who was playing what, and to assess strengths and weaknesses of each actor's multiple roles.[69]

At the other extreme was *The Black Jacobins* on the grandest possible scale: Yvonne Brewster's major 1986 London production, featuring a vast cast of twenty-three actors and a total crew of forty-six. Leading black actors of the time, including Norman Beaton, Mona Hammond, Trevor Laird, and Brian Bovell, turned down lucrative parts in order to do this play with a historical context, avoiding stereotyped comic caricatures or angry young men in inner-city-type roles. Generally seen as a milestone on the "same level as anything done by the Royal Shakespeare and the National," the play and its playwright were proclaimed by Caryl Phillips as deserving "reclassification near the head, if not at the head of what could be termed 'black British drama.'"[70]

As highlighted in a press release, the final performance on March 15, 1986, coincided with the anniversary of Paul Robeson's first performance as Louverture. Some reviews held the fifty-year gap against the play as evidence that it was now "dated," "outdated," and "discoloured around the edges," with an "odour of theatrical mothballs."[71] However, many positive reviews claimed that the play had not at all become dated and retained a topical relevance.[72] In the event, performances also coincided with the ousting of Haitian dictator Jean-Claude "Baby Doc" Duvalier on February 7, 1986. Immediately issuing a press release, Talawa Theatre Company noted that the play "places a unique perspective on Haiti's past with today's recent events."[73] Banners on posters for the show now proclaimed in bold capitals "**HAITI—HISTORY REPEATED!**," while Brewster's program note emphasized timeliness: "That this production should coincide with another Haitian Revolution has caused a shiver or two."[74] These "eerie" coincidences of the Haitian play "hard on the heels of Baby Doc Duvalier's ousting" were mainly seen as exciting and probably made the play's ending ring less melancholic, although some critics noted the historical irony with a weary note of déjà-vu.[75]

Gibbons staged his third production of the play in Trinidad in 1993, locating it within the specific moment of the 1991–94 coup. This was political theater to galvanize audiences into action by getting them to sign a petition calling for President Aristide's return and an end to political violence. The program bore a message from Aristide and also a note about the initiatives of the Haiti Action Support Team to raise wider Caribbean solidarity with Haiti. Performed not on a traditional stage but in the yard of the Scherzando

Steelband in Curepe, the play tried to shake the Caribbean out of its usual indifference to the plight of Haiti.[76] Actors playing *tontons macoutes* drove the audience out of their seats during the intermission, while others called on them to act now—"My friend, what are you going to do about Haiti?"—breaking down barriers between actor and spectator, past and present, stage and stalls, and foregrounding the crowd.[77]

Speaking to the contemporary moment was also the raison d'être of the 2004 production of the play in Barbados. This production was timed to coincide with the celebration of the bicentenary of Haitian independence, with the Barbados UWI Cave Hill campus's farewell to Rex Nettleford—dance authority, choreographer, and vice-chancellor of the University of the West Indies—and with the Association of Caribbean Historians' annual conference, relocated from Haiti. Hilary Beckles, pro-vice chancellor and principal of UWI Cave Hill Campus and an eminent Caribbean historian, concluded his introduction in the play program by calling Nettleford "a Jamaican Jacobin." Another Haitian coup d'état took place that year, which saw Aristide leave for exile a second time. In a speech at the gala performance, Nettleford commented on the fact that more than five hundred Haitians had been given refuge at that time.[78] Director Harclyde Walcott highlighted in the program that Haiti was still being "forced to continue its struggle for freedom, for self-actualisation."

Walcott recalls directing the play as a "straight" historical play, sticking to the script with "no adventurism."[79] His focus was on making the word-heavy text play by bringing it to life. One reason why this play is not mounted often, according to Walcott, is the fact that it requires such a large cast of thirty to forty people, of whom at least one-third need to be white. It was apparently a difficult feat to convince white performers that roles would be worth the effort, not portraying them "as devils who should be driven into the sea." No white masks were used, and Walcott recruited two octogenarians, a sixteen-year-old, and some people who had never acted or had not done so for fifty years. Nettleford congratulated Walcott on "getting so many people of every hue in the cast." It was a star-studded cast with very favorable reviews for the lead roles. Walcott says he would like to direct the epilogue, in the spirit of *Accidental Death of an Anarchist* (1970) and Dario Fo's notion of "continuous substitution," which involves the play-making process of adapting political and cultural references to fit the production context.[80] As it is, Walcott says the play does not actually end in terms of drama, even without the epilogue. Walcott hardly ever mounts the same play twice, but is tempted to do *The*

Black Jacobins as a musical or opera, or to mount all the Caribbean plays about the Haitian Revolution back-to-back.

Under Gibbons and Marvin George, Haitian-centered work continues to be developed in Trinidad through the carnival band Jouvay Ayiti (Daybreak Haiti).[81] The story of *The Black Jacobins* is being used to create a type of mas/mass action, using the medium of mas from Trinidad carnival combined with Haitian carnival *rara*. Now the Jouvay Ayiti band is performing under the banner "Return of *The Black Jacobins*," and the plan is to take "Return of *The Black Jacobins*" to Haiti for its first performance on Haitian soil.

Afterlives of *The Black Jacobins* play are also the afterlives of the earlier 1936 *Toussaint Louverture* play. In Liverpool on October 27, 2013, readings from *Toussaint Louverture* were performed for the first time in almost eighty years. Appropriately, the lead role was played by Tayo Aluko, who performs a one-man show, *Call Mr. Robeson*, about Paul Robeson, who first played the leading role in James's 1936 play. In addition, Tayo Aluko and friends also performed readings of the never-before-performed or published epilogue from the 1967 *Black Jacobins* play.[82] Students at Bowdoin College also performed an abridged version of *Toussaint Louverture* on November 20, 2014.[83]

"*The Black Jacobins* Moves in Mysterious Ways Its Wonders to Perform"

James would often tell the story of the impacts of *The Black Jacobins* across the world in different places, such as Haiti and South Africa. The heading above is adapted from James's account in the 1980 foreword of "one of the most remarkable experiences" of his book in apartheid South Africa.[84] There, as Marty Glaberman pointed out, the book became an "underground textbook," which was clandestinely copied and distributed in installments to the next readers.[85] Grant Farred has told of how he first came across the history in precisely this manner: "On an August Friday in 1979 when I was in high school, I was asked to come to the vice principal's office. Richard Owen Dudley [...] gave me one of those mimeographed chapters [...] and he said to me, 'Read this, and come to me on Monday morning and tell me what this is about.'"[86] This is precisely the same type of serious study of history that James promoted throughout his life.

Dudley was one of the leaders of the Non-European Unity Movement (NEUM), for which James was an important figure.[87] As Corinne Sandwith has noted, "Many of the founder members of the NEUM had some sort of affiliation with Trotskyist ideas so anyone who articulated an anti-Stalinist view from the Left was particularly interesting to them."[88] Sandwith has traced some important readings of James in early apartheid South Africa by the likes of Dudley and Marxist critic Dora Taylor.[89] Taylor reviewed *The Black Jacobins* in the popular Cape Town publication *Trek*.[90] Her review offers a window into James's history from the vantage point of apartheid South Africa. She signals that James's main "achievement lies in his analysis of the political and economic forces of the age providing the background of that revolt, the close relationship between the progress of the French Revolution and the fate of the slaves in San Domingo, and the influence of French and British colonial rivalry during twelve years of the struggle for freedom." Literary criticism is political for both James and Taylor. Her "Re-view" analysis makes James's history speak to contemporary political concerns where she is.

Taylor and the Unity Movement shared a preoccupation with radical cultural projects involving the reading and discussion of literature.[91] The South African NEUM activists' development of a radical educational program chimes with the independent education study circles associated with James and his own political organizations in places like Detroit, Montreal, and London. James and *The Black Jacobins* were interpolated in these ways into local South African antiapartheid struggles as they offered alternative views with which to counter and "write back" to the "single commanding [discursive] narrative" of imperialism-colonialism.[92] James and *The Black Jacobins* are appropriated and rewritten in their turn to critique and reconfigure the contemporary South African political scene.[93] According to Sean Jacobs, founder of the blog *Africa Is a Country*, *The Black Jacobins* has had a resurgence throughout South Africa in recent years.[94] A lecture series by David Austin from October 9–12, 2017, titled C. L. R. James—Life and Lasting Legacy, marked eighty years of *The Black Jacobins* in South Africa.[95]

One place where *The Black Jacobins* worked its wonders was Haiti itself. Such was its impact there, according to James, that it became "a sort of Bible" where it was "read and deeply admired."[96] The interconnections between the famous history and Haiti are complex and multilayered. From the start, James's history is intertwined with earlier French-language accounts of the revolution by Haitian historians, including Pauléus Sannon, Thomas Madiou, Beaubrun Ardouin, and Alfred Nemours, offering accounts of these histories and their sources in English for the first time in many cases. James would often focus on the journey of his work back to the Caribbean and Haiti of its inspiration via Paris, for example in a conversation with Stuart

Hall in 1986. The French translation in 1949 transported *Les Jacobins noirs* back to Haiti. Michel Acacia, Haitian sociologist, tells how back in 1949 there were not many books on the revolution, apart from Sannon's three-volume 1920 history.[97] Even if at this point in the mid-twentieth century there was in Haiti a distinct privileging of histories of the Haitian Revolution written by Haitians, as Matthew J. Smith has noted, James's history would have attracted notice among Haitian intellectuals as it is a sympathetic portrayal of Haiti and its revolution—uncommon among other books written by foreigners at that time.[98]

Crucially, the 1949 publication of the French translation came right on cue in the lead-up to a major commemoration: the tricinquantenaire—the 150th anniversary of the Haitian Revolution in 1954.[99] Tricinquantenaire-induced historical fever, as Michel-Rolph Trouillot has noted, was given a boost by James's history.[100] *Les Jacobins noirs* contributed to the profusion of new titles being introduced at this time by Haitian historians: works by the likes of Étienne Charlier and Jean Fouchard. An important part of James's legacy lies in the impact he had on the focus, style, and political orientation of Haitian historians, extending the life of the historical imagination, particularly in the land of the work's inspiration. From 1949 onward, *Les Jacobins noirs* opened up new Marxist perspectives in Haitian history, with Charlier the first to explicitly espouse a Marxist viewpoint. Congratulating the Haitian historian on his 1954 book, James wrote that he had learned much from him, especially about "the revolutionary and creative power of untaught slaves," but contested Charlier's claim that Louverture was a man of the ancien régime.[101] Certainly, James's book also influenced Haitian historians' foregrounding of Louverture, whose role had been downplayed by some Haitian historiography. According to James himself in a 1971 interview, Haitians had discovered "a new conception of the role of Toussaint in the revolution."[102] On the subject of Haitian maroons, James also introduced the translation of his protégé Fouchard's work to new English readers.

James planned to travel to Haiti in the 1950s. Already in 1953, he sent a copy of the *Toussaint Louverture* script to the Haitian embassy in London. Although it is not clear what exactly James's proposition was, it can be inferred from Secretary Gérard Jean-Baptiste's reply that James was planning to visit the birthplace of his material and hoping to see his play performed in Haiti itself.[103] Throughout 1958, he corresponded with two Haitian intellectuals—Félix Morisseau-Leroy and Jean Brierre—about coming to Haiti that same year.[104] Morisseau-Leroy contacted newly elected Haitian president François

Duvalier himself, who conveyed his "pleasure" at the prospect of inviting "the famous author of *Les Jacobins noirs*" to Haiti, adding that Haiti owed James a great debt of gratitude.[105] In the end, James returned to Trinidad in April 1958 after twenty-six years of absence to involve himself with politics there, postponing the Haiti trip indefinitely. Intriguingly, however, James would later make brief reference to a Haiti trip when interviewed by his assistant Anna Grimshaw about the history, describing Haiti as a "wild place, a dictatorship," adding, "I went there once but that was not a place to go and stay."[106] If James did ever make a trip to Haiti, I agree with Matthew J. Smith's assessment that it would likely have been during the rule of Jean-Claude "Baby Doc" Duvalier after the death of Papa Doc in 1971, although another possibility is that James briefly visited Haiti in the early years of his life, in the 1920s or early 1930s before coming to Britain.

Already in 1958, Papa Doc's dictatorial tendencies were clear, and James was no doubt aware of the July–September 1958 coup attempt by Alix Pasquet and other Haitian exiles. Explicitly, James would refer to the "brutality, savagery, even personal cruelties" of the Duvalierist regime.[107] From his papers and writings, it is clear that James always kept up to date with events in Haiti. When reviewing *The Black Jacobins*, he referred to Haitians as "the Black Sansculottes of 1964," and wrote, "This is now."[108] Directly condemning the "jungle politics" of Papa Doc Duvalier, who had just declared himself president for life, James also denounced Papa Doc's tontons macoutes as "armed gangsters" and damned foreign powers for propping up the dictator.

By 1980, *Les Jacobins noirs* was out of print.[109] Only from 1983 onward would the title become widely available again, thanks to the second French edition by Éditions Caribéennes. Around the turn of the twenty-first century and the build-up of historical fever about the 2004 bicentennial of Haitian independence, a new Haitian edition was published by Fardin in 2008 as part of their Collection du bicentenaire Haïti 1804–2004. This facsimile of the 1983 Éditions Caribéennes text contains the same translations by Naville and Fivel-Demoret. The 2008 Fardin Haitian edition suggests that this is still a popular and sought-after title in Haiti.

Certainly, the title of the book is well known throughout Haiti, even among those who have not actually read it.[110] This is especially important in a place like Haiti—a country with a high illiteracy rate, but where the book and its culture are venerated. From a Haitian perspective, James's memorable title has been criticized, notably by Michel-Rolph Trouillot, who signaled that it sidelines the Haitian Revolution, as if it were an appendix to the

French Revolution. For Michel Hector, president of the Société haïtienne d'Histoire et de Géographie, *Les Jacobins noirs* is more than just a memorable title, it is a *livre-phare*, a beacon book for a new approach to the Haitian Revolution and the founding of the nation-state.[111] This beacon was used by Hector to underpin his 2009 plea for a conference to be organized sometime during 2010 to renew the teaching of Haitian history, using James's work as a basis. Unfortunately, the Haitian earthquake struck on January 12, 2010, disrupting these plans.

Selma James has written of how James's book was called on again after the earthquake, with many people turning to *The Black Jacobins* because they wanted to know who the Haitians were.[112] She writes of how this history "reignited Haiti and its revolutionary past" for new readers. As the first democratically elected Haitian president, Aristide, told Selma James on his return to Haiti in 2011, *The Black Jacobins* "had put Haiti on the map" because "people didn't know where it was before," also revealing that former South African president Thabo Mbeki had said he knew that the antiapartheid forces would win when he read the history.[113] From the perspective of successive pasts and presents, and for the futures in those pasts and presents, James was always translating Haiti and its revolution for Anglophones and speakers of other languages from the 1930s onward, inspiring new generations of today's black and Haitian Jacobins, both inside and outside Haiti itself.

Impacts were also felt elsewhere, with *The Black Jacobins* inspiring the political work of activists across the world, including student protesters against French rule in Martinique. James's papers include famous handwritten tracts defiantly saying no to the French colonial exploitation of the Caribbean by organizations including the Association Générale des Étudiants Martiniquais in 1958, and the Organisation de la Jeunesse Anticolonialiste de la Martinique from 1962 onward, and a copy of *Combat Ouvrier* from October 11, 1972, about the French Antilles.[114] It is significant that James supported these causes looking for the autonomy of the French Caribbean, as he always had a wider vision of a truly pan-Caribbean federation, including Haiti and "those two lost souls Martinique and Guadeloupe."[115]

Another place where James passed on the torch to new generations was in Montreal. David Austin has documented the C. L. R. James Study Circle (CLRJSC), which provided a political and intellectual home for James among West Indian students from the mid-1960s onward.[116] James gave important lectures in Montreal and also a series of private political classes there for CLRJSC members. James played an active role in the group's activities, including the Congress of Black Writers in October 1968, where James was applauded, and he kept abreast of the pivotal Sir George Williams University Affair—a student occupation of a computer lab that started as a protest against low marks for black students.[117] Among those arrested would be prominent CLRJSC members, including Rosie (Roosevelt) Douglas, who would later become prime minister of Dominica, and Anne Cools from Barbados, who would subsequently become a Canadian senator.[118] Part of James's legacy, then, lies in the ferment embodied by these two significant events in Montreal and their aftermath. Many of James's followers would later become active political figures in their respective countries, with Walter Rodney, Rosie Douglas, and Tim Hector capturing the political imagination and guiding the activity of Caribbean people from different islands.[119]

Multimedia *Black Jacobins*

The impacts of *The Black Jacobins* spread to various media beginning in the late twentieth century. During James's lifetime, he actively pursued new stagings of the play as well as a film version. As he wrote to Trinidadian director and playwright Marina Maxwell in 1967, he was on the verge of sending the play to the Rank Organization where, he said, "I understand there is an excellent possibility that they will take out an option." He also approached Sepia Films and British Lion Films about such a possibility.[120] Sound and video recordings of James speaking are scattered throughout the world. One major recording was James's lectures on *The Black Jacobins*, delivered at the Institute of the Black World, Atlanta, June 14–18, 1971.[121] Recordings of these lectures can be found today at the Schomburg Center for Research on Black Culture, New York; Michigan State University Libraries; and the West Indian and Special Collection, University of the West Indies Library, Mona. Some of these lectures were transcribed and published in the journal *Small Axe* in 2000.[122]

Mike Dibb, veteran English filmmaker, has made two landmark documentaries about James, including *Beyond a Boundary* in 1976, a film based on James's classic book about cricket by the same title.[123] Dibb also made the 1986 documentary *C. L. R. James in Conversation with Stuart Hall* for British TV Channel 4, which covers James's life and political development, including *The Black Jacobins*.[124] Other pioneering films featuring James include *Talking History* (1983), directed by H. O. Nazareth and featuring James in conversation with E. P. Thompson, and six lectures by James on Shakespeare, cricket, American society, Solidarity in Poland, the Caribbean, and Africa (1982), which were broadcast on Channel 4 on November 2, 1982.[125]

James was profiled in David Austin's outstanding three-part radio documentary *C. L. R. James: The Black Jacobin*, broadcast on the CBC radio program *Ideas* in December 2008, which features in-depth interviews with Robert Hill, Stuart Hall, Selma James, Aldon Lynn Nielsen, Paget Henry, and Tariq Ali, among others.[126] Hill outlines how *The Black Jacobins* was modeled on Tolstoy's *War and Peace* and is, in fact, the Caribbean *War and Peace*: "the equivalent of what Tolstoy's epic is for Russian literature." Hall shows how James's focus on a "world-historical moment which has the Caribbean at its center" rewrites the "history of Western Capitalism from the margins [. . .] rewriting some of the central episodes of the modern world. That's what he did." Tariq Ali made it clear how James's *Black Jacobins* had helped him respond to events in Haiti today, including the coups against popular Haitian president Aristide in 1991–94 and 2004. Likewise, Selma James has also frequently used *The Black Jacobins* to talk about what is happening with Aristide and Haiti now in the twenty-first century.

In March 2016, the first feature-length documentary on C. L. R. James was released.[127] It explores his life, writings, and politics, especially in England, but also in the Caribbean and the United States. *The Black Jacobins* is covered at length as one of James's most celebrated works and is explored as a masterpiece of historical scholarship and political analysis. The film mixes archive footage of James himself with testimony from some of the people closest to him, and from James scholars from across the world and a range of disciplines. This film was uniquely produced in James's own image, as pioneer of the history of the dispossessed from the bottom up. It was a collective effort by over two hundred volunteer camera operators, presenters, and researchers, mostly trained from scratch by the charity Worldwrite. This was in the spirit of James's conviction that "every cook can govern"—the title of one of his works, which in turn became the documentary film's title.[128] The film's release in March 2016 marked the culmination of Worldwrite's multimedia project, which resulted in a C. L. R. James online knowledge portal, featuring footage of conferences, lectures, and performances, as well as a timeline of James's life and further information on an extensive range of his works.[129]

As for adapting *The Black Jacobins* for the screen, it has recently been announced that Kwame Kwei-Armah—artistic director of London's Young Vic Theatre and himself a playwright, director, and actor—is to adapt James's *The Black Jacobins* history for a ten-part television series.[130] Having optioned the book in November 2018, Foz Allan, the creative director of UK-based Bryncoed Productions, will produce the series. While it is still early days for the *Black Jacobins* television adaptation, Kwei-Armah and Allan are discussing ways of shaping and framing the dramatic action and storytelling.[131] According to Kwei-Armah, "Some books change you; other books change everybody who reads them. *The Black Jacobins* is one such book." He sums up his own personal transformation as "viscerally tilting" his axis so much that it "changed the way I see the world we live in today."[132] Once again, it is the history's transformative potential that is highlighted above all else.[133]

Monumental Afterlives and Legacy

James is remembered in some significant physical sites. There have been frequent attempts to construct, maintain, and transform physical sites of memory that have an association with James, and to make these places available to visit. Both before and during James's own lifetime, the lives of the man himself and his most famous work have been extended into monumental, canonical, and more stable points of reference. Projected and established monumental afterlives include libraries, institutes, foundations, centers, auditoriums, and archive collections bearing and honoring his name, including the C. L. R. James Library in Hackney, London, in 1985; the Nello James Centre in Manchester in 1967; the former C. L. R. James Institute in New York City in 1984; plans and efforts to establish a projected C. L. R. James Foundation or Institute in London between 1983 and 1996; the C. L. R. James Educational Centre (also known as the Butler-Rienzi Labour College), San Fernando, Trinidad; the C. L. R. James Auditorium at the Cipriani College of Labour and Co-operative Studies in Valsayn, St. Joseph, Trinidad, home to the annual C. L. R. James Memorial Lecture; and the C. L. R. James Cricket Research Centre Library, University of the West Indies, Cave Hill Campus, Barbados.[134] In London, there was even a C. L. R. James Supplementary School in London, which was set up in 1969 by Ansel Wong and Jack Hines to give extra tuition for children of West Indian origin, an initiative to which James chose to put his name.[135] James was also honored by English Heritage, which mounted a blue plaque at his last home in Brixton. Recently, James's picture was chosen for the Brixton Pound £10 note. There has been an intensification of the call to remember C. L. R. James in public spaces, especially as those who knew him best are dying out.

All these commemorations of James's life and work celebrate the importance of James the writer as monument. Already during his own lifetime, James was considered a living monument, and in 1980 he himself remarked, "I have been labelled the Greatest Living Marxist, and the Greatest Living Pan-Africanist, I am treated with great distinction in the capitals of Western Civilization."[136] John La Rose, writer, political activist, and founder of New Beacon Books, also saw James as a living monument who "established a link for us in his own person between the past and our activities in the present."[137] Particularly since the 1980s when James the living monument was in his eighties, monumental sites of memory associated with him have created stable points of reference for all those interested in James. This is already having a considerable influence on the legacies of James and *The Black Jacobins*. One of the strengths of these legacies has been that his work, while not tied down to any one place or country and operating internationally across borderlines, has been at the same time rooted in certain locations that were important for James during his lifetime, such as "the front line" in Brixton, where he spent his final days in the 1980s on Railton Road in a flat above the Race Today Collective, or at the Oilfields Workers' Trade Union in San Fernando, where James had a base in Trinidad. James's photo still adorns the window of the former Race Today Collective premises, which is now part of the Brixton Advice Centre.

Nevertheless, some of these monuments to James's life and work are not so stable, as their fate has shown. Cases of the actual fragility of monuments include the furor over the renaming of the C. L. R. James Library in Dalston, Hackney, London, and the fates of the Nello James Centre in Manchester and the C. L. R. James Institute in New York. In 1985 Dalston library was renamed the C. L. R. James Library, which was seen as a statement of African and Caribbean people's contribution to world literature and as a symbol of Hackney's progress in tackling racism during its "anti-racist year," 1985.[138] To celebrate the new name, Hackney Council produced a sixteen-page booklet titled "C. L. R. James: The Black Jacobin."[139] There was also a C. L. R. James Week to coincide with the renaming ceremony on March 29, 1985.[140] This renaming constituted a memorial initiative from below: apt for memorializing James, the pioneer of history from below.[141] Some argued that James's own connections to Hackney were somewhat tenuous, but Hackney was a "socialist borough," and James provided a radical black anticolonial figurehead for Dalston library, which helped the library to be more representative of the racial profile of its own community and more relevant to Hackney as an antiracism battleground. Events in 1985 linked to the renaming drew in large crowds.[142]

In 2010 when the council announced that the library was moving to a new £4.4 million development nearby, they also let it be known that "C. L. R. James" would be dropped from the name.[143] The Black and Ethnic Minority Arts Network, based in Hackney, launched a campaign to save the name, along with support from local alliance Hackney Unites. The campaign centered on a petition declaring that "having C. L. R. James's name on the library is an honour—to the library" and that to remove it would be an "act of vandalism." Winning local and international support with over 2,500 signatures, the petition pressured Hackney Council into revoking the name change. While this particular monument endured despite such threats, others have not been as enduring.

The C. L. R. James Institute, which was founded in New York in 1983 by Jim Murray according to James's wishes, has disappeared. Due to the ephemerality of the internet, the former institute website no longer functions, highlighting issues of preservation of virtual resources linked to James. Following Murray's death in 2003, the institute was run by Ralph Dumain. However, the institute's papers have been transferred to Columbia University, where they are finally open for consultation. This and other archive collections linked to James are already fueling new generations of scholarship.

In some cases, then, C. L. R. James's name on these places has come dangerously close to being lost for good. Even the outward physical stability of buildings can prove frail and temporary when premises move. A case in point is James's childhood house in Tunapuna, overlooking the cricket pitch that he describes so vividly in *Beyond a Boundary*. This house, featured in the documentary *Every Cook Can Govern* in 2016, has now sadly been torn down. Commemorative acts that renew, rearticulate, and reinforce points of reference are needed to keep James's name alive in the community. In contrast with the materiality and locatedness of monuments and renamed buildings, James's books, articles, and other writings are highly portable. Nevertheless, many of his writings remain ephemeral due to the collaborative nature of his work. Because of the types of political organizations in which James was involved, his work was often collective and unpublished, with copies being sent out across the world. Compared to the work of other well-known political figures and writers, this has led to a situation where the published work represents only a tiny percentage of the full output of one of the great intellectual figures of the twentieth century.[144]

Recent conferences and films about James's life and work are also adding new pages to his legacy, including conferences in London organized by the London Socialist Historians Group in 2008 ("Seventy Years of *The Black Jacobins*," February 2, 2008) and the C. L. R. James Legacy Project in 2013, and symposia held in Glasgow (*"Beyond a Boundary*: 50 Years On," May 9–11, 2013, University of Glasgow), Liverpool ("*The Black Jacobins* Revisited: Rewriting History," October 27–28, 2013, University of Liverpool), and New York ("C. L. R. James Now!" November 4, 2016, CUNY Graduate School).

Conclusion: *The Black Jacobins* as Multilayered Palimpsest

French historian Pierre Nora has suggested that particular sites become the locus of collective memory.[145] His concept of *lieux de mémoire* is useful for this examination of how James and his works have been treated as monuments. According to Nora, a lieu de mémoire is "any significant entity, be it material or non-material in nature, which human will or the work of time has rendered into a symbolic element of the memorial heritage of any community."[146] Lieux are not necessarily always places here but refer to where memory is crystallized in buildings, artifacts, books, monuments, images, and so on. The lieux are the vestiges and outer shells of living memories, and Nora's conception is marked by a fin de siècle pessimism, for example, when he remarks, "We speak so much of memory because there is so little left of it."[147]

Aspects of Nora's lieux de mémoire approach to the writing of history are problematic and have been severely criticized, including Nora's Francocentric insistence on lieux de mémoire applying to France alone, and only to an eternal and unchanging French national identity. Recently, there have been attempts to take the idea out of its French and European frameworks and test it in a wider range of colonial and postcolonial situations.[148] Nora's concept needs to be extended in order to document James-related physical sites of memory, which constitute a transnational constellation because memories of James go beyond national boundaries, as did he. It was important for James to write a history about colonials taking place because colonialism and geopolitics have always been driven by desire for conquest of malleable space.[149]

One important concern for James was the memorialization of slavery and colonization, and especially how colonized peoples fought against them. We have seen how he literally wrote back to colonial narratives, biased historiography, and racist articles dealing with supposedly terrible Haitian atrocities. His repeated rewriting of his Haitian narrative was an ongoing process of contestation and decolonization, cracking the colonial edifice by writing back to the colonial powers' grand-scale self-fashioning that helped to legitimize colonial rule.[150]

Post/colonial sites of memory have been conceptualized as a palimpsest by Jay Winter.[151] To conclude, I use the model of the palimpsest to connect the various versions of *The Black Jacobins* and the memorial sites associated with James. Palimpsests are embedded in these physical sites: the constant process by which they are made and change in meaning. His writing about the Haitian Revolution can be seen as an overwritten palimpsest, with new layers added on top of the vestiges of the previous written traces. *The Black Jacobins* can be thought of as a palimpsest precisely because its 1938 "foundation would remain imperishable," with the history remaining substantially the same for subsequent editions and the embedded vestiges becoming important parts of the new whole. Like a palimpsest, *The Black Jacobins* is overwritten and reflects the multiple stories James told about colonial history and the anticolonial struggles of the colonized in order to build a (federal) West Indian nation. The contradictory stories that James would tell in drafts of his autobiography never settled into finished form. An apt visualization for this never-ending process is James's tombstone in Tunapuna, Trinidad, which takes the form of an always-open book to memorialize James as a man of letters (figure 5.4).

This book has traced the development of James's Haitian Revolution–related writings through *The Black Jacobins* and beyond, through articles, histories, and plays. I would like to examine the rewriting of *The Black Jacobins* project in the light of James's analysis in *Notes on Dialectics*, a document originally worked out in 1948 in letter form.[152] In a 1980 interview, James would declare that *Notes* was his most important work, and proclaimed that the greatest contributions of his life's work had been "number one, to clarify and extend the heritage of Marx and Lenin. And number two, to explain and expand the idea of what constitutes the new society."[153] This conclusion now ends by charting the dialectical development of *The Black Jacobins* and James's other Haitian Revolution writings, arguing that James's rewriting of *The Black Jacobins* is itself a dialectical development. My conclusion is that *The Black Jacobins* and James's other writings on the Haitian Revolution are in a state of continuous motion and change. Rewriting for James is a truly dialectical method.

FIG. 5.4 C. L. R. James's tombstone in Tunapuna, Trinidad. Photo courtesy of Rianella Gooding.

Rewriting animates *The Black Jacobins* project in all its movement, from the very beginning of James's 1931 article invoking the biography of Toussaint Louverture. From the word go, James's Haitian Revolution writings can be thought of as rewriting historical misrepresentations, engaging with the Caribbean quarrel with history, and writing back to correct falsifications and distortions in previous accounts of the revolution. On another level, James can also be thought of as rewriting Marx, Lenin, and Trotsky by clarifying, extending, explaining, and expanding their heritage as outlined in that same interview in 1980.[154] As in all Marxist accounts of history, revolution occupies a special place in James's writing. *The Black Jacobins* provided a remarkable exemplar of Marxist historical writing, breaking new ground by applying Marx's method to a major new historical subject: the Haitian Revolution. At the crux of the whole *Black Jacobins* project is the Haitian

Revolution, itself seen as an event that rewrote history, creating an opening like Louverture's act of self-renaming, and causing far-reaching historical change. What rewriting encapsulates is the dynamic of revolutionary process. In this way, rewriting links *The Black Jacobins*—the history book that changed the way history was written—to the Haitian Revolution, which rewrote world history.

There are the rewritten versions of the plays and the history—the events of rewriting across the history of James's work on the Haitian Revolution. Indeed, the concrete rewriting of *The Black Jacobins* resembles the composition James outlines in *Notes on Dialectics* for Marx's *Capital*, which can be extrapolated to the dynamics of James's Haitian Revolution–related writing: if we examine *The Black Jacobins*, we see how James wrote a draft, then reorganized it completely, and then reorganized that. Here I am adapting James's comments about Marx's writing of *Capital* to *The Black Jacobins*.[155] Rewriting is also the dialectical method used by James throughout his projects on the Haitian Revolution. My task has been to trace the process of *The Black Jacobins*' own development, working out its form of movement and method of change. Change allows James to show that its mutability manifests what the Haitian Revolution is.

Here the essential dialectical movement is reflected in the form of rewriting. Rewriting is the concrete method for dealing with *The Black Jacobins*' matter, but also its manner. The content has the form, and the form has the content. Rewriting also links theory and practice. James always refused to separate theory from concrete struggle and practice. Rewriting enables James to get away from "the thin air of the most abstract of abstractions" and into practice.[156] James applies his theory to his historical writing with the dialectic as the central connection between the theory and practice of history that his work embodies, and his productive dialogue with new historical approaches. This book has attempted to give a sense of the continuous process of change and the dynamic, constantly changing nature of the work itself. On the dialogue between theory and practice in James's Haitian Revolution–related work, this study has sought to show how James applies his theories to the practice of history, giving, for example, special emphasis to the ideas of the Johnson-Forest approach about organization and the activity, spontaneity, and self-mobilization of the masses. When the different versions of James's writings on the Haitian Revolution are compared and contrasted, insights emerge that call for, teach, illustrate, and develop the free activity of the ordinary slaves and their popular leaders, and the reader is given the sense of watching dialogue, organization, spontaneity, and independent mass action develop.

Throughout *Notes on Dialectics*, any method constituting a finite or fixed nature is damned. James comments unfavorably, for example, about the "specific dialectic of American politics [remaining] a closed book (a vile phrase)."[157] If any closed book is vile, rewriting can be thought of as helping to keep the book of James's Haitian Revolution writings open, like the always-open book that is his tombstone in Tunapuna. James's rewriting repeatedly acts against fixed and static, finite and limited forms—qualities consistently associated with negative Stalinist categories and falsification throughout *Notes on Dialectics*.[158] Instead, the strong pattern drawn by James's reflexive rewriting turns back upon itself and has for an image the circle, which has neither beginning nor end.[159] Following James's commentary in *Notes on Dialectics*, his writing on the Haitian Revolution can be thought of like the practice of continually enlarging circles, a series of circles with each one including and yet excluding the previous circle.[160]

Chapter 4 used Augusto Boal's productive concept of reading unfinished open drafts of the play as the radical opposite of bourgeois finished theater, and this perspective about unfinished openness can be applied to James's writings about the Haitian Revolution as a whole. James's work on this subject—like the Haitian Revolution itself—can never be finished, nor ever end neatly and complacently in a closed state of serene repose like an image of the complete, finished bourgeois world. Instead, as we have seen, all of James's Haitian Revolution writings are intensely dialogic and polemical, always entering into dialogue and asking for explanations, and actively and transitively trying to fill in the gaps in the historical records. The open and unfinished form and contents of James's Haitian Revolution writings, including *The Black Jacobins*, reflect processes of dynamic political action, transformation, and re-creation, which are always becoming.

The Black Jacobins in all its multiple forms was a major achievement, making James one of the prime creators of West Indian history, politics, and literature. Collectively, the text-network created a blueprint, guide, and catalyst for action. This involved coming to terms with the legacies of Caribbean colonial history and rewriting it in order to constitute creatively a Caribbean character and voice. To rewrite the colonizer's history in *The Black Jacobins*, James turned inward to make the Caribbean see itself. From the start, James is concerned with self-representation and increasingly involves himself with showing a pattern of Caribbean identity development. Simultaneously, James stretches inward to reach further outward.[161]

Two masters of Trinidadian calypso—Black Sage (Phillip Murray) and Short Pants (Llewellyn McIntosh)—are known for their extempo on the subject of C. L. R. James versus Eric Williams.[162] The extempo calypso style involves improvising witty comments in the moment, challenging each other to a debate where each one riffs on the other's lines. Like the extempoing calypsonians who have remade James's famous book in their turn, James adds layer upon layer of constitutive elements to *The Black Jacobins*, actualizing his vision. New writing is superimposed on top of previous writing, leaving visible traces of the rewriting and transforming the work as a whole. These successive layers of rewriting and the original vestiges can be seen as a palimpsest or layered repository of the Caribbean pasts, presents, and futures that James built up over a period of almost six decades as part of the dynamic process of making *The Black Jacobins*.[163] Following James's own example, this palimpsestually multilayered text-network can be reactivated to change presents and new futures in light of successive pasts.

NOTES

Introduction

1. See the image of this advertisement in Charles Forsdick and Christian Høgsbjerg, eds., *The Black Jacobins Reader* (Durham, NC: Duke University Press, 2017), 15.
2. C. L. R. James, *The Life of Captain Cipriani* (Nelson: Coulton, 1932); C. L. R. James, *The Case for West Indian Self-Government* (London: Hogarth, 1933). See also Bridget Brereton, "Introduction," in C. L. R. James, *The Life of Captain Cipriani: An Account of British Government in the West Indies* (Durham, NC: Duke University Press, 2014), 1–29.
3. C. L. R. James, *Mariners, Renegades, and Castaways: The Story of Herman Melville and the World We Live In* (1953; repr., Hanover, NH: University Press of New England, 2001). James discusses the rewriting in C. L. R. James to Hill and Wang, November 9, 1960, University of the West Indies "C. L. R. James Collection [Sc 82]" (henceforth UWI), Box 7, Folder 180. James later wrote that he was "rewriting *Mariners, Renegades and Castaways* to make it more suitable for general reading" (C. L. R. James to Hill and Wang, January 23, 1961, UWI Box 7, Folder 180).
4. C. L. R. James, *A History of Negro Revolt* (London: FACT, 1938); C. L. R. James, *A History of Pan-African Revolt* (Washington, DC: Drum and Spear Press, 1969).
5. "As Franco's Moors have once more proved." James, *A History of Negro Revolt* (1938), 13; removed from James, *A History of Pan-African Revolt* (1969), 11.
6. C. L. R. James, *World Revolution, 1917–1936: The Rise and Fall of the Communist International* (London: Secker and Warburg, 1937; repr., Westport, CT: Hyperion, 1973). It is not clear whether this was with James's permission or not, or what role he played in the publication process.
7. C. L. R. James, *State Capitalism and World Revolution*, 4th ed. (1950; Chicago: Kerr, 1986).
8. Daryl Cumber Dance, "Conversation with C. L. R. James" (1980), in *New World Adams: Conversations with Contemporary West Indian Writers* (Leeds: Peepal Tree, 1992), 119.
9. See Grace Lee Boggs, "C. L. R. James: Organizing in the U.S.A., 1938–1953," in *C. L. R. James: His Intellectual Legacies*, ed. Selwyn R. Cudjoe and William Cain (Amherst:

University of Massachusetts Press, 1995), 163–72; Grace Lee Boggs, *Living for Change: An Autobiography* (Minneapolis: University of Minnesota Press, 1998).

10. See Joe Kelleher, *Theatre and Politics* (Basingstoke, UK: Palgrave Macmillan, 2009), 10.

11. On the multivoiced medium of drama, see Paul Breslin, "'The First Epic of the New World': But How Shall It Be Written," in *Tree of Liberty: Cultural Legacies of the Haitian Revolution in the Atlantic World*, ed. Dorris L. Garraway (Charlottesville: University of Virginia Press, 2008), 241.

12. David Scott, *Conscripts of Modernity: The Tragedy of Colonial Enlightenment* (Durham, NC: Duke University Press, 2004), 51; Charles Forsdick and Christian Høgsbjerg, "Introduction: Rethinking *The Black Jacobins*," in *The Black Jacobins Reader*, 1–52; Brett St Louis, *Rethinking Race, Politics, and Poetics: C. L. R. James's Critique of Modernity* (London: Routledge, 2007); Grant Farred, ed., *Rethinking C. L. R. James* (Oxford: Blackwell, 1996); Paul Buhle, "Rethinking the Rethinking," *C. L. R. James Journal* 6, no. 1 (1998): 61–71; Anthony Bogues, "Afterword," *Small Axe* 8 (2000): 113–17; Selwyn R. Cudjoe, "The Audacity of It All: C. L. R. James's Trinidadian Background," in Paget Henry and Paul Buhle, *C. L. R. James's Caribbean* (London: Macmillan Caribbean, 1992), 39–55; Selwyn R. Cudjoe, "C. L. R. James and the Trinidad and Tobago Intellectual Tradition, or, Not Learning Shakespeare under a Mango Tree," *New Left Review* 223 (1997): 114–25. See also Paul Buhle, "Afterword," in *C. L. R. James: The Artist as Revolutionary* (1988; repr., London: Verso, 2017), 174–211.

13. See Susan Gillman, "Black Jacobins and New World Mediterraneans," in *Surveying the American Tropics: A Literary Geography from New York to Rio*, ed. Maria Cristina Fumagalli, Peter Hulme, Owen Robinson, and Lesley Wylie (Liverpool: Liverpool University Press, 2013), 174. Eric Williams, *From Columbus to Castro: The History of the Caribbean, 1492–1969* (London: André Deutsch, 1970).

14. The second play has been published as *The Black Jacobins* in C. L. R. James, *The C. L. R. James Reader*, ed. Anna Grimshaw (Oxford: Blackwell, 1992); "The Black Jacobins," in *A Time and a Season: Eight Caribbean Plays*, ed. Errol Hill (Port-of-Spain: University of the West Indies, Trinidad, Extramural Studies Unit, 1976), 382–450. Page references refer to the 1976 edition of the play. See Nicole King, *C. L. R. James and Creolization: Circles of Influence* (Jackson: University Press of Mississippi, 2001), 30–51; Nicole King, "C. L. R. James, Genre and Cultural Politics," in *Beyond Boundaries: C. L. R. James and Postnational Studies*, ed. Christopher Gair (London: Pluto, 2006), 13–38; Reinhard Sander, "C. L. R. James and the Haitian Revolution," *World Literature Written in English* 26, no. 2 (1986): 277–90; Reinhard Sander, *The Trinidad Awakening: West Indian Literature of the Nineteen-Thirties* (New York: Greenwood, 1988), 91–114; Frank Rosengarten, *Urbane Revolutionary: C. L. R. James and the Struggle for a New Society* (Jackson: University Press of Mississippi, 2008), 220–32.

15. Other scholarship on C. L. R. James and *The Black Jacobins* that has been influential to this study include: Anthony Bogues, *Black Heretics, Black Prophets: Radical Politi-*

cal Intellectuals (New York: Routledge, 2003); Anthony Bogues, "The Black Jacobins and the Long Haitian Revolution: Archives, History, and the Writing of Revolution," in Forsdick and Høgsbjerg, The Black Jacobins, 197–214; Anthony Bogues, Caliban's Freedom: The Early Political Thought of C. L. R. James (London: Pluto, 1997); Brian Meeks, Radical Caribbean: From Black Power to Abu Bakr (Mona, Jamaica: University of the West Indies Press, 1996); Andrew Smith, C. L. R. James and the Study of Culture (London: Palgrave Macmillan, 2010); Cedric J. Robinson, Black Marxism: The Making of the Black Radical Tradition (London: Zed, 1983).

16. C. L. R. James, The Black Jacobins: Toussaint Louverture and the San Domingo Revolution (London: Allison and Busby, 1980), vi.

17. Paula Morgan, qtd. in Kwynn Johnson, "Place as Palimpsest—Yon kote tankou Palimpseste," Caribbean Quarterly 63, nos. 2–3 (2017): 169–76. My understanding of palimpsests is influenced by Trinidadian artist Kwynn Johnson's exploration of place and meaning in contemporary Cap Haïtien through her physical and symbolic etchings of that landscape. Her 2017 visual artwork Place as Palimpsest/Yon kote tankou Palimpseste builds on the set she created, along with Carol Williams, for a 2004 staging of Derek Walcott's play The Haitian Earth. Johnson developed Place as Palimpsest as a storyboard of Walcott's play, which also speaks to other Haitian concerns, notably dictatorship and the twenty-first-century outbreak of cholera.

18. Gérard Genette, Palimpsests: Literature in the Second Degree (Lincoln: University of Nebraska Press, 1997).

19. Gérard Genette, Paratexts: Thresholds of Interpretation (Cambridge: Cambridge University Press, 1997).

20. I follow Richard Watts's skillful combination of Genette and postcolonial theory in his analysis of paratexts in Francophone postcolonial literature. Richard Watts, Packaging Post/Coloniality: The Manufacture of Literary Identity in the Francophone World (Lanham, MD: Lexington, 2005).

21. See, for example, Robert Fraser, Book History through Postcolonial Eyes: Rewriting the Script (London: Routledge, 2008); Sarah Brouillette, Postcolonial Writers in the Global Literary Marketplace (Basingstoke, UK: Palgrave Macmillan, 2007); Graham Huggan, The Postcolonial Exotic: Marketing the Margins (London: Routledge, 2001); Watts, Packaging Post/Coloniality.

22. For criticisms of genetic criticism, see Marion Schmid, Processes of Literary Creation: Flaubert and Proust (Oxford: Legenda, 1998), 3n4, 23–27, 29; Dirk Van Hulle, Manuscript Genetics, Joyce's Know-How, Beckett's Nohow (Gainesville: University Press of Florida, 2008), 9, 17, 29.

23. On genetic criticism, see William Kinderman and Joseph E. Jones, Genetic Criticism and the Creative Process: Essays from Music, Literature, and Theater (Rochester, NY: University of Rochester Press, 2009); Jed Deppman, Daniel Ferrer, and Michael Groden, Genetic Criticism: Texts and Avant-Textes (Philadelphia: University of Pennsylvania Press, 2004); Van Hulle, Manuscript Genetics.

24. On genetic criticism and theater, see Almuth Grésillon, Marie-Madeleine Mervant-Roux, and Dominique Budor, eds., *Genèses théâtrales* (Paris: CNRS, 2010); Josette Féral, ed., "Genetics of Performance," special issue, *Theatre Research International* 33, no. 3 (2008); Nathalie Léger and Almuth Grésillon, eds., "Théâtre," special issue, *Genesis* 26 (2005).

25. Almuth Grésillon, *Éléments de critique génétique: Lire les manuscrits modernes* (Paris: Presses universitaires de France, 1994).

26. See, however, the issue of the journal *Genesis* that does look at the trajectory of rewriting after publication: Rudolf Mahrer, ed., "Après le texte: De la réécriture après publication," special issue, *Genesis* 44 (2017).

27. Claire Riffard and Daniel Delas, eds., "Afrique–Caraïbe," special issue, *Genesis* 33 (2011).

28. On theatrical genesis, see Grésillon, Mervant-Roux, and Budor, *Genèses théâtrales*.

29. UWI Box 9, Folder 228, 24; UWI Box 9, Folder 229.

30. William Gibson, *The Seesaw Log: A Chronicle of the Stage Production* (New York: Knopf, 1959).

31. Augusto Boal, *Theater of the Oppressed* (London: Pluto, 2008).

32. Boal, *Theater of the Oppressed*, 28.

33. Afterlife is a metaphorical notion used here to invoke the relations between the source text and its avatars. My work on the afterlives of *The Black Jacobins* builds on work by Terence Cave, Ann Rigney, Richard Scholar, and Anna Holland, among others, outlining critical methods for engaging with this usable metaphor of afterlives. See Terence Cave, *Mignon's Afterlives* (Oxford: Oxford University Press, 2011); Ann Rigney, *The Afterlives of Walter Scott: Memory on the Move* (Oxford: Oxford University Press, 2012); Anna Holland and Richard Scholar, eds., *Pre-Histories and Afterlives: Studies in Critical Method* (Oxford: Legenda, 2009). Useful for my purposes have also been Kristin Ross, *May '68 and Its Afterlives* (Chicago: University of Chicago Press, 2004); and Eric Hobsbawm, *Echoes of the Marseillaise: Two Centuries Look Back on the French Revolution* (London: Verso, 1990).

34. C. L. R. James, "Lectures on *The Black Jacobins*," *Small Axe* 8 (2000): 65–112.

35. See Brouillette, *Postcolonial Writers in the Global Literary Marketplace*, 11–12, 67–69, 104; Christopher Watkin, "Rewriting the Death of the Author: Rancièrian Reflections," *Philosophy and Literature* 39 (2015): 32–46; Seán Burke, *The Death and Return of the Author: Criticism and Subjectivity in Barthes, Foucault, and Derrida* (Edinburgh: Edinburgh University Press, 1992).

36. On the special qualities of theater as literature, see Raphael Samuel, "Introduction: Theatre and Politics," in *Theatres of the Left, 1880–1935: Workers' Theatre Movements in Britain and America*, ed. Raphael Samuel, Ewan MacColl, and Stuart Cosgrove (London: Routledge and Kegan Paul, 1985), xiii; Kelleher, *Theatre and Politics*, 10, 13.

37. See C. L. R. James, *The Future in the Present: Selected Writings*, vol. 1 (London: Allison and Busby, 1977); Alun Munslow, *Narrative and History* (Basingstoke, UK: Palgrave Macmillan, 2007), 48.

38. On showing versus telling forms of historical representation, see Munslow, *Narrative and History*, 60.
39. See Hayden White, *The Content of the Form: Narrative Discourse and Historical Representation* (Baltimore, MD: Johns Hopkins University Press, 1987).
40. Kara M. Rabbitt, "C. L. R. James's Figuring of Toussaint Louverture: *The Black Jacobins* and the Literary Hero," in Cudjoe and Cain, *C. L. R. James*, 118–35; David Geggus, *Haitian Revolutionary Studies* (Bloomington: Indiana University Press, 2002), 31.
41. On this literary feel, see King, *C. L. R. James and Creolization*; King, "C. L. R. James, Genre and Cultural Politics," 13–38.
42. C. L. R. James, *Beyond a Boundary* (Durham, NC: Duke University Press, 2013), 121, 151.
43. Samuel, "Introduction," xiii; Kelleher, *Theatre and Politics*, 10, 13.
44. James, *The Black Jacobins* (1980), v.
45. Bernard Moitt, "Transcending Linguistic and Cultural Frontiers in Caribbean Historiography: C. L. R. James, French Sources, and Slavery in San Domingo," in Cudjoe and Cain, *C. L. R. James*, 136.
46. Thomas Madiou, *Histoire d'Haïti*, 2 vols. (Port-au-Prince: J. Courtois, 1847–48); Alexis Beaubrun Ardouin, *Études sur l'histoire d'Haïti, suivies de la vie du général J. M. Borgella*, 11 vols. (Paris: n.p., 1853–60; repr., Port-au-Prince: François Dalencourt, 1958).
47. Michel-Rolph Trouillot, "Haitian Historiography," in *General History of the Caribbean*, vol. 6, *Methodology and Historiography of the Caribbean*, ed. B. W. Higman (Paris: Unesco; London: Macmillan Education, 1999), 458.
48. C. L. R. James, *The Black Jacobins* (New York: Vintage, 1963), 387. References in this chapter are to the 1963 edition.
49. Michel Hector, "Pour un colloque sur l'enseignement de l'histoire en Haïti," *Revue de la Société haïtienne d'histoire et de géographie* 237 (2009): 47–60.
50. Trouillot, "Haitian Historiography," 462.
51. James himself used the historical term "mulatto" to refer to mixed-race black and white people throughout his writings.
52. See Geggus, *Haitian Revolutionary Studies*, 33.
53. Victor Schœlcher, *Vie de Toussaint Louverture* (1889; repr., Paris: Karthala, 1982).
54. Pamphile de Lacroix, *Mémoires pour servir à l'Histoire de la Révolution de Saint-Domingue* (Paris: Pillet aîné, 1819); Chris Bongie, "Introduction: Bug-Jargal, 1791: Language and History in Translation," in *Bug-Jargal*, trans. and ed. Chris Bongie (Ontario: Broadview, 2004), 9–47; Susan Gillman and Kirsten Silva Gruesz, "Worlding America: The Hemispheric Text-Network," in *The Blackwell Companion to American Literary Studies*, ed. Robert S. Levine and Caroline Levander (Oxford: Blackwell, 2011), 228–47.
55. Marlene L. Daut, *Tropics of Haiti: Race and the Literary History of the Haitian Revolution in the Atlantic World, 1789–1865* (Liverpool: Liverpool University Press, 2015), 522.

56. Nick Nesbitt, "Fragments of a Universal History: Global Capital, Mass Revolution, and the Idea of Equality in *The Black Jacobins*," in Forsdick and Høgsbjerg, *The Black Jacobins Reader*, 139–61.

57. See Alfred Auguste Nemours, *Histoire militaire de la guerre d'indépendance de Saint-Domingue*, 2 vols. (Paris: n.p., 1925); Alfred Auguste Nemours, *Histoire de la captivité et de la mort de Toussaint-Louverture* (Paris: n.p., 1929).

58. Trouillot, "Haitian Historiography," 461.

59. See Trouillot, "Haitian Historiography." Alfred Auguste Nemours, *Histoire de la famille et de la descendance de Toussaint-Louverture* (Port-au-Prince: Éditions Presses nationales d'Haïti, 2008).

60. Charles Forsdick, "The Black Jacobin in Paris," *Journal of Romance Studies* 5, no. 3 (2005): 17.

61. See Trouillot, "Haitian Historiography," 469.

62. Jean Fouchard, *Les Marrons de la liberté* (Paris: Éditions de l'École, 1972); C. L. R. James, "Preface," in Jean Fouchard, *The Haitian Maroons: Liberty or Death* (New York: Blyden, 1981), v–vii.

63. On the importance of these historiographical contributions by *The Black Jacobins*, see James, *The C. L. R. James Reader*, 5–7; VèVè A. Clark, "Haiti's Tragic Overture: (Mis)Representations of the Haitian Revolution in World Drama," in *Representing the French Revolution: Literature, Historiography, and Art*, ed. James A. W. Heffernan (Hanover, NH: University Press of New England), 239, 242.

64. See, for example, all the accolades for *The Black Jacobins* listed by Aldon Lynn Nielsen in his *C. L. R. James: A Critical Introduction* (Jackson: University Press of Mississippi, 1997), 52. According to Anna Grimshaw, this work "raised implicitly, a challenge to certain assumptions which were commonplace on the revolutionary Left. First of all, he cast doubt on the assumption that the revolution would take place first in Europe, and in the advanced capitalist countries, and that this would act as a model and a catalyst for the later upheavals in the underdeveloped world. Secondly, there were clear indications that the lack of specially-trained leaders, a vanguard, did not hold back the movement of the San Domingo revolution" (James, *The C. L. R. James Reader*, 7). Robert Hill's assessment is that *The Black Jacobins* "revolutionized historical writing in ways dealing both with conception and method"; Robert A. Hill, "In England, 1932–1938," in *C. L. R. James: His Life and Work*, ed. Paul Buhle (London: Allison and Busby, 1986), 79. Some associates of James have claimed, however, that such testimonies are overblown. See Farrukh Dhondy, *C. L. R. James* (London: Weidenfeld and Nicolson, 2001), 125–27, 163–66; Louise Cripps, *C. L. R. James: Memories and Commentaries* (London: Cornwall, 1997), 188–99.

65. Laurent Dubois, *Avengers of the New World: The Story of the Haitian Revolution* (Cambridge, MA: Harvard University Press, 2004), 298–99; Geggus, *Haitian Revolutionary Studies*, 207–15; Laurent Dubois and Julius Scott, eds., *Origins of the Black Atlantic: Rewriting Histories* (London: Routledge, 2010). Important studies of the Haitian Revolution and Toussaint Louverture include a graphic history by Rocky Cotard

and Laurent Dubois, "The Slave Revolution That Gave Birth to Haiti," *The Nib*, February 5, 2018, https://thenib.com/haitian-revolution; Jeremy Popkin, *A Concise History of Haiti* (Hoboken, NJ: Wiley-Blackwell, 2011); John Garrigus, *Before Haiti: Race and Citizenship in French Saint-Domingue* (Basingstoke, UK: Palgrave Macmillan, 2006); David P. Geggus, *The Impact of the Haitian Revolution in the Atlantic World* (Columbia: University of South Carolona Press, 2001); David B. Gaspar and David P. Geggus, eds., *A Turbulent Time: The French Revolution and the Greater Caribbean* (Bloomington: Indiana University Press, 2002); David P. Geggus and Norman Fiering, eds., *The World of the Haitian Revolution* (Bloomington: Indiana University Press, 2009); Deborah Jenson, *Beyond the Slave Narrative: Politics, Sex, and Manuscripts in the Haitian Revolution* (Liverpool: Liverpool University Press, 2011); Malick W. Ghachem, *The Old Regime and the Haitian Revolution* (Cambridge: Cambridge University Press, 2012); Charles Forsdick and Christian Høgsbjerg, *Toussaint Louverture: A Black Jacobin in the Age of Revolutions* (London: Pluto, 2017).

66. On the corresponding onomastic revolution taking place in the French language in France in response to the French Revolution—involving new titles such as *citoyen*, new calendar months such as *pluviôse*, renumbering years starting with "An I" (Year I), and new place names such as the Champ de Mars, see Steven Blakemore, "Revolution in Language: Burke's Representation of Linguistic Terror," in Heffernan, *Representing the French Revolution*, 3–23; Ronald Paulson, *Representations of Revolution (1789–1820)* (New Haven, CT: Yale University Press, 1983), 15–19; and Keith Michael Baker, *Inventing the French Revolution: Essays on French Political Culture in the Eighteenth Century* (Cambridge: Cambridge University Press, 1990), 203–7.

67. See David Geggus, "The Naming of Haiti," *New West Indian Guide* 71 (1997): 43–68.

68. Regarding the French Revolution, Paulson observes: "In terms of language, revolution makes words mean something else. [. . .] To fit in with the change of events, words, too, had to change their usual meanings." Paulson, *Representations of Revolution*, 15.

69. Haitian Declaration of Independence, January 1, 1804, Duke University Libraries, Digital Collections, http://library.duke.edu/digitalcollections/rubenstein_hdims01001/; Dubois, *Avengers of the New World*, 298; Laurent Dubois, *Haiti: The Aftershocks of History* (New York: Picador, 2012), 16.

70. Dubois, *Avengers of the New World*, 298; Geggus, *Haitian Revolutionary Studies*, 208. See also Louis Félix, *Mémoires pour servir à l'histoire d'Haïti* (Paris: n.p., 1851).

71. Marlene L. Daut, "Un-Silencing the Past: Boisrond-Tonnerre, Vastey, and the Rewriting of the Haitian Revolution," *South Atlantic Review* 74, no. 1 (2009): 35–64; Daut, *Tropics of Haiti*, 73–109.

72. Susan Buck-Morss, *Hegel, Haiti, and Universal History* (Pittsburgh: University of Pittsburgh Press, 2009); Sibylle Fischer, *Modernity Disavowed: Haiti and the Cultures of Slavery in the Age of Revolution* (Durham, NC: Duke University Press, 2004); Michel-Rolph Trouillot, *Silencing the Past: Power and the Production of History* (Boston: Beacon, 1995), 84, 88.

73. Nick Nesbitt, *Universal Emancipation: The Haitian Revolution and the Radical Enlightenment* (Charlottesville: University of Virginia Press, 2008). As Dubois and Scott make clear, even Diderot's famous ghostwritten passage in the Abbé Reynal's multivolume history of European colonialism was written firmly from the present and reads more as "a call/warning." Laurent Dubois and Julius Scott, "An African Revolutionary in the Atlantic World," in *Revolution! The Atlantic World Reborn*, ed. Thomas Bender, Laurent Dubois, and Richard Rabionwitz (New York: New York Historical Society, 2011), 144.

74. Sylvia Wynter discusses the fundamental importance for Jamaica of becoming "the agent and creative *subject* of our [history]," instead of being "the *object* of the history of other nations." Sylvia Wynter, *Jamaica's National Heroes* (Kingston: Jamaica National Commission, 1971). See also Anthony Bogues, "History, Decolonization and the Making of Revolution: Reflections on Writing the Popular History of the Jamaican Events of 1938," *Interventions* 12, no. 1 (2010): 76–87.

75. Eric Williams, *Capitalism and Slavery* (1944; repr., Chapel Hill: University of North Carolina Press, 1994).

76. Trouillot, "Haitian Historiography," 468.

77. Étienne Charlier, *Aperçu sur la formation historique de la nation haïtienne* (Port-au-Prince: Presses libres, 1954).

78. Trouillot, "Haitian Historiography," 469.

79. For ways in which François Duvalier imposed his history book, *Le Problème des classes à travers l'histoire d'Haïti*, 2nd ed. (Port-au-Prince: Au service de la jeunesse, 1959), during his dictatorship, see Hector, "Pour un colloque sur l'enseignement de l'histoire en Haïti," 47–60.

80. Trouillot, *Silencing the Past*, 26.

81. Trouillot, *Silencing the Past*, 105.

82. Fischer, *Modernity Disavowed*.

83. Naipaul claims that history "is built around achievement, and nothing was created in the West Indies." V. S. Naipaul, *The Middle Passage* (London: André Deutsch, 1961), 29.

84. Édouard Glissant, *Monsieur Toussaint* (Paris: Gallimard, 1961); Édouard Glissant, *Caribbean Discourse: Selected Essays*, trans. J. Michael Dash (Charlottesville: University Press of Virginia, 1989).

85. Leopold von Ranke, *Geschichten der romanischen und germanischen Völker von 1494 bis 1535* (Leipzig: Reimer, 1824).

86. Carolyn Fick, "C. L. R. James, *The Black Jacobins*, and *The Making of Haiti*," in Forsdick and Høgsbjerg, *The Black Jacobins Reader*, 60–69; Carolyn Fick, *The Making of Haiti: The Saint Domingue Revolution from Below* (Knoxville: University of Tennessee Press, 1990). Since 1990, Fick has revised and expanded her work in the 2013–2014 French-language editions of the book: Carolyn Fick, *Haïti, naissance d'une nation: La révolution de Saint-Domingue vue d'en bas*, trans. Frantz Voltaire (Rennes: Éditions Les Perséides, 2013; Montreal: Éditions du CIDIHCA, 2014). Frantz Voltaire, the Director of the Centre International de Documentation et d'Information Haïtienne, Caribéenne et Afro-canadienne, re-presents the book for new Francophone Haitian and Afro-Canadian readerships.

87. Fick, "Acknowledgements," in *The Making of Haiti*, xiv.

88. Fick, "C. L. R. James," 62, 64. C. L. R. James to Étienne Charlier, August 24, 1955, UWI Box 7, Folder 190.

89. Fick, *The Making of Haiti*, 4.

90. Alyssa Goldstein Sepinwall, *Haitian History: New Perspectives* (London: Routledge, 2013), 16.

91. Boal, *Theater of the Oppressed*.

1. Toussaint Louverture Takes Center Stage

1. C. L. R. James, "The Intelligence of the Negro: A Few Words with Dr. Harland," *The Beacon* 1, no. 5 (August 1931): 6–10; Sidney C. Harland, "Race Admixture," *The Beacon* 1, no. 4 (July 1931): 25–29.

2. C. L. R. James, *Toussaint Louverture: The Story of the Only Successful Slave Revolt in History: A Play in Three Acts*, ed. Christian Høgsbjerg (Durham, NC: Duke University Press, 2013), 54, 131. Further citations appear as page references in the text.

3. On *The Beacon*, see Brinsley Samaroo, "Introduction," in *The Beacon: Volumes I–IV, 1931–1939* (New York: Kraus, 1977), i–xiii; Reinhard Sander, "Introduction: The Beacon and the Emergence of West Indian Literature," in *The Beacon: Volumes I–IV, 1931–1939* (New York: Kraus, 1977), xv–xxv; Reinhard Sander, ed., *From Trinidad: An Anthology of Early West Indian Writing* (London: Hodder and Stoughton, 1978), 227–37.

4. See Edward Baugh, "The West Indian Writer and His Quarrel with History," *Tapia*, part 1 (February 20, 1977): 6–7; part 2 (February 27, 1977): 6–7, 11. Reprinted with minor editorial changes and corrections in *Small Axe* 38 (2012): 60–74. See also Alison Donnell, "All Friends Now? Critical Conversations, West Indian Literature, and 'The Quarrel with History,'" *Small Axe* 38 (2012): 75–85; Laurence A. Breiner, "Too Much History, or Not Enough," *Small Axe* 38 (2012): 86–98; Nadi Edwards, "Contexts, Criticism, and Quarrels: A Reflection on Edward Baugh's 'The West Indian Writer and His Quarrel with History,'" *Small Axe* 38 (2012): 99–107; and Edward Baugh, "Reflections on 'The Quarrel with History,'" *Small Axe* 38 (2012): 108–18. See also Laurent Dubois, "History's Quarrel: The Future of the Past in the French Caribbean," in *Beyond Fragmentation: Perspectives on Caribbean History*, ed. Juanita de Barros, Audra Diptee, and David V. Trotman (Princeton, NJ: Markus Wiener, 2006), 213–30.

5. T. Lothrop Stoddard, *The French Revolution in San Domingo* (Boston: Houghton Mifflin, 1914); James Anthony Froude, *The English in the West Indies; or, The Bow of Ulysses* (London: Longmans, Green, 1888).

6. C. L. R. James, "The West Indian Intellectual," in J. J. Thomas, *Froudacity: West Indian Fables Explained* (London: New Beacon, 1969), 23–49. On Thomas, see Faith Smith, *Creole Recitations: John Jacob Thomas and Colonial Formation in the Late Nineteenth-Century Caribbean* (Charlottesville: University of Virginia Press, 2002). On Thomas's striking silence about the Haitian Revolution itself, see Christian Høgsbjerg, *C. L. R. James in Imperial Britain* (Durham, NC: Duke University Press, 2014), 165–66; Christian Høgsbjerg, "Introduction," in C. L. R. James, *Toussaint Louverture* (Durham, NC: Duke University Press, 2013), 31n30.

7. "Froudacious" Froude is what James calls the historian in his 1969 introduction to *Froudacity*. On predecessor Thomas's use of the terms "Froudacity" and "Froudacious," see Smith, *Creole Recitations*, 155.

8. Robert A. Hill, "C. L. R. James: The Myth of Western Civilization," in *Enterprise of the Indies*, ed. George Lamming (Port-of-Spain: Trinidad and Tobago Institute of the West Indies, 1999), 255–59.

9. Hannibal Price, *De la réhabilitation de la race noire par la République d'Haïti* (Port-au-Prince: J. Verrollot, 1900); Louis Joseph Janvier, *La République d'Haïti et ses visiteurs, 1840–1882* (Paris: Marpon and Flammarion, 1883); Anténor Firmin, *The Equality of Human Races*, trans. Asselin Charles (Urbana: University of Illinois Press, 2002).

10. James, "The Intelligence of the Negro," 7. See Joseph Arthur de Gobineau, *Essai sur l'inégalité des races humaines* (Paris: n.p., 1853–55).

11. Harland would then retaliate in an even more racially charged and pompous intervention: Sidney C. Harland, "Magna est veritas et praevalebit: A Reply to Mr. C. L. R. James," *The Beacon* 1, no. 7 (October 1931): 18–20.

12. On the rewriting and creolization of this passage, see Paul Breslin, *Nobody's Nation: Reading Derek Walcott* (Chicago: University of Chicago Press, 2001), 189–92; Paul Breslin, "I Met History Once but He Ain't Recognize Me," *TriQuarterly* 68 (1987): 168–83.

13. See Breiner, "Too Much History, or Not Enough," 89.

14. James, *The Black Jacobins* (1980), xv.

15. James, "Discovering Literature in Trinidad: The 1930s," in C. L. R. James, *Spheres of Existence* (London: Allison and Busby, 1980), 237.

16. James would target Crown Colony government in the British West Indies in some of his earliest work published after his arrival in Britain. See James, *The Life of Captain Cipriani* (1932); and the shorter related pamphlet, James, *The Case for West Indian Self-Government* (1933).

17. Buhle, *C. L. R. James*, 22; Høgsbjerg, "Introduction," in James, *Toussaint Louverture*, 4–5, 30n19.

18. Høgsbjerg, *C. L. R. James in Imperial Britain*, 6, 99; Cripps, *C. L. R. James*, 22–36.

19. See King, *C. L. R. James and Creolization*, 30–51; King, "C. L. R. James, Genre and Cultural Politics," 13–38; Sander, "C. L. R. James and the Haitian Revolution," 277–90; Rosengarten, *Urbane Revolutionary*, 220–32.

20. James, "Author's Note," *Toussaint Louverture* (theater program) (2013), 161. A copy of the original 1936 program can be found in UWI Box 8, Folder 219.

21. Conversations with Robert A. Hill in May 2009, and with Selma James in summer 2010.

22. C. L. R. James to Gallimard, September 9, 1953, UWI Box 7, Folder 187; Gérard Jean-Baptiste, Haitian Embassy in London, to C. L. R. James, September 15, UWI Box 7, Folder 190; P. D. Mascolo of Gallimard to C. L. R. James, November 5, 1953, UWI Box 7, Folder 187.

23. Fionnghuala Sweeney, "The Haitian Play: C. L. R. James' *Toussaint Louverture* (1936)," *International Journal of Francophone Studies* 14, nos. 1–2 (2011): 143–63.

24. See Sweeney, "The Haitian Play"; Høgsbjerg, "Introduction," in James, *Toussaint Louverture*; Mary Lou Emery, *Modernism, the Visual, and Caribbean Literature* (Cambridge: Cambridge University Press, 2007), 143, 259–60.

25. C. L. R. James, "Toussaint Louverture (Act 2, Scene 1)," *Life and Letters Today* 14, no. 3 (1936): 7–18.

26. See Høgsbjerg, "Introduction," in James, *Toussaint Louverture*, 1. See John Saville, *Memoirs from the Left* (London: Merlin, 2003), 138–39, for background information on how historian John Saville acquired the Haston papers for the University of Hull. On leading British Trotskyist Jock Haston, see John McIlroy, "James Richie (Jock) Haston," in *Dictionary of Labour Biography*, vol. 12, ed. Keith Gildart and David Howell (Basingstoke, UK: Palgrave Macmillan, 2005), 124–36. See also Sam Bornstein and Al Richardson, *Against the Stream: A History of the Trotskyist Movement in Britain, 1924–1938* (London: Socialist Platform, 1986), 251–52.

27. See Russell J. Linnemann, *Alain Locke: Reflections on a Modern Renaissance Man* (Baton Rouge: Louisiana State University Press, 1982); Johnny Washington, *Alain Locke and Philosophy: A Quest for Cultural Pluralism* (Westport, CT: Greenwood, 1986).

28. Sweeney, "The Haitian Play," 149.

29. Errol Hill to Michelle A. Stephens, September 23, 1998, Errol Hill Papers (ML-77), Raunder Special Collections Library, Dartmouth College, Box 48, Folder 48; Michelle Stephens, *Black Empire: The Masculine Global Imaginary of Caribbean Intellectuals in the United States, 1914–1962* (Durham, NC: Duke University Press, 2005.

30. Constance Webb, *Richard Wright: A Biography* (New York: Putnam, 1968); Constance Webb, *Not without Love: Memoirs* (Hanover, NH: University Press of New England, 2003).

31. James, "Lectures on *The Black Jacobins*," 70.

32. From memoirs written by James's comrades, it is clear that at least by 1936, James's working method revolved around a typist or copyist. Dorothy Pizer, partner of James's fellow Pan-Africanist comrade of Trinidadian birth, George Padmore, was working as personal secretary to James during the period when he was writing *World Revolution, 1917–1936: The Rise and Fall of the Communist International*, published in 1937 and, according to James's preface to that book, written over the course of 1936.

33. This is also the conclusion that Sweeney comes to based on the cover sheet information. Sweeney, "The Haitian Play," 149.

34. Columbia University script of *Toussaint Louverture* in C. L. R. James Papers (MS#1529), Rare Book and Manuscript Library, Columbia University, New York, in

Box 5, Folder 18, 82; UWI Box 12, Folder 275, 82. For an explanation of the transcription conventions used here, see the note in the introduction.

35. See Patrice Pavis, *Dictionary of the Theatre: Terms, Concepts, and Analysis* (Toronto: University of Toronto Press, 1988), 55–56; Felix Schelling, *The English Chronicle Play: A Study in the Popular Historical Literature Environing Shakespeare* (New York: Macmillan, 1902), 209–10.

36. See James's correspondence in UWI Box 7, Folder 183.

37. References in the final section of this chapter to these three scripts will follow this notation system.

38. Page references in parentheses refer to James, *Toussaint Louverture* (2013).

39. Paul B. Miller, "Enlightened Hesitations: C. L. R. James, Toussaint Louverture, and the Black Masses," in *Elusive Origins: The Enlightenment in the Modern Caribbean Historical Imagination* (Charlottesville: University of Virginia Press, 2010), 29–83.

40. See entry for "Ferrand de la Baudière" in Charles Theodore Beauvais and Antoine-Alexandre Barbier, *Dictionnaire historique; ou, Biographie universelle classique*, vol. 1 (Paris: C. Gosselin, 1829), 1064.

41. On the U.S. occupation of Haiti, see Mary Renda, *Taking Haiti: Military Occupation and the Culture of U.S. Imperialism, 1915–1940* (Chapel Hill: University of North Carolina Press, 2001). Another backdrop was the Spanish Civil War. See C. L. R. James, "Introduction" in Mary Low and Juan Breá, *Red Spanish Notebook: The First Six Months of the Revolution and the Civil War* (London: Secker and Warburg, 1937), v–vii.

42. Raphael Dalleo, "'The Independence So Hardly Won Has Been Maintained': C. L. R. James and the U.S. Occupation of Haiti," in *American Imperialism's Undead: The Occupation of Haiti and the Rise of Caribbean Anticolonialism* (Charlottesville: University of Virginia Press, 2016), 25–43; Raphael Dalleo, "'The Independence So Hardly Won Has Been Maintained': C. L. R. James and the U.S. Occupation of Haiti," *Cultural Critique* 87 (2014): 38–59; Christian Høgsbjerg, "Reflections on C. L. R. James and the U.S. Occupation of Haiti" (paper presented at "After Revolution: Versions and Revisions of Haiti," Conference, July 9–10, 2015); Christian Høgsbjerg, "C. L. R. James and Italy's Conquest of Abyssinia," *Socialist History* 28 (2006): 17–36.

43. Santiago Colás, "Silence and Dialectics: Speculations on C. L. R. James and Latin America," in *Rethinking C. L. R. James*, ed. Grant Farred (Oxford: Blackwell, 1996), 131–64.

44. Dalleo, "'The Independence So Hardly Won,'" 32; James, *Toussaint Louverture* (2013), 161.

45. Magdaline Shannon, *Jean Price-Mars, the Haitian Elite and the American Occupation, 1915–1935* (New York: St. Martin's, 1996), 18; Høgsbjerg, "Reflections on C. L. R. James and the U.S. Occupation of Haiti," 3–4, 10.

46. Dalleo, "'The Independence So Hardly Won,'" 31.

47. Dalleo, "'The Independence So Hardly Won,'" 32.

48. Dalleo, "'The Independence So Hardly Won,'" 30.

49. Dalleo, "'The Independence So Hardly Won.'"

50. James, *The Black Jacobins* (1980), v–vi.
51. Dalleo, *American Imperialism's Undead*, 32.
52. Høgsbjerg, "Reflections on C. L. R. James and the U.S. Occupation of Haiti," 4–5, 8.
53. Charles Dupuis, "Le général Nemours," *Le Nouvelliste*, November 29, 2004, http://www.myclipboard.com/vastey/nemoursnouvelliste.htm.
54. George Padmore, *Haiti, an American Slave Colony* (Moscow: Centrizdat, 1931). See Leslie James, *George Padmore and Decolonization from Below: Pan-Africanism, the Cold War, and the End of Empire* (Basingstoke, UK: Palgrave Macmillan, 2015).
55. See Matthew Quest, "George Padmore's and C. L. R. James's *International African Opinion*," in *George Padmore: Pan African Revolutionary*, ed. Rupert Lewis and Fitzroy Baptiste (Kingston: Ian Randall, 2009), 105–32. On Pan-Africanism, see also Hakim Ali and Marika Sherwood, *The 1945 Manchester Pan-African Congress Revisited* (London: New Beacon, 1995); Hakim Ali and Marika Sherwood. *Pan-African History: Political Figures from Africa and the Diaspora Since 1787* (London: Routledge, 2003).
56. S. K. B. Asante, *Pan-African Protest: West Africa and the Italo-Ethiopian Crisis 1934–1941* (London: Longman, 1977), 46.
57. C. L. R. James, "Abyssinia and the Imperialists," *Keys* 3, no. 3 (January–March 1936). Reprinted in James, *The C. L. R. James Reader*, 63–66.
58. James, "Abyssinia and the Imperialists."
59. Høgsbjerg has highlighted the hypocrisy of U.S. Consul Lear in James's first play. Høgsbjerg, "Reflections on C. L. R. James and the U.S. Occupation of Haiti."
60. These quotations have been entirely added in both the NALIS and *Life and Letters Today* scripts, but the bold font here indicates the later changes in *Life and Letters Today*.
61. See the 1936 reviews published alongside the play text in Høgsbjerg's 2013 critical edition of James, *Toussaint Louverture*, 164–86.
62. See, for example, Asante, one of the leading commentators on Pan-Africanism, according to whom Haiti was "virtually disregarded as [a source] of inspiration and hope to black peoples" because it was an "artificial" state created by "artificial" means, and maintained by methods equally "artificial." Asante, *Pan-African Protest*, 15–16.
63. C. L. R. James, "Is This Worth a War? The League's Scheme to Rob Abyssinia of Its Independence," *New Leader*, October 4, 1935.
64. Dance, "Conversation with C. L. R. James," 114.
65. The Stage Society was responsible for the first performances of plays by George Bernard Shaw and Arnold Bennett, and had a reputation for trying out more radical or internationalist plays through Sunday performances—Sunday, traditionally being the dead day in theater—enabling plays to be put on for little money, and for censorship to be circumvented. See Michael J. Sidnell, *Dances of Death: The Group Theatre of London in the Thirties* (London: Faber and Faber, 1984), 168, 260; Colin Chambers, *The Story of Unity Theatre* (London: Lawrence and Wishart, 1989), 33–34; Høgsbjerg, "Introduction," in James, *Toussaint Louverture*, 20–21.
66. C. L. R. James, "Paul Robeson: Black Star," in *Spheres of Existence: Selected Writings*, vol. 2 (London: Allison and Busby, 1980), 256–64.

67. Philip S. Foner, *Paul Robeson Speaks: Writings, Speeches, Interviews, 1918–1974* (London: Quartet, 1978), 30, 107–8, 121; Paul Robeson, *Here I Stand* (London: Cassell, 1988), 51; Martin Bauml Duberman, *Paul Robeson* (London: Bodley Head, 1989), 190.

68. Duberman, *Paul Robeson*, 190.

69. Charles Forsdick and Christian Høgsbjerg, "Sergei Eisenstein and the Haitian Revolution: 'The Confrontation between Black and White Explodes into Red,'" *History Workshop Journal* 78, no. 1 (2014): 157–85.

70. James, "Paul Robeson," 259; Duberman, *Paul Robeson*, 190.

71. James, "Paul Robeson," 261.

72. Peter Noble, *The Negro in Films* (London: Skelton Robinson, 1948), 8, 27, 111, 165.

73. Robeson, *Here I Stand*, 31; James, "Paul Robeson," 261.

74. Noble, *The Negro in Films*, 87.

75. Noble, *The Negro in Films*, 117; Duberman, *Paul Robeson*, 194.

76. Robert A. Hill, "In England, 1932–1938," 73–74.

77. Duberman, *Paul Robeson*, 197.

78. James, "Paul Robeson," 258.

79. See James, *Toussaint Louverture* (2013), 70; James, "Paul Robeson," 257–58.

80. James, "Paul Robeson," 257.

81. James, "Paul Robeson," 258.

82. "Paul Robeson in Negro Play—A Dignified Study," *Morning Post*, March 17, 1936; "Toussaint Louverture," *Glasgow Herald*, March 18, 1936; A[lan] D[ent], "Mr. Paul Robeson as Toussaint: A Documentary Play," *Manchester Guardian*, March 17, 1936; G[eorge] W. B[ishop], "'Toussaint Louverture,' a Play by C. L. R. James," *Sunday Times*, March 22, 1936.

83. James, "Paul Robeson," 258.

84. Hannen Swaffer, "Two Great Negroes," *The People*, March 22, 1936; "Toussaint L'Ouverture, at the Stage Society," *New Statesman*, March 21, 1936.

85. "Robeson a Success in Drama by Negro," *New York Times*, March 16, 1936; syndicated in Jamaica's *Daily Gleaner*, March 28, 1936.

86. Ivor Brown, "Criticisms in Cameo: The Stage," *The Sketch*, March 25, 1936.

87. Emery, *Modernism, the Visual, and Caribbean Literature*, 128–29.

88. See the following reviews: "Stage Society: 'Toussaint Louverture' by C. L. R. James," *The Times*, March 17, 1936; P. L. M[annock], "Paul Robeson as Slave Leader," *Daily Herald*, March 17, 1936; Ivor Brown, "Stage Society: 'Toussaint Louverture' by C. L. R. James," *Observer*, March 22, 1936; "Our London Letter: Black Episode," *Liverpool Post*, March 17, 1936.

89. E[dna] R[obinson], "Toussaint Louverture; The Story of the Only Successful Slave Revolt in History," *Nelson Leader*, March 27, 1936.

90. See Noble, *The Negro in Films*, 27.

91. C. L. R. James, "Introduction," in *Caribbean Plays*, vol. 2, ed. Errol Hill (St. Augustine: University of the West Indies, 1965), viii.

92. See Duberman, *Paul Robeson*, 196; James, "Paul Robeson," 261.

93. James, "Paul Robeson," 256.

94. See Roger Dorsinville, *De fatras bâton à Toussaint Louverture* (Alger: Enal, 1983); John Beard, *The Life of Toussaint L'Ouverture* (London: Ingram, Cooke, 1853).

95. Duberman, *Paul Robeson*, 196.

96. Hill, "In England," 73.

97. James, "Introduction," in Hill, *Caribbean Plays*.

98. Emphasis added. Here I am combining two quotations: one from James's introduction to Hill's anthology *Caribbean Plays*, and one from James's 1966 essay "Kanhai: A Study in Confidence," where he declares of this exceptional West Indian cricketer, "In Kanhai's batting what I have found is a unique pointer of the West Indian quest for identity, for ways of expressing our potential bursting at every seam." This last quotation is also cited by Hill, "C. L. R. James," 258. James, "Kanhai: A Study in Confidence," in C. L. R. James, *At the Rendezvous of Victory: Selected Writings*, vol. 3 (London: Allison and Busby, 1984), 166–71.

99. Abbé Guillaume-Thomas Raynal, *Histoire philosophique et politique des établissemens et du commerce des Européens dans les deux Indes*, 3rd ed., 10 vols. (Geneva: Jean-Léonard Pellet, 1780–1784). As Srinivas Aravamudan has pointed out, the Black Spartacus passages in Raynal were actually copied from Louis-Sébastien Mercier's *L'An deux mille quatre cent quarante* (1771). See Srinivas Aravamudan, *Tropicopolitans: Colonialism and Agency, 1688–1804* (Durham, NC: Duke University Press, 1999), 302. Diderot's version in the multivolume work edited by Raynal turns this into a warning that all the black slaves lack is a "Black Spartacus" to lead them.

100. According to Norman Marshall, *Toussaint Louverture* in its Stage Society production was possibly Peter Godfrey's "best work." Norman Marshall, *The Other Theatre* (London: Lehmann, 1947), 76.

101. James, "Paul Robeson," 258.

102. Trouillot, "Haitian Historiography," 466–68.

103. Here, my notation system follows the running heads of these three UWI scripts where 2.1.14 indicates act 2, scene 1, page 14.

104. King, *C. L. R. James and Creolization*, 40.

105. Here, Dessalines is not struck through and both Moïse's and Dessalines's names appear together.

106. Herbert Lindenberger, *Historical Drama: The Relation of Literature and Reality* (Chicago: University of Chicago Press, 1975), 156–57.

107. Laurent Dubois notes the significance of Macoya/Macaya's explanation for his loyalty to three kings through which James identifies the key role played by the African-born majority in the Haitian Revolution. James does not seem so respectful of the principle of kingship in this part of the play, however. See Laurent Dubois, "Foreword," in James, *Toussaint Louverture*, ix; John K. Thornton, "I Am the Subject of the King of Congo: African Political Ideology and the Haitian Revolution," *Journal of World History* 4 (1993): 181–214.

108. Kikite is a name that appears in the famous Haitian story "Fefe ak Kikit" (about a boy called Fefe and a chicken called Kikit), and it is also the name of a goddess in the Vodou pantheon. See Nirvah Jean-Jacques, *Fefe ak Kikit* (Coconut Creek, FL: Educa Vision, 2001).

2. Making History (1938)

1. C. L. R. James, *The Black Jacobins: Toussaint Louverture and the San Domingo Revolution* (London: Secker and Warburg, 1938), 301. Further references to this book appear in parentheses in the text.
2. On Trotsky's use of theatrical metaphor, see Peter Beilharz, "Trotsky as Historian," *History Workshop Journal* 20 (1985): 36–55.
3. This is how, for example, the Facing Reality Book Service announces the revised 1963 Vintage edition in its flyer. See UWI Box 8, Folder 219.
4. On differences between showing and telling as forms of historical representation, see Alun Munslow, *Narrative and History* (Basingstoke, UK: Palgrave Macmillan, 2007), 60.
5. See Munslow, *Narrative and History*, 6, 9.
6. Regarding film and photography, Munslow has discussed how "neither comes with their references sliding across the bottom of the screen or written alongside it." Munslow, *Narrative and History*, 67.
7. C. L. R. James, letter to *New Statesman*, March 28, 1936.
8. Manning Marable, *Black Leadership* (New York: Columbia University Press, 1998), 91.
9. Kent Worcester, *C. L. R. James: A Political Biography* (Albany: State University of New York Press, 1996), 40; Høgsbjerg, *C. L. R. James in Imperial Britain*, 114–20.
10. Bill Schwarz, "Not Even Past Yet," *History Workshop Journal* 57 (2004): 104–5. See Christian Høgsbjerg, "'A Thorn in the Side of Great Britain': C. L. R. James and the Caribbean Labour Rebellions of the 1930s," *Small Axe* 35 (2011): 24–42.
11. Christian Høgsbjerg, "The Black International as Social Movement Wave: C. L. R. James's *History of Pan-African Revolt*," in *Marxism and Social Movements*, ed. Colin Barker, Laurence Cox, John Krinsky, and Alf Gunvald Nilsen (Brill: Leiden, 2013), 317–37; Brent Hayes Edwards, *The Practice of Diaspora: Literature, Translation, and the Rise of Black Internationalism* (Cambridge, MA: Harvard University Press, 2003); Michael O. West and William G. Martin, "Haiti, I'm Sorry: The Haitian Revolution and the Forging of the Black International," in *From Toussaint to Tupac: The Black International Since the Age of Revolution*, ed. Michael O. West, William G. Martin, and Fanon Che Wilkins (Chapel Hill: University of North Carolina Press, 2009), 87; Minkah Makalani, *In the Cause of Freedom: Radical Black Internationalism from Harlem to London, 1917–1939* (Chapel Hill: University of North Carolina Press, 2011).
12. C. L. R. James, *A History of Negro Revolt* (London: Race Today, 1985), 5.
13. James, *A History of Negro Revolt* (1938), 9; James, *The Black Jacobins* (1938), 66.
14. Schwarz, "Not Even Past Yet," 104–5.

15. On this dialectic tension, see Colás, "Silence and Dialectics," 131–63.
16. In an undated draft of an unpublished preface to *The Black Jacobins*, James explicitly makes the point that Toussaint was seeking dominion status. UWI Box 20, Folder 387.
17. C. L. R. James, "'Civilising' the 'Blacks': Why Britain Needs to Maintain Her African Possessions," *New Leader*, May 29, 1936, 5.
18. Brereton, "Introduction," 1–29.
19. See Frederic Warburg, *An Occupation for Gentlemen* (London: Hutchison, 1959), 214–15. See also Ethel Mannin, *Comrade, O Comrade; or Low-Down on the Left* (London: Jarrolds, 1947), 5; and Bornstein and Richardson, *Against the Stream*, 219.
20. See C. L. R. James, *World Revolution, 1917–1936: The Rise and Fall of the Communist International*, ed. Christian Høgsbjerg (Durham, NC: Duke University Press, 2017). See Christian Høgsbjerg, "Introduction," in James, *World Revolution* (2017), 1–57; Christian Høgsbjerg, "'A Kind of Bible of Trotskyism': Reflections on C. L. R. James's *World Revolution*," *C. L. R. James Journal* 19, nos. 1–2 (2013): 243–75; Duncan Hallas, *The Comintern* (London: Bookmarks, 1985), 8.
21. Hamish Henderson, "Introduction," in Antonio Gramsci, *Gramsci's Prison Letters*, ed. Hamish Henderson (London: Zwan, 1988), 19. Quoted in Høgsbjerg, "Introduction," in James, *World Revolution* (2017), 44, 57n201.
22. Bornstein and Richardson, *Against the Stream*, 264; K. Tilak [Leslie Goonewardene], *Rise and Fall of the Comintern* (Bombay: n.p., 1947). See Høgsbjerg, "Introduction," in James, *World Revolution* (2017), 42, 57n190.
23. On Trotsky, see John Molyneux, *Leon Trotsky's Theory of Revolution* (Brighton, UK: Harvester, 1981).
24. I am paraphrasing Trotsky's biographer here about Trotsky in relation to Marx. See Isaac Deutscher, *The Prophet: The Life of Leon Trotsky* (London: Verso, 2015), 1272.
25. However, few works of Marxist historiography had been published by 1930—the publication date of Trotsky's *History*—and even by 1938 when James's history was first published. As Neil Davidson has noted, this is odd given that the most common synonym for Marxism is "historical materialism"; Neil Davidson, "History from Below," *Jacobin*, January 12, 2018, https://www.jacobinmag.com/2018/01/leon-trotsky-russian-revolution-stalin-lenin. But while Marx did write works such as *The Eighteenth Brumaire of Louis Bonaparte* that most resemble conventional history writing, these are "brilliant journalistic assessments written in the immediate aftermath of events," as Davidson has noted. As James himself summed up, Marx "wrote specifically on history only as the occasion presented itself, and always to the point and no more." C. L. R. James, "Trotsky's Place in History" (1940), in *C. L. R. James and Revolutionary Marxism: Selected Writings of C. L. R. James, 1939–1949*, ed. Scott McLemee and Paul Le Blanc (Amherst, NY: Humanity, 1994), 124. Trotsky it is, then, who becomes the "first great Marxist *historian*," as summed up by Perry Anderson, *Arguments within English Marxism* (London: Verso, 1980), 154, emphasis in original.
26. Høgsbjerg, *C. L. R. James in Imperial Britain*, 44; Jeffrey Hill, *Nelson: Politics, Economy, Community* (Edinburgh: Keele University Press, 1997), 77–78, 81, 86; Jill Liddington,

The Life and Times of a Respectable Rebel: Selina Cooper, 1864–1946 (London: Virago, 1984), 35; Stuart MacIntyre, *Little Moscows: Communism and Working-Class Militancy in Inter-War Britain* (London: Croom Helm, 1980), 14.

27. James, "Trotsky's Place in History," 108.

28. James, "Trotsky's Place in History," 125.

29. On the influence of Michelet and Trotsky's prefaces, see Scott, *Conscripts of Modernity*, 34–35; Rosengarten, *Urbane Revolutionary*, 225.

30. On the theme of beginnings, see Edward Said's seminal and wide-ranging essay *Beginning: Intention and Method* (Baltimore, MD: Johns Hopkins University Press, 1975). On endings, see Barbara Herrnstein Smith, *Poetic Closure: A Study of How Poems End* (Chicago: University Press of Chicago, 1968); and Frank Kermode, *The Sense of an Ending: Studies in the Theory of Fiction* (Oxford: Oxford University Press, 1967).

31. Peter Beilharz, *Trotsky, Trotskyism and the Transition to Socialism* (London: Croom Helm, 1987), 52; Beilharz, "Trotsky as Historian," 49.

32. Michel Étienne Descourtilz, *Voyage d'un naturaliste* (Paris: n.p., 1809); Justin Girod-Chantrans, *Voyage d'un Suisse dans différentes colonies d'Amérique pendant la dernière guerre* (Neuchâtel: Imprimerie de la société typographique, 1785).

33. Pierre de Vaissière, *Saint-Domingue* (Paris: Perrin, 1909), 217.

34. C. L. R. James, "Section 4, 1932–1938," autobiography, Columbia University Library, C. L. R. James Papers, Box 4, Folder 15; C. L. R. James, "My Knowledge of Damas Is Unique," in *Léon-Gontran Damas, 1912–1978: Founder of Negritude: A Memorial Casebook*, ed. Daniel L. Racine (Washington, DC: University Press of America, 1979), 131.

35. James, "Lectures on *The Black Jacobins*," 70.

36. James, "Lectures on *The Black Jacobins*." Also see Høgsbjerg, *C. L. R. James in Imperial Britain*, 82–89; Hill, "In England," 67–68; Edwards, *The Practice of Diaspora*, 276, 377n99.

37. Matthieu Renault, *C. L. R. James: La vie révolutionnaire d'un "Platon noir"* (Paris: La Découverte, 2015), 67.

38. On Paris during this crucial interwar period, see Michael Goebel, *Anti-Imperial Metropolis: Interwar Paris and the Seeds of Third World Nationalism* (Cambridge: Cambridge University Press, 2015). In Paris, Cripps recalls being offered and refusing the position of Trotsky's secretary by someone who was murdered shortly afterward. Cripps, *C. L. R. James*, 48–54. Trotsky himself would also be murdered in 1940.

39. James, Autobiography, UWI Box 14, Folder 309. James recalls his first meetings with Pierre Naville in 1930s Paris in the context of a much later 1967 meeting with Césaire in Cuba at a birthday party for James, which Naville also attended.

40. C. L. R. James, *Fight* 1, no. 7 (June 1937): 14–15. Unfortunately, James's optimism for the France of 1938 and beyond was not borne out in the event.

41. Gary Wilder, *The French Imperial Nation-State: Negritude and Colonial Humanism between the Two World Wars* (Chicago: University of Chicago Press, 2005), 152.

42. Wilder, *The French Imperial Nation-State*, 150, 156.

43. See Forsdick, "The Black Jacobin in Paris," 16–17. On Césaire and James's 1968 meeting in Cuba, see Andrew Salkey, *Havana Journal* (Harmondsworth: Penguin, 1971); James, Autobiography, UWI Box 14, Folders 306, 309, 311.
44. This is how Damas is described in Femi Ojo-Ade, *Being Black, Being Human* (Ile-Ife, Nigeria: Obafemi Awolowo University Press, 1996), 327. It is an indirect reference to Stanislav Adotevi, *Négritude et négrologues* (Paris: Union générale d'éditions, 1972).
45. Wilder, *The French Imperial Nation-State*, 153. See also Léon-Gontran Damas, *Pigments* (Paris: G.L.M., 1937). On Damas, see F. Bart Miller, *Rethinking Negritude through Léon-Gontran Damas* (Amsterdam: Rodopi, 2014); Monique Blérard, Kathleen Gyssels, and Marc Lony, *Léon-Gontran Damas: Poète, écrivain patrimonial et postcolonial: Quels héritiers, quels héritages au seuil du XXIe siècles* (Matoury, French Guiana: Ibis Rouge, 2014); Kathleen Gyssels, *Black Label, ou, Les Déboires de Léon-Gontran Damas* (Paris: Passage[s], 2016).
46. James, "My Knowledge of Damas Is Unique," 131–32. James recalls that Damas did not introduce him to Césaire or Senghor. See also Renault, *C. L. R. James*, 67.
47. Wilder, *The French Imperial Nation-State*, 153, 156.
48. On Senghor's quest for "the spirit of Paris," see Wilder, *The French Imperial Nation-State*, 155, 157; Léopold Sédar Senghor, "Paris," in *Liberté I: Négritude et humanisme* (Paris: Stock, 1964), 313.
49. On the close relationship between George Padmore and Tiemoko Garan Kouyaté, see Edwards, *The Practice of Diaspora*, 241–305. See also Wilder, *The French Imperial Nation-State*; J. Ayo Langley, "Pan-Africanism in Paris, 1924–36," *Journal of Modern African Studies* 7, no. 1 (1969): 69–94.
50. See Langley, "Pan-Africanism in Paris," 91.
51. MARHO, ed., *Visions of History* (Manchester: Manchester University Press, 1984), 269–70.
52. C. L. R. James, "George Padmore, Black Marxist Revolutionary—a Memoir," in *At the Rendezvous of Victory: Selected Writings*, vol. 3 (London: Allison and Busby, 1984), 258; Edwards, *The Practice of Diaspora*, 276.
53. "1932–1938," Autobiography, UWI Box 16, Folder 338.
54. James, "Foreword," in *The Black Jacobins* (1980), v–vii. Reynold K. Raymond, "La Fondation Alfred Nemours inaugurée," *Le Nouvelliste*, May 7, 2009, http://lenouvelliste.com/lenouvelliste/article/69428/La-Fondation-Alfred-Nemours-Inauguree; Charles Dupuis, "Société: Le Général Nemours," *Le Nouvelliste*, November 24, 2004, http://www.myclipboard.com/vastey/nemoursnouvelliste.htm; Jane Toth and William A. Tremblay, "The Alfred Nemours Collection of Haitian History: A Catalogue," *Caribbean Studies*, 2, no. 3 (1962): 61–70.
55. James also remained neutral over conflicting interpretations of which side won a particular Haitian Revolution battle, stating in a note, "The result of the battle remains for the writer undecided" (255n1). This was an instance where Nemours's narrative conflicts with most Haitian history.

56. Likewise, Maximilien Robespierre has always acted as an icon and symbol. See Ann Rigney, "Icon and Symbol: The Historical Figure Called Maximilien Robespierre," in Heffernan, *Representing the French Revolution*, 106–22.
57. On this tendency, see Forsdick, "The Black Jacobin in Paris," 17.
58. Horace Pauléus Sannon, *Histoire de Toussaint Louverture*, 3 vols. (Port-au-Prince: A. A. Héraux, 1920–1933).
59. Trouillot, "Historiography of Haiti," 462–63.
60. On this tendency, see Trouillot, "Historiography of Haiti," 462–63.
61. Jean Price Mars, *Ainsi parla l'oncle* (Port-au-Prince: Imprimerie de Compiègne, 1928; repr., Montreal: Mémoire d'encrier, 2005).
62. This has been suggested by Høgsbjerg, "Reflections on C. L. R. James."
63. Nesbitt also notes James's frequent use of the word "mass" itself. See Nesbitt, "Fragments of a Universal History," 142.
64. One critic, Charles Post, has criticized the NHC for their arguments that plantation slavery in the Caribbean and United States enabled the development of industrial capitalism by providing the raw materials that could be transformed industrially and used to generate capital in Britain and the United States; Charles Post, "Slavery and the New History of Capitalism," *Catalyst* 1, no. 1 (2017): 173–92. He argues that the relationship of master and slave is completely different, and that under slavery, the planters did not purchase nor sell the labor power of the slaves. Instead they purchased and sold the laborers, the slaves themselves. See the following NHC studies: Walter Johnson, *River of Dark Dreams: Slavery and Empire in the Cotton Kingdom* (Cambridge, MA: Harvard University Press, 2013); Edward Baptist, *The Half Has Never Been Told: Slavery and the Making of American Capitalism* (New York: Basic Books, 2014); Sven Beckert, *Empire of Cotton: A Global History* (New York: Alfred A. Knopf, 2014). On NHC, see Jennifer Schuessler, "In History Departments, It's Up with Capitalism," *New York Times*, April 6, 2013; Seth Rockman, "What Makes the History of Capitalism Newsworthy?" *Journal of the Early Republic* 34 (2014): 439–66; Sven Beckert, "Interchange: The History of Capitalism," *Journal of American History* 101, no. 2 (2014): 503–36. On the relationship between capitalism and slavery since Williams's book by that title, see also Eugene D. Genovese, *The Political Economy of Slavery: Studies in the Economy and Society of the Slave South* (Middletown, CT: Wesleyan University Press, 1989); Charles Post, *The American Road to Capitalism: Studies in Class Structure, Economic Development and Political Conflict, 1620–1877* (Chicago: Haymarket, 2012); Robin Blackburn, "White Gold, Black Labour," *New Left Review* 95 (2015): 151–60; Robin Blackburn, *The Making of New World Slavery: From the Baroque to the Modern* (London: Verso, 1997); Ellen Meiksins Wood, *The Empire of Capital* (London: Verso, 2003); Peter James Hudson, "The Racist Dawn of Capitalism," *Boston Review*, March 14, 2016; John Clegg, "Capitalism and Slavery," *Critical Historical Studies* 2, no. 2 (2015): 281–304.
65. On Marx's *Capital*, see Harry Cleaver, *Reading Capital Politically* (Brighton, UK: Harvester, 1979).

66. See Robert J. C. Young, "Rereading the Symptomatic Reading," in *The Concept in Crisis*, ed. Nick Nesbitt (Durham, NC: Duke University Press, 2017), 35–48; Emily Apter, "Translation and Event: Rereading *Reading Capital*," in Nesbitt, *The Concept in Crisis*, 49–69. See Louis Althusser, Étienne Balibar, Roger Establet, Jacques Rancière, and Pierre Macherey, *Reading Capital: The Complete Edition*, trans. Ben Brewster and David Fernbach (London: Verso, 2016).

67. On French colonial historians on capitalism and slavery shaping the James-Williams thesis on abolition, see Alyssa Goldstein Sepinwall, "Beyond *The Black Jacobins*: Haitian Revolutionary Historiography Comes of Age," *Journal of Haitian Studies* 23, no. 1 (2017): 4–34; C. L. R. James, "Correspondence [27 February 1950]," *Les Temps Modernes* 56 (June 1950).

68. On the intellectual relationship between James and Williams and their overthrowing of conventional history, see Aaron Kamugisha, "C. L. R. James, *The Black Jacobins* and the Making of the Modern Atlantic World," in *Ten Books That Shaped the British Empire: Creating an Imperial Commons*, ed. Antoinette Burton and Isabel Hofmeyr (Durham, NC: Duke University Press, 2014), 190–215.

69. James, Autobiography, UWI Box 14, Folder 309.

70. Stuart Hall has dismissed rumors about James sketching out the thesis on the back of an envelope as "apocryphal." Stuart Hall, "Breaking Bread with History: C. L. R. James and *The Black Jacobins*," interview with Bill Schwarz, *History Workshop Journal* 46 (1998): 21. Instead, James's own reminiscences suggest that the thesis plan was more substantial than the back of an envelope, stretching to two or three pages. James, Autobiography, UWI Box 14, Folder 309.

71. UWI Box 14, Folder 309, 6–8. *Capitalism and Slavery*, first published in 1944, was based on a substantially different doctoral thesis submitted by Williams in 1938.

72. See Hilary Beckles, "'The Williams Effect': Eric Williams's *Capitalism and Slavery* and the Growth of West Indian Political Economy," in *British Capitalism and Caribbean Slavery*, ed. Barbara L. Solow and Stanley L. Engerman (Cambridge: Cambridge University Press, 1987), 303–16.

73. Williams, *Capitalism and Slavery*, 268.

74. Ivar Oxaal, *Black Intellectuals Come to Power: The Rise of Creole Nationalism in Trinidad and Tobago* (Cambridge, MA: Schenkman, 1968), xii, 74–75, 76.

75. See Michael Craton, "What and Who to Whom and What: The Significance of Slave Resistance," in *British Capitalism and Caribbean Slavery*, ed. Barbara L. Solow and Stanley L. Engerman (Cambridge: Cambridge University Press), 1989, 259–60.

76. Selwyn Ryan, *Eric Williams: The Myth and the Man* (Kingston, Jamaica: University of the West Indies Press, 2009), 43–44.

77. Williams, *Capitalism and Slavery*, 268.

78. Williams, *Capitalism and Slavery*, 258. However, Lowell J. Ragatz is singled out as Williams's master and monumental guide throughout *Capitalism and Slavery*, and it is to Ragatz that Williams dedicates the whole history (iv). Indeed, such is the debt of Williams's *Capitalism and Slavery* to Ragatz's work that scholars often refer to "the

Williams-Ragatz thesis." See, for example, Andrew O'Shaughnessy, "Eric Williams as Economic Historian," in *Capitalism and Slavery Fifty Years Later: Eric Eustace Williams—a Reassessment of the Man and His Work*, ed. Heather Cateau and S. H. H. Carrington (New York: Peter Lang, 2000), 103; Seymour Drescher, "*Capitalism and Slavery*: After Fifty Years," in Cateau and Carrington, *Capitalism and Slavery*, 81–98.

79. James, Autobiography, UWI Box 14, Folder 309.

80. Alternatively, James could have highlighted, as Barbadian writer George Lamming has done, Williams's linguistic abilities in French, which presumably equipped him for the role of James's unofficial research assistant during research trips to Paris. Lamming has noted how rare and valuable Williams's foreign language abilities would have been at that time. George Lamming, "The Legacy of Eric Williams," *Callaloo* 20, no. 4 (1997): 733. See Matthew Quest, "The 'Not So Bright' Protégés and the Comrades Who 'Never Quarreled,'" *Journal of Communist Theory*, October 4, 2013, http://insurgentnotes.com/2013/10/the-not-so-bright-proteges/; Eric Williams, *Inward Hunger: The Education of a Prime Minister* (London: André Deutsch, 1969).

81. Paul Le Blanc, "Introduction: C. L. R. James and Revolutionary Marxism," in McLemee and Le Blanc, *C. L. R. James and Revolutionary Marxism*, 22. See also Leon Trotsky, *The Permanent Revolution and Results and Prospects* (New York: Pathfinder, 1972); Paul Blackledge, "Trotsky's Contribution to the Marxist Theory of History," *Studies in East European Thought* 58, no. 1 (2006): 1–31. See Michael Löwy, *The Politics of Combined and Uneven Development: The Theory of Permanent Revolution* (London: NLB, 1981).

82. Later, James would fiercely attack the notion of permanent revolution, making it one of his main targets in *Notes on Dialectics* (1948), where he described it as "precisely lacking in life, spirit, colour, content," and as the idea that always propelled Trotsky toward the Mensheviks (a moderate minority) and against Leninism (quoted in Le Blanc, "Introduction," 22). As Le Blanc points out, James's criticism of permanent revolution is less harsh in some later works. James would even go so far as to criticize Trotsky's theory of the revolutionary party as "permanent blunder" or "a fiction." C. L. R. James, *Marxism for Our Time: C. L. R. James on Revolutionary Organization*, ed. Martin Glaberman (Jackson: University of Mississippi, 1999), 58.

83. See Matt Perry, *Marxism and History* (Basingstoke, UK: Palgrave, 2002), 67.

84. See Leon Trotsky, "Class Relations in the Chinese Revolution," *New International* 4, nos. 3–4 (1938 [1927]): 87–89, 123–24; Leon Trotsky, *Problems of the Chinese Revolution* (New York: Pioneer, 1932); Leon Trotsky, "On the Canton Insurrection: Three Letters to Preobrazhensky," *New International* 3, no. 2 (1936 [1928]); Leon Trotsky, *The Third International after Lenin* (1928; London: Union Books, 2008); Leon Trotsky, "The Sino-Soviet Conflict and the Opposition," *The Militant* 2, no. 14, September 15, 1929; Leon Trotsky, "Peasant War in China and the Proletariat," *The Militant*, October 15, 1932,1; October 22, 1932, 4; Leon Trotsky, "A Strategy of Action and Not of Speculation, Letter to Peking Friends," *Class Struggle* 3, no. 6 (June 1933 [October 1932]); Leon Trotsky, "On the War in China," *Class Struggle* 3, no. 2 (February 1933); Leon

Trotsky, "On the Sino-Japanese War," *Internal Bulletin* 1 (October 1937); Leon Trotsky, "Introduction," in Harold R. Isaacs, *The Tragedy of the Chinese Revolution* (London: Secker and Warburg, 1938), xi–xxv. Trotsky's writings on the Chinese Revolution of 1925–27 are available at Marxists Internet Archive, https://www.marxists.org/archive/trotsky/china/index.htm. See Neil Davidson, "From Uneven to Combined Development," in Bill Dunn and Hugo Radice, *100 Years of Permanent Revolution: Results and Prospects* (London: Pluto, 2006), 10–26; Tariq Ali, *Introducing Trotsky and Marxism* (Cambridge: Icon, 2000), 40, 43, 47, 106; Perry, *Marxism and History*, 22, 167; Tony Cliff, *Trotsky, 1927–40* (London: Bookmarks, 1993); Duncan Hallas, *Trotsky's Marxism and Other Essays* (Chicago: Haymarket, 2003).

85. Forsdick and Høgsbjerg, "Introduction," 13.

86. Davidson, "History from Below."

87. See Blackledge, "Trotsky's Contribution," 21.

88. Nick Nesbitt's incisive reading of the place of French Revolutionary Robespierre and French historian Albert Mathiez in *The Black Jacobins* complicates my reading of James moving straightforwardly toward a model of history from below. Nesbitt notes that the idea of leaders of genius is lacking from James's interpretation of the French Revolution. Nesbitt argues that James should have drawn on Mathiez's rehabilitation of Robespierre, making him the equivalent of Louverture and Lenin. What James does wrong, according to Nesbitt, is to reduce Robespierre to the role of "sinister dictator"—"a reductive caricature." See Nesbitt, "Fragments of a Universal History," 139–61. In both the 1938 and 1963 history editions, James makes brief references to Mathiez, mentioning his "life-long service to the rehabilitation of Robespierre," and that Mathiez was repelled by the great mass movements, despite recognizing their importance (James, *The Black Jacobins*, 1938, 319; 1963, 384). Certainly, Robespierre is never celebrated by James as he is by Mathiez.

89. See Blackledge, "Trotsky's Contribution," 20–21; Perry, *Marxism and History*, 28.

90. Anderson, *Arguments within English Marxism*, 154. See Albert Soboul, *Les Sans-culottes parisiens en l'an 2* (Paris: Clavreuil, 1958); George Rudé, *The Crowd in the French Revolution* (Oxford: Clarendon, 1959); E. P. Thompson, *The Making of the English Working Class* (London: V. Gollancz, 1963); Eric Hobsbawm, "History from Below—Some Reflections," in *History from Below: Studies in Popular Protest and Popular Ideology*, ed. Frederick Krantz (Oxford: Blackwell, 1988), 13–27.

91. Stoddard, *The French Revolution in San Domingo*, 46, 49.

92. One key source always cited approvingly and uncritically by Stoddard is Moreau de Saint-Méry, Creole planter, responsible for racialist typologies of "miscegenation," with which Stoddard is obsessed. In contrast, James signals in his annotated bibliography that Moreau de Saint-Méry's account displays "all the white bias of his time, e.g. the natural inferiority of mulattoes to whites, etc." (320). See Médéric-Louis-Élie Moreau de Saint-Méry, *Description topographique, physique, civile, politique et historique de la partie française de l'isle Saint-Domingue. Avec des observations générales sur sa* *population, sur le caractère & les mœurs de ses divers habitans; sur son climat, sa culture … accompagnées des détails les plus propres à faire connaître l'état de cette colonie à l'époque du 18 octobre 1789; et d'une carte de la totalité de l'isle* (Philadelphia: Author, 1797).

93. On traces of discursive sedimentation in Orientalist discourse, see Adel Iskander and Hakem Rustom, *Edward Said: A Legacy of Emancipation and Representation* (Berkeley: University of California Press, 2010), 179; Abdelrahman Hussein, *Edward Said: Criticism and Society* (London: Verso, 2002), 138.

94. Warren L. Berggren to C. L. R. James, undated, UWI Box 10, Folder 242. Berggren was director of community health at the Albert Schweitzer hospital, Port-au-Prince. His letter asked James for his source on the "jaw sickness" (newborn tetanus), which killed so many babies during colonial times.

95. Hill, "C. L. R. James," 256–57.

96. Stoddard, *The French Revolution in San Domingo*, 53.

97. Stoddard, *The French Revolution in San Domingo*, 246, 382.

98. On James's representation of Toussaint and the black masses, see Cora Kaplan, "Black Heroes/White Writers: Toussaint L'Ouverture and the Literary Imagination," *History Workshop Journal* 46 (1998): 32–62.

99. James's footnote reference for the unknown anarchist is to a "Lacroix Memorandum" in Les Archives Nationales (298n1).

100. Extracts from letter to the *New Leader* of June 3, 1936, quoted in James, "Black Intellectuals in Britain," 159.

101. Davidson, "History from Below." On this negative type of revisionism, see also Beilharz, "Trotsky as Historian," 49.

102. See Brian Pearce, "Trotsky as an Historian," *The Newsletter*, August 27, 1960, Marxists Internet Archive Library, https://www.marxists.org/archive/pearce/1960/08/trotsky-historian.htm.

103. Scott, *Conscripts of Modernity*.

104. Scott, *Conscripts of Modernity*, 97, 131.

105. See C. L. R. James, "Romanticising History," *New Society*, February 15, 1979.

106. Here, I am, of course, adapting to literature and the "literary" E. P. Thompson's famous statement about the emplacement of popular culture within Marxist historiography. E. P. Thompson, *Customs in Common: Studies in Traditional Popular Culture* (New York: New Press, 1991), 7.

107. On the subject of refashioning, see David Scott, *Refashioning Futures: Criticism after Postcoloniality* (Princeton, NJ: Princeton University Press, 1985).

108. See Jeremy Glick, "'Taking Up Arms against a Sea of Troubles': Tragedy as History and Genre in the Black Radical Tradition" (PhD diss., Rutgers University, 2007), http://dx.doi.org/doi:10.7282/T38K79HJ. Part of this argument is subsequently made in Glick's later book, *The Black Radical Tragic* (New York: New York University Press, 2016).

109. James, *Toussaint Louverture* (2013), 128.

110. See Scott, *Conscripts of Modernity*, 132–69.

111. See Miller, *Elusive Origins*, 81.

112. See James, *The Black Jacobins* (1938), 72, 119, 153, 171, 183, 212, 240, 247.
113. Italics in the extracts below are mine.
114. See Glick, "'Taking Up Arms against a Sea of Troubles,'" 54.
115. James to Charlier, August 24, 1955, UWI Box 7, Folder 190.
116. In an interview, James highlighted the future-oriented dimensions of the penultimate chapter (chapter 32) in Marx's *Capital*, vol. I, "The Historical Tendency of Capitalist Accumulation," as a dynamic he sought to emulate throughout his own work: "It's a masterpiece of summing up and pointing out the implications for the future. I tried to do the same." MAHRO, *Visions of History*, 271.
117. See S. H. Rigby, *Marxism and History: A Critical Introduction* (Manchester: Manchester University Press, 1998).
118. James, *The Life of Captain Cipriani*; James, *The Case for West Indian Self-Government*.
119. This insistence on the need for guidance from Europe, like Toussaint Louverture from his European light Raynal, is a problematic issue that James himself would later address in the preface of the 1963 revised edition. James, "Preface to the Vintage Edition," *The Black Jacobins* (1963), vii. See also Alberto Moreiras, "Historicality and Historiography: Haiti and the Limits of World History," http://www.studiculturali.it/laboratori/laboratori_v_d.php?recordID=60&laboratorioID=Summer%20School%20Critica/Crisi.
120. See Wilder, *The French Imperial Nation-State*, 281, 289.
121. Rabbitt has briefly touched on the Césairean overtones of "upright" at the end of *The Black Jacobins*. See Rabbitt, "C. L. R. James's Figuring of Toussaint Louverture," 130. On the significance of the repetition of the word "debout" in Césaire's *Cahier*, see Gregson Davis, *Aimé Césaire* (Cambridge: Cambridge University Press, 1997), 57.

3. Rewriting History (1963)

1. Hall, "Breaking Bread with History," 22.
2. See Forsdick and Høgsbjerg, "Introduction," 32, 36.
3. Scott, *Conscripts of Modernity*.
4. Scott, *Conscripts of Modernity*.
5. Gillman, "Black Jacobins," 175.
6. James, *The Black Jacobins* (1963), vii.
7. James, "Lectures on *The Black Jacobins*," 72.
8. Reinhart Koselleck, *Futures Past* (Cambridge, MA: MIT Press, 1985).
9. Gary Wilder, "Untimely Vision: Aimé Césaire, Decolonization, Utopia," *Public Culture* 21, no. 1 (2009): 104–5; Gary Wilder, *Freedom Time: Negritude, Decolonization, and the Future of the World* (Durham, NC: Duke University Press, 2015), 13, 15; Gillman, "Black Jacobins," 178–79. See also Kenneth Surin, "'The Future Anterior': C. L. R. James and Going *Beyond a Boundary*," in *Rethinking C. L. R. James*, ed. Grant Farred (Oxford: Blackwell, 1996), 187–204.
10. C. L. R. James to Morris Philipson, November 30, 1961, UWI Box 7, Folder 182.

11. On paratexts, see Genette, *Paratexts*. On paratexts in postcolonial contexts, see Watts, *Packaging Post/Coloniality*. On James's use of paratexts, see Gillman, "Black Jacobins."

12. See C. L. R. James, *Beyond a Boundary* (London: Stanley Paul, 1963); Roy McCree, "The Boundaries of Publication: The Making of *Beyond a Boundary*," in *Marxism, Colonialism, and Cricket: C. L. R. James's Beyond a Boundary*, ed. David Featherstone, Christopher Gair, Christian Høgsbjerg, and Andrew Smith (Durham, NC: Duke University Press, 2018), 72–87; Selwyn R. Cudjoe, *Beyond Boundaries: The Intellectual Tradition of Trinidad and Tobago in the Nineteenth Century* (Amherst: University of Massachusetts Press, 2003).

13. C. L. R. James to Frederick A. Praeger, September 19, 1960, UWI Box 7, Folder 180.

14. C. L. R. James to Messrs. Hill and Wang, November 9, 1960, UWI Box 7, Folder 180.

15. Morris Philipson to C. L. R. James, November 7, 1960, UWI Box 7, Folder 181.

16. C. L. R. James to Morris Philipson, December 10, 1960, UWI Box 7, Folder 181.

17. C. L. R. James to Morris Philipson, March 11, 1961, UWI Box 7, Folder 181.

18. James to Philipson, December 10, 1960.

19. On James's letters during this period to Robert Lusty, publisher at Hutchison, as part of the process of making *Beyond a Boundary*, see McCree, "The Boundaries of Publication."

20. C. L. R. James, *Party Politics in the West Indies: Formerly PNM Go Forward* (San Juan, Trinidad: Vedic Enterprises, 1962); J. R. Johnson [C. L. R. James], Grace C. Lee, and Pierre Chaulieu [Cornelius Castoriadis], *Facing Reality* (Detroit: Correspondence Publishing Company, 1958; repr. Chicago: Kerr, 2006); C. L. R. James, *Nkrumah and the Ghana Revolution* (Westport, CT: Lawrence Hill, 1977).

21. Morris Philipson to C. L. R. James, February 24, 1961, UWI Box 7, Folder 181.

22. James to Philipson, March 11, 1961.

23. James to Philipson, March 11, 1961.

24. C. L. R. James to Morris Philipson, June 23, 1961, UWI Box 7, Folder 181.

25. James to Philipson, June 23, 1961.

26. James to Philipson, November 30, 1961, UWI Box 7, Folder 182.

27. James to Philipson, November 30, 1961.

28. C. L. R. James to Morris Philipson, January 18, 1962, UWI Box 7, Folder 182.

29. The new preface to the Vintage edition is not preserved in the 2001 Penguin edition, which is the most readily available edition of *The Black Jacobins* today. See C. L. R. James, *The Black Jacobins: Toussaint Louverture and the San Domingo Revolution* (Harmondsworth: Penguin, 2001).

30. Page numbers in parentheses, here and throughout, refer to the 1963 and 1938 editions respectively. For an explanation of the transcription conventions used, see the note in the introduction.

31. James, "Lectures on *The Black Jacobins*," 103.

32. James, "Lectures on *The Black Jacobins*," 90.

33. In the quotations below, text in bold indicates 1963 additions and strikethrough points out 1963 deletions.
34. C. L. R. James to Frederick A. Praeger, September 19, 1960, UWI Box 7, Folder 180; James to Philipson, December 10, 1960.
35. See 18n12/11, 41/30, 43n9/31, 51/38, 55n33/41, 82n8/64, 265n22/222.
36. See Gillman, "Black Jacobins," 176.
37. James also provided similar "written in 1938" oral footnotes in the 1971 lecture "How I Wrote *The Black Jacobins.*" James, "Lectures on *The Black Jacobins*," 72.
38. James to Philipson, November 30, 1961.
39. See Lisa Jackson-Schebetta, *"Traveler, There Is No Road": Theater, the Spanish Civil War, and the Decolonial Imagination in the Americas* (Iowa City: University of Iowa Press, 2017), 20, 121, 157, 181.
40. See 16n11/9n1, 141/113, 358n14/216n1.
41. See 22/14, 55/41, 73/56.
42. James to Philipson, March 11, 1961.
43. C. L. R. James, *You Don't Play with Revolution: The Montreal Lectures of C. L. R. James*, ed. David Austin (Oakland, CA: AK Press, 2009), 183.
44. On James's refiguring of Toussaint Louverture, see also Charles Forsdick, "Refiguring Resistance: Historiography, Fiction, and the Afterlives of Toussaint Louverture," in Forsdick and Høgsbjerg, *The Black Jacobins Reader*, 215–34.
45. See 137/110 and 148/119.
46. See also 221/183.
47. See B. W. Higman, *Writing West Indian Histories* (London: Macmillan Education, 1999).
48. Scott, *Conscripts of Modernity*, 11, 132.
49. Scott, *Conscripts of Modernity*, 137.
50. Scott, *Conscripts of Modernity*, 45, 123, 168.
51. Alex Callinicos, *Theories and Narratives: Reflections on the Philosophy of History* (Durham, NC: Duke University Press, 1995). See also Hayden White, "Historical Emplotment and the Problem of Truth," in *Probing the Limits of Representation: Nazism to the Final Solution*, ed. Saul Friedlander (Cambridge, MA: Harvard University Press, 1992), 37–53; Perry, *Marxism and History*, 136–54.
52. James, "Lectures on *The Black Jacobins*," 103–9; James, "Black Sansculottes," 160.
53. Thompson, *The Making of the English Working Class* (1963); Soboul, *Les Sansculottes parisiens* (1958); Rudé, *The Crowd in the French Revolution* (1959). There is a valuable 1983 film directed by H. O. Nazareth and entitled *Talking History: C. L. R. James in Conversation with E. P. Thompson*. See also E. P. Thompson, *Making History: Writings on History and Culture* (New York: New Press, 1994); Bryan Palmer, *The Making of E. P. Thompson: Marxism, Humanism, and History* (Toronto: New Hogtown, 1981); Stephen Woodhams, *History in the Making: Raymond Williams, Edward Thompson, and Radical Intellectuals, 1936–1956* (London: Merlin, 2001).

54. See Fick, "C. L. R. James, *The Black Jacobins*, and *The Making of Haiti*," 63–64. As Fick notes, this "was a daunting task, all the more so because these slaves and their leaders left no written records of their own." See Georges Lefebvre, *La Révolution française: La fuite du roi* (Paris: Tournier and Constans, 1947).

55. James, "Black Sansculottes," 159–62. See Alberto Toscano, "Black Sansculottes and Ambitious Marionettes: Cedric J. Robinson, C. L. R. James and the Critique of Political Leadership," *Viewpoint Magazine*, February 16, 2017.

56. Matthew Quest has also wondered about whether the title of the proposed rewritten account might change in "On 'Both Sides' of the Haitian Revolution? Rethinking Direct Democracy and National Liberation in *The Black Jacobins*," in Forsdick and Høgsbjerg, *The Black Jacobins Reader*, 236. See also R. B. Rose, *The Making of the Sans-Culottes* (Manchester: Manchester University Press, 1983); R. B. Rose, *The Enragés* (Melbourne: Melbourne University Press, 1965); Gwyn A. Williams, *Artisans and Sans-Culottes: Popular Movements in France and Britain during the French Revolution* (London: Edward Arnold, 1968).

57. James, "Lectures on *The Black Jacobins*," 107–8.

58. On similar hunting down of "bandits," see Eric Hobsbawm, *Bandits* (London: Weidenfeld and Nicolson, 1969).

59. James, "Lectures on *The Black Jacobins*," 108.

60. James, "Lectures on *The Black Jacobins*," 108, 100.

61. Fick, "C. L. R. James, *The Black Jacobins*, and *The Making of Haiti*," 64.

62. James, "Lectures on *The Black Jacobins*," 103.

63. See Quest, "On 'Both Sides' of the Haitian Revolution," 251. See also Rose, *The Making of the Sans-Culottes*; Rose, *The Enragés*.

64. James, "Lectures on *The Black Jacobins*," 102–3.

65. Nemours, *Histoire de la Captivité et la mort de Toussaint-Louverture*, 90–105.

66. Geggus, *Haitian Revolutionary Studies*, 96, 137–49.

67. James, "Lectures on *The Black Jacobins*," 111.

68. On how the tragic and the chorus feature in both versions of *The Black Jacobins* history, see Glick, "'Taking Up Arms,'" 73, 120; Glick, *The Black Radical Tragic*, 85, 92.

69. See Martin Glaberman, ed., *Marxism for Our Times: C. L. R. James on Revolutionary Organization* (Jackson: University Press of Mississippi, 1999); Kimathi Mohammed, *Organization and Spontaneity: The Theory of the Vanguard Party and Its Application to the Black Movement in the U.S. Today* (Atlanta, GA: On Our Own Authority!, 2013).

70. Grace Lee Boggs, "Thinking and Acting Dialectically: C. L. R. James, the American Years," *Monthly Review* 45, no. 5 (1993): 38–46.

71. See Dan Georgakas, "*The Black Jacobins* in Detroit: 1963," in Forsdick and Høgsbjerg, *The Black Jacobins Reader*, 55–57; Dan Goergakas and Marvin Surkin, *Detroit: I Do Mind Dying: A Study in Urban Revolution* (London: Redwords, 1998).

72. Paul Romano [Phil Singer] and Ria Stone [Grace Lee Boggs], *The American Worker* (Detroit: Bewick, 1947 [Schomburg Center for Research in Black Culture,

New York Public Library, New York, Manuscripts, Archives, and Rare Books Division, SC87–89, Box 2, Folder 7]); Martin Glaberman, *Punching Out* (Detroit: Bewick, 1952). See Rosengarten, *Urbane Revolutionary*, 71, 73–74.

73. See C. L. R. James, "Education, Propaganda, Agitation," in Glaberman, *Marxism for Our Times*, 16–17.

74. Mbiyu Koinange, *The People of Kenya Speak for Themselves* (Detroit: Kenya Publication Fund, 1955).

75. Robert A. Hill, "Literary Executor's Afterword," in C. L. R. James, *American Civilization*, ed. Anna Grimshaw and Keith Hart (Oxford: Blackwell, 1993), 345.

76. James, "Lectures on *The Black Jacobins*," 99–100.

77. See also James, "Black Sansculottes," 161.

78. James, "Lectures on *The Black Jacobins*," 76.

79. Daniel Guérin, *La Lutte de classes sous la première République: Bourgeois et "bras nus," 1793–1797* (Paris: Gallimard, 1946). Attempts such as Daniel Guérin's to project backward and cast the workers as categories of proletariat or preproletariat have been criticized by Georges Lefebvre and Albert Soboul as appropriate only to a later stage of development. See Georges Lefebvre, review of *La Lutte de class sous la première République: Bourgeois et "bras nus" (1793–1797)*, by Daniel Guérin, *Annales historiques de la Révolution française* 19 (1947): 173–79; Albert Soboul, "Classes et luttes de classes sous la Révolution française," *La Pensée* 53 (1954): 39. As for Rose, he condemned Guérin's view of the enragés as "at best a half-truth, and at worst an anachronism." Rose, *The Enragés*, 7–8, 93; Rose, *The Making of the Sans-Culottes*, 93.

80. James, "Lectures on *The Black Jacobins*," 77.

81. See Hill, "Literary Executor's Afterword," 342, 345.

82. Hill, "Literary Executor's Afterword," 342.

83. James, "Lectures on *The Black Jacobins*," 78.

84. James, "Lectures on *The Black Jacobins*," 76.

85. James, "Lectures on *The Black Jacobins*," 77. As further evidence of his "hard reading," James also accidentally left behind a library copy of Soboul's book during his 1968 visit to Nigeria (C. L. R. James to Dexter Lyndersay, July 3, 1968, UWI Box 10, Folder 241).

86. Høgsbjerg makes this point about possible correspondence between Price Mars and James in his paper "Reflections on C. L. R. James and the U.S. Occupation of Haiti."

87. Aimé Césaire, *Toussaint Louverture* (Paris: Présence Africaine, 1961). On Aimé Césaire and Toussaint Louverture, see John Patrick Walsh, "Toussaint Louverture at a Crossroads: The Mémoire of the 'First Soldier of the Republic of Saint-Domingue,'" *Journal of Haitian Studies* 17, no. 1 (2011): 88–105.

88. Madison Smartt Bell, "Afterword to *The Black Jacobins*'s Italian Edition," in Forsdick and Høgsbjerg, *The Black Jacobins Reader*, 318.

89. Scott, *Conscripts of Modernity*, 107.

90. Scott, *Conscripts of Modernity*, 123.

91. Scott, *Conscripts of Modernity*.

92. Gillman, "Black Jacobins," 174.

93. Renault, *C. L. R. James*, 195.

94. Raphael Dalleo, "'The Independence So Hardly Won Has Been Maintained': C. L. R. James and the U.S. Occupation of Haiti," *Cultural Critique* 87 (2014): 38–59. Høgsbjerg has also presented an unpublished paper on this topic: "Reflections on C. L. R. James and the U.S. Occupation of Haiti."

95. Constantin Mayard, "Haïti" (speech delivered January 28, 1934) (Poitiers: L'Action intellectuelle, 1934).

96. This speech is wrongly attributed to 1938, when it dates, in fact, from 1934; Mayard, "Haïti."

97. Aimé Césaire, *Cahier d'un retour au pays natal* (1939; Paris: Présence Africaine, 1956).

98. See for example UWI Box 14, Folder 310; UWI Box 20, Folder 377.

99. Harold Bloom, *A Map of Misreading* (Oxford: Oxford University Press, 2003).

100. Bloom, *A Map of Misreading*, 3–4. On postcolonial strong readings, see Biodun Jeyifo, "Whose Theatre, Whose Africa? Wole Soyinka's *The Road* on the Road," *Modern Drama* 45, no. 3 (2002): 449–65.

101. "Eia pour le Kaïlcédrat royal!" See Aimé Césaire, *Cahier d'un retour au pays natal*, ed. Abiola Irele (Ibadan: New Horn Press, 1994), 118.

102. See Césaire, *Cahier d'un retour au pays natal* (1994), 122.

103. Césaire, *Cahier d'un retour au pays natal* (1994), 36.

104. Selma James, *Sex, Race, and Class—The Perspective of Winning: A Selection of Writings, 1952–2011* (Oakland, CA: PM Press, 2012).

105. C. L. R. James, *At the Rendezvous of Victory: Selected Writings*, vol. 3 (London: Allison and Busby, 1984). Margaret Busby made a major contribution to making James's writings available to new readers in the UK. See Margaret Busby, "C. L. R. James: A Biographical Introduction," in Gaverne Bennett and Christian Høgsbjerg, eds., *Celebrating C. L. R. James in Hackney, London* (London: Redwords, 2015).

106. UWI Box 14, Folder 209; UWI Box 20, Folder 377.

107. UWI Box 20, Folder 387; UWI Box 16, Folder 336.

108. James makes similar references regarding Chaguaramas and the need to strike serious blows at the old colonial system in a speech in UWI Box 20, Folder 377.

109. UWI Box 20, Folder 177. See also James, "Black Sansculottes," 160. In a 1973 speech, James would also speak about the significance of the Cuban Revolution within the line of West Indian development; UWI Box 14, Folder 309.

110. See C. L. R. James, "Dr. Eric Williams, First Premier of Trinidad and Tobago; a Biographical Sketch [1960]," in *Eric E. Williams Speaks*, ed. Selwyn R. Cudjoe (Wellesley, MA: Calaloux, 1993), 327–51.

111. UWI Box 20, Folder 377.

112. See Colin Palmer, *Eric Williams and the Making of the Modern Caribbean* (Chapel Hill: University of North Carolina Press, 2006), 137.

113. On James's writings of this period, Frank Rosengarten has also noted how new terms such as "nation" and "community" appear constantly in James's writings of the

early 1960s, completely overshadowing the Marxist terms he had previously used. See Rosengarten, *Urbane Revolutionary*, 119.

114. Scott, *Conscripts of Modernity*, 145. See also James, *Party Politics in the West Indies* for his damning postmortem of the failure of the West Indies Federation.

115. UWI Box 20, Folder 377.

116. UWI Box 20, Folder 377.

117. UWI Box 20, Folder 377. On James and gender, see Hazel V. Carby, *Race Men* (Cambridge, MA: Harvard University Press, 1998); Belinda Edmondson, *Making Men: Gender, Literary Authority, and Women's Writing in Caribbean Narrative* (Durham, NC: Duke University Press, 1999). Elsewhere, however, James did comment on African American women's writing. See C. L. R. James, "Three Black Women Writers: Toni Morrison, Alice Walker, Ntozake Shange" (1981), reprinted in James, *The C. L. R. James Reader*, 411–17.

118. UWI Box 14, Folder 310.

4. Reshaping the Past as Drama (1967)

1. There are two nearly identical published play texts in Errol Hill, ed., *A Time and a Season: Eight Caribbean Plays* (Port-of-Spain: University of the West Indies, Trinidad, Extramural Studies Unit, 1976), 382–450; James, *The C. L. R. James Reader*, 67–111. *The Black Jacobins* play was also produced by BBC Radio in 1971 and for the stage by (among others) Dexter Lyndersay, Arts Theatre, University of Ibadan, Nigeria, December 14–16, 1967; Rawle Gibbons and University Players at Mona, Jamaica, in 1975; Rawle Gibbons and the Yard Theatre in Trinidad in 1979; by Eugene Williams and the Graduate Theatre Company of the Jamaica School of Drama in Kingston in 1982; by Yvonne Brewster for Talawa Theatre Company's maiden production at the Riverside Studios in London in 1986; by Rawle Gibbons and Danielle Lyndersay at the Theatre Arts Faculty, University of the West Indies, St. Augustine, Trinidad, in 1993; and by Harclyde Walcott at the University of the West Indies, Cave Hill Campus, Barbados, in 2004. Extracts directed by Wendell Manwarren were also performed at Bocas Lit Fest, Trinidad, April 29, 2018.

2. On James's rethinking of direct democracy in *The Black Jacobins*, see Quest, "On 'Both Sides' of the Haitian Revolution?," 235–52.

3. See King, *C. L. R. James and Creolization*, 30–51; King, "C. L. R. James, Genre and Cultural Politics," 13–38; Sander, "C. L. R. James and the Haitian Revolution," 277–90; Sander, *The Trinidad Awakening*, 104–13.

4. See Selwyn R. Cudjoe, "C. L. R. James Misbound," *Transition* 58 (1992): 127.

5. Scott McLemee, "Afterword—American Civilization and World Revolution: C. L. R. James in the United States, 1938–1953 and Beyond," in McLemee and Le Blanc, *C. L. R. James and Revolutionary Marxism*, 239n9.

6. Emery, *Modernism, the Visual, and Caribbean Literature*, 259n63.

7. On this, Rosengarten cites McLemee, and Emery cites Jim Murray (C. L. R. James Institute). See Rosengarten, *Urbane Revolutionary*, 255n2; Emery, *Modernism, the*

Visual, and Caribbean Literature, 259–60n63; McLemee and Blanc, *C. L. R. James and Revolutionary Marxism*, 234n9. On the C. L. R. James Institute, see Jim Murray, "The C. L. R. James Institute and Me," *Interventions* 1, no. 3 (1999): 389–96.

8. See Lindenberger, *Historical Drama*, 156–57.

9. James, *Beyond a Boundary*, 196.

10. On alternative modes of historical expression, see Munslow, *Narrative and History*, 67, 84; Breslin, "'The First Epic of the New World,'" 241.

11. On the Johnson-Forest Tendency, see James D. Young, *The World of C. L. R. James: The Unfragmented Vision* (Glasgow: Clydeside, 1999), 162–79; Rosengarten, *Urbane Revolutionary*, 61–84; McLemee and Le Blanc, *C. L. R. James and Revolutionary Marxism*, 8–18, 48–51. On Haitian history from below, see the James-mentored study by Fick, *The Making of Haiti*; Fouchard, *The Haitian Maroons*, v–vii, which has a preface by James. Generally, see Jim Sharpe, "History from Below," in *New Perspectives on Historical Writing*, ed. Peter Burke (Cambridge: Polity, 1991), 24–41; Krantz, *History from Below*.

12. Rabbitt, "C. L. R. James's Figuring of Toussaint Louverture," 120; Geggus, *Haitian Revolutionary Studies*, 31; King, *C. L. R. James*, 31–32; Rosengarten, *Urbane Revolutionary*, 226.

13. James, *Beyond a Boundary*, 151; Nicole King notes, for example, "For my part, I recognized James's affinity for fiction and narrative in nearly everything he wrote," in *C. L. R. James and Creolization*, xiii.

14. Samuel, "Introduction," xiii; Kelleher, *Theatre and Politics*, 10, 13.

15. Diana Taylor, *The Archive and the Repertoire: Performing Cultural Memory in the Americas* (Durham, NC: Duke University Press, 2003); Joseph Roach, *Cities of the Dead: Circum-Atlantic Performance* (New York: Columbia University Press, 1996); Rebecca Schneider, *Performing Remains: Art and War in Times of Theatrical Reenactment* (London: Routledge, 2011).

16. Errol G. Hill, "The Emergence of a National Drama in the West Indies," *Caribbean Quarterly* 18, no. 4 (1972): 9–10.

17. See, for example, Nicolas Donin and Daniel Ferrer, eds., "Créer à plusieurs mains," special issue, *Genesis* 41 (2015).

18. James, Preface to *The Black Jacobins* (1980), v.

19. Hill, "The Emergence of a National Drama," 11.

20. See C. L. R. James to William Gorman, February 4, 1967, UWI Box 10, Folder 240. I am grateful to Raj Chetty for directing my attention back to the February 4, 1967, letter, which I saw in 2009. See Raj Chetty, "Race Fundamentalism: Caribbean Theater and the Challenge to Black Diaspora" (PhD diss., University of Washington, 2013), 86.

21. See Priscilla Allen, "The Major and Minor Themes of Melville's *White-Jacket*" (PhD diss., Cornell University, 1966); Priscilla Allen, "Evidence of the Slavery Dilemma in *White-Jacket*," *American Quarterly* 18 (1966): 477–92; Priscilla Allen, "*White-Jacket*: Melville and the Man-of-War Microcosm," *American Quarterly* 25 (1973): 32–47. Al-

len's daughter Natalia Ely told me about her mother's plays, which dated roughly from the 1970s–80s, including *Louisa*, based on Louisa May Alcott's *Little Women*: *No Limit to the Heartlessness*, based on Ivy Compton-Burnett's *The Mighty and Their Fall*. Other plays included *The Horses of Destruction* and *The Migration*.

22. Selma James, Priscilla Allen, and Sylvine Schmidt, *Wages for Housework Notebook No. 1* (New York: New York Collective, 1975). On Facing Reality, see Paul Lawrence Berman, "Facing Reality," in Buhle, *C. L. R. James*, 212–19.

23. See Chetty, "Race Fundamentalism," 86–87.

24. I am very grateful to Jenny Morgan for identifying his handwriting on the British Library script of *The Black Jacobins* play and for sharing her memories of life with him: https://jennymorganfilmswrites.wordpress.com/2018/12/03/a-small-slice-of-private-life/. I would also like to thank David Cork and his wife, Feride, for discussing their memories of Clem and James with me.

25. The Workers' and Farmers' Party was formed in October 1965 by James, Stephen Maharaj (former Democratic Labour Party leader), Dalip Gopeesingh, and George Weekes of the Oilfields Workers' Trade Union (OWTU). See Walton Look Lai, "C. L. R. James and Trinidadian Nationalism," in Henry and Buhle, *C. L. R. James's Caribbean*, 199; Jerome Teelucksingh, *Ideology, Politics, and Radicalism of the Afro-Caribbean* (London: Palgrave Macmillan, 2016), 53; Robert A. Hill, "Preface," in James, *You Don't Play with Revolution*, xv; David Austin, "Introduction: In Search of a National Identity: C. L. R. James and the Promise of the Caribbean," in James, *You Don't Play with Revolution*, 14–15; Rosengarten, *Urbane Revolutionary*, 110, 118, 124, 128–31.

26. See Clem Maharaj, *The Dispossessed* (Portsmouth, NH: Heinemann, 1992). David Cork remembers that Maharaj attended a writing course with Barbadian writer George Lamming. David Cork, telephone conversation with Rachel Douglas, January 18, 2019.

27. See, for example, the digitized British Library script here: https://www.bl.uk/collection-items/typescript-of-the-black-jacobins-play-by-c-l-r-james-1967.

28. UWI Box 9, Folder 228; UWI Box 9, Folder 229.

29. Dexter Lyndersay to C. L. R. James, November 9, 1967, UWI Box 10, Folder 240.

30. Dexter Lyndersay's annotated program for the 1993 Trinidad production of C. L. R. James, *The Black Jacobins*. I am grateful to Danielle Lyndersay for sending this to me. For an explanation of the transcription conventions used here, see the note in the introduction.

31. Dexter Lyndersay pointed out that he had never laid eyes on the script for the 1936 play in his review of the 1993 Trinidad production. Source: Danielle Lyndersay and Rawle Gibbons.

32. See Grésillon, Mervant-Roux, and Budor, *Genèses théâtrales*.

33. Dexter Lyndersay to C. L. R. James, October 8, 1967, UWI Box 10, Folder 240.

34. Dexter Lyndersay to C. L. R. James, October 31, 1967, UWI Box 10, Folder 240.

35. Dexter Lyndersay to C. L. R. James, November 9, 1967, UWI Box 10, Folder 240.

36. See Molley Ahye, *Cradle of Caribbean Dance: Beryl McBurnie and the Little Carib Theatre* (Petit Valley: Heritage Cultures, 1983).

37. Lyndersay to James, October 31, 1967.
38. Lyndersay to James, November 9, 1967.
39. C. L. R. James Papers, Box 5, Folder 16, Columbia University Library.
40. The epilogue has met with some praise as well as criticism. In a letter to James, British playwright and founder of the Roundhouse Arnold Wesker, despite complaining that there was "something wooden" about the play, wrote that he thought James was right "to set [his] preference for the views of Moïse and to use the device at the end of drawing a parallel between then and now." Arnold Wesker to C. L. R. James, May 16, 1968, UWI Box 7, Folder 190.
41. Lyndersay to James, October 31, 1967.
42. Lyndersay to James, October 31, 1967.
43. Lyndersay to James, November 9, 1967.
44. C. L. R. James to Dexter Lyndersay, November 23, 1967, UWI Box 7, Folder 190.
45. Dexter Lyndersay to C. L. R. James, November 14, 1967, UWI Box 10, Folder 240.
46. Lyndersay to James, October 31, 1967.
47. Almuth Grésillon, *La Mise en œuvre: Itinéraires génétiques* (Paris: CNRS, 2008).
48. Dexter Lyndersay to C. L. R. James, December 8, 1967, UWI Box 10, Folder 240.
49. James, "Paul Robeson," 257–58; Stuart Hall, "A Conversation with C. L. R. James," in Farred, *Rethinking C. L. R. James*, 33.
50. See Wole Soyinka, *The Man Died: Prison-Notes of Wole Soyinka* (Harmondsworth: Penguin, 1975); Wole Soyinka, *Ibadan: The Penkelemes Years: A Memoir, 1946–65* (London: Methuen, 2001). See also Derek Wright, *Wole Soyinka Revisited* (New York: Twayne, 1993); Biodun Jeyifo, *Wole Soyinka: Politics, Poetics, Postcolonialism* (Cambridge: Cambridge University Press, 2004); Biodun Jeyifo, ed., *Conversations with Wole Soyinka* (Jackson: University Press of Mississippi, 2001); Biodun Jeyifo, ed., *Perspectives on Wole Soyinka: Freedom and Complexity* (Jackson: University Press of Mississippi, 2001). Soyinka was arrested for writing press articles opposing the Nigerian Civil War, forming the "third force" to attempt to avert civil war, and visiting the Biafra secessionist leader Colonel Ojakuwa. During his detention, a forged confession alleged that he had given active support to federal authorities' archrival rebel leader by assisting with purchase of an aircraft, charges Soyinka vehemently denied, although he was never formally charged.
51. Lyndersay to James, December 8, 1967.
52. James to Lyndersay, November 23, 1967.
53. Lyndersay to James, December 8, 1967. In the event, James did miss the play premiere in December 1967 but was able to travel to Nigeria early the next year, less than a month after his trip to Cuba around February 24, 1968. In Ibadan, James delivered a lecture series. There are references to this Nigeria trip in various letters located in the following archive locations: C. L. R. James to Dexter Lyndersay, July 3, 1968, UWI Box 10, Folder 241; UWI Box 16, Folder 305; UWI Box 14, Folder 306. See also Rosengarten, *Urbane Revolutionary*, 144.
54. Theater program, University of Ibadan, UWI Box 8, Folder 219.

55. To indicate handwritten additions to the play text, I use bold font in this and following quotations in this chapter.
56. See Jeyifo, *Conversations with Wole Soyinka*, 17, 31, 61.
57. Lyndersay to James, November 9, 1967; Gibson, *The Seesaw Log*.
58. Lyndersay to James, November 9, 1967.
59. UWI Box 9, Folder 229.
60. I am grateful to Martin Banham for sharing this material with me before depositing it at the University of Leeds. Harold Preston's script has now been cataloged at the University of Leeds, Special Collections, Banham Collection, MS 1748/4.
61. James, *Toussaint Louverture* (2013), 54, 131.
62. James, "Lectures on *The Black Jacobins*," 111.
63. James, *The Black Jacobins*, in Hill, *A Time and a Season*, 384. Subsequent references are to this play edition.
64. On the top-heaviness of *The Black Jacobins* history, see Miller, *Elusive Origins*, 57–83; Rabbitt, "C. L. R. James's Figuring of Toussaint Louverture," 128–30; Nana Wilson-Tagoe, *Historical Thought and Literary Representation in West Indian Literature* (Gainesville: University Press of Florida, 1998), 27–28; Fick, *The Making of Haiti*, 4.
65. UWI Box 9, Folder 230.
66. See Lindenberger, *Historical Drama*, 150–52.
67. Lindenberger, *Historical Drama*, 148.
68. Boal, *Theater of the Oppressed*, xix, 33, 41, 183.
69. James refers to the commentary about the Haitian troops marching to this song found in Jean-Baptiste Lemonnier-Delafosse, *Seconde campagne de Saint-Domingue . . . Précédée de Souvenirs historiques et succincts de la première campagne* (Le Havre: Imprimerie de Brindeau, 1946), 84–86. C. L. R. James, "The Making of the Caribbean People," in *You Don't Play with Revolution*, 44–45; C. L. R. James, "The Haitian Revolution in the Making of the Modern World," in *You Don't Play with Revolution*, 58. On this song's complex history, see Jean-Pierre Le Glaunec, *L'Armée indigène: La défaite de Napoléon en Haïti* (Montreal: Lux, 2014). Recent uses include Michel "Sweet Micky" Martelly, former Haitian president's "Grenadier," and calls to support the Haitian football team.
70. James, *The Black Jacobins* (1976), 436.
71. See similar emphasis in Fick, *The Making of Haiti*, 228, 231, 248.
72. Boal, *Theater of the Oppressed*, 58.
73. James, *The Black Jacobins* (1976), 449–50.
74. Frantz Fanon, *Black Skin, White Masks* (London: Pluto, 1986). See C. L. R. James, "Fanon and the Caribbean," in *International Tribute to Frantz Fanon: Record of the Special Meeting of the United Nations Special Committee against Apartheid, 3 November 1978* (New York: United Nations Center against Apartheid, 1979); Max Silverman, ed., *Frantz Fanon's Black Skin, White Masks: New Interdisciplinary Essays* (Manchester: Manchester University Press, 2005).

75. James, *The Black Jacobins* (1976), 433. Historically, "Grenadiers" is associated with François Capois/Capoix-la-mort, not Samedi Smith. See Le Glaunec, *L'Armée indigène*.

76. King reads the naming of "Samedi Smith" as James invoking Vodou *lwa* Baron Samedi (King, *C. L. R. James and Creolization*, 40). But Samedi Smith, however mythologized, did exist as an identifiable individual and is not just a construct of James's literary imagination. See Fick, *The Making of Haiti*, 225–26, 231.

77. See Hobsbawm, *Bandits*, 10, 20; Fick, *The Making of Haiti*, 111–12, 216, 242.

78. James, *The Black Jacobins* (1976), 434.

79. On these leaders, see Fick, *The Making of Haiti*, 59, 222–23, 226.

80. Hobsbawm, *Bandits*, 82.

81. Like Captain Cipriani, whose political biography James published in 1932 on the question of West Indian self-government, Samedi Smith is a self-professed "champion of the barefooted man."

82. James, *The Black Jacobins* (1976), 393. See James, "The Haitian Revolution," 54.

83. See Fick, *The Making of Haiti*, 75, 86.

84. James, *The Black Jacobins* (1976), 391, 432.

85. James, *The Black Jacobins* (1976), 432–33.

86. James, *The Black Jacobins* (1976), 443.

87. James, *The Black Jacobins* (1976), 445–49.

88. James, *The Black Jacobins* (1976), 450.

89. C. L. R. James to Étienne Charlier, August 24, 1955. UWI Box 7, Folder 190.

90. James, *The Black Jacobins* (1976), 395.

91. On gaps and silences in historical records relating to Haiti and the Caribbean, see Trouillot, *Silencing the Past*; Fischer, *Modernity Disavowed*; Higman, *Writing West Indian Histories*; and Wilson-Tagoe, *Historical Thought and Literary Representation*.

92. James, *The Black Jacobins* (1976), 403.

93. James to Charlier, August 24, 1955.

94. James produced at least two alternative versions of this most reworked scene, including an introductory commentary outlining his decision to rewrite it entirely, and proposing to print as appendixes all alternative versions in an afterword to the published play text, in which he planned to "discuss how the play was arrived at." UWI Box 9, Folders 228 and 229.

95. James, *The Black Jacobins* (1976), 428.

96. On Toussaint's flaws in the revised 1963 history edition, see Scott, *Conscripts of Modernity*.

97. See Fick, *The Making of Haiti*, 209–10.

98. On this policy, see Fick, *The Making of Haiti*, 209, 247.

99. James, *The Black Jacobins* (1976), 428.

100. See Lindenberger, *Historical Drama*, 156–57.

101. James, *The Black Jacobins* (1976), 440.

102. James, *The Black Jacobins* (1976), 450.
103. As Glick points out, it is significant that James does not call these three speakers Toussaint2, Christophe2, Dessalines2, and Moïse2 because neatly conflating the speakers with the corresponding revolutionary "would problematically short-circuit the interpretive operation" (Glick, *The Black Radical Tragic*, 125).
104. David Murphy, *Sembene: Imagining Alternatives in Film and Fiction* (Oxford: James Currey, 2000), 105, 110–13, 117, 120.
105. On comedy and this play, see also Chetty, "Race Fundamentalism"; Raj Chetty, "The Tragicomedy of Anticolonial Overcoming: *Toussaint Louverture* and *The Black Jacobins* on Stage," *Callaloo* 37, no. 1 (2014): 69–88.
106. Karl Marx, *The Eighteenth Brumaire of Louis Bonaparte* (New York: Mondial, 2005).
107. See Ann Curthoys and John Docker, *Is History Fiction?* (Sydney: University of New South Wales Press, 2010), 124, 196–98; Dominick LaCapra, *Rethinking Intellectual History: Texts, Contexts, Language* (Ithaca, NY: Cornell University Press, 1983), 272, 286–87.
108. Jeffrey Mehlman, *Revolution and Repetition* (Berkeley: University of California Press, 1977), 19.
109. See Curthoys and Docker, *Is History Fiction?*, 124.
110. This more Caribbean epilogue version can be found in UWI Box 9, Folder 230.
111. UWI Box 9, Folder 230.
112. See Jeyifo, *Conversations with Wole Soyinka*, 17, 31, 61.
113. See UWI Box 9, Folders 228 and 229, Schomburg, Columbia, and Penn State 1 and 2 for this epilogue version.
114. Lyndersay to James, October 8, 1967.
115. Copies of "Alternative to p. 46 of Epilogue" can be found in UWI Box 9, Folders 228 and 229.
116. On the long postcolonial tradition of big-man politics and trade unionism, see Jeyifo, *Wole Soyinka*, xvi–xx, 58, 97–99, 285. On James's foregrounding of Toussaint's exceptionalism, see Hill, "C. L. R. James," 256–57.
117. One version of the epilogue was performed by Tayo Aluko and friends at the Liverpool Bluecoat, October 27, 2013. The performance can be viewed on YouTube: https://www.youtube.com/watch?v=F3tgbdezFCE&feature=youtu.be.
118. See Jeyifo, "Whose Theatre, Whose Africa?," 449–50.
119. My argument here diverges from Genette's dismissal of the postface/epilogue as capable of "only a curative or corrective function" because of its position at the end. Genette, *Paratexts*, 237–39.
120. C. L. R. James, "Lecture on Federation," June 1958, Marxists Internet Archive Library, https://www.marxists.org/archive/james clr/works/1958/06/federation.htm.
121. See Boal, *Theater of the Oppressed*, 122, 141, 155.
122. Boal, *Theater of the Oppressed*, 141.
123. UWI Box 10, Folder 240.
124. Boal, *Theater of the Oppressed*, 28.

5. Afterlives of *The Black Jacobins*

1. Gillman, "Black Jacobins," 171, 172.
2. There was even an opera and a calypso song directly inspired by *The Black Jacobins*. See David Blake and Anthony Ward, *Toussaint, or The Aristocracy of the Skin: Opera in Three Acts* (Sevenoaks, UK: Novello, 1977). The opera was first performed in 1977 and then revived in 1983 by the English National Opera. David Rudder's 1988 calypso song is titled "Haiti, I'm Sorry."
3. This chapter on the afterlives of *The Black Jacobins* builds on work by Cave, Rigney, Forsdick, Scholar, and Holland, among others. See Cave, *Mignon's Afterlives*; Rigney, *The Afterlives of Walter Scott*; Holland and Scholar, *Pre-Histories and Afterlives*. The following works have been useful for my purposes: Ross, *May '68 and Its Afterlives*; and Hobsbawm, *Echoes of the Marseillaise*.
4. Forsdick and Høgsbjerg, "Introduction," 33.
5. See Robin Bunce and Paul Field, *Darcus Howe: A Political Biography* (London: Bloomsbury, 2014), 217–19; Robin Bunce, *Renegade: The Life and Times of Darcus Howe* (London: Bloomsbury, 2017). See City Lights, "Black History Month: Creation for Liberation," *Abandon All Despair Ye Who Enter Here*, February 25, 2013, http://www.blogcitylights.com/2013/02/25/black-history-month-creation-for-liberation.
6. See David A. Bailey, Alissandra Cummins, Axel Lapp, and Allison Thompson, eds., *Curating in the Caribbean* (Berlin: Green Box, 2012).
7. Ras Akyem-i Ramsay, interview by Rachel Douglas, June 29, 2018.
8. Adisa "Aja" Adwele, "Brekin' Open the *Blakk-Jacobin*," in *Painting Poetry: Poetic Interpretations of Art* (Bridgetown, Barbados: Acute Vision, 2015).
9. See Lubaina Himid, *Scenes from the Life of Toussaint L'Ouverture*, Arts Council Collection, 1987, http://www.artscouncilcollection.org.uk/explore/artist/himid-lubaina.
10. Kimathi Donkor, interview by Rachel Douglas, August 24, 2018.
11. C. L. R. James, *The Black Jacobins: Toussaint Louverture and the San Domingo Revolution* (New York: Vintage, 1963), 346.
12. James, *The Black Jacobins* (1963), 352.
13. For an incisive reading of *Caribbean Passion: Haiti 1804* and in particular the painting *Toussaint L'Ouverture at Bedourete*, see Philip Kaisary, *The Haitian Revolution in the Literary Imagination* (Charlottesville: University of Virginia Press, 2014), 84–95.
14. See Celeste-Marie Bernier, "Tracing Transatlantic Slavery in Kimathi Donkor's UK Diaspora," *Nka: Journal of Contemporary African Art* 41 (2017): 108–24; Kimathi Donkor, Selected Projects 2002–2017, http://kimathidonkor.net/Projects/; Charles Forsdick, "Visualising Toussaint Louverture," British Museum, March 12, 2018, https://blog.britishmuseum.org/visualising-toussaint-louverture/; Caroline Menezes, "Retelling History through Art: An Interview with Kimathi Donkor," *Studio International*, January 16, 2013, https://www.studiointernational.com/index.php/retelling-history-through-art-an-interview-with-kimathi-donkor; Eddie Chambers, "Reading the Riot Act," *Visual Culture in Britain* 14, no. 2 (2013): 238–56.

15. See Bernier, "Tracing Transatlantic Slavery" for images of these artworks.

16. *A Revolutionary Legacy: Haiti and Toussaint Louverture*, British Museum, February 22–April 22, 2018, https://www.britishmuseum.org/about_us/past_exhibitions/2018/a_revolutionary_legacy.aspx.

17. The display suggests that the credit to "Loren Eutemy" may be a misspelling of Loring Eutemey, an African American graphic artist who designed many jazz sleeves.

18. Gina Athena Ulysse, "Haiti and Toussaint Louverture: The Response Must Be a Remix," British Museum, March 13, 2018, https://blog.britishmuseum.org/haiti-and-toussaint-louverture-the-response-must-be-a-remix/. See also Gina Athena Ulysse, *Why Haiti Needs New Narratives: A Post-Quake Chronicle* (Middletown, CT: Wesleyan University Press, 2014).

19. On Dessalines's apotheosis to Vodou lwa, see Joan Dayan, *Haiti, History, and the Gods* (Berkeley: University of California Press, 1995). See also Lindsay J. Twa, "Jean-Jacques Dessalines: Demon, Demigod, and Everything in Between," Romantic Circles, October 2011, https://www.rc.umd.edu/praxis/circulations/HTML/praxis.2011.twa.html; Deborah Jenson, "Jean-Jacques Dessalines and the African Character of the Haitian Revolution," *William and Mary Quarterly* 69, no. 3 (2012): 615–38.

20. Donald Cosentino, "Divine Revolution: The Art of Édouard Duval-Carrié," Fowler Museum at UCLA, https://www.fowler.ucla.edu/product/divine-revolution-the-art-of-edouard-duval-carrie/; Ulrick Jean-Pierre, *Ulrick: The Documentary*, 2016, http://www.ulrickdoc.com/home.html.

21. For information on the exhibit, see https://news.brown.edu/events/detail/many-faces-toussaint-l-ouverture-and-haitian-revolution; and https://www.brown.edu/initiatives/slavery-and-justice/many-faces-toussaint-l-ouverture-and-haitian-revolution-conversation-haitian-artist-edouard-duval-ca. "The Many Faces of Toussaint Louverture" was also the title of a chapter on portraiture of Louverture. See Helen Weston, "The Many Faces of Toussaint Louverture," in *Slave Portraiture in the Atlantic World*, ed. Agnes Lugo-Ortiz and Angela Rosenthal (Cambridge: Cambridge University Press, 2013), 345–71.

22. Anthony Bogues, "Curatorial Note," in *The Many Faces of Toussaint L'Ouverture and the Haitian Revolution*, exhibition catalog (Providence, RI: Center for the Study of Slavery and Justice, Brown University, 2014), 2.

23. Édouard Duval-Carrié, interview by Rachel Douglas, January 27, 2019.

24. See Bogues, *The Many Faces*, 1.

25. See Zack Bu, "In Conversation: Duval-Carrié—'It's Like Building a Hero,'" *The Brown Daily Herald*, October 7, 2014. http://www.browndailyherald.com/2014/10/07/conversation-duval-carrie-like-building-hero/.

26. Fritz Daguillard, *Enigmatic in His Glory: Toussaint Louverture, 1743–1803* (Port-au-Prince: Musée du Panthéon Nationale Haïtien, 2003), 7; Celeste-Marie Bernier, *Characters of Blood: Black Heroism in the Transatlantic Imagination* (Charlottesville: University of Virginia Press, 2012), 35.

27. David P. Geggus, "The Changing Faces of Toussaint Louverture: Literary and Pictorial Depictions," https://www.brown.edu/Facilities/John_Carter_Brown_Library/exhibitions/toussaint/pages/iconography.html.

28. On this famous picture, see Grégory Pierrot and Paul Youngquist, "Introduction," in Marcus Rainsford, *An Historical Account of the Black Empire of Hayti* (Durham, NC: Duke University Press, 2013), xvii–lvi; Geggus, "The Changing Faces"; Bernier, *Characters of Blood*, 27–88.

29. See Forsdick, "Visualising Toussaint Louverture."

30. See Youngquist and Pierrot, "Introduction," xlvii.

31. Daguillard, *Enigmatic*, 21.

32. Bernier, *Characters of Blood*, 37.

33. See Donald Consentino, *Divine Revolution: The Art of Édouard Duval-Carrié* (Los Angeles: UCLA Fowler Museum of Cultural History, 2005).

34. Duval-Carrié has also based work on a recently discovered portrait of Louverture attributed to Alexandre Girardin. See Duval-Carrié, *Toussaint Blue* (2014) and *Toussaint Pink* (2014), in Bogues, *The Many Faces*, 12. See also Patrick Sylvain, "Is This the Authentic Face of Toussaint Louverture?," https://www.bostonhaitian.com/2011/authentic-face-toussaint-louverture; Geggus, "The Changing Faces."

35. See Josh MacPhee, "Judging Books By Their Covers," July 25, 2011, https://justseeds.org/jbbtc-68-the-black-jacobins/.

36. On early British representations of Toussaint Louverture, see Grégory Pierrot, "'Our Hero': Toussaint Louverture in British Representations," *Criticism* 50, no. 4 (2008): 581–607.

37. See, for example, Forsdick and Høgsbjerg, "Introduction," 34.

38. C. L. R. James, *Les Jacobins noirs: Toussaint Louverture et la révolution de Saint-Domingue*, trans. Pierre Naville (Paris: Gallimard, 1949); 2nd ed., trans. Pierre Naville and Claude-Fivel Demoret (Paris: Éditions Caribéennes, 1983); 3rd ed. (Paris: Éditions Amsterdam, 2008); C. L. R. James, *I giacobini neri: La prima rivolta contro l'uomo bianco*, trans. Raffaele Petrillo (Milan: Feltrinelli, 1968); 2nd ed., ed. Filippo del Lucchese and Miguel Mellino, trans. Raffaele Petrillo and Filippo del Lucchese (Rome: Derive Approdi, 2006); C. L. R. James, *Die schwarzen Jakobiner: Toussaint L'Ouverture und die San-Domingo-Revolution* (Berlin: Verlag Neues Leben, 1984); C. L. R. James, *Schwarze Jakobiner: Toussaint L'Ouverture und die Unabhängigkeitsrevolution in Haiti* (Cologne: Pahl-Rugenstein, 1984); C. L. R. James, *Burakku jakoban: Tusan ruveruchūru to haichi kakumei* (1991; reprint, Tokyo: Omura-Shoten, 2002); C. L. R. James, *Os jacobinos negros: Toussaint Louverture e a revolução de São Domingos* (São Paulo: Boitempo, 2001; repr., 2010); C. L. R. James, *Los jacobinos negros: Toussaint Louverture y la revolución de Haití* (Madrid, Mexico City: Turner, Fondo de Cultura Económica, 2003); C. L. R. James, "De Toussaint Louverture a Fidel Castro," *Casa de las Américas* 91 (1975): 64–69; C. L. R. James, *Los jacobinos negros: Toussaint Louverture y la revolución de Saint-Domingue*, trans. Rosa López Oceguera (Havana: Casa de las Américas, 2010).

39. James tells in his autobiography drafts of his regular meetings with Naville "every three or four months" in Paris where the Trotksyist movement was based, with James usually representing the British section. "Section 4 1932–1938," autobiography, C. L. R. James Papers, Box 4, Folder 15, Columbia University Library; James, "My Knowledge of Damas Is Unique," 131. Naville was also an early surrealist and sociologist. See Michael Löwy, *Morning Star: Surrealism, Marxism, Anarchism, Situationism, Utopia* (Austin: University of Texas Press, 2009), 43–62.

40. My reading of Naville's preface is informed by the interpretation of Césaire's 1948 speech in Gary Wilder, "Race, Reason, Impasse: Césaire, Fanon, and the Legacy of Emancipation," *Radical History Review* 90 (2004): 31–61. See also C. L. R. James, "Fanon and the Caribbean," in *International Tribute to Frantz Fanon*, 43–46.

41. Gaston Monnerville, Léopold Sédar-Senghor, and Aimé Césaire, *Commémoration du centenaire de l'abolition de l'esclavage: Discours prononcés à la Sorbonne le 27 Avril 1948* [Centennial commemoration of the abolition of slavery: Presentations at the Sorbonne April 27, 1948] (Paris: Presses Universitaires des France, 1948), 27–28.

42. Steve Wright, *Storming Heaven: Class Composition and Struggle in Italian Autonomist Marxism* (London: Pluto, 2002), 89, 96, 114–26.

43. Ferruccio Gambino, "Only Connect," in Buhle, *C. L. R. James*, 195–98; Christian Høgsbjerg, "'A Bohemian Freelancer?' C. L. R. James, His Early Relationship to Anarchism and the Intellectual Origins of Autonomism," in *Libertarian Socialism: Politics in Black and Red*, ed. Alex Prichard, Ruth Kinna, Saku Pinta, and David Berry (Basingstoke, UK: Palgrave Macmillan, 2012), 11–17. See Francesca Pozzi, Gigi Roggero, and Guido Borio, *Futuro anteriore: Dai "Quaderni rossi" ai movimenti globali: Riccheze e limiti dell'operaismo italiano* (Rome: Derive Approdi, 2002); Francesca Pozzi, Gigi Roggero, and Guido Borio, *Gli operaisti* (Rome: Derive Approdi, 2005); "Intervista a Ferruccio Gambino" [Interview with Ferruccio Gambino], by Guido Borio, Francesca Pozzi, and Gigi Roggero, June 10, 2001, http://www.autistici.org/operaismo/gambino/5_1.htm.

On Italian Workerism, see Chamsy El-Ojeili, "Many Flowers, Little Fruit? The Dilemmas of Workerism," *Thesis Eleven* 79 (2004): 112–23; Ferdinando Fasce, "American Labor History, 1973–1983: Italian Perspectives," *Reviews in American History* 14, no. 4 (1986): 597–613. George Rawick was one important collaborator who worked with the Italian Workerists. See his James-inspired composite documentary project about slaves' reactions to slaves: George P. Rawick, *The American Slave: A Composite Autobiography*, vol. 1, *From Sundown to Sunup: The Making of the Black Community* (Westport, CT: Greenwood, 1972); George P. Rawick, *Listening to Revolt: The Selected Writings of George Rawick*, ed. David Roediger (Chicago: Charles H. Kerr, 2010).

44. On this problematic subtitle with reference to the second 2006 Italian edition, see Alessandro Portelli, "Gli schiavi dei Lumi alla presa della Bastigli riproposto il volume di C. L. R. James, *I giacobini neri*, un classico della storiografia sociale," December 10, 2006, https://alessandroportelli.blogspot.com/2006/12/gli-schiavi-dei-lumi-alla-presa-della.html.

45. Raffaele Petrillo, interview by Rachel Douglas, July 21, 2014.
46. Sandro Chignola, *François Dominique Toussaint Louverture, la libertà del popolo nero: Scritti politici* (Turin: La Rosa, 1997).
47. Madison Smartt Bell, "Afterword to *The Black Jacobins*'s Italian Edition," in Forsdick and Høgsbjerg, *The Black Jacobins Reader*, 313–21; see also Madison Smartt Bell, *Toussaint Louverture: A Biography* (New York: Pantheon, 2007).
48. C. L. R. James to Dr. de la Osa, February 18, 1961, UWI Box 7, Folder 183; René Depestre to C. L. R. James, July 20, 1961, UWI Box 7, Folder 183.
49. James, "De Toussaint Louverture a Fidel Castro." See also Joseph Pereira, "The Influence of the Casa de las Américas on English Caribbean Literature," *Caribbean Quarterly* 31, no. 1 (1985): 93–105; Judith A. Weiss, *Casa de las Américas: An Intellectual Review in the Cuban Revolution* (Madrid: Editorial Castalia, 1977).
50. Rosa López Oceguera, email correspondence with Rachel Douglas, July 1, 2017.
51. On the Cuban black scare and racial issues in Cuba, see Esteban Morales Domínguez, *Race in Cuba: Essays on the Revolution and Racial Inequality* (New York: Monthly Review Press, 2013); Gerald Horne, *Race to Revolution: The U.S. and Cuba during Slavery and Jim Crow* (New York: Monthly Review Press, 2014); Andrea Easley Morris, *Afro-Cuban Identity in Post-Revolutionary Novel and Film: Inclusion, Loss, and Cultural Resistance* (Lewisburg, PA: Bucknell University Press, 2011).
52. See the English-language version of John H. Bracey's introduction to the Cuban edition of *Los jacobinos negros* in Forsdick and Høgsbjerg, *The Black Jacobins Reader*, 322–27.
53. Rosa López Oceguera, email correspondence with Rachel Douglas, August 31, 2015.
54. Jahnheinz Jahn to C. L. R. James, January 9, 1969, UWI Box 10, Folder 242; Sergio Bologna, interview by Rachel Douglas, August 20, 2014.
55. Udo Baron, *Kalter Krieg und heisser Frieden: Der Einfluss der SED und ihrer westdeutschen Verbündeten auf die Partei "Die Grünen"* (Münster: Lit Verlag, 2003). See also Günter Bohnsack, *Hauptverwaltung Aufklärung: Die Legende stirbt: Das Ende von Wolfs Geheimdienst* (Berlin: Edition Ost, 1997), 111; Roland Kirbach, "Von den Genossen verlassen," *Die Zeit*, December 2, 1989, http://www.zeit.de/1989/52/von-den-genossen-verlassen; "Ewige Wahrheiten," *Der Spiegel*, no. 23 (June 5, 1989), 42–46, http://www.spiegel.de/spiegel/print/d-13492945.html.
56. See Salkey, *Havana Journal*, 58–59.
57. See C. L. R. James to seven Japanese publishers, September 1968, UWI Box 10, Folder 241.
58. Yoshio Aoki, interview by Rachel Douglas, July 10, 2017.
59. See Jacob Gorender, "O épico e o trágico na história do Haiti," *Estudos avançados* 18, no. 50 (2004): 295–302; Jacob Gorender, *A escravidão reabilitada* (São Paolo, Editora Ática, 1990).
60. See Marvin George and Rawle Gibbons, "*Jouvay Ayiti*: Haiti's New Day from Mas to Mas Action," *Caribbean Quarterly* 62, no. 1 (2016): 69–81; Rawle Gibbons,

"Traditional Enactments of Trinidad: Towards a Third Theatre" (M.Phil. thesis, University of the West Indies, St. Augustine, 1979); Louis Regis, "Rawle Gibbons and the Theory and Practice of the Third Theatre," *Caribbean Quarterly* 63, nos. 2–3 (2017): 183–202.

61. Judy Stone, "Yard Theatre Triumphs in *Jacobins*," *Trinidad Guardian*, August 3, 1979.

62. Synopsis, *The Monday Play*, BBC Radio 4, December 13, 1971, http://genome.ch.bbc.co.uk/e27608e472cc48acbe8a3e7083cd2e03.

63. *The Black Jacobins* radio play script (December 13, 1971), BBC Written Archives Centre, Play Library, 37. Martin Esslin, "The Mind as Stage—Radio Drama," *Theatre Quarterly* 1, no. 3 (1971): 5–11.

64. BBC *Black Jacobins* radio play script, 49. The bold font here indicates what has been added to the radio play script for blind radio. For an explanation of the transcription conventions used here, see the note in the introduction.

65. Judy Stone, "Yard Theatre Triumphs in 'Jacobins,'" *Trinidad and Tobago Guardian*, 1979; Judy Stone, "Caribbean," in *The Continuum Companion to Twentieth Century Theatre*, ed. Colin Chambers (London: Continuum, 2002), 135; Judy Stone, *Theatre* (London: Macmillan Caribbean, 1994); Martin Banham, Errol Hill, and George Woodyard, *The Cambridge Guide to African and Caribbean Theatre* (Cambridge: Cambridge University Press, 1994); Marina Maxwell, "Toward a Revolution in the Arts," *Savacou* 2 (1970): 30; Christopher B. Balme, *Decolonizing the Stage: Theatrical Syncretism and Post-Colonial Drama* (Oxford: Clarendon, 1999), 233n15–16; Edward Kamau Brathwaite, "The Love Axe/l (Developing a Caribbean Aesthetic 1962–1974)," *Bim* 16, no. 61 (1977): 181–82; Gibbons, "Traditional Enactments of Trinidad."

66. Stone, "Yard Theatre Triumphs."

67. Beverley Brown, "Don't Miss the *Jacobins*," *Jamaica Daily News*, August 28, 1982, UWI Box 8, Folder 223; Michael Reckord, "*Black Jacobins*—GOOD WORK," UWI Box 6, Folder 157; "Graduate Theatre Company Presents *Black Jacobins*," July 6, 1982, UWI Box 6, Folder 157. Eugene Williams to C. L. R. James, June 11, 1982, UWI Box 6, Folder 157.

68. Eugene Williams, interview by Rachel Douglas, September 11, 2015. See also Eugene Williams, "The Anancy Technique: A Gateway to Postcolonial Performance," *Caribbean Quarterly* 63, nos. 2–3 (2017): 215–33.

69. Reckord, "*Black Jacobins*"; Brown, "Don't Miss the *Jacobins*."

70. Caryl Phillips, "Commentary: The Most Unhappy Man of Men," *Times Literary Supplement*, March 14, 1986. One negative review describes it as one of those "school plays whose chief virtue is that it has roles for all the Upper Sixth and few fifth formers as well," Peter Hepple, "Riverside: *The Black Jacobins*," *The Stage*, March 6, 1986. However, Tony Sewell criticizes Brian Bovell as Moïse, claiming that he "seemed to lack the range to leave the 'street hero' behind and become what this play demanded—a classical performer." Tony Sewell, "Trevor's Revolution," *The Voice*, February 22, 1986. One of the most damning reviews of the characters came from Sheila Fox, *City Limits*,

March 7–13, 1986, who negatively remarks on "the characters" as being "little more than shadow puppets thrown up against a vast historical screen." Generally, however the vast historical screen was seen as positive.

71. See Nicholas de Jongh, "Slaves to Fortune," *The Guardian*, February 29, 1986; Mark Honigsbaum, *Hampstead and Highgate Express*, March 7, 1986.

72. Angela Price, "Slave Uprising Topical—Half a Century Later," *Uxbridge and Hillingdon Gazette*, March 6, 1986. The final sentence of one review reads: "It hasn't dated at all." M. L., "Black History Lesson," *Where to Go London*, March 6, 1986. See also "Performance More Than Stands the Test of Time," *Weekly Gleaner*, March 14, 1986.

73. Riverside Studios, Press Release 2, February 7, 1986, Victoria and Albert Theatre and Performance Archives, Talawa Theatre Company 8.2.1 Press Releases.

74. Yvonne Brewster, *The Black Jacobins* program, February 1986, UWI Box 8, Folder 219.

75. See, for example, Della Couling, "Theatre," *The Tablet*, March 22, 1986; Tom Vaughan, "Haiti—the Roots of Rebellion," *Morning Star*, February 17, 1986. There is a sense of déjà-vu in Eric Shorter, "The Black Jacobins," *Daily Telegraph*, February 28, 1986; Michael Coveney, "*The Black Jacobins*/Riverside Studios," *Financial Times*, February 27, 1986.

76. Rawle Gibbons, interview by Rachel Douglas, July 11, 2014. Rawle Gibbons, "Dechoukaj! *The Black Jacobins* and Liberating Caribbean Theatre" (unpublished manuscript, September 1, 2014).

77. Faith Smith, "*Black Jacobins*: Review," *Trinidad and Tobago Review*, June 1993, 27; Raymond Ramcharitar, "*Black Jacobins*: A View from the Inside," *Trinidad and Tobago Review*, May 1993, 24.

78. See Dionne Jackson Miller, "Jamaica Welcomes Hundreds of Haitian Refugees," *Albion Monitor*, May 6, 2004, http://www.albionmonitor.com/0405a/copyright/jamaicahaitirefugee.html.

79. Harclyde Walcott, interview by Rachel Douglas, September 8, 2015.

80. On "continuous substitution," see Tony Mitchell, *Dario Fo: People's Court Jester* (London: Bloomsbury, 2014), 267; Alan Cumming and Tim Supple, "A Note on the Present Text," in Dario Fo, *Accidental Death of an Anarchist* (London: Methuen, 1991), xxiii–xxiv.

81. See George and Gibbons, "*Jouvay Ayiti*," 69–81.

82. A video of the performance can be viewed here: "Reading of Toussaint Louverture Play," Worldwrite, YouTube, July 24, 2017, https://www.youtube.com/watch?v=F3tgbdezFCE&feature=youtu.be.

83. A video of the performance can be viewed here: http://bowdoin.ensemblevideo.com/hapi/v1/contents/permalinks/Ne36KdJy/view.

84. James, "Foreword," *The Black Jacobins* (1980), vii.

85. Martin Glaberman, quoted in Rosengarten, *Urbane Revolutionary*, 229; Scott McLemee, "C. L. R. James: A Biographical Introduction," *American Visions* (April–May 1996), available here: https://groups.yahoo.com/neo/groups/zimbabwefree/conversations/messages/3836. Sean Jacobs, interview by Rachel Douglas, Septem-

ber 27, 2017. On censorship during the apartheid era, see Peter D. McDonald, *The Literature Police: Apartheid Censorship and Its Cultural Consequences* (Oxford: Oxford University Press, 2009).

86. Grant Farred, interview by Rachel Douglas, September 7, 2014.

87. See Richard Owen Dudley, "About Ourselves," *Educational Journal*, October 1948, 2–4; Alan Wieder, *Teacher and Comrade: Richard Dudley and the Fight for Democracy in South Africa* (Albany: State University of New York Press, 2008).

88. Corinne Sandwith, personal correspondence with Rachel Douglas, October 6, 2017.

89. Corinne Sandwith, *World of Letters: Reading Communities and Cultural Debates in Early Apartheid South Africa* (Pietermaritzburg: University of KwaZulu-Natal Press, 2014), 97, 158.

90. Dora Taylor, "Literary Re-view," *Trek*, August 29, 1941. Many thanks to Corinne Sandwith for sending me a copy of this column.

91. Benita Parry has questioned and criticized the "privileged place" given to literary texts by Taylor and the NEUM radicals, noting that their work "tended to take a rather mechanistic form." Benita Parry, quoted in Sandwith, *World of Letters*, 161; Benita Parry, "Reconciliation and Remembrance," *Pretexts* 5, nos. 1–2 (1995): 86.

92. Sandwith, *World of Letters*, 158.

93. On these South African tactics of "writing back," "rewriting," and education programs, see Sandwith, *World of Letters*, 158, 233, 261.

94. Interview with Sean Jacobs, September 27, 2017. See his blog *Africa Is a Country*, http://africasacountry.com/.

95. See "C. L. R. James: Life and Lasting Legacy," Tshisimani Centre for Activist Education, http://tshisimani.org.za/event/radical-thinkers-series-clr-james/.

96. James to Morris Phillipson, November 30, 1961, UWI Box 7, Folder 182.

97. Michel Acacia, interview by Rachel Douglas, July 21, 2014.

98. Matthew J. Smith, interview by Rachel Douglas, October 19, 2014. See also "'To Place Ourselves in History': The Haitian Revolution in British West Indian Thought before *The Black Jacobins*," in Forsdick and Høgsbjerg, *The Black Jacobins Reader*, 178–93.

99. See James's response to Louis Ménard's review of the French edition *Les Jacobins noirs*: C. L. R. James, "Correspondance [27 February 1950]," *Les Temps Modernes* 56 (June 1950).

100. Trouillot, "Haitian Historiography," 468–70.

101. James to Charlier, August 24, 1955, UWI Box 7, Folder 190.

102. "C. L. R. James and Studs Terkel Discuss *The Black Jacobins* on WFMT Radio (Chicago), 1970," reprinted in Forsdick and Høgsbjerg, *The Black Jacobins Reader*, 344. See also Forsdick, "Refiguring Resistance," 227.

103. Gérard Jean-Baptiste to C. L. R. James, September 15, 1953, UWI Box 7, Folder 190.

104. C. L. R. James to Félix Morisseau-Leroy, May 30, 1958, UWI Box 7, Folder 190; C. L. R. James to Jean Brierre, March 1, 1958, UWI Box 7, Folder 190.

105. Lamartinière Honorat to Félix Morisseau-Leroy, April 16, 1958, UWI Box 7, Folder 190.

106. C. L. R. James and Anna Grimshaw, interview on *Toussaint Louverture*, C. L. R. James Papers, Box 12, Folder 14, Columbia University Library.

107. James, *The Black Jacobins* (1963), 408.

108. James, "Black Sansculottes," 159.

109. Max Manigat, "Le Livre haïtien en diaspora: Problèmes et perspectives," *Études littéraires* 13, no. 2 (1980): 335–45.

110. Acacia, interview by Douglas.

111. Hector, "Pour un colloque sur l'enseignement de l'Histoire en Haïti," 53.

112. Selma James, "*The Black Jacobins*, Past and Present," in Forsdick and Høgsbjerg, *The Black Jacobins Reader*, 74.

113. On Thabo Mbeki's Haiti/*Black Jacobins* comments, Sean Jacobs underlines that this was part of Mbeki's political project to write South Africa back into the rest of Africa and the Black Atlantic once he became president of South Africa (Jacobs, interview with Douglas). See Sean Jacobs and Richard Calland, eds., *Thabo Mbeki's World: The Politics and Ideology of the South African President* (Pietermaritzburg: University of Natal Press, 2002); Sean Jacobs and Herman Wasserman, *Shifting Selves: Post-Apartheid Essays on Mass Media, Culture, and Identity* (Cape Town: Kwela, 2003).

114. UWI Box 18, Folder 353; see also Julien Valère Loza, *Les Étudiants martiniquais en France: Histoire de leur organisation et de leurs luttes* (Saint-Estève, Martinique: Éditions 2M, 2003); Louis-Georges Placide, *Les Émeutes de décembre 1959 en Martinique: Un repère historique* (Paris: L'Harmattan, 2009); *La Martinique aux Martiniquais. L'Affaire de l'OJAM*, dir. Camille Mauduech (Paris: Les Films du Marigot, 2011); Laurent Jalabert, "Les Mouvements sociaux en Martinique dans les années 1960 et la réaction des pouvoirs publics," *Études caribéennes* 17 (2010), https://etudescaribeennes.revues.org/4881; Marcel Manville, *Les Antilles sans fards* (Paris: L'Harmattan, 1992); Romain Fanchonne, *Radioscopie de la communauté antillaise* (Paris: Société des Écrivains, 2013); Félix Fernand Germain, "Dangerous Liaisons: The Lives and Labor of Working-Class Antilleans" (PhD diss., University of California, Berkeley, 2007).

115. UWI Box 14, Folder 310. On the process of departmentalization and its ultimate failures in the French Caribbean, see Kristen Stromberg Childers, *Seeking Imperialism's Embrace: National Identity, Decolonization, and Assimilation in the French Caribbean* (Oxford: Oxford University Press, 2016); Nick Nesbitt, "Departmentalization and the Logic of Decolonization," *L'Esprit Créateur* 47, no. 1 (2007): 32–43; Charles Forsdick, "Haiti and Departmentalization: The Spectral Presence of Toussaint Louverture," *International Journal of Francophone Studies* 11, no. 3 (2008): 327–44; Robert Aldrich and John Connell, *The Last Colonies* (Cambridge: Cambridge University Press, 2006).

116. See Austin, "Introduction," in James, *You Don't Play with Revolution*, 1–26; David Austin, "*The Black Jacobins*: A Revolutionary Study of Revolution, and of a Caribbean Revolution," in Forsdick and Høgsbjerg, *The Black Jacobins Reader*, 256–77; David Austin, *Fear of a Black Nation: Race, Sex, and Security in Sixties Montreal* (Toronto: Between the Lines, 2013); Alfie Roberts, *A View for Freedom: Alfie Roberts Speaks on the Caribbean, Cricket, Montreal, and C. L. R. James* (Montreal: Alfie Roberts Institute, 2005).

117. Marguerite Alfred to C. L. R. James, February 15, 1969, UWI Box 7, Folder 197. See Dennis Forsythe, "Let the Niggers Burn!" *The Sir George Williams Affair and Its Caribbean Aftermath* (Montreal: Our Generation Press, 1971); Sean Mills, *The Empire Within: Postcolonial Activism in Sixties Montreal* (Montreal: McGill-Queen's University Press, 2010).

118. See David Austin, "Anne Cools: Radical Feminist and Trailblazer?" *MaComère* (fall 2010): 68–76. Cools was also tasked with pursuing the Cuban edition of *The Black Jacobins*, which would be a long time in the making.

119. See Paul Buhle, *Tim Hector: A Caribbean Radical's Story* (Kingston, Jamaica: Ian Randle, 2006); Kate Quinn, ed., *Black Power in the Caribbean* (Gainesville: University Press of Florida, 2014); Walter Rodney, *How Europe Underdeveloped Africa* (Washington, DC: Howard University Press, 1981); Walter Rodney, "The African Revolution," in Buhle, *C. L. R. James*, 30–48.

120. C. L. R. James to Marina Maxwell, October 29, 1967, UWI Box 7, Folder 190. See correspondence in UWI Box 10, Folder 241.

121. On the significance of this recording, see Aldon Lynn Nielsen, "On the Wings of Atlanta," in Forsdick and Høgsbjerg, *The Black Jacobins Reader*, 297–310.

122. James, "Lectures on *The Black Jacobins*."

123. *Beyond a Boundary*, dir. Mike Dibb (London: Omnibus, 1976), https://www.youtube.com/watch?v=E2eatQ7A9e8&feature=youtu.be.

124. *C. L. R. James in Conversation with Stuart Hall*, dir. Mike Dibb (London: Channel 4, 1976), https://www.youtube.com/watch?v=_GfoKUxgZfI.

125. *The C. L. R. James Lectures*, dir. H. O. Nazareth (London: Penumbra Films, 1983).

126. David Austin, "The Black Jacobin: A Biography of C. L. R. James," CBC Radio, May 3, 10, and 17, 2005, https://curio.ca/en/show/ideas-1703/2005/.

127. *Every Cook Can Govern: The Life, Impact and Works of C. L. R. James*, dir. Ceri Dingle and Rob Harris (London: Worldwrite, 2016).

128. See C. L. R. James, *Every Cook Can Govern: A Study of Democracy in Ancient Greece: Its Meaning for Today* (Detroit, MI: Correspondence, 1956).

129. See "C. L. R. James: Film and Knowledge Portal," http://www.clrjames.uk/.

130. Peter White, "Kwame Kwei-Armah to Adapt Haitian Revolution Story for TV with Foz Allan's Bryncoed," Deadline, November 25, 2018. https://deadline.com/2018/11/kwame-kwei-armah-the-black-jacobins-1202508415/.

131. Foz Allan, interview with Rachel Douglas, January 18, 2019.

132. White, "Kwame Kwei-Armah."

133. One biopic about Toussaint Louverture that has been many years in the making is Danny Glover's long-awaited movie with Louverture Films, of which he is cofounder and chief executive. In 2012, Philippe Niang's French TV miniseries about the Haitian Revolution was released. See Alyssa Goldstein Sepinwall, "Happy as a Slave: The *Toussaint Louverture* Miniseries," *Fiction and Film for French Historians: A Cultural Bulletin* 4, no. 1 (2013), https://h-france.net/fffh/maybe-missed/happy-as-a-slave-the-toussaint-louverture-miniseries/.

134. On plans for a C. L. R. James Foundation in London, see Darcus Howe Papers, Box 3, Folders 1–3, Columbia University Library. See David Abdulah giving the OWTU C. L. R. James Memorial Lecture, March 29, 2017 here: https://www.youtube.com/watch?v=sdDbY8qE-; on the library, see C. L. R. James Cricket Research Centre, University of the West Indies, http://www.cavehill.uwi.edu/clrjameslibrary.

135. Rob Waters, "Student Politics, Teaching Politics, Black Politics: An Interview with Ansel Wong," *Race and Class* 58, no. 1 (2016): 17–33.

136. C. L. R. James, "Letter to A.D.," October 8, 1980, Box 2, C. L. R. James Collection, Quinton O'Connor Library, Oilfield Workers Trade Union, Trinidad. Quoted in Bennett and Høgsbjerg, "Introduction: The C. L. R. James Library," in Bennett and Høgsbjerg, *Celebrating C. L. R. James*, 38. James's biographer Paul Buhle describes how James became "a living monument of sorts." Buhle, *C. L. R. James: The Artist as Revolutionary*, 133–34.

137. Errol Lloyd, "The Origins of the Book Fair and Book Fair Festival: An Interview with John La Rose, London, April 1982," in *A Meeting of the Continents: The International Book Fair of Radical Black and Third World Books Revisited: History, Memories, Organisation and Programmes 1982–1995*, ed. Sarah White, Roxy Harris, and Sharmilla Beezmohn (London: New Beacon and George Padmore Institute, 2005), 4. See also John La Rose, "C. L. R. James—The Revolutionary as Artist," in *Unending Journey: Selected Writings* (London: New Beacon and George Padmore Institute, 2014), 50–53.

138. Bennett and Høgsbjerg, *Celebrating C. L. R. James*, 96.

139. Hackney Council, "C. L. R. James."

140. According to Stephen Howe, there was an "uncomfortable irony" as the council was closing down other libraries, and because "[t]heir derelict and municipally-vandalised interiors, piles of books mouldering in the dust, formed a miserable kind of tribute to the passionate bibliophile James"; Stephen Howe, "C. L. R. James: Visions of History, Visions of Britain," in *West Indian Intellectuals in Britain*, ed. Bill Schwarz (Manchester: Manchester University Press, 2003), 162–63. However, it was in the late 1980s when the council was under new administration that it began closing down other libraries—this was not the case in 1985 when the C. L. R. James Library came into being. Gaverne Bennett and Christian Høgsbjerg have summed up this renaming as being "where black self-organisation from below came together with municipal socialism and wider anti-racist campaigning that should be remembered, celebrated and commemorated." Bennett and Høgsbjerg, *Celebrating C. L. R. James*, 39.

141. Indra Sengupta, ed., *Memory, History, and Colonialism: Engaging with Pierre Nora in Colonial and Postcolonial Contexts* (London: German Historical Institute London, 2009), 69.

142. Christian Høgsbjerg, "Interview with Mackenzie Frank: 2015," in Bennett and Høgsbjerg, *Celebrating C. L. R. James*, 78.

143. See Bennett and Høgsbjerg, *Celebrating C. L. R. James*, 101–3.

144. *The Black Jacobins* continues to be a text reactivated by new generations who make James's famous title resonate again. See, for example, Gerald Horne, *Confronting Black Jacobins: The U.S., the Haitian Revolution, and the Origins of the Dominican Republic* (New York: Monthly Review Press, 2015).
145. Pierre Nora, ed., *Les Lieux de mémoire*, 7 vols. (Paris: Gallimard, 1984–1992).
146. Nora, *Les Lieux de mémoire*, vol. 3, bk. 1, 20. This definition also has an entry in *Le Grand Robert*, see Nora, "L'ère de la commémoration," *Les Lieux de mémoire*, vol. 3, bk. 3, 1004.
147. Nora, *Les Lieux de mémoire*, vol. 1, xvii.
148. See many of the essays in Sengupta, *Memory, History, and Colonialism*.
149. See Aleida Assmann, "How History Takes Place," in Sengupta, *Memory, History, and Colonialism*, 151–65.
150. See Astrid Erll, "The 'Indian Mutiny' as a Shared Site of Memory: A Media Culture Perspective on Britain and India," in Sengupta, *Memory, History, and Colonialism*, 121.
151. Jay M. Winter, "In Conclusion: Palimpsests," in Sengupta, *Memory, History, and Colonialism*, 167–73.
152. On James and dialectics, see C. L. R. James, *Notes on Dialectics* (London: Allison and Busby, 1980); C. L. R. James, *This "Thing on Dialectic": Notes and Comments, August–September 1948*, ed. Robert A. Hill (London: Pluto, 2005); C. L. R. James, "Dialectical Materialism and the Fate of Humanity" [1947], reprinted in James, *The C. L. R. James Reader*, 153–81; John McClendon, *C. L. R. James's "Notes on Dialectics": Left Hegelianism or Marxism-Leninism* (Lanham, MD: Lexington, 2005); Rick Roderick, "Further Adventures of the Dialectic," in Cudjoe and Cain, *C. L. R. James*, 205–11.
153. See James Early, Ethelbert Miller, Paul Buhle, and Noel Ignatin, "Interview, C. L. R. James," in Buhle, *C. L. R. James*, 164–67.
154. See Early, Miller, Buhle, and Ignatin, "Interview," 164–67.
155. James, *Notes on Dialectics*, 204.
156. James, *Notes on Dialectics*, 130.
157. James, *Notes on Dialectics*, 184.
158. James, *Notes on Dialectics*, 104–5.
159. On James and circles, see also King, *C. L. R. James and Creolization*.
160. James, *Notes on Dialectics*, 103–5.
161. I am playing on the title of Rex Nettleford, *Inward Stretch, Outward Reach: A Voice from the Caribbean* (Basingstoke, UK: Macmillan Caribbean, 1993). See also Keithley Woolward, ed., "The Caribbean Stage: From Traditional Theatre to Modern Performances," special issue, *Caribbean Quarterly* 63, nos. 2–3 (2017).
162. On the extempo debate about James's relationship with Williams, see Ashlee Burnett's blog: *Ashlee Burnett*, May 17, 2017, https://ashleeburnett.wordpress.com/2017/05/17/20/.
163. See Kwynn Johnson's reflections on place as palimpsest via her storyboard drawings for the set design of Derek Walcott's staging of *The Haitian Earth* (1984) at the Haitian bicentennial conference (2004) held at UWI, St Augustine, Trinidad. Johnson, "Place as Palimpsest."

BIBLIOGRAPHY

Archival Sources

BBC Written Archives Centre, Reading, UK. Play Library.
British Library, London. Andrew Salkey Archive.
Columbia University Library, New York. Rare Book and Manuscript Library, Butler Library. C. L. R. James Papers, MS#1529; C. L. R. James Institute Records, MS#1469; Robert A. Hill Papers, MS#1681; Darcus Howe Papers, MS#1476; Anna Grimshaw Papers, MS#1553; and Margaret Busby Papers, MS#1516.
Dartmouth College, Hanover, NH. Rauner Special Collections Library. Errol Hill Papers.
Glasgow Caledonian University Archive of the Trotskyist Tradition. Glasgow.
Howard University, Washington, DC. Moorland-Spingarn Research Center, Manuscript Division, Alain Locke Papers.
Hull History Centre, Hull, UK. Jock Haston Papers.
Institute of Commonwealth Studies, University of London, London, U.K. Special Collections, Senate House Library. C. L. R. James Papers.
National Library and Information Systems Authority (NALIS), Port of Spain, Trinidad and Tobago. Heritage Library Division, Special Collections and Rare Books Room, Sir Learie Constantine Collection.
Oilfield Workers' Trade Union, San Fernando, Trinidad and Tobago. Quinton O' Connor Memorial Library. C. L. R. James Collection.
Pennsylvania State University Libraries, State College, PA. Special Collections Library.
People's History Museum, Manchester, UK. Labour History Archive and Study Centre.
Schomburg Center for Research in Black Culture, New York Public Library, New York. Manuscripts, Archives, and Rare Books Division.
University of the West Indies (UWI), St. Augustine, Trinidad and Tobago. The Alma Jordan Library, West Indiana and Special Collections, C. L. R. James Collection (Sc 82).
Wayne State University (WSU), Detroit, MI. Walter P. Reuther Library. Archives of Labor and Urban Affairs. Martin and Jessie Glaberman Papers; Raya Dunayevskaya Papers; James and Grace Lee Boggs Papers.

Yale University, New Haven, CT. Beinecke Rare Book and Manuscript Library, Richard Wright Papers.

Works by C. L. R. James

James, C. L. R. "Abyssinia and the Imperialists." *Keys* 3, no. 3 (January–March 1936). Reprinted in James, *The C. L. R. James Reader*, 63–66.

James, C. L. R. *At the Rendezvous of Victory: Selected Writings*. Vol. 3. London: Allison and Busby, 1984.

James, C. L. R. *Beyond a Boundary*. London: Stanley Paul, 1963.

James, C. L. R. "The Black Jacobins." In *A Time and a Season: Eight Caribbean Plays*, edited by Errol Hill, 382–450. Port-of-Spain: University of the West Indies, Trinidad, Extramural Studies Unit, 1976.

James, C. L. R. *The Black Jacobins*. In James, *The C. L. R. James Reader*, 67–111.

James, C. L. R. *The Black Jacobins: Toussaint Louverture and the San Domingo Revolution*. London: Secker and Warburg, 1938.

James, C. L. R. *The Black Jacobins: Toussaint Louverture and the San Domingo Revolution*. New York: Vintage, 1963.

James, C. L. R. *The Black Jacobins: Toussaint Louverture and the San Domingo Revolution*. London: Allison and Busby, 1980.

James, C. L. R. *The Black Jacobins: Toussaint Louverture and the San Domingo Revolution*. Harmondsworth: Penguin, 2001.

James, C. L. R. "Black Sansculottes." In James, *At the Rendezvous of Victory*, 159–62.

James, C. L. R. *Burakku jakoban: Tusan ruveruchūru to haichi kakumei*. 1991. Reprint, Tokyo: Omura-Shoten, 2002.

James, C. L. R. *The Case for West Indian Self-Government*. London: Hogarth, 1933.

James, C. L. R. "'Civilising' the 'Blacks': Why Britain Needs to Maintain Her African Possessions." *New Leader*, May 29, 1936, 5.

James, C. L. R. "C. L. R. James and Studs Terkel Discuss *The Black Jacobins* on WFMT Radio (Chicago), 1970." Reprinted in Forsdick and Høgsbjerg, *The Black Jacobins Reader*, 329–52.

James, C. L. R. *The C. L. R. James Reader*. Edited by Anna Grimshaw. Oxford: Blackwell, 1992.

James, C. L. R. "Correspondence [27 February 1950]." *Les Temps Modernes* 56 (June 1950).

James, C. L. R. "De Toussaint Louverture a Fidel Castro." *Casa de las Américas* 91 (1975): 64–69.

James, C. L. R. "Dialectical Materialism and the Fate of Humanity" [1947]. Reprinted in James, *The C. L. R. James Reader*, 153–81.

James, C. L. R. "Discovering Literature in Trinidad: The 1930s." In James, *Spheres of Existence*, 237–44.

James, C. L. R. "Education, Propaganda, Agitation." In Glaberman, *Marxism for Our Times*, 3–42.

James, C. L. R. *Every Cook Can Govern: A Study of Democracy in Ancient Greece: Its Meaning for Today*. Detroit: Correspondence, 1956.

James, C. L. R. "Fanon and the Caribbean." In *International Tribute to Frantz Fanon: Record of the Special Meeting of the United Nations Special Committee against Apartheid, 3 November 1978*, 43–46. New York: United Nations Centre against Apartheid, 1979.

James, C. L. R. *The Future in the Present: Selected Writings*. Vol. 1. London: Allison and Busby, 1977.

James, C. L. R. "George Padmore, Black Marxist Revolutionary—A Memoir." In James, *At the Rendezvous of Victory*, 251–63.

James, C. L. R. *I giacobini neri: La prima rivolta contro l'uomo bianco*. Translated by Raffaele Petrillo. Milan: Feltrinelli, 1968.

James, C. L. R. *I giacobini neri: La prima rivolta contro l'uomo bianco*. 2nd ed. Edited by Filippo del Lucchese and Miguel Mellino. Translated by Raffaele Petrillo and Filippo del Lucchese. Rome: Derive Approdi, 2006.

James, C. L. R. "The Haitian Revolution in the Making of the Modern World." In James, *You Don't Play with Revolution*, 51–70.

James, C. L. R. *A History of Negro Revolt*. London: FACT, 1938.

James, C. L. R. *A History of Negro Revolt*. London: Race Today, 1985.

James, C. L. R. *A History of Pan-African Revolt*. Washington, DC: Drum and Spear Press, 1969.

James, C. L. R. "The Intelligence of the Negro: A Few Words with Dr. Harland." *The Beacon* 1, no. 5 (August 1931): 6–10.

James, C. L. R. "Interview, C. L. R. James with James Early, Ethelbert Miller, Paul Buhle, Noel Ignatin." In Buhle, *C. L. R. James*, 164–67.

James, C. L. R. "Introduction." In *Carribean Plays*, vol. 2, edited by Errol Hill, v–viii. St. Augustine: University of the West Indies, 1965.

James, C. L. R. "Introduction." In Mary Low and Juan Breá, *Red Spanish Notebook: The First Six Months of the Revolution and the Civil War*, v–vii. London: Secker and Warburg, 1937.

James, C. L. R. *Os jacobinos negros: Toussaint Louverture e a revolução de São Domingos*. 2001. Reprint, São Paulo: Boitempo, 2010.

James, C. L. R. *Los jacobinos negros: Toussaint Louverture y la revolución de Haití*. Madrid: Turner; Mexico City: Fondo de Cultura Económica, 2003.

James, C. L. R. *Los jacobinos negros: Toussaint Louverture y la revolución de Saint-Domingue*. Translated by Rosa López Oceguera. Havana: Casa de las Américas, 2010.

James, C. L. R. *Les Jacobins noirs: Toussaint Louverture et la révolution de Saint-Domingue*. Translated by Pierre Naville. Paris: Gallimard, 1949.

James, C. L. R. *Les Jacobins noirs: Toussaint Louverture et la révolution de Saint-Domingue*. 2nd ed. Translated by Pierre Naville and Claude-Fivel Demoret. Paris: Éditions Caribéennes, 1983.

James, C. L. R. *Les Jacobins noirs: Toussaint Louverture et la révolution de Saint-Domingue*. 3rd ed. Paris: Éditions Amsterdam, 2008.

James, C. L. R. "Kanhai: A Study in Confidence." In James, *At the Rendezvous of Victory*, 166–71.

James, C. L. R. "Lecture on Federation." June 1958. Marxists Internet Archive Library. https://www.marxists.org/archive/james-clr/works/1958/06/federation.htm.

James, C. L. R. "Lectures on *The Black Jacobins*." *Small Axe* 8 (2000): 65–112.

James, C. L. R. *The Life of Captain Cipriani*. Nelson: Coulton, 1932.

James, C. L. R. "The Making of the Caribbean People." *Radical America* 4, no. 4 (1970): 36–49.

James, C. L. R. "The Making of the Caribbean People." In James, *You Don't Play with Revolution*, 29–49.

James, C. L. R. *Mariners, Renegades, and Castaways: The Story of Herman Melville and the World We Live In*. 1953. Reprint, Hanover, NH: University Press of New England, 2001.

James, C. L. R. *Marxism for Our Times: C. L. R. James on Revolutionary Organization*. Edited by Martin Glaberman. Jackson: University Press of Mississippi, 1999.

James, C. L. R. "My Knowledge of Damas Is Unique." In *Léon-Gontran Damas, 1912–1978: Father of Negritude: A Memorial Casebook*, edited by Daniel L. Racine, 131–34. Washington, DC: University Press of America, 1979.

James, C. L. R. *Nkrumah and the Ghana Revolution*. Westport, CT: Lawrence Hill, 1977.

James, C. L. R. *Notes on Dialectics*. Detroit: Friends of Facing Reality, 1971.

James, C. L. R. *Notes on Dialectics: Hegel, Marx, Lenin*. London: Allison and Busby, 1980.

James, C. L. R. *Party Politics in the West Indies: Formerly PNM Go Forward*. San Juan, Trinidad: Vedic Enterprises, 1962.

James, C. L. R. "Paul Robeson: Black Star." In James, *Spheres of Existence*, 256–64.

James, C. L. R. "Preface." In Jean Fouchard, *The Haitian Maroons: Liberty or Death*, v–vii. New York: Blyden, 1981.

James, C. L. R. "Romanticising History." *New Society*, February 15, 1979.

James, C. L. R. *Schwarze Jakobiner: Toussaint L'Ouverture und die Unabhängigkeitsrevolution in Haiti*. Cologne: Pahl-Rugenstein, 1984.

James, C. L. R. *Die schwarzen Jakobiner: Toussaint L'Ouverture und die San-Domingo-Revolution*. Berlin: Verlag Neues Leben, 1984.

James, C. L. R. *Spheres of Existence: Selected Writings*. Vol. 2. London: Allison and Busby, 1980.

James, C. L. R. *State Capitalism and World Revolution*. 1st ed. New York: Socialist Workers Party, 1950.

James, C. L. R. *State Capitalism and World Revolution*. 4th ed. Chicago: Kerr, 1986.

James, C. L. R. *This "Thing on Dialectic": Notes and Comments, August–September 1948*. Edited by Robert A. Hill. London: Pluto, 2005.

James, C. L. R. "Three Black Women Writers: Toni Morrison, Alice Walker, Ntozake Shange." 1981. Reprinted in James, *The C. L. R. James Reader*, 411–17.

James, C. L. R. "Toussaint Louverture (Act 2, Scene 1)." *Life and Letters Today* 14, no. 3 (1936): 7–18.

James, C. L. R. *Toussaint Louverture: The Story of the Only Successful Slave Revolt in History: A Play in Three Acts*. Edited by Christian Høgsbjerg. Durham, NC: Duke University Press, 2013.

James, C. L. R. "Trotsky's Place in History." In McLemee and Le Blanc, *C. L. R. James and Revolutionary Marxism*, 92–130.

James, C. L. R. "The West Indian Intellectual." In John Jacob Thomas, *Froudacity: West Indian Fables Explained*, 23–49. London: New Beacon, 1969.

James, C. L. R. *World Revolution, 1917–1936: The Rise and Fall of the Communist International*. London: Secker and Warburg, 1937. Reprint, Westport, CT: Hyperion, 1973.

James, C. L. R. *World Revolution, 1917–1936: The Rise and Fall of the Communist International*. Edited by Christian Høgsbjerg. Durham, NC: Duke University Press, 2017.

James, C. L. R. *You Don't Play with Revolution: The Montreal Lectures of C. L. R. James*. Edited by David Austin. Oakland, CA: AK Press, 2009.

Johnson, J. R. [C. L. R. James], Grace C. Lee, and Pierre Chaulieu [Cornelius Castoriadis]. *Facing Reality*. Detroit: Correspondence Publishing Company, 1958. Reprint, Chicago: Kerr, 2006.

Secondary Sources

Adotevi, Stanislav. *Négritude et négrologues*. Paris: Union générale d'éditions, 1972.

Adwele, Adisa "Aja." *Painting Poetry: Poetic Interpretations of Art*. Bridgetown, Barbados: Acute Vision, 2015.

Ahye, Molly. *Cradle of Caribbean Dance: Beryl McBurnie and the Little Carib Theatre*. Petit Valley: Heritage Cultures, 1983.

Akala. *The Ruins of Empires*. London: Illa State Publishing, 2014.

Aldrich, Robert, and John Connell. *The Last Colonies*. Cambridge: Cambridge University Press, 2006.

Ali, Hakim, and Marika Sherwood. *The 1945 Manchester Pan-African Congress Revisited*. London: New Beacon, 1995.

Ali, Hakim, and Marika Sherwood. *Pan-African History: Political Figures from Africa and the Diaspora Since 1787*. London: Routledge, 2003.

Ali, Tariq. *Introducing Trotsky and Marxism*. Cambridge: Icon, 2000.

Allen, Priscilla. "Evidence of the Slavery Dilemma in *White-Jacket*." *American Quarterly* 18 (1966): 477–92.

Allen, Priscilla. "The Major and Minor Themes of Melville's *White-Jacket*." PhD diss., Cornell University, 1966.

Allen, Priscilla. "*White-Jacket*: Melville and the Man-of-War Microcosm." *American Quarterly* 25 (1973): 32–47.

Althusser, Louis, Étienne Balibar, Roger Establet, Jacques Rancière, and Pierre Macherey. *Reading Capital: The Complete Edition*. Translated by Ben Brewster and David Fernbach. London: Verso, 2016.

Anderson, Perry. *Arguments within English Marxism*. London: Verso, 1980.

Apter, Emily. "Translation and Event: Rereading *Reading Capital*." In Nesbitt, *The Concept in Crisis*, 49–69.

Aravamudan, Srinivas. *Tropicopolitans: Colonialism and Agency, 1688–1804*. Durham, NC: Duke University Press, 1999.

Ardouin, Alexis Beaubrun. *Études sur l'histoire d'Haïti, suivies de la vie du général J. M. Borgella*. 11 vols. Paris: n.p., 1853–60. Reprint, Port-au-Prince: François Dalencourt, 1958.

Asante, S. K. B. *Pan-African Protest: West Africa and the Italo-Ethiopian Crisis, 1934–1941*. London: Longman, 1977.

Assmann, Aleida. "How History Takes Place." In Sengupta, *Memory, History, and Colonialism*, 151–65.

Austin, David. "Anne Cools: Radical Feminist and Trailblazer?" *MaComère*, fall 2010, 68–76.

Austin, David. "The Black Jacobin: A Biography of C. L. R. James." CBC Radio, Toronto. First broadcast on May 3, 10, and 17, 2005.

Austin, David. "*The Black Jacobins*: A Revolutionary Study of Revolution, and of a Caribbean Revolution." In Forsdick and Høgsbjerg, *The Black Jacobins Reader*, 256–77.

Austin, David. *Fear of a Black Nation: Race, Sex, and Security in Sixties Montreal*. Toronto: Between the Lines, 2013.

Austin, David. "Introduction: In Search of a National Identity: C. L. R. James and the Promise of the Caribbean." In James, *You Don't Play with Revolution*, 1–28.

Bailey, David A., Alissandra Cummins, Axel Lapp, and Allison Thompson, eds. *Curating in the Caribbean*. Berlin: Green Box, 2012.

Baker, Keith Michael. *Inventing the French Revolution: Essays on French Political Culture in the Eighteenth Century*. Cambridge: Cambridge University Press, 1990.

Balme, Christopher B. *Decolonizing the Stage: Theatrical Syncretism and Post-Colonial Drama*. Oxford: Clarendon, 1999.

Banham, Martin Errol Hill, and George Woodyard. *The Cambridge Guide to African and Caribbean Theatre*. Cambridge: Cambridge University Press, 1994.

Baptist, Edward. *The Half Has Never Been Told: Slavery and the Making of American Capitalism*. New York: Basic Books, 2014.

Baron, Udo. *Kalter Krieg und heisser Frieden: Der Einfluss der SED und ihrer westdeutschen Verbündeten auf die Partei "Die Grünen."* Münster: Lit Verlag, 2003.

Baugh, Edward. "Reflections on 'The Quarrel with History.'" *Small Axe* 38 (2012): 108–18.

Baugh, Edward. "The West Indian Writer and His Quarrel with History." *Tapia*, part 1, February 20, 1977, 6–7; part 2, February 27, 1977, 6–7, 11. Reprint, *Small Axe* 38 (2012): 60–74.

Beard, John. *The Life of Toussaint L'Ouverture*. London: Ingram, Cooke, 1853.

Beauvais, Charles Theodore, and Antoine-Alexandre Barbier. *Dictionnaire historique; ou, Biographie universelle classique*. Vol. 1. Paris: C. Gosselin, 1829.

Beckert, Sven. *Empire of Cotton: A Global History*. New York: Alfred A. Knopf, 2014.

Beckert, Sven. "Interchange: The History of Capitalism." *Journal of American History* 101, no. 2 (2014): 503–36.

Beckles, Hilary. "'The Williams Effect': Eric Williams's *Capitalism and Slavery* and the Growth of West Indian Political Economy." In Solow and Engerman, *British Capitalism and Caribbean Slavery*, 303–16.

Beilharz, Peter. "Trotsky as Historian." *History Workshop Journal* 20 (1985): 36–55.

Beilharz, Peter. *Trotsky, Trotskyism, and the Transition to Socialism*. London: Croom Helm, 1987.

Bell, Madison Smartt. "Afterword to *The Black Jacobins*'s Italian Edition." In Forsdick and Høgsbjerg, *The Black Jacobins Reader*, 313–21.

Bell, Madison Smartt. *Toussaint Louverture: A Biography*. New York: Pantheon, 2007.

Bennett, Gaverne, and Christian Høgsbjerg, eds. *Celebrating C. L. R. James in Hackney, London*. London: Redwords, 2015.

Bennett, Gaverne, and Christian Høgsbjerg. "Introduction: The C. L. R. James Library." In Bennett and Høgsbjerg, *Celebrating C. L. R. James*, 11–40.

Bernier, Celeste-Marie. *Characters of Blood: Black Heroism in the Transatlantic Imagination*. Charlottesville: University of Virginia Press, 2012.

Bernier, Celeste-Marie. "Tracing Transatlantic Slavery in Kimathi Donkor's UK Diaspora." *Nka: Journal of Contemporary African Art* 41 (2017): 108–24.

Blackburn, Robin. "*The Black Jacobins* and New World Slavery." In Cudjoe and Cain, *C. L. R. James*, 81–97.

Blackburn, Robin. *The Making of New World Slavery: From the Baroque to the Modern, 1492–1800*. London: Verso, 1997.

Blackburn, Robin. "White Gold, Black Labour." *New Left Review* 95 (2015): 151–60.

Blackledge, Paul. "Trotsky's Contribution to the Marxist Theory of History." *Studies in East European Thought* 58, no. 1 (2006): 1–31.

Blake, David, and Anthony Ward. *Toussaint, or The Aristocracy of the Skin: Opera in Three Acts*. Sevenoaks, UK: Novello, 1977.

Blakemore, Steven. "Revolution in Language: Burke's Representation of Linguistic Terror." In Heffernan, *Representing the French Revolution*, 3–23.

Blérard, Monique, Kathleen Gyssels, and Marc Lony. *Léon-Gontran Damas: Poète, écrivain patrimonial et postcolonial: Quels héritiers, quels héritages au seuil du XXIe siècles?* Matoury, French Guiana: Ibis Rouge, 2014.

Bloom, Harold. *A Map of Misreading*. Oxford: Oxford University Press, 2003.

Boal, Augusto. *Theater of the Oppressed*. London: Pluto, 2008.

Boggs, Grace Lee. "C. L. R. James: Organizing in the U.S.A., 1938–1953." In Cudjoe and Cain, *C. L. R. James*, 163–72.

Boggs, Grace Lee. *Living for Change: An Autobiography*. Minneapolis: University of Minnesota Press, 1998.

Boggs, Grace Lee. "Thinking and Acting Dialectically: C. L. R. James, the American Years." *Monthly Review* 45, no. 5 (1993): 38–46.

Bogues, Anthony. "Afterword." *Small Axe* 8 (2000): 113–17.

Bogues, Anthony. *Black Heretics, Black Prophets: Radical Political Intellectuals*. New York: Routledge, 2003.

Bogues, Anthony. "*The Black Jacobins* and the Long Haitian Revolution: Archives, History, and the Writing of Revolution." In Forsdick and Høgsbjerg, *The Black Jacobins*, 197–214.

Bogues, Anthony. *Caliban's Freedom: The Early Political Thought of C. L. R. James*. London: Pluto, 1997.

Bogues, Anthony. "History, Decolonization and the Making of Revolution: Reflections on Writing the Popular History of the Jamaican Events of 1938." *Interventions* 12, no. 1 (2010): 76–87.

Bogues, Anthony. *The Many Faces of Toussaint L'Ouverture and the Haitian Revolution*. Providence, RI: Center for the Study of Slavery and Justice, Brown University, 2014.

Bohnsack, Günter. *Hauptverwaltung Aufklärung: Die Legende stirbt. Das Ende von Wolfs Geheimdienst*. Berlin: Edition Ost, 1997.

Bornstein, Sam, and Al Richardson. *Against the Stream: A History of the Trotskyist Movement in Britain, 1924–1938*. London: Socialist Platform, 1986.

Bracey, John H. Introduction to *The Black Jacobins*. In Forsdick and Høgsbjerg, *The Black Jacobins Reader*, 322–27.

Brathwaite, Edward Kamau. "The Love Axe/1 (Developing a Caribbean Aesthetic 1962–1974)." *Bim* 16, no. 61 (1977): 181–82.

Breiner, Laurence A. "Too Much History, or Not Enough." *Small Axe* 38 (2012): 86–98.

Brereton, Bridget. "Introduction." In C. L. R. James, *The Life of Captain Cipriani*, 1–29. Durham, NC: Duke University Press, 2014.

Breslin, Paul. "'The First Epic of the New World': But How Shall It Be Written." In *Tree of Liberty: Cultural Legacies of the Haitian Revolution in the Atlantic World*, edited by Doris L. Garraway, 223–48. Charlottesville: University of Virginia Press, 2008.

Breslin, Paul. "I Met History Once but He Ain't Recognize Me." *Tri-quarterly* 68 (1987): 168–83.

Breslin, Paul. *Nobody's Nation: Reading Derek Walcott*. Chicago: University of Chicago Press, 2001.

Brouillette, Sarah. *Postcolonial Writers in the Global Literary Marketplace*. Basingstoke: Palgrave Macmillan, 2007.

Bu, Zack. "In Conversation: Duval-Carrié: 'It's Like Building a Hero.'" *The Brown Daily Herald*, October 7, 2014. http://www.browndailyherald.com/2014/10/07/conversation-duval-carrie-like-building-hero/.

Buck-Morss, Susan. *Hegel, Haiti, and Universal History*. Pittsburgh: University of Pittsburgh Press, 2009.

Buhle, Paul, ed. *C. L. R. James: His Life and Work*. London: Allison and Busby, 1986.

Buhle, Paul. *C. L. R. James: The Artist as Revolutionary*. London: Verso, 1988. Reprint, London: Verso, 2017.

Buhle, Paul. "Rethinking the Rethinking." *C. L. R. James Journal* 6, no. 1 (1998): 61–71.

Buhle, Paul. *Tim Hector: A Caribbean Radical's Story*. Kingston, Jamaica: Ian Randle, 2006.

Bunce, Robin. *Renegade: The Life and Times of Darcus Howe*. London: Bloomsbury, 2017.

Bunce, Robin, and Paul Field. *Darcus Howe: A Political Biography*. London: Bloomsbury, 2014.

Burke, Seán. *The Death and Return of the Author: Criticism and Subjectivity in Barthes, Foucault, and Derrida*. Edinburgh: Edinburgh University Press, 1992.

Busby, Margaret. "C. L. R. James: A Biographical Introduction." In Bennett and Høgsbjerg, *Celebrating C. L. R. James*, 51–58.

Callinicos, Alex. *Theories and Narratives: Reflections on the Philosophy of History*. Durham, NC: Duke University Press, 1995.

Carby, Hazel V. *Race Men*. Cambridge, MA: Harvard University Press, 1998.

Cateau, Heather, and Selwyn Carrington, eds. *Capitalism and Slavery Fifty Years Later*. New York: Peter Lang, 2000.

Cave, Terence. *Mignon's Afterlives*. Oxford: Oxford University Press, 2011.

Césaire, Aimé. *Cahier d'un retour au pays natal*. 1939. Reprint, Paris: Présence Africaine, 1956.

Césaire, Aimé. *Cahier d'un retour au pays natal*. Edited by Abiola Irele. Ibadan, Nigeria: New Horn, 1994.

Césaire, Aimé. *Toussaint Louverture*. Paris: Présence Africaine, 1961.

Chambers, Colin. *The Story of Unity Theatre*. London: Lawrence and Wishart, 1989.

Chambers, Eddie. "Reading the Riot Act." *Visual Culture in Britain* 14, no. 2 (2013): 238–56.

Charlier, Étienne. *Aperçu sur la formation historique de la nation haïtienne*. Port-au-Prince: Presses libres, 1954.

Chetty, Raj. "Race Fundamentalism: Caribbean Theater and the Challenge to Black Diaspora." PhD diss., University of Washington, 2013.

Chetty, Raj. "The Tragicomedy of Anticolonial Overcoming: *Toussaint Louverture* and *The Black Jacobins* on Stage." *Callaloo* 14, no. 1 (2014): 69–88.

Chignola, Sandro. *François Dominique Toussaint Louverture, la libertà del popolo nero: Scritti politici*. Turin: La Rosa, 1997.

Childers, Kristen Stromberg. *Seeking Imperialism's Embrace: National Identity, Decolonization, and Assimilation in the French Caribbean*. Oxford: Oxford University Press, 2016.

Clark, VèVè A. "Haiti's Tragic Overture: (Mis)Representations of the Haitian Revolution in World Drama." In Heffernan, *Representing the French Revolution*, 237–60.

Cleaver, Harry. *Reading Capital Politically*. Brighton, UK: Harvester, 1979.

Clegg, John. "Capitalism and Slavery." *Critical Historical Studies* 2, no. 2 (2015): 281–304.

Cliff, Tony. *Trotsky, 1927–40*. London: Bookmarks, 1993.

Colás, Santiago. "Silence and Dialectics: Speculations on C. L. R. James and Latin America." In Farred, *Rethinking C. L. R. James*, 131–63.

Consentino, Donald. *Divine Revolution: The Art of Édouard Duval-Carrié*. Los Angeles: UCLA Fowler Museum of Cultural History, 2005.

Cools, Anne. "Womanhood." *McGill Free Press*, Black Spark edition, February 1971, 8.

Cotard, Rocky, and Laurent Dubois. "The Slave Revolution That Gave Birth to Haiti." *The Nib*, February 5, 2018. https://thenib.com/haitian-revolution.

Craton, Michael. "What and Who to Whom and What: The Significance of Slave Resistance." In Solow and Engerman, *British Capitalism*, 259–82.

Cripps, Louise. *C. L. R. James: Memories and Commentaries*. London: Cornwall, 1997.

Cudjoe, Selwyn R. "The Audacity of It All: C. L. R. James's Trinidadian Background." In Henry and Buhle, *C. L. R. James's Caribbean*, 39–55.

Cudjoe, Selwyn R. *Beyond Boundaries: The Intellectual Tradition of Trinidad and Tobago in the Nineteenth Century*. Amherst: University of Massachusetts Press, 2003.

Cudjoe, Selwyn R. "C. L. R. James Misbound." *Transition* 58 (1992): 124–36.

Cudjoe, Selwyn R., and William E. Cain, eds. *C. L. R. James: His Intellectual Legacies*. Amherst: University of Massachusetts Press, 1995.

Curthoys, Ann, and John Docker. *Is History Fiction?* Sydney: University of New South Wales Press, 2010.

Daguillard, Fritz. *Enigmatic in His Glory: Toussaint Louverture, 1743–1803*. Port-au-Prince: Musée du Panthéon Nationale Haïtien, 2003.

Dalleo, Raphael. *American Imperialism's Undead: The Occupation of Haiti and the Rise of Caribbean Anticolonialism*. Charlottesville: University of Virginia Press, 2016.

Dalleo, Raphael. "'The Independence So Hardly Won Has Been Maintained': C. L. R. James and the U.S. Occupation of Haiti." *Cultural Critique* 87 (2014): 38–59.

Damas, Léon-Gontran. *Pigments*. Paris: G.L.M., 1937.

Dance, Daryl Cumber. "Conversation with C. L. R. James." 1980. In *New World Adams: Conversations with Contemporary West Indian Writers*, 109–19. Leeds: Peepal Tree, 1992.

Daut, Marlene L. *Tropics of Haiti: Race and the Literary History of the Haitian Revolution in the Atlantic World, 1789–1865*. Liverpool: Liverpool University Press, 2015.

Daut, Marlene L. "Un-Silencing the Past: Boisrond-Tonnerre, Vastey, and the Rewriting of the Haitian Revolution." *South Atlantic Review* 74, no. 1 (2009): 35–64.

Davidson, Neil. "From Uneven to Combined Development." In Dunn and Radice, *100 Years of Permanent Revolution*, 10–26.

Davidson, Neil. "History from Below." *Jacobin*, January 12, 2018. https://www.jacobinmag.com/2018/01/leon-trotsky-russian-revolution-stalin-lenin.

Davis, Gregson. *Aimé Césaire*. Cambridge: Cambridge University Press, 1997.

Dayan, Colin. *Haiti, History, and the Gods*. Berkeley: University of California Press, 1984.

Deppman, Jed, Daniel Ferrer, and Michael Groden. *Genetic Criticism: Texts and Avant-Textes*. Philadelphia: University of Pennsylvania Press, 2004.

Descourtilz, Michel Étienne. *Voyage d'un naturaliste*. Paris: n.p., 1809.

Deutscher, Isaac. *The Prophet: The Life of Leon Trotsky*. London: Verso, 2015.

Donin, Nicolas, and Daniel Ferrer, eds. "Créer à plusieurs mains." Special issue, *Genesis* 41 (2015).

Donnell, Alison. "All Friends Now? Critical Conversations, West Indian Literature, and 'The Quarrel with History.'" *Small Axe* 38 (2012): 75–85.

Dorsinville, Roger. *De fatras bâton à Toussaint Louverture*. Alger: Enal, 1983.

Drescher, Seymour. "*Capitalism and Slavery*: After Fifty Years." In Cateau and Carrington, *Capitalism and Slavery*, 81–98.

Duberman, Martin Bauml. *Paul Robeson*. London: Bodley Head, 1989.

Dubois, Laurent. *Avengers of the New World: The Story of the Haitian Revolution*. Cambridge, MA: Harvard University Press, 2004.

Dubois, Laurent. "Foreword." In C. L. R. James, *Toussaint Louverture*, edited by Christian Høgsbjerg, vii–x. Durham, NC: Duke University Press, 2013.

Dubois, Laurent. *Haiti: The Aftershocks of History*. New York: Picador, 2012.

Dubois, Laurent. "History's Quarrel: The Future of the Past in the French Caribbean." In *Beyond Fragmentation: Perspectives on Caribbean History*, edited by Juanita de Barros, Audra Diptee, and David V. Trotman, 213–30. Princeton, NJ: Markus Wiener, 2006.

Dubois, Laurent, and Julius Scott. "An African Revolutionary in the Atlantic World." In *Revolution! The Atlantic World Reborn*, edited by Thomas Bender, Laurent Dubois, and Richard Rabinowitz, 139–58. New York: New York Historical Society, 2011.

Dubois, Laurent, and Julius Scott, eds. *Origins of the Black Atlantic: Rewriting Histories*. London: Routledge, 2010.

Dudley, Richard Owen. "About Ourselves." *Educational Journal*, October 1948, 2–4.
Dunn, Bill, and Hugo Radice, eds. *100 Years of Permanent Revolution: Results and Prospects*. London: Pluto, 2006.
Duvalier, François. *Le Problème des classes à travers l'histoire d'Haïti*. 2nd ed. Port-au-Prince: Au service de la jeunesse, 1959.
Early, James, Ethelbert Miller, Paul Buhle, and Noel Ignatin. "Interview, C. L. R. James." In Buhle, *C. L. R. James*, 164–67.
Edmondson, Belinda. *Making Men: Gender, Literary Authority, and Women's Writing in Caribbean Narrative*. Durham, NC: Duke University Press, 1999.
Edwards, Brent Hayes. *The Practice of Diaspora: Literature, Translation, and the Rise of Black Internationalism*. Cambridge, MA: Harvard University Press, 2003.
Edwards, Nadi. "Contexts, Criticism, and Quarrels: A Reflection on Edward Baugh's 'The West Indian Writer and His Quarrel with History.'" *Small Axe* 38 (2012): 99–107.
El-Ojeili, Chamsy. "Many Flowers, Little Fruit? The Dilemmas of Workerism." *Thesis Eleven* 79 (2004): 112–23.
Emery, Mary Lou. *Modernism, the Visual, and Caribbean Literature*. Cambridge: Cambridge University Press, 2007.
Erll, Astrid. "The 'Indian Mutiny' as a Shared Site of Memory: A Media Culture Perspective on Britain and India." In Sengupta, *Memory, History, and Colonialism*, 117–48.
Esslin, Martin. "The Mind as Stage—Radio Drama." *Theatre Quarterly* 1, no. 3 (1971): 5–11.
Fanchonne, Romain. *Radioscopie de la communauté antillaise*. Paris: Société des Écrivains, 2013.
Fanon, Frantz. *Black Skin, White Masks*. London: Pluto, 1986.
Farred, Grant. "First Stop, Port-au-Prince: Mapping Postcolonial Africa through Toussaint L'Ouverture and His Black Jacobins." In Lowe and Lloyd, *The Politics of Culture in the Shadow of Capital*, 227–47.
Farred, Grant, ed. *Rethinking C. L. R. James*. Oxford: Blackwell, 1996.
Fasce, Ferdinando. "American Labor History, 1973–1983: Italian Perspectives." *Reviews in American History* 14, no. 4 (1986): 597–613.
Féral, Josette, ed. "Genetics of Performance." Special issue, *Theatre Research International* 33, no. 3 (2008).
Fick, Carolyn. "C. L. R. James, *The Black Jacobins*, and *The Making of Haiti*." In Forsdick and Høgsbjerg, *The Black Jacobins Reader*, 60–69.
Fick, Carolyn. *Haïti, naissance d'une nation: La Révolution de Saint-Domingue vue d'en bas*. Translated by Frantz Voltaire. Rennes: Éditions Les Perséides; Montreal: Éditions du CIDIHCA, 2013–14.
Fick, Carolyn. *The Making of Haiti: The Saint Domingue Revolution from Below*. Knoxville: University of Tennessee Press, 1990.
Firmin, Anténor. *The Equality of Human Races*. Translated by Asselin Charles. Urbana: University of Illinois Press, 2002.
Fischer, Sibylle. *Modernity Disavowed: Haiti and the Cultures of Slavery in the Age of Revolution*. Durham, NC: Duke University Press, 2004.

Fo, Dario. *Accidental Death of an Anarchist*. Adapted by Alan Cumming and Tim Supple. London: Methuen, 1991.

Foner, Philip S. *Paul Robeson Speaks: Writings, Speeches, Interviews, 1918–1974*. London: Quartet, 1978.

Forsdick, Charles. "The Black Jacobin in Paris." *Journal of Romance Studies* 5, no. 3 (2005): 9–24.

Forsdick, Charles. "Haiti and Departmentalization: The Spectral Presence of Toussaint Louverture." *International Journal of Francophone Studies* 11, no. 3 (2008): 327–44.

Forsdick, Charles. "Refiguring Resistance: Historiography, Fiction, and the Afterlives of Toussaint Louverture." In Forsdick and Høgsbjerg, *The Black Jacobins Reader*, 215–34.

Forsdick, Charles. "Visualising Toussaint Louverture." British Museum, March 12, 2018. https://blog.britishmuseum.org/visualising-toussaint-louverture/.

Forsdick, Charles, and Christian Høgsbjerg, eds. *The Black Jacobins Reader*. Durham, NC: Duke University Press, 2017.

Forsdick, Charles, and Christian Høgsbjerg. "Introduction: Rethinking *The Black Jacobins*." In Forsdick and Høgsbjerg, *The Black Jacobins Reader*, 1–52.

Forsdick, Charles, and Christian Høgsbjerg. "Sergei Eisenstein and the Haitian Revolution: 'The Confrontation between Black and White Explodes into Red.'" *History Workshop Journal* 78, no. 1 (2014): 157–85.

Forsdick, Charles, and Christian Høgsbjerg. *Toussaint Louverture: A Black Jacobin in the Age of Revolutions*. London: Pluto, 2017.

Forsythe, Dennis. *"Let the Niggers Burn!" The Sir George Williams Affair and Its Caribbean Aftermath*. Montreal: Our Generation, 1971.

Fouchard, Jean. *Les Marrons de la liberté*. Paris: Éditions de l'École, 1972. Translated by A. Faulkner Watts as *The Haitian Maroons: Liberty or Death*. New York: Blyden, 1981.

Fraser, Robert. *Book History through Postcolonial Eyes: Rewriting the Script*. London: Routledge, 2008.

Froude, James Anthony. *The English in the West Indies; or, The Bow of Ulysses*. London: Longmans, Green, 1888.

Fuentes, Marisa J. *Dispossessed Lives: Enslaved Women, Violence, and the Archive*. Philadelphia: University of Pennsylvania Press, 2016.

Galton, Francis. *Hereditary Genius: An Inquiry into Its Laws and Consequences*. London: Macmillan, 1869.

Gambino, Ferruccio. "Only Connect." In Buhle, *C. L. R. James*, 195–99.

Garrigus, John. *Before Haiti: Race and Citizenship in French Saint-Domingue*. Basingstoke: Palgrave Macmillan, 2006.

Gaspar, David B., and David P. Geggus, eds. *A Turbulent Time: The French Revolution and the Greater Caribbean*. Bloomington: Indiana University Press, 1997.

Geggus, David P. "The Changing Faces of Toussaint Louverture: Literary and Pictorial Depictions." https://www.brown.edu/Facilities/John_Carter_Brown_Library/exhibitions/toussaint/pages/iconography.html.

Geggus, David P. *Haitian Revolutionary Studies*. Bloomington: Indiana University Press, 2002.

Geggus, David P. *The Impact of the Haitian Revolution in the Atlantic World*. Columbia: University of South Carolina Press, 2001.

Geggus, David P. "The Naming of Haiti." *New West Indian Guide* 71 (1997): 43–68.

Geggus, David P., and Norman Fiering, eds. *The World of the Haitian Revolution*. Bloomington: Indiana University Press, 2009.

Genette, Gérard. *Palimpsests: Literature in the Second Degree*. Translated by Channa Newman and Claude Doubinsky. Lincoln: University of Nebraska Press, 1997.

Genette, Gérard. *Paratexts: Thresholds of Interpretation*. Translated by Jane E. Lewin. Cambridge: Cambridge University Press, 1997.

Genovese, Eugene D. *The Political Economy of Slavery: Studies in the Economy and Society of the Slave South*. Middletown, CT: Wesleyan University Press, 1989.

Georgakas, Dan. "*The Black Jacobins* in Detroit: 1963." In Forsdick and Høgsbjerg, *The Black Jacobins Reader*, 55–57.

Georgakas, Dan, and Marvin Surkin. *Detroit: I Do Mind Dying: A Study in Urban Revolution*. London: Redwords, 1998.

George, Marvin, and Rawle Gibbons. "*Jouvay Ayiti*: Haiti's New Day from Mas to Mas Action." *Caribbean Quarterly* 62, no. 1 (2016): 69–81.

Germain, Félix Fernand. "Dangerous Liaisons: The Lives and Labor of Working-Class Antilleans." PhD diss., University of California, Berkeley, 2007.

Ghachem, Malick W. *The Old Regime and the Haitian Revolution*. Cambridge: Cambridge University Press, 2012.

Gibbons, Rawle. "Dechoukaj! *The Black Jacobins* and Liberating Caribbean Theatre." Unpublished manuscript. September 1, 2014.

Gibbons, Rawle. "Traditional Enactments of Trinidad: Towards a Third Theatre." M.Phil. thesis, University of the West Indies, St. Augustine, 1979.

Gibson, William. *The Seesaw Log: A Chronicle of the Stage Production*. New York: Knopf, 1959.

Gillman, Susan. "Black Jacobins and New World Mediterraneans." In *Surveying the American Tropics: A Literary Geography from New York to Rio*, edited by Maria Cristina Fumagalli, Peter Hulme, Owen Robinson, and Lesley Wylie, 159–82. Liverpool: Liverpool University Press, 2013.

Gillman, Susan, and Kirsten Silva Gruez. "Worlding America: The Hemispheric Text-Network." In *The Blackwell Companion to American Literary Studies*, edited by Robert S. Levine and Caroline Levander, 228–47. Oxford: Blackwell, 2011.

Girod-Chantrans, Justin. *Voyage d'un Suisse dans différentes colonies d'Amérique pendant la dernière guerre*. Neuchâtel: Imprimerie de la Société Typographique, 1785.

Glaberman, Martin, ed. *Marxism for Our Times: C. L. R. James on Revolutionary Organization*. Jackson: University Press of Mississippi, 1999.

Glaberman, Martin. *Punching Out*. Detroit: Bewick, 1952.

Glick, Jeremy. *The Black Radical Tragic*. New York: New York University Press, 2016.

Glick, Jeremy. "'Taking Up Arms against a Sea of Troubles': Tragedy as History and Genre in the Black Radical Tradition." PhD diss., Rutgers University, 2007.
Glissant, Édouard. *Caribbean Discourse: Selected Essays*. Translated by Michael J. Dash. Charlottesville: University of Virginia Press, 1989.
Glissant, Édouard. *Monsieur Toussaint*. Paris: Gallimard, 1961.
Gobineau, Joseph Arthur de. *Essai sur l'inégalité des races humaines*. Paris: n.p., 1853–55.
Goebel, Michael. *Anti-Imperial Metropolis: Interwar Paris and the Seeds of Third World Nationalism*. Cambridge: Cambridge University Press, 2015.
Gorender, Jacob. *A escravidão reabilitada*. São Paulo: Editora Ática, 1990.
Gorender, Jacob. "O épico e o trágico na história do Haiti." *Estudos avançados* 18, no. 50 (2004): 295–302.
Grésillon, Almuth. *Éléments de critique génétique: Lire les manuscrits modernes*. Paris: Presses universitaires de France, 1994.
Grésillon, Almuth. *La Mise en œuvre: Itinéraires génétiques*. Paris: CNRS, 2008.
Grésillon, Almuth, Marie-Madeleine Mervant-Roux, and Dominique Budor, eds. *Genèses théâtrales*. Paris: CNRS, 2010.
Guérin, Daniel. *La Lutte de classes sous la première République: Bourgeois et "bras nus," 1793–1797*. Paris: Gallimard, 1946.
Gyssels, Kathleen. *Black Label, ou, Les Déboires de Léon-Gontran Damas*. Paris: Passage(s), 2016.
Hackney Council. "C. L. R. James: The Black Jacobin." London: Hackney Council, 1985.
Hall, Stuart. "Breaking Bread with History: C. L. R. James and *The Black Jacobins*." Interview with Bill Schwarz. *History Workshop Journal* 46 (1998): 17–32.
Hall, Stuart. "A Conversation with C. L. R. James." In Farred, *Rethinking C. L. R. James*, 15–44.
Hallas, Duncan. *The Comintern*. London: Bookmarks, 1985.
Hallas, Duncan. *Trotsky's Marxism and Other Essays*. Chicago: Haymarket, 2003.
Harland, Sidney C. "Magna est veritas et praevalebit: A Reply to Mr. C. L. R. James." *The Beacon* 1, no. 7 (October 1931): 18–20.
Harland, Sidney C. "Race Admixture." *The Beacon* 1, no. 4 (July 1931): 25–29.
Hector, Michel. "Pour un colloque sur l'enseignement de l'histoire en Haïti." *Revue de la Société haïtienne d'histoire et de géographie* 237 (2009): 47–60.
Heffernan, James A. W., ed. *Representing the French Revolution: Literature, Historiography, and Art*. Hanover, NH: University Press of New England, 1992.
Henderson, Hamish. "Introduction." In Antonio Gramsci, *Gramsci's Prison Letters*, 1–23. London: Zwan, 1988.
Henry, Paget, and Paul Buhle, eds. *C. L. R. James's Caribbean*. London: Macmillan Caribbean, 1992.
Higman, B. W. *Writing West Indian Histories*. London: Macmillan Education, 1999.
Hill, Errol G. "The Emergence of a National Drama in the West Indies." *Caribbean Quarterly* 18, no. 4 (1972): 9–40.

Hill, Jeffrey. *Nelson: Politics, Economy, Community*. Edinburgh: Keele University Press, 1997.

Hill, Robert A. "C. L. R. James: The Myth of Western Civilization." In *Enterprise of the Indies*, edited by George Lamming, 255–59. Port-of-Spain: Trinidad and Tobago Institute of the West Indies, 1999.

Hill, Robert A. "In England, 1932–1938." In Buhle, *C. L. R. James*, 61–80.

Hill, Robert A. "Literary Executor's Afterword." In James, *American Civilization*, 293–366.

Hill, Robert A. "Preface." In James, *You Don't Play with Revolution*, xiii–xvi.

Hobsbawm, Eric. *Bandits*. London: Weidenfeld and Nicolson, 1969.

Hobsbawm, Eric. *Echoes of the Marseillaise: Two Centuries Look Back on the French Revolution*. London: Verso, 1990.

Hobsbawm, Eric. "History from Below—Some Reflections." In Krantz, *History from Below*, 13–27.

Høgsbjerg, Christian. "The Black International as Social Movement Wave: C. L. R. James's *History of Pan-African Revolt*." In *Marxism and Social Movements*, edited by Colin Barker, Laurence Cox, John Krinsky, and Alf Gunvald Nilsen, 317–37. Brill: Leiden, 2013.

Høgsbjerg, Christian. "'A Bohemian Freelancer?' C. L. R. James, His Early Relationship to Anarchism and the Intellectual Origins of Autonomism." In *Libertarian Socialism: Politics in Black and Red*, edited by Alex Prichard, Ruth Kinna, Saku Pinta, and David Berry, 11–17. Basingstoke: Palgrave Macmillan, 2012.

Høgsbjerg, Christian. "C. L. R. James and Italy's Conquest of Abyssinia." *Socialist History* 28 (2006): 17–36.

Høgsbjerg, Christian. *C. L. R. James in Imperial Britain*. Durham, NC: Duke University Press, 2014.

Høgsbjerg, Christian. "Interview with Mackenzie Frank: 2015." In Bennett and Høgsbjerg, *Celebrating C. L. R. James*, 67–80.

Høgsbjerg, Christian. "Introduction." In Høgsbjerg, *World Revolution*, 1–57.

Høgsbjerg, Christian. "Introduction." In James, *Toussaint Louverture*, 1–39. Durham, NC: Duke University Press, 2013.

Høgsbjerg, Christian. "'A Kind of Bible of Trotskyism': Reflections on C. L. R. James's *World Revolution*." *C. L. R. James Journal* 19, nos. 1–2 (2013): 243–75.

Høgsbjerg, Christian. "Reflections on C. L. R. James and the U.S. Occupation of Haiti." Paper presented at After Revolution: Versions and Re-visions of Haiti Conference, Institute for Black Atlantic Research, University of Central Lancashire, Preston, July 9–10, 2015.

Høgsbjerg, Christian. "'A Thorn in the Side of Great Britain': C. L. R. James and the Caribbean Labour Rebellions of the 1930s." *Small Axe* 35 (2011): 24–42.

Holland, Anna, and Richard Scholar, eds. *Pre-Histories and Afterlives: Studies in Critical Method*. Oxford: Legenda, 2009.

Horne, Gerald. *Confronting Black Jacobins, the U.S., the Haitian Revolution, and the Origins of the Dominican Republic*. New York: Monthly Review Press, 2015.

Horne, Gerald. *Race to Revolution: The U.S. and Cuba during Slavery and Jim Crow.* New York: Monthly Review Press, 2014.

Howe, Stephen. "C. L. R. James: Visions of History, Visions of Britain." In Schwarz, *West Indian Intellectuals in Britain*, 153–74.

Hudson, Peter James. "The Racist Dawn of Capitalism." *Boston Review*, March 14, 2016.

Huggan, Graham. *The Postcolonial Exotic: Marketing the Margins.* London: Routledge, 2001.

Hussein, Abdelrahman. *Edward Said: Criticism and Society.* London: Verso, 2002.

Iskander, Adel, and Hakem Rustom. *Edward Said: A Legacy of Emancipation and Representation.* Berkeley: University of California Press, 2010.

Jackson-Schebetta, Lisa. *"Traveler, There Is No Road": Theater, the Spanish Civil War, and the Decolonial Imagination in the Americas.* Iowa City: University of Iowa Press, 2017.

Jacobs, Sean, and Richard Calland, eds. *Thabo Mbeki's World: The Politics and Ideology of the South African President.* Pietermaritzburg: University of Natal Press, 2002.

Jacobs, Sean, and Herman Wasserman. *Shifting Selves: Post-Apartheid Essays on Mass Media, Culture, and Identity.* Cape Town: Kwela, 2003.

Jalabert, Laurent. "Les Mouvements sociaux en Martinique dans les années 1960 et la réaction des pouvoirs publics." *Études caribéennes* 17 (2010). https://etudescaribeennes.revues.org/4881.

James, Leslie. *George Padmore and Decolonization from Below: Pan-Africanism, the Cold War, and the End of Empire.* London: Palgrave Macmillan, 2015.

James, Selma. "*The Black Jacobins*, Past and Present." In Forsdick and Høgsbjerg, *The Black Jacobins Reader*, 73–91.

James, Selma. *Sex, Race, and Class—The Perspective of Winning: A Selection of Writings, 1952–2011.* Oakland, CA: PM Press, 2012.

James, Selma, Priscilla Allen, and Sylvine Schmidt. *Wages for Housework Notebook No. 1.* New York: New York Collective, 1975.

Janvier, Louis Joseph. *La République d'Haïti et ses visiteurs, 1840–1882.* Paris: Marpon and Flammarion, 1883.

Jean-Jacques, Nirvah. *Fefe ak Kikit.* Coconut Creek, FL: Educa Vision, 2001.

Jenson, Deborah. *Beyond the Slave Narrative: Politics, Sex, and Manuscripts in the Haitian Revolution.* Liverpool: Liverpool University Press, 2011.

Jeyifo, Biodun, ed. *Conversations with Wole Soyinka.* Jackson: University Press of Mississippi, 2001.

Jeyifo, Biodun, ed. *Perspectives on Wole Soyinka: Freedom and Complexity.* Jackson: University Press of Mississippi, 2001.

Jeyifo, Biodun. "Whose Theatre, Whose Africa? Wole Soyinka's *The Road* on the Road." *Modern Drama* 45, no. 3 (2002): 449–65.

Jeyifo, Biodun. *Wole Soyinka: Politics, Poetics, Postcolonialism.* Cambridge: Cambridge University Press, 2004.

Johnson, Kwynn. "Place as Palimpsest—*Yon kote tankou Palimpseste.*" *Caribbean Quarterly* 63, nos. 2–3 (2017): 169–76.

Johnson, Walter. *River of Dark Dreams: Slavery and Empire in the Cotton Kingdom.* Cambridge, MA: Harvard University Press, 2013.

Kaisary, Philip. *The Haitian Revolution in the Literary Imagination: Radical Horizons, Conservative Constraints.* Charlottesville: University of Virginia Press, 2014.

Kamugisha, Aaron. "C. L. R. James's *The Black Jacobins* and the Making of the Modern Atlantic World." In *Ten Books That Shaped the British Empire: Creating an Imperial Commons,* edited by Antoinette Burton and Isabel Hofmeyr, 190–215. Durham, NC: Duke University Press, 2014.

Kaplan, Cora. "Black Heroes/White Writers: Toussaint L'Ouverture and the Literary Imagination." *History Workshop Journal* 46 (1998): 32–62.

Kelleher, Joe. *Theatre and Politics.* Basingstoke: Palgrave Macmillan, 2009.

Kermode, Frank. *The Sense of an Ending: Studies in the Theory of Fiction.* Oxford: Oxford University Press, 1967.

Kinderman, William, and Joseph E. Jones. *Genetic Criticism and the Creative Process: Essays from Music, Literature, and Theater.* Rochester, NY: University of Rochester Press, 2009.

King, Nicole. *C. L. R. James and Creolization: Circles of Influence.* Jackson: University Press of Mississippi, 2001.

King, Nicole. "C. L. R. James, Genre and Cultural Politics." In *Beyond Boundaries: C. L. R. James and Postnational Studies,* edited by Christopher Gair, 13–38. London: Pluto, 2006.

Koinange, Mbiyu. *The People of Kenya Speak for Themselves.* Detroit: Kenya Publication Fund, 1955.

Koselleck, Reinhart. *Futures Past.* Cambridge, MA: MIT Press, 1985.

Krantz, Frederick, ed. *History from Below: Studies in Popular Protest and Popular Ideology.* Oxford: Blackwell, 1988.

LaCapra, Dominick. *Rethinking Intellectual History: Texts, Contexts, Language.* Ithaca, NY: Cornell University Press, 1983.

Lacroix, Pamphile de. *Mémoires pour servir à l'Histoire de la Révolution de Saint-Domingue.* Paris: Pillet aîné, 1819.

Lamming, George. "The Legacy of Eric Williams." *Callaloo* 20, no. 4 (1997): 731–36.

Langley, J. Ayo. "Pan-Africanism in Paris, 1924–36." *Journal of Modern African Studies* 7, no. 1 (1969): 69–94.

La Rose, John. *Unending Journey: Selected Writings.* London: New Beacon and George Padmore Institute, 2014.

Le Blanc, Paul. "Introduction: C. L. R. James and Revolutionary Marxism." In McLemee and Le Blanc, *C. L. R. James and Revolutionary Marxism,* 1–37.

Lefebvre, Georges. Review of *La Lutte de classes sous la première République: Bourgeois et "bras nus" (1793–1797),* by Daniel Guérin. *Annales historiques de la Révolution française* 19 (1947): 173–79.

Lefebvre, Georges. *La Révolution française: La fuite du roi*. Paris: Tournier and Constans, 1947.

Léger, Nathalie, and Almuth Grésillon, eds. "Théâtre." Special issue, *Genesis* 26 (2005).

Le Glaunec, Jean-Pierre. *L'Armée indigène: La défaite de Napoléon en Haïti*. Montreal: Lux, 2014.

Lemonnier-Delafosse, Jean-Baptiste. *Seconde campagne de Saint-Domingue... Précédée de Souvenirs historiques et succincts de la première campagne*. Le Havre: Imprimerie de Brindeau, 1946.

Lewis, Rupert, and Fitzroy Baptiste, eds. *George Padmore: Pan African Revolutionary*. Kingston: Ian Randall, 2009.

Liddington, Jill. *The Life and Times of a Respectable Rebel: Selina Cooper, 1864–1946*. London: Virago, 1984.

Lindenberger, Herbert. *Historical Drama: The Relation of Literature and Reality*. Chicago: University of Chicago Press, 1975.

Linnemann, Russell J. *Alain Locke: Reflections on a Modern Renaissance Man*. Baton Rouge: Louisiana State University Press, 1982.

Lloyd, Errol. "The Origins of the Book Fair and Book Fair Festival: An Interview with John La Rose, London, April 1982." In *A Meeting of the Continents: The International Book Fair of Radical Black and Third World Books Revisited: History, Memories, Organisation and Programmes 1982–1995*, edited by Sarah White, Roxy Harris, and Sharmilla Beezmohn, 3–14. London: New Beacon and the George Padmore Institute, 2005.

Löwy, Michael. *Morning Star: Surrealism, Marxism, Anarchism, Situationism, Utopia*. Austin: University of Texas Press, 2009.

Löwy, Michael. *The Politics of Combined and Uneven Development: The Theory of Permanent Revolution*. London: NLB, 1981.

Loza, Julien Valère. *Les Étudiants martiniquais en France: Histoire de leur organisation et de leurs luttes*. Saint-Estève, Martinique: Éditions 2M, 2003.

MacIntyre, Stuart. *Little Moscows: Communism and Working-Class Militancy in Inter-War Britain*. London: Croom Helm, 1980.

MacPhee, Josh. "Judging Books by Their Covers." Justseeds, July 25, 2011. https://justseeds.org/jbbtc-68-the-black-jacobins/.

Madiou, Thomas. *Histoire d'Haïti*. 2 vols. Port-au-Prince: Impr. J. Courtois, 1847–1848.

Maharaj, Clem. *The Dispossessed*. Portsmouth, NH: Heinemann, 1992.

Mahrer, Rudolf, ed. "Après le texte: De la réécriture après publication." Special issue, *Genesis* 44 (2017).

Makalani, Minkah. *In the Cause of Freedom: Radical Black Internationalism from Harlem to London, 1917–1939*. Chapel Hill: University of North Carolina Press, 2011.

Manigat, Max. "Le Livre haïtien en diaspora: Problèmes et perspectives." *Études littéraires* 13, no. 2 (1980): 335–45.

Mannin, Ethel. *Comrade, O Comrade; or Low-Down on the Left*. London: Jarrolds, 1947.

Manville, Marcel. *Les Antilles sans fards*. Paris: L'Harmattan, 1992.

Marable, Manning. *Black Leadership*. New York: Columbia University Press, 1998.
MARHO, ed. *Visions of History*. Manchester: Manchester University Press, 1984.
Marshall, Norman. *The Other Theatre*. London: Lehmann, 1947.
Marx, Karl. *Capital*. 3 vols. London: Penguin, 1990.
Marx, Karl. *The Eighteenth Brumaire of Louis Bonaparte*. In Karl Marx and Friedrich Engels, *Selected Works*. London: Lawrence and Wishart, 1991.
Marx, Karl. *The Eighteenth Brumaire of Louis Bonaparte*. New York: Mondial, 2005.
Marx, Karl, and Friedrich Engels. *The Communist Manifesto*. London: Arcturus, 2010.
Mathiez, Albert. *After Robespierre: The Thermidorean Reaction*. New York: Knopf, 1931.
Mathiez, Albert. *Autour de Robespierre*. Paris: Payot, 1925.
Mathiez, Albert. *Études sur Robespierre 1758–1794*. Paris: Éditions sociales, 1958.
Mathiez, Albert. *The Fall of Robespierre*. London: Williams and Norgate, 1927.
Mathiez, Albert. *The French Revolution*. New York: Knopf, 1928.
Mathiez, Albert. *Robespierre terroriste*. Paris: La Renaissance du livre, 1918.
Maxwell, Marina. "Toward a Revolution in the Arts." *Savacou* 2 (1970): 19–32.
Mayard, Constantin. "Haïti." Speech delivered on January 28, 1934. Poitiers: L'Action intellectuelle, 1934. http://gallica.bnf.fr/ark:/12148/bpt6k57965104.
McClendon, John H. *C. L. R. James's "Notes on Dialectics": Left Hegelianism or Marxism-Leninism*. Lanham, MD: Lexington, 2005.
McCree, Roy. "The Boundaries of Publication: The Making of *Beyond a Boundary*." In *Marxism, Colonialism, and Cricket: C. L. R. James's Beyond a Boundary*, edited by David Featherstone, Christopher Gair, Christian Høgsbjerg, and Andrew Smith, 72–87. Durham, NC: Duke University Press, 2018.
McDonald, Peter D. *The Literature Police: Apartheid Censorship and Its Cultural Consequences*. Oxford: Oxford University Press, 2009.
McIlroy, John. "James Richie (Jock) Haston." In *Dictionary of Labour Biography*, vol. 12, edited by Keith Gildart and David Howell, 124–36. Basingstoke: Palgrave Macmillan, 2005.
McLemee, Scott. "Afterword—American Civilization and World Revolution: C. L. R. James in the United States, 1938–1953 and Beyond." In McLemee and Le Blanc, *C. L. R. James and Revolutionary Marxism*, 209–38.
McLemee, Scott. "C. L. R. James: A Biographical Introduction." *American Visions*, April–May 1996.
McLemee, Scott, and Paul Le Blanc, eds. *C. L. R. James and Revolutionary Marxism: Selected Writings of C. L. R. James, 1939–1949*. Amherst, NY: Humanity, 1994.
Meeks, Brian. *Radical Caribbean: From Black Power to Abu Bakr*. Mona, Jamaica: University of the West Indies Press, 1996.
Mehlman, Jeffrey. *Revolution and Repetition*. Berkeley: University of California Press, 1977.
Menezes, Caroline. "Retelling History through Art: An Interview with Kimathi Donkor." *Studio International*, January 16, 2013. https://www.studiointernational.com/index.php/retelling-history-through-art-an-interview-with-kimathi-donkor.

Miller, F. Bart. *Rethinking Negritude through Léon-Gontran Damas.* Amsterdam: Rodopi, 2014.

Miller, Paul B. *Elusive Origins: The Enlightenment in the Modern Caribbean Historical Imagination.* Charlottesville: University of Virginia Press, 2010.

Mills, Sean. *The Empire Within: Postcolonial Activism in Sixties Montreal.* Montreal: McGill-Queen's University Press, 2010.

Mitchell, Tony. *Dario Fo: People's Court Jester.* London: Bloomsbury, 2014.

Mohammed, Kimathi. *Organization and Spontaneity: The Theory of the Vanguard Party and Its Application to the Black Movement in the U.S. Today.* Atlanta, GA: On Our Own Authority!, 2013.

Moitt, Bernard. "Transcending Linguistic and Cultural Frontiers in Caribbean Historiography: C. L. R. James, French Sources, and Slavery in San Domingo." In Cudjoe and Cain, *C. L. R. James,* 136–60.

Molyneux, John. *Leon Trotsky's Theory of Revolution.* Brighton: Harvester, 1981.

Monnerville, Gaston, Léopold Sédar-Senghor, and Aimé Césaire. *Commémoration du centenaire de l'abolition de l'esclavage: Discours prononcés à la Sorbonne le 27 Avril 1948* [Centennial commemoration of the abolition of slavery: Presentations at the Sorbonne April 27, 1948]. Paris: Presses Universitaires des France, 1948.

Morales Domínguez, Esteban. *Race in Cuba: Essays on the Revolution and Racial Inequality.* New York: Monthly Review Press, 2013.

Moreau de Saint-Méry, Médéric-Louis-Élie. *Description topographique, physique, civile, politique et historique de la partie française de l'isle Saint-Domingue. Avec des observations générales sur sa population, sur le caractère & les mœurs de ses divers habitans; sur son climat, sa culture . . . accompagnées des détails les plus propres à faire connaître l'état de cette colonie à l'époque du 18 octobre 1789; et d'une carte de la totalité de l'isle.* Philadelphia: Author, 1797.

Moreiras, Alberto. "Historicality and Historiography: Haiti and the Limits of World History." Studi Culturali, http://www.studiculturali.it/laboratori/laboratori_v_d.php?recordID=60&laboratorioID=Summer%20School%20Critica/Crisi.

Morris, Andrea Easley. *Afro-Cuban Identity in Post-Revolutionary Novel and Film: Inclusion, Loss, and Cultural Resistance.* Lewisburg, PA: Bucknell University Press, 2011.

Munslow, Alun. *Narrative and History.* Basingstoke: Palgrave Macmillan, 2007.

Murphy, David. *Sembene: Imagining Alternatives in Film and Fiction.* Oxford: James Currey, 2000.

Murray, Jim. "The C. L. R. James Institute and Me." *Interventions* 1, no. 3 (1999): 389–96.

Naipaul, V. S. *The Middle Passage.* London: André Deutsch, 1961.

Nemours, Alfred Auguste. *Histoire de la captivité et de la mort de Toussaint-Louverture.* Paris: n.p., 1929.

Nemours, Alfred Auguste. *Histoire de la famille et de la descendance de Toussaint-Louverture.* Port-au-Prince: Éditions Presses nationales d'Haïti, 2008.

Nemours, Alfred Auguste. *Histoire militaire de la guerre d'indépendance de Saint-Domingue.* 2 vols. Paris: n.p., 1925.

Nesbitt, Nick. "Departmentalization and the Logic of Decolonization." *L'Esprit Créateur* 47, no. 1 (2007): 32–43.

Nesbitt, Nick. "Fragments of a Universal History: Global Capital, Mass Revolution, and the Idea of Equality in *The Black Jacobins*." In Forsdick and Høgsbjerg, *The Black Jacobins Reader*, 139–61.

Nesbitt, Nick, ed. *The Concept in Crisis: Reading Capital Today*. Durham, NC: Duke University Press, 2017.

Nesbitt, Nick. *Universal Emancipation: The Haitian Revolution and the Radical Enlightenment*. Charlottesville, VA: University of Virginia Press, 2008.

Nettleford, Rex. *Inward Stretch, Outward Reach: A Voice from the Caribbean*. Basingstoke: Macmillan Caribbean, 1993.

Ngũgĩ wa Thiong'o. *Moving the Centre: The Struggle for Cultural Freedoms*. Oxford: James Currey, 1993.

Nicholls, David. *From Dessalines to Duvalier: Race, Colour, and National Independence in Haiti*. Cambridge: Cambridge University Press, 1979.

Nielsen, Aldon Lynn. *C. L. R. James: A Critical Introduction*. Jackson: University Press of Mississippi, 1997.

Nielsen, Aldon Lynn. "On the Wings of Atlanta." In Forsdick and Høgsbjerg, *The Black Jacobins Reader*, 297–310.

Noble, Peter. *The Negro in Films*. London: Skelton Robinson, 1948.

Nora, Pierre, ed. *Les Lieux de mémoire*. 7 vols. Paris: Gallimard, 1984–92.

Ojo-Ade, Femi. *Being Black, Being Human*. Ile-Ife, Nigeria: Obafemi Awolowo University Press, 1996.

O'Shaughnessy, Andrew. "Eric Williams as Economic Historian." In Cateau and Carrington, *Capitalism and Slavery*, 99–117.

Oxaal, Ivar. *Black Intellectuals Come to Power: The Rise of Creole Nationalism in Trinidad and Tobago*. Cambridge, MA: Schenkman, 1968.

Padmore, George. *Haiti, an American Slave Colony*. Moscow: Centrizdat, 1931.

Palmer, Bryan. *The Making of E. P. Thompson: Marxism, Humanism, and History*. Toronto: New Hogtown, 1981.

Palmer, Colin A. *Eric Williams and the Making of the Modern Caribbean*. Chapel Hill: University of North Carolina Press, 2006.

Parry, Benita. "Reconciliation and Remembrance." *Pretexts* 5, nos. 1–2 (1995): 86.

Paulson, Ronald. *Representations of Revolution (1789–1820)*. New Haven, CT: Yale University Press, 1983.

Pavis, Patrice. *Dictionary of the Theatre: Terms, Concepts, and Analysis*. Toronto: University of Toronto Press, 1988.

Pearce, Brian. "Trotsky as an Historian." *The Newsletter*, August 27, 1960. Marxists Internet Archive Library. https://www.marxists.org/archive/pearce/1960/08/trotsky-historian.htm.

Pereira, Joseph. "The Influence of the Casa de las Américas on English Caribbean Literature." *Caribbean Quarterly* 31, no. 1 (1985): 93–105.

Perry, Matt. *Marxism and History*. Basingstoke: Palgrave, 2002.
Pierrot, Grégory. "'Our Hero': Toussaint Louverture in British Representations." *Criticism* 50, no. 4 (2008): 581–607.
Pierrot, Grégory, and Paul Youngquist. "Introduction." In Marcus Rainsford, *An Historical Account of the Black Empire of Hayti*, xvii–lvi. Durham, NC: Duke University Press, 2013.
Placide, Louis-Georges. *Les Émeutes de décembre 1959 en Martinique: Un repère historique*. Paris: L'Harmattan, 2009.
Popkin, Jeremy. *A Concise History of Haiti*. Hoboken, NJ: Wiley-Blackwell, 2011.
Portelli, Alessandro. "Gli schiavi dei Lumi alla presa della Bastigli riproposto il volume di C. L. R. James, *I giacobini neri*, un classico della storiografia sociale." December 10, 2006. https://alessandroportelli.blogspot.com/2006/12/gli-schiavi-dei-lumi-alla-presa-della.html.
Post, Charles. "Slavery and the New History of Capitalism." *Catalyst* 1 (2017): 173–92.
Post, Charles. *The American Road to Capitalism: Studies in Class Structure, Economic Development and Political Conflict, 1620–1877*. Chicago: Haymarket, 2012.
Pozzi, Francesca, Gigi Roggero, and Guido Borio. *Futuro anteriore: Dai "Quaderni rossi" ai movimenti globali: Riccheze e limiti dell'operaismo italiano*. Rome: Derive Approdi, 2002.
Pozzi, Francesca, Gigi Roggero, and Guido Borio. *Gli operaisti*. Rome: Derive Approdi, 2005.
Price, Hannibal. *De la réhabilitation de la race noire par la République d'Haïti*. Port-au-Prince: J. Verrollot, 1900.
Price Mars, Jean. *Ainsi parla l'oncle*. Port-au-Prince: Imprimerie de Compiègne, 1928. Reprint, Montreal: Mémoire d'encrier, 2005.
Quest, Matthew. "George Padmore's and C. L. R. James's *International African Opinion*." In Lewis and Baptiste, *George Padmore*, 105–32.
Quest, Matthew. "The 'Not So Bright' Protégés and the Comrades Who 'Never Quarreled.'" *Journal of Communist Theory*, October 4, 2013. http://insurgentnotes.com/2013/10/the-not-so-bright-proteges/.
Quest, Matthew. "On 'Both Sides' of the Haitian Revolution? Rethinking Direct Democracy and National Liberation in *The Black Jacobins*." In Forsdick and Høgsbjerg, *The Black Jacobins Reader*, 235–55.
Quinn, Kate, ed. *Black Power in the Caribbean*. Gainesville: University Press of Florida, 2014.
Rabbitt, Kara M. "C. L. R. James's Figuring of Toussaint Louverture: *The Black Jacobins* and the Literary Hero." In Cudjoe and Cain, *C. L. R. James*, 118–35.
Ranke, Leopold von. *Geschichten der romanischen und germanischen Völker von 1494 bis 1535*. Leipzig: Reimer, 1824.
Rawick, George P. *The American Slave: A Composite Autobiography*. Vol. 1: *From Sundown to Sunup: The Making of the Black Community*. Westport, CT: Greenwood, 1972.

Rawick, George P. *Listening to Revolt: The Selected Writings of George Rawick.* Edited by David Roediger. Chicago: Charles H. Kerr, 2010.

Raynal, Abbé Guillaume-Thomas. *Histoire philosophique et politique des établissemens et du commerce des Européens dans les deux Indes.* 3rd ed. 10 vols. Geneva: Jean-Léonard Pellet, 1780–1784.

Regis, Louis. "Rawle Gibbons and the Theory and Practice of the Third Theatre." *Caribbean Quarterly* 63, nos. 2–3 (2017): 183–202.

Renault, Matthieu. *C. L. R. James: La vie révolutionnaire d'un "Platon noir."* Paris: La Découverte, 2015.

Renda, Mary A. *Taking Haiti: Military Occupation and the Culture of U.S. Imperialism, 1915–1940.* Chapel Hill: University of North Carolina Press, 2001.

Riffard, Claire, and Daniel Delas, eds. "Afrique–Caraïbe." Special issue, *Genesis* 33 (2011).

Rigby, S. H. *Marxism and History: A Critical Introduction.* Manchester: Manchester University Press, 1998.

Rigney, Ann. "Icon and Symbol: The Historical Figure Called Maximilien Robespierre." In Heffernan, *Representing the French Revolution*, 106–22.

Rigney, Ann. *The Afterlives of Walter Scott: Memory on the Move.* Oxford: Oxford University Press, 2012.

Roach, Joseph. *Cities of the Dead: Circum-Atlantic Performance.* New York: Columbia University Press, 1996.

Roberts, Alfie. *A View for Freedom: Alfie Roberts Speaks on the Caribbean, Cricket, Montreal, and C. L. R. James.* Montreal: Alfie Roberts Institute, 2005.

Robeson, Paul. *Here I Stand.* London: Cassell, 1988.

Robinson, Cedric J. *Black Marxism: The Making of the Black Radical Tradition.* London: Zed, 1983.

Rockman, Seth. "What Makes the History of Capitalism Newsworthy?" *Journal of the Early Republic* 34 (2014): 439–66.

Roderick, Rick. "Further Adventures of the Dialectic." In Cudjoe and Cain, *C. L. R. James*, 205–11.

Rodney, Walter. "The African Revolution." In Buhle, *C. L. R. James*, 30–48.

Rodney, Walter. *How Europe Underdeveloped Africa.* Washington, DC: Howard University Press, 1981.

Romano, Paul [Phil Singer], and Ria Stone [Grace Lee Boggs]. *The American Worker.* Detroit: Bewick, 1947.

Rose, R. B. *The Enragés.* Melbourne: Melbourne University Press, 1965.

Rose, R. B. *The Making of the Sans-Culottes.* Manchester: Manchester University Press, 1983.

Rosengarten, Frank. *Urbane Revolutionary: C. L. R. James and the Struggle for a New Society.* Jackson: University Press of Mississippi, 2008.

Ross, Kristin. *May '68 and Its Afterlives.* Chicago: University of Chicago Press, 2004.

Rudé, George. *The Crowd in the French Revolution*. Oxford: Clarendon, 1959.
Ryan, Selwyn. *Eric Williams: The Myth and the Man*. Kingston, Jamaica: University of the West Indies Press, 2009.
Said, Edward. *Beginning: Intention and Method*. Baltimore, MD: Johns Hopkins University Press, 1975.
Salkey, Andrew. *Havana Journal*. Harmondsworth, UK: Penguin, 1971.
Samaroo, Brinsley. "Introduction." In *The Beacon: Volumes I–IV, 1931–1939*, i–xiii. New York: Kraus, 1977.
Samuel, Raphael. "Introduction: Theatre and Politics." In *Theatres of the Left, 1880–1935: Workers' Theatre Movements in Britain and America*, edited by Raphael Samuel, Ewan MacColl, and Stuart Cosgrove, xiii–xx. London: Routledge and Kegan Paul, 1985.
Sander, Reinhard. "C. L. R. James and the Haitian Revolution." *World Literature Written in English* 26, no. 2 (1986): 277–90.
Sander, Reinhard, ed. *From Trinidad: An Anthology of Early West Indian Writing*. London: Hodder and Stoughton, 1978.
Sander, Reinhard. "Introduction: *The Beacon* and the Emergence of West Indian Literature." In *The Beacon: Volumes I–IV, 1931–1939*, xv–xxv. New York: Kraus, 1977.
Sander, Reinhard. *The Trinidad Awakening: West Indian Literature of the Nineteen-Thirties*. New York: Greenwood, 1988.
Sandwith, Corinne. *World of Letters: Reading Communities and Cultural Debates in Early Apartheid South Africa*. Pietermaritzburg, South Africa: University of KwaZulu-Natal Press, 2014.
Sannon, Horace Pauléus. *Histoire de Toussaint Louverture*. 3 vols. Port-au-Prince: A. A. Héraux, 1920–1933.
Saville, John. *Memoirs from the Left*. London: Merlin, 2003.
Schelling, Felix. *The English Chronicle Play: A Study in the Popular Historical Literature Environing Shakespeare*. New York: Macmillan, 1902.
Schmid, Marion. *Processes of Literary Creation: Flaubert and Proust*. Oxford: Legenda, 1998.
Schneider, Rebecca. *Performing Remains: Art and War in Times of Theatrical Reenactment*. London: Routledge, 2011.
Schœlcher, Victor. *Vie de Toussaint Louverture*. 1889. Reprint, Paris: Karthala, 1982.
Schuessler, Jennifer. "In History Departments, It's Up with Capitalism." *New York Times*, April 6, 2013. http://www.nytimes.com/2013/04/07/education/in-history-departments-its-up-with-capitalism.html.
Schwarz, Bill. "Not Even Past Yet." *History Workshop Journal* 57 (2004): 101–15.
Schwarz, Bill, ed. *West Indian Intellectuals in Britain*. Manchester, UK: Manchester University Press, 2003.
Scott, David. *Conscripts of Modernity: The Tragedy of Colonial Enlightenment*. Durham, NC: Duke University Press, 2004.

Scott, David. *Refashioning Futures: Criticism after Postcoloniality*. Princeton, NY: Princeton University Press, 1999.

Scott, David. "The Theory of Haiti: *The Black Jacobins* and the Poetics of Universal History." In Forsdick and Høgsbjerg, *The Black Jacobins Reader*, 115–38.

Senghor, Léopold Sédar. *Liberté I: Négritude et humanisme*. Paris: Stock, 1964.

Sengupta, Indra, ed. *Memory, History, and Colonialism: Engaging with Pierre Nora in Colonial and Postcolonial Contexts*. London: German Historical Institute London, 2009.

Sepinwall, Alyssa Goldstein. "Beyond *The Black Jacobins*: Haitian Revolutionary Historiography Comes of Age." *Journal of Haitian Studies* 23, no. 1 (2017): 4–34.

Sepinwall, Alyssa Goldstein. *Haitian History: New Perspectives*. London: Routledge, 2013.

Sepinwall, Alyssa Goldstein. "Happy as a Slave: The *Toussaint Louverture* Miniseries." *Fiction and Film for French Historians: A Cultural Bulletin* 4, no. 1 (2013). https://h-france.net/fffh/maybe-missed/happy-as-a-slave-the-toussaint-louverture-miniseries/.

Shannon, Magdaline. *Jean Price-Mars, the Haitian Elite and the American Occupation, 1915–1935*. New York: St. Martin's, 1996.

Sharpe, Jim. "History from Below." In *New Perspectives on Historical Writing*, edited by Peter Burke, 24–41. Cambridge: Polity, 1991.

Sherwood, Marika. *Manchester and the 1945 Pan-African Congress*. London: Savannah, 1995.

Sherwood, Marika. *Origins of Pan-Africanism: Henry Sylvester Williams, Africa and the African Diaspora*. London: Routledge, 2011.

Sidnell, Michael J. *Dances of Death: The Group Theatre of London in the Thirties*. London: Faber and Faber, 1984.

Silverman, Max, ed. *Frantz Fanon's Black Skin, White Masks: New Interdisciplinary Essays*. Manchester: Manchester University Press, 2005.

Smith, Andrew. *C. L. R. James and the Study of Culture*. Basingstoke, UK: Palgrave Macmillan, 2010.

Smith, Barbara Herrnstein. *Poetic Closure: A Study of How Poems End*. Chicago: University of Chicago Press, 1968.

Smith, Faith. *Creole Recitations: John Jacob Thomas and Colonial Formation in the Late Nineteenth-Century Caribbean*. Charlottesville: University of Virginia Press, 2002.

Smith, Matthew J. "'To Place Ourselves in History': The Haitian Revolution in British West Indian Thought before *The Black Jacobins*." In Forsdick and Høgsbjerg, *The Black Jacobins Reader*, 178–93.

Soboul, Albert. "Classes et luttes de classes sous la Révolution française." *La Pensée* 53 (1954): 39.

Soboul, Albert. *Les Sans-culottes parisiens en l'an 2*. Paris: Clavreuil, 1958.

Solow, Barbara L., and Stanley L. Engerman, eds. *British Capitalism and Caribbean Slavery: The Legacy of Eric Williams*. Cambridge: Cambridge University Press, 1989.

Soyinka, Wole. *Ibadan: The Penkelemes Years: A Memoir, 1946–65*. London: Methuen, 2001.

Soyinka, Wole. *The Man Died: Prison-Notes of Wole Soyinka*. Harmondsworth: Penguin, 1975.

Stephens, Michelle. *Black Empire: The Masculine Global Imaginary of Caribbean Intellectuals in the United States, 1914–1962*. Durham, NC: Duke University Press, 2005.

St Louis, Brett. *Rethinking Race, Politics, and Poetics: C. L. R. James's Critique of Modernity*. London: Routledge, 2007.

Stoddard, T. Lothrop. *The French Revolution in San Domingo*. Boston: Houghton Mifflin, 1914.

Stone, Judy. "Caribbean." In *The Continuum Companion to Twentieth Century Theatre*, edited by Colin Chambers, 135. London: Continuum, 2002.

Stone, Judy. *Theatre*. London: Macmillan Caribbean, 1994.

Surin, Kenneth. "'The Future Anterior': C. L. R. James and Going *Beyond a Boundary*." In Farred, *Rethinking C. L. R. James*, 187–204.

Sweeney, Fionnghuala. "The Haitian Play: C. L. R. James' *Toussaint Louverture* (1936)." *International Journal of Francophone Studies* 14, nos. 1–2 (2011): 143–63.

Taylor, Diana. *The Archive and the Repertoire: Performing Cultural Memory in the Americas*. Durham, NC: Duke University Press, 2003.

Teelucksingh, Jerome. *Ideology, Politics, and Radicalism of the Afro-Caribbean*. London: Palgrave Macmillan, 2016.

Thompson, E. P. *Customs in Common: Studies in Traditional Popular Culture*. New York: New Press, 1991.

Thompson, E. P. *Making History: Writings on History and Culture*. New York: New Press, 1994.

Thompson, E. P. *The Making of the English Working Class*. London: Victor Gollancz, 1963.

Thornton, John K. "I Am the Subject of the King of Congo: African Political Ideology and the Haitian Revolution." *Journal of World History* 4 (1993): 181–214.

Tilak, K. [Leslie Goonewardene]. *Rise and Fall of the Comintern*. Bombay: n.p., 1947.

Toscano, Alberto. "Black Sansculottes and Ambitious Marionettes: Cedric J. Robinson, C. L. R. James and the Critique of Political Leadership." *Viewpoint Magazine*, February 16, 2017. https://www.viewpointmag.com/2017/02/16/black-sansculottes-and-ambitious-marionettes-cedric-j-robinson-c-l-r-james-and-the-critique-of-political-leadership.

Toth, Jane, and William A. Tremblay. "The Alfred Nemours Collection of Haitian History: A Catalogue." *Caribbean Studies* 2, no. 3 (1962): 61–70.

Trotsky, Leon. "A Strategy of Action and Not of Speculation, Letter to Peking Friends." *Class Struggle* 3, no. 6 (June 1933 [October 1932]).

Trotsky, Leon. "Class Relations in the Chinese Revolution." *New International* 4, nos. 3–4 (1938 [1927]): 87–89, 123–24.

Trotsky, Leon. *History of the Russian Revolution*. 1930. London: Penguin, 2017.

Trotsky, Leon. "Introduction." In Harold R. Isaacs, *The Tragedy of the Chinese Revolution*, xi–xxv. London: Secker and Warburg, 1938.

Trotsky, Leon. "On the Canton Insurrection: Three Letters to Preobrazhensky." *New International* 3, no. 2 (1936 [1928]).

Trotsky, Leon. "On the Sino-Japanese War." *Internal Bulletin* 1 (October 1937).

Trotsky, Leon. "On the War in China." *Class Struggle* 3, no. 2 (February 1933).

Trotsky, Leon. "Peasant War in China and the Proletariat." *The Militant*, October 15, 1932, 1; October 22, 1932, 4.

Trotsky, Leon. *The Permanent Revolution and Results and Prospects*. New York: Pathfinder, 1972.

Trotsky, Leon. *Problems of the Chinese Revolution*. New York: Pioneer, 1932.

Trotsky, Leon. "The Sino-Soviet Conflict and the Opposition." *The Militant* 2, no. 14 (September 15, 1929).

Trotsky, Leon. *The Third International after Lenin*. 1928. London: Union, 2008.

Trouillot, Michel-Rolph. "Haitian Historiography." In *General History of the Caribbean*, vol. 6, *Methodology and Historiography of the Caribbean*, edited by B. W. Higman, 451–77. Paris: UNESCO; London: Macmillan Education, 1999.

Trouillot, Michel-Rolph. *Silencing the Past: Power and the Production of History*. Boston: Beacon, 1995.

Twa, Lindsay J. "Jean-Jacques Dessalines: Demon, Demigod, and Everything in Between." Romantic Circles, October 2011. https://www.rc.umd.edu/praxis/circulations/HTML/praxis.2011.twa.html.

Ulysse, Gina Athena. "Haiti and Toussaint Louverture: The Response Must Be a Remix." British Museum, March 13, 2018. https://blog.britishmuseum.org/haiti-and-toussaint-louverture-the-response-must-be-a-remix/.

Ulysse, Gina Athena. *Why Haiti Needs New Narratives: A Post-Quake Chronicle*. Middletown, CT: Wesleyan University Press, 2015.

Vaissière, Pierre de. *Saint-Domingue*. Paris: Perrin, 1909.

Van Hulle, Dirk. *Manuscript Genetics, Joyce's Know-How, Beckett's Nohow*. Gainesville: University Press of Florida, 2008.

Walsh, John Patrick. *Free and French in the Caribbean: Toussaint Louverture, Aimé Césaire, and Narratives of Loyal Opposition*. Bloomington: Indiana University Press, 2013.

Walsh, John Patrick. "Toussaint Louverture at a Crossroads: The Mémoire of the 'First Soldier of the Republic of Saint-Domingue.'" *Journal of Haitian Studies* 17, no. 1 (2011): 88–105.

Warburg, Frederic. *An Occupation for Gentlemen*. London: Hutchison, 1959.

Washington, Johnny. *Alain Locke and Philosophy: A Quest for Cultural Pluralism*. Westport, CT: Greenwood, 1986.

Waters, Rob. "Student Politics, Teaching Politics, Black Politics: An Interview with Ansel Wong." *Race and Class* 58, no. 1 (2016): 17–33.

Watkin, Christopher. "Rewriting the Death of the Author: Rancièrian Reflections." *Philosophy and Literature* 39 (2015): 32–46.

Watts, Nic, and Sakina Karimjee. *Toussaint Louverture: The Story of the Only Successful Slave Revolt in History*. London: Verso, forthcoming.
Watts, Richard. *Packaging Post/Coloniality: The Manufacture of Literary Identity in the Francophone World*. Lanham, MD: Lexington, 2005.
Webb, Constance. *Not without Love: Memoirs*. Hanover, NH: University Press of New England, 2003.
Webb, Constance. *Richard Wright: A Biography*. New York: Putnam, 1968.
Weiss, Judith A. *Casa de las Américas: An Intellectual Review in the Cuban Revolution*. Madrid: Editorial Castalia, 1977.
West, Michael O., and William G. Martin. "Haiti, I'm Sorry: The Haitian Revolution and the Forging of the Black International." In *From Toussaint to Tupac: The Black International since the Age of Revolution*, edited by Michael O. West, William G. Martin, and Fanon Che Wilkins, 72–104. Chapel Hill: University of North Carolina Press, 2009.
Weston, Helen. "The Many Faces of Toussaint Louverture." In *Slave Portraiture in the Atlantic World*, edited by Agnes Lugo-Ortiz and Angela Rosenthal, 345–71. Cambridge: Cambridge University Press, 2013.
White, Hayden. *The Content of the Form: Narrative Discourse and Historical Representation*. Baltimore, MD: Johns Hopkins University Press, 1987.
White, Hayden. "Historical Emplotment and the Problem of Truth." In *Probing the Limits of Representation: Nazism to the Final Solution*, edited by Saul Friedlander, 37–53. Cambridge, MA: Harvard University Press, 1992.
Wieder, Alan. *Teacher and Comrade: Richard Dudley and the Fight for Democracy in South Africa*. Albany: State University of New York Press, 2008.
Wilder, Gary. *Freedom Time: Negritude, Decolonization, and the Future of the World*. Durham, NC: Duke University Press, 2015.
Wilder, Gary. *The French Imperial Nation-State: Negritude and Colonial Humanism between the Two World Wars*. Chicago: University of Chicago Press, 2005.
Wilder, Gary. "Race, Reason, Impasse: Césaire, Fanon, and the Legacy of Emancipation." *Radical History Review* 90 (2004): 31–61.
Wilder, Gary. "Untimely Vision: Aimé Césaire, Decolonization, Utopia." *Public Culture* 21, no. 1 (2009): 101–40.
Williams, Eric. *Capitalism and Slavery*. 1944. Reprint, Chapel Hill: University of North Carolina Press, 1994.
Williams, Eric. *From Columbus to Castro: The History of the Caribbean, 1492–1969*. London: André Deutsch, 1970.
Williams, Eric. *Inward Hunger: The Education of a Prime Minister*. London: André Deutsch, 1969.
Williams, Eugene. "The Anancy Technique: A Gateway to Postcolonial Performance." *Caribbean Quarterly* 63, nos. 2–3 (2017): 215–33.
Williams, Gwyn A. *Artisans and Sans-culottes: Popular Movements in France and Britain during the French Revolution*. London: Edward Arnold, 1968.

Wilson-Tagoe, Nana. *Historical Thought and Literary Representation in West Indian Literature*. Gainesville: University Press of Florida, 1998.

Winter, Jay M. "In Conclusion: Palimpsests." In Sengupta, *Memory, History, and Colonialism*, 167–73.

Wood, Ellen Meiksins. *The Empire of Capital*. London: Verso, 2003.

Woodhams, Stephen. *History in the Making: Raymond Williams, Edward Thompson, and Radical Intellectuals, 1936–1956*. London: Merlin, 2001.

Woolward, Keithley, ed. "The Caribbean Stage: From Traditional Theatre to Modern Performances." Special issue, *Caribbean Quarterly* 63, nos. 2–3 (2017).

Worcester, Kent. *C. L. R. James: A Political Biography*. Albany: State University of New York Press, 1996.

Wright, Derek. *Wole Soyinka Revisited*. New York: Twayne, 1993.

Wright, Steve. *Storming Heaven: Class Composition and Struggle in Italian Autonomist Marxism*. London: Pluto, 2002.

Wynter, Sylvia. *Jamaica's National Heroes*. Kingston: Jamaica National Commission, 1971.

Young, James D. *The World of C. L. R. James: The Unfragmented Vision*. Glasgow: Clydeside, 1999.

Young, Robert J. C. "Rereading the Symptomatic Reading." In Nesbitt, *The Concept in Crisis*, 35–48.

Filmography

Beyond a Boundary. Directed by Mike Dibb. London: Omnibus, 1976. https://www.youtube.com/watch?v=E2eatQ7A9e8&feature=youtu.be.

C. L. R. James in Conversation with Stuart Hall. Directed by Mike Dibb. London: Channel 4, 1986. https://www.youtube.com/watch?v=_GfoKUxgZfI.

Every Cook Can Govern: The Life, Impact and Works of C. L. R. James. Directed by Ceri Dingle and Rob Harris. London: Worldwrite, 2016. http://www.clrjames.uk/.

La Martinique aux Martiniquais: L'Affaire de l'OJAM. Directed by Camille Mauduech. Paris: Les Films du Marigot, 2011.

Talking History: C. L. R. James in Conversation with E. P. Thompson. Directed by H. O. Nazareth. London: Penumbra Films, 1983. https://www.youtube.com/watch?v=MI7n7M6nAOA.

The C. L. R. James Lectures. Directed by H. O. Nazareth. London: Penumbra Films, 1983.

INDEX

abolition, 21, 83–85, 111, 143; in French colonies, 45–46, 63, 134–35, 169, 189; not granted benevolently, 21, 84, 143
Abyssinia. *See* Ethiopia
"Abyssinia and the Imperialists" (James), 51, 52, 55
Acacia, Michel, 12, 200
Africa, 51, 56, 69, 70, 72, 91, 99–101, 102–3, 108, 110–11, 178, 204. *See also* antiapartheid struggle; Mbeki, Thabo; South Africa
afterlives, 2, 4, 7, 12, 22, 28, 178–213, 218n33, 252n3
Akala, 188
Ali, Tariq, 204
Allan, Foz (Kwame Kwei-Armah), 204–5
Allen, Priscilla (Prisca), 140, 246–47n21, 247n22
alternative scenes for *The Black Jacobins* 1967 play, 10, 137, 144–45, 147–49, 158–60
Althusser, Louis, 83, 235n66
Aluko, Tayo, 198
America: naval base at Chaguaramas (Trinidad), 129–30; occupation of Haiti, 48–53, 73, 126, 178, 226nn41–42; civil rights movement in, 102, 117; James on society in, 73, 178, 204; James organizing in, 112, 120–21, 141, 190

American Civilization (James), 122
antiapartheid struggle, 4, 12, 198–99, 202, 260n114
Aoki, Yoshio, 193
Aperçu sur la formation historique de la nation haïtienne (Charlier), 22, 200
appendix: "From Toussaint Louverture to Fidel Castro" (1963), 9, 101–8, 112, 125–32, 175–76; translation of, 189, 190–93
Andwele, Adisa: "Aja," 180
Apter, Emily, 82
Ardouin, Alexis Beaubrun, 15, 81, 199
Arise Sir John (Donkor), 185
Aristide, Jean-Bertrand, 193, 196, 197, 202, 204
Aristotle, 115
Arnold, A. James, 7
Arts Theatre Group, 4, 144, 146
At the Rendezvous of Victory (James), 128–29
Austin, David, 199, 202–3, 204
autobiography (James, unpublished), 12, 33, 75–76, 84–85, 129–30

Bach, Hans, 192
Bailey, David A., 180
Bandung Conference, 172
Barbados, 180, 195, 197, 203, 205
Barthes, Roland, 11–14

Baudière, Ferrand de, 44–45, 134
Baugh, Edward: "The West Indian Writer and His Quarrel with History," 30–31, 223n4
Beaton, Norman, 196
Beckles, Hilary, 197, 235n72
Bell, Madison Smartt, 125, 190
Bernier, Celeste-Marie, 187, 252–53n14
Beyond a Boundary (Dibb), 203
Beyond a Boundary (James), 33, 75–76, 104, 106, 203, 207, 208
bibliography (*The Black Jacobins*): in 1938 history edition, 16, 18, 71, 81, 82, 87, 88, 104; updated for 1963 history edition, 121–25; translations of, 189–90, 192, 193
Black and Ethnic Minority Arts Network, 207
The Black Jacobins (James, 1967 Nigerian production), 4, 11, 24, 25, 27–28, 133–77; Caribbeanness of, 152; read as *Toussaint Louverture* (1936 play), 34, 140. *See also* epilogue; Lyndersay, Dexter; prologue
The Black Jacobins (James, 1975 Jamaican production), 195. *See also* Gibbons, Rawle
The Black Jacobins (James, 1979 Trinidad production), 194–95. *See also* Gibbons, Rawle
The Black Jacobins (James, 1982 Jamaican production), 195–96. *See also* Williams, Eugene
The Black Jacobins (James, 1986 London production), 180, 193, 194, 196. *See also* Brewster, Yvonne
The Black Jacobins (James, 1993 Trinidad production), 145, 194–96. *See also* Gibbons, Rawle
The Black Jacobins (James, 2004 Barbados production), 195, 197–98. *See also* Walcott, Harclyde

"Black Jacobins: Negritude in a Post-Global 21st Century," 180
The Black Jacobins: Toussaint L'Ouverture and the San Domingo Revolution (C. L. R. James): Haitian trajectory, 4, 28, 198, 199–202; 1938 edition, 26–27, 69–100; 1963 edition, 26, 27, 102–32; 1980 foreword, 14, 17, 18, 32, 50, 80, 143, 198; translations and foreign editions, 188–93
Black Power movement, 102, 117, 195
Black Sage [pseud. for Phillip Murray], 213
"The Black Sansculottes" (James), 117, 129, 201
Blakk-Jacobin (Ramsay), 180–81
Bloom Harold, 127
Boal, Augusto, 11, 25, 165, 177, 212
Boggs, Grace Lee, 3–4, 121
Bogues, Anthony, 186, 253n22
Bois Caïman ceremony, 45, 134
Boisrond-Tonnerre, Louis, 20
Bologna, Sergio, 190, 192
Bonaparte, Louis, 172–73. *See also* farce; Marx, Karl
Bonaparte, Napoleon, 17, 45–46, 115, 148, 149, 158, 159, 184
Bongie, Chris, 16
book history, 6–11, 27, 140
Boukman, Dutty, 44, 180
Bovell, Brian, 196, 257–58n71
Bowdoin College, 198
Bracey, John, 191
Braun, Eva, 115
"Brekin' Open the *Blakk-Jacobin*" (Andwele), 180
Brewster, Yvonne, 11, 137, 193, 194, 196
British Lion Films, 203
British Museum, 179, 186
Bullet, Madame, 137, 154–55, 159, 161, 170–71, 194

Bullet, Monsieur, 41, 44, 45, 134, 135, 154, 164
Byron, Jhon Picard, 12

Cahier d'un retour au pays natal (Césaire), 101, 112, 125–29, 191
Caliban, 20
Callinicos, Alex, 115, 241n51
Call Mr. Robeson (Aluko), 198
calypso, 213, 252n2. *See also* extempo
Candomblé, 193
Capital (Marx), 82–83, 211, 234n65, 235n66, 239n116
Capitalism and Slavery (Williams), 21 70, 82–85, 234n64, 235–36n78
Caribbean, 10, 14, 21, 23, 32–33, 199, 204; identity, 73, 128, 212–13; labor revolts, 73. *See also* West Indies; *individual islands*
Caribbean Passion: Haiti 1804 (Donkor), 182–84, 252n13
Carpentier, Alejo, 191
Casa de las Américas (Cuban journal), 191
Casa de las Américas (Cuban publisher), 11, 191–92
The Case for West Indian Self-Government (James), 2, 33, 74, 100
Castro, Fidel, 5, 102, 106–7, 125, 126, 131, 178, 191, 192. *See also* Cuba
Cathcart, Hugh, 72, 92–93
Cave, Terence, 12, 179
Célestine, 135, 147, 161
Césaire, Aimé, 9, 79, 101, 112, 124–29, 130, 131, 180, 189, 191, 232n39, 233n43
Chaguaramas (U.S. naval base), 129–30, 244n108. *See also* America
Charlier, Étienne, 22, 24, 98, 168, 169, 200
Chetty, Raj, 246n20
Chignola, Sandro, 190
chorus, 23, 25, 27, 29, 120, 122, 155, 164–66. *See also* crowds

Christophe, Henri, 46, 52, 55, 57, 65–66; as composite revolutionary, 180; in 1967 play, 133, 154; demythologization of, 141; leadership style, 165, 168–79; surrender to French, 47–48, 137–39
chronicle play, 39, 40
Cipriani, Arthur Andrew, 2, 33–34, 74, 131
Cipriani College of Labour and Co-operative Studies, 205
Clarkson, Thomas, 84
C. L. R. James Cricket Research Centre, 205
C. L. R. James Educational Centre (Butler-Rienzi Labour College), 205
C. L. R. James in Conversation with Stuart Hall, 203
C. L. R. James Institute (New York), 36, 140, 205, 206, 207.
C. L. R. James Library, Hackney, London, 205, 206–7, 262n141
C. L. R. James: Man of the People exhibition (1986), 180
The C. L. R. James Reader (James, Grimshaw), 140, 145, 153
C. L. R. James Study Circle (CLRJSC), 202–3
C. L. R. James Supplementary School, 205
Code Noir, 21
Colás, Santiago, 48–49
collaboration, 140–52, 178
Columbus, Christopher, 76, 178
Combat Ouvrier, 202
combined and uneven development, law of, 70, 85–87, 236–37n84. *See also* permanent revolution, theory of; Trotsky, Leon
comedy, 172–73. *See also* farce; genre
Comintern, 75
The Communist Manifesto (Marx and Engels), 111–12
Communist Party, 80, 91, 191

Index | 297

Congress of Black Writers, 202–3
Constantine, Learie, 37
Cools, Anne, 203
Craton, Michael, 84
Creation for Liberation, 11, 180
cricket, 104, 141, 203, 204, 207
Cripps, Louise, 78, 232n38
crowds, 25, 114, 141, 154, 155, 164–66, 169, 175. *See also* chorus
Cuba: black scare, 191, 256n51; James visits, 248n53; Cuban Revolution, 126, 129, 191, 192, 244n109. *See also* Castro, Fidel; appendix
Cudjoe, Selwyn R., 140
Cummins, Alissandra, 180
Curating in the Caribbean (Bailey, Cummins, Lapp, Thompson), 180
Curepe Scherzando panyard, 194, 196–97

Daguillard, Fritz, 187
Dalleo, Raphael, 48–50, 126
Damas, Léon-Gontran, 79–80, 233nn44–45
Daut, Marlene, 16–17, 20
David, Jacques-Louis: *Napoleon Crossing the Alps*, 184
Delné, Claudy, 12
Delpech, François-Séraphin, 187
Depestre, René, 191
Derance, 118
Dessalines, Jean-Jacques 20, 22, 45–48, 52, 54, 55, 62–66, 86–87, 133–39, 154; as composite revolutionary, 180; flaws, 99, 141; and Haitian flag, 55, 194; leadership style, 165–66, 169–70; as Stalin, 93; and Toussaint, 69, 96, 138, 149, 156, 166, 171; as Vodou god, 186; crowning of, 176;
Detroit, 10, 121, 164, 190, 199, 242n71
dialectics, 27, 127, 178, 209–12, 263n153; silences and, 48–49, 73, 178
Dibb, Mike, 203

Dominica, 203
Dominican Republic, 106
Donkor, Kimathi, 182–86, 252n13
Douglas, Rosie (Roosevelt), 203
Drake, Francis, 185
Drake-u-liar (Donkor), 185
Dubois, Laurent, 19–20, 190, 229n107
Dudley, Richard Owen, 198–99
Dumain, Ralph, 207
Dunayevskaya, Raya, 3–4
Duval-Carrié, Édouard, 186–88, 254n34
Duvalier, François "Papa Doc," 22, 129, 191, 200–201, 222n79
Duvalier, Jean-Claude "Baby Doc," 22, 196, 201

Éditions Amsterdam (French publisher), 189–90
Éditions Caribéennes (French publisher), 189, 201
The Eighteenth Brumaire of Louis Bonaparte (Marx), 11, 77, 112, 172–73, 231n25
Eisenstein, Sergei, 56–57
Elizabeth I, 185–86
Elizabeth II, 185
Elizabeth Rex Lives (Donkor), 185–86
Ellison, Ralph: *Invisible Man*, 193
Emery, Mary Lou, 35, 58, 140, 245n7
Engels, Friedrich, 83, 111–12
Enlightenment, 20–21, 60, 63, 222n73, 226n39
epilogue (*The Black Jacobins*, 1967), 27–28, 139, 140, 152, 157–60, 171–76, 197; Caribbean version of, 156, 173–75; rejection of, 147–48, 162, 174, 176; rewriting of, 173–76; updatability of, 174–76
Ethiopia, 48–53, 55, 57, 80, 91–92
Eutemy, Loren [Loring Eutemey], 188, 253n17
Every Cook Can Govern (James), 204

298 | Index

Every Cook Can Govern (Worldwrite), 204, 207
extempo, 213, 263n161

Facing Reality, 10, 112, 120–21, 140, 143. *See also* Johnson-Forest Tendency
Facing Reality (James, Lee, Castoriadis), 106
FACT, 73
Fanon, Frantz, 166, 249n74
farce, 172–73. *See also* genre
Fardin (Haitian publisher), 201
Farred, Grant, 12, 198, 259n87
fascism; German, 56; Italian, 48–53, 55, 69, 91–92, 190
Feltrinelli (Italian publisher), 190
Fernández Retamar, Roberto, 191
Fick, Carolyn, 24–25, 118, 222–23n86. *See also* history from below
Firmin, Anténor, 30
Fivel-Demoret, Claude, 189, 201
Fo, Dario: *Accidental Death of an Anarchist*, 197
Fondo de Cultura Económica (Mexican publisher), 191
footnotes (*The Black Jacobins*, 1963), 109–11, 116–19
Forest, Freddie [pseud. for Raya Dunayevskaya], 3
Forsdick, Charles, 81, 179, 241n44
Fort de Joux, 120
Fouchard, Jean, 18, 24–25, 200
France: French connections, 27; Paris, 78–82, 199–200. *See also* French Revolution
Franco, Francisco, 3, 110–11
French Revolution, 21, 118–19, 200–201; bibliography (1963) on, 122–24; bicentenary of, 193; *bras nus* in, 123, 165; Convention (1794), 45–46, 169; *enragés* in, 25, 119, 122, 123, 165; Evêché, 119; Marxist historiography of, 24, 99; motto (Liberty, Equality, Fraternity), 44, 167, 170; Paris Commune, 118–19; popular movements in, 122–24. *See also* France; sansculottes
From Columbus to Castro (Williams), 5
Froude, James Anthony, 19, 30, 32, 87–88. *See also* Thomas, John Jacob: *Froudacity*

Gallimard (French publisher), 21, 35, 39, 61, 189
Gambino, Ferrucio, 11, 190
Geggus, David, 19–20, 120, 141
Le Général Toussaint enfumé (Duval-Carrié), 187
genetic criticism, 6–11, 27; *avant-texte*, 7–8; Institut des textes et manuscrits modernes (ITEM), 8–9; theatrical, 10–11
Genette, Gérard, 6. *See also* palimpsest
genre, 14, 141–42, 172–73, 178
George, Marvin, 198, 257n61
German Democratic Republic (GDR), 192, 256n56
Gibbons, Rawle, 11, 193–95, 198, 257n61
Gibson, William, 10, 145
Gillman, Susan, 5, 16, 102–3, 125, 178
Girondins, 119
Glaberman, Martin, 121, 198, 204
Glick, Jeremy, 95, 238n108; 239n114; 242n68, 251n103
Glissant, Édouard, 23
Gobineau, Joseph Arthur de, 31
Godfrey, Peter, 60
Goonewardene, Leslie, 75
Gorender, Jacob, 193
Gorman, William, 140, 143
Green, John Richard, 108
Grésillon, Almuth, 7, 150
Grimshaw, Anna, 140, 145, 153, 201, 220n64
Gruesz, Kirsten Silva, 16

Guadeloupe, 131, 202
Guérin, Daniel, 123–24, 243n79

Hackney Council, 206–7
Hackney Unites, 207
Haiti: *The Black Jacobins* influence in, 199–202; coups, 193, 197, 201, 204; earthquake (2010), 193, 202; and federation, 131, 202; James's planned trip to, 200–201; maroons, 18, 200; modern-day, 178, 204
Haiti Action Support Team, 196
Haitian Revolution: bicentenary (2004), 184–85, 193; and independence, 171, 176; extreme left wing of, 119; popular movements within, 120; modern politicians and, 173; scorched-earth strategy, 51, 91; success of, 19, 55–56, 92; *tricinquantenaire* (150th) anniversary of, 21–22, 35, 61, 200; and world history, 21, 211
Hall, Stuart, 102, 199–200, 203, 204, 235n70
hamartia, 114–15
Hammond, Mona, 196
Harland, Sidney, 19, 26, 29–34, 44, 87–89, 210
Harris, Wilson, 130
Hassan, Leila, 11, 180. *See also* Race Today Collective
Haston, Jock, 36, 225n26
Hector, Michel, 12, 202
Hector, Tim, 203
Hegel, Georg Wilhelm Friedrich, 103, 172. *See also* speculative thought
Henry, Paget, 204
Herodotus, 108
Hill, Errol, 36, 137, 142, 145, 153, 163, 225n29
Hill, Robert A., 11, 30, 35, 57, 60, 61, 90, 122, 204
Hilliard, Nicholas, 185

Himid, Lubaina, 181–83
Hines, Jack, 205
history from below, 23–26, 86–87, 117–18, 122, 141, 169, 206. *See also* total history
A History of Negro Revolt (James), 3, 70, 72–75
A History of Pan-African Revolt (James), 3, 72, 74
The History of the Russian Revolution (Trotsky), 72, 75–76, 86–87, 93, 111
Hitler, Adolf, 110, 115. *See also* World War II
Hobsbawm, Eric, 24, 87, 165, 167
Høgsbjerg, Christian: on afterlives, 179; and Hull script, 4–5; and NALIS script, 35; on *A History of Negro Revolt*, 73; on James's 1936 play, 4, 5, 35; on Nemours, 50; on U.S. occupation of Haiti, 48, 226n42, 227n59
Howe, Darcus, 11–12, 180, 262n135; *See also* Race Today Collective

illiteracy, 47–48, 149, 169, 201
Imprenta Nacional (Cuba), 191
India, 55, 111
Institute of the Black World (IBW), 12, 203
"The Intelligence of the Negro: A Few Words with Dr. Harland" (James), 26, 29–34, 87–89, 210
International African Friends of Abyssinia (IAFA), 51. *See also* Ethiopia; Pan-Africanism
International African Opinion, 51
International African Service Bureau (IASB), 51, 100
Independent Labour Party (ILP), 34
International Slavery Museum, 184–85
Iphigénie (Racine), 157

Jacobs, Sean, 12, 199, 260n114
Jahn, Jahnheinz, 192

James, C. L. R.: as actor, 61; car accident (1961), 106; contributions to Marxism, 3, 85, 112, 116, 120–21; deportation from United States, 3, 10, 35; coming to Marxism, 14, 69–70, 141; Francophilia, 49–50; house arrest in Trinidad (1965), 36, 119; response to Harland in *The Beacon* (1931), 26, 29–34, 87–89, 210; silences of, 17, 182. *See also individual works*

James, C. L. R., correspondence of, 35; with Brierre, 200; with Charlier, 98, 168, 169, 200; with Gallimard, 35, 61; with Haitian Embassy London, 35, 61; with Lyndersay, 140, 145–52; with Maxwell, 203; with Morisseau-Leroy, 200–201

James, Selma, 11, 35, 61, 106, 128, 143, 202, 204

Janvier, Louis Joseph, 30
Jaurès, Jean, 122–23
Jean-Pierre, Ulrick, 186
Johnson-Forest Tendency, 3, 4, 10, 19, 27, 68, 112, 120–21, 141, 211; significance, 246n11; spontaneity, 166, 211–12. *See also* Facing Reality
Johnson, Kwynn, 263n162. *See also* palimpsest; Walcott, Derek
Johnson, J. R. [pseud. for C. L. R. James], 3
Jouvay Ayiti, 198
Juan, Adelaida de, 191

Kaisary, Philip, 252n13
Kamugisha, Aaron, 235n68
Karimjee, Sakina, 188
Kenya, 111
The Keys, 51
Kina, Jean, 120
Kina, Zamor, 120
King, Nicole, 5, 34, 63, 141–42, 263n160
Koselleck, Reinhart, 103

Kouyaté, Tiemoko Garan, 80, 233n49
Kremlin, 191
Kropotkin, Peter, 124
Kwei-Armah, Kwame (Foz Allen), 204–5

Lacroix, Pamphile de, 16, 89, 91, 116, 238n99
Laird, Trevor, 196
Lamming, George, 130, 131, 236n80, 247n26
La Rose, John, 206, 262n138
Latin America, 193
Lawrence, Jacob, 186, 188
League of Coloured Peoples (LCP), 51
League of Nations, 49
Lear, Tobias, 52–53; in 1967 play, 154
Le Blanc, Paul, 86, 236n81, 236n82
Leclerc, Charles, 17, 42, 43, 46, 81 116, 118, 136, 138–39, 148, 158
Leclerc, Pauline Bonaparte, 68, 138, 158
"Lectures on *The Black Jacobins*" (James), 12, 103, 109, 113, 116–20, 122–24, 166, 168, 203
Lefebvre, Georges, 117–18, 123–24, 242n54, 243n79
Lenin, Vladimir, 76, 93–94, 100, 111, 112, 209–10
liberation theology, 193
lieux de mémoire, 208
The Life of Captain Cipriani (James), 2, 33, 74
The Life of Toussaint L'Ouverture (Lawrence), 186
Lindenberger, Herbert, 64
Little Carib Theatre, 146–47
Locke, Alain LeRoy, 36, 225n27
London, 34, 50–51, 56, 161, 180, 190, 194, 196, 199, 205–6
London Socialist Historians Group, 208
López Oceguera, Rosa, 11, 191–92
Louverture, Isaac, 187

Louverture, Toussaint, 133, 154; in *The Beacon*, 26; biography, 30, 32, 39, 74, 210; as black Spartacus, 60, 229n99; as exceptional, 91–92, 96; demythologization, 141; "descent into his depths" speech, 156, 159; flaws, 27, 93–97, 113–16, 156, 170; as freeman and slave owner, 190; imprisonment and death, 95; as Legba, 188; as Lenin, 93–94; leadership style, 45, 48, 98, 169–70; refiguring of, 27, 105, 112, 241n44; rise of, 95; rural code of, 171; self-renaming of, 109, 186, 210; sons and wife of, 45–47, 67–68; strategy, 96, 113–14; tensions with masses, 86–87, 112, 117; visual representations of, 180–88; and West Indian identity, 130; writing out of, 12, 26, 168

Lucchese, Filippo del, 190

Lycée Schœlcher (Martinique), 129. *See also* Césaire, Aimé

Lyndersay, Dexter, 10, 78, 140, 145–52, 154, 156–57, 158, 161–63, 174, 176

Macaulay, Thomas Babington, 108

Macaya, 61, 167, 229n107

Madiou, Thomas, 15, 81, 98, 199

Madras textile mill strike, 75

Maharaj, Clem, 143–44, 160–61, 247n24, 247n26

Maharaj, Stephen, 143. *See also* Workers' and Farmers' Party

Maitland, Thomas, 45, 52–53, 154, 162–63; British plans to restore slavery, 44, 66. *See also* Preston, Harold

The Many Faces of Toussaint Louverture (exhibition), Brown University, 186–87

Marable, Manning, 73

Marat, 155, 167–68.

Marie-Jeanne, 133, 143, 147, 154–55, 157, 160–61

Mariners, Renegades, and Castaways (James), 2–3, 215n3

Martin, William G., 73

Martinique, 131, 202, 260n115

marvelous realism, 191

Marx, Karl, 76, 77, 82–85, 111–12; 172–73, 209–10. *See also* Capital; *The Eighteenth Brumaire of Louis Bonaparte*

Marxism, 2, 3, 111–12; James coming to, 14, 69, 75–76; James's contributions to, 85, 116, 117, 120, 210; Marxist historical explanations, 13, 19, 83; Marxist models, 75, 100, 172; removal of Marxist language (1963), 27, 105

Marxist Group, 34

mas-action, 193, 198. *See also* Gibbons, Rawle; George, Marvin

masses, 97–99, 105, 112, 113, 114, 116–21, 164–66

Mathiez, Albert, 17, 237n88

Maurin lithograph, 187–88

Maurin, Nicolas, 187

Max, 155, 167–68. *See also* Robespierre, Maximilien

Maxwell, Marina, 194, 203

Mbeki, Thabo, 202, 260n114

McBurnie, Beryl, 146–47

McIntosh, Llewellyn, 213. *See also* calypso; extempo

McLemee, Scott, 140

Mehlman, Jeffrey, 172

Melville, Herman, 143

Michelet, Jules, 108, 122

Middlesbrough Institute of Modern Art, 181

Moïse, 26, 93–94, 97–98, 133, 141, 147, 154–55, 168–71, 173–76, 194; added to *Toussaint Louverture* play, 61–66, 68; name-calling others, 157; showdown with Louverture, 144–45, 156, 158, 162

Moitt, Bernard, 14

Molière, 33

Montreal, 199, 202–3, 204
Morisseau-Leroy, Félix, 22, 200–201
multivoicedness, 4, 141
Murray, Jim, 140, 207. *See also* C. L. R. James Institute
Murray, Phillip, 213. *See also* calypso; extempo music, 146
Mussolini, Benito, 91, 190. *See also* fascism: Italian
Mynanda, Lukanyo, 12
My Own, My Native Land (James, projected memoir), 105–6

Naipaul, V. S., 23, 130, 131, 222n83
narrativism, 13, 70, 94, 115–16, 140
Naville, Pierre, 78–79, 123, 189, 201, 232n39, 255nn40–41
Nazareth, H. O, 203–4
Negri, Antonio, 190
Negritude, 79–80, 101, 124, 126–27, 180, 191, 192. *See also* Césaire, Aimé; Damas, Léon-Gontran
Nello James Centre, Manchester, 205, 206
Nelson, Lancashire, 33–34, 37, 76
Nemours, Alfred Auguste, 17–18, 50, 80–81, 120, 199, 233n55
Nesbitt, Nick, 17, 234n63, 237n88
Nettleford, Rex, 197, 263n162
New Beacon Books, 206
New Historians of Capitalism (NHC), 82, 234n64
Nielsen, Aldon Lynn, 204, 220n64, 261n122
Nigeria, 4, 133, 144–52, 156, 162, 166, 174, 248n53
Nkrumah and the Ghana Revolution (James, 1977), 106
Nkrumah, Kwame, 66
Noble, Peter, 57
Non-European Movement (NEUM), 198–99, 259n92

Nora, Pierre, 208
Notes on Dialectics (James), 209–12
Nurse, Malcolm. *See* Padmore, George

Oilfields Workers' Trade Union (OWTU), 206
old colonial system, 126–29, 191
operaismo, 190, 192, 255n44
Orisun Theatre Drummers, 147, 152
Orléans, 155, 167–68
Orléans, Louis Philippe Joseph d' [pseud. Philippe Égalité], 167–68.
Ortiz, Fernando, 131
Osa, Dr. de la (Cuban minister of foreign affairs), 191
Oxaal, Ivar, 84
Oyelana, Tunji, 147, 152. *See also* Nigeria

Padmore, George, 50, 80, 191, 227n54
Pahl-Rugenstein (German publisher), 192
palimpsest, 5–6, 10, 82–83, 116, 144, 145, 161, 189, 208–9, 213, 217n17
Pan-Africanism, 51, 55–56, 79, 80, 186, 191
Panier, Jean, 118, 167, 168
paratexts, 2, 5–6, 77, 104, 175–76, 217n20, 240n11, 251n119
Parry, Benita, 259n92
Party Politics in the West Indies (James), 106
Pasquet, Alix, 201
"Paul Robeson: Black Star" (James), 56, 60
Paulson, Ronald, 19–20
The People of Kenya Speak for Themselves (Koinange), 121
People's National Movement (PNM), 129–30, 151
permanent revolution, theory of, 3, 70, 85–87, 236nn81–82. *See also* combined and uneven development, law of; Trotsky, Leon

Pétion, Alexandre, 55, 99, 139
Petrillo, Raffaele, 11, 190
Philipson, Morris, 103–8
Phillips, Caryl, 196
Pitt, William, 111
Poland, 204
popular leaders, 26, 63, 86, 112, 116–18, 122, 124, 145, 147, 155–56, 166–68, 211
preface to *The Black Jacobins* (1938), 76–77, 92, 108, 193
preface to *The Black Jacobins* (1963), 103–5, 108
Preston, Harold, 153, 162–63, 249n60
Price, Hannibal, 30
Price Mars, Jean, 82, 124, 127, 131
prologue (*The Black Jacobins*, 1967), 78, 137, 139, 146–48, 158, 159, 161–62, 163, 164. *See also* Lyndersay, Dexter

Queen's Royal College (QRC), 129, 195
Quest, Matthew, 242n56

Rabbitt, Kara M., 141, 239n121
Race Today Collective, 11, 73, 180, 206
Racine, Jean, 157
Ramsay, Ras Akyem-i, 180–81
Ran Away by George (Donkor), 185
Rank Organization, 203
Ranke, Leopold von, 23
rara, 198
rasanblaj, 186
Raynal, Abbé, 60, 63, 100, 135, 137, 159, 229n99, 239n119
Reid, Claude, 195
Reid, Vic, 130
"Remixed Ode to Rebel's Spirit: Lyrical Meditations on Haiti and Toussaint Louverture" (Ulysse performance), 186
A Revolutionary Legacy: Haiti and Toussaint Louverture (British Museum exhibition), 186

rewriting, 2, 5–6, 12, 21, 74, 76, 210–11; falsifications and, 88–89, 165, 210; negative, 22; reflections on, 13; linguistic reshaping, 19–21
Rigney, Ann, 12
Roach, Joseph, 142
Robeson, Eslanda, 36
Robeson, Paul, 26, 29, 56–61, 81, 196, 198
Robespierre, Maximilien, 17, 97, 123, 167, 234n56, 237n88. *See also* Max
Rodney, Walter, 203
Romano, Paul [pseud. for Phil Singer], 121
Rosengarten, Frank, 5, 34, 244–45n113
Roy, Ajit, 75
Rudder, David, 252n2
Rudé, George, 24–25, 87, 117, 165
Russian Revolution: 71–72, 75, 86, 93–94, 99, 111
Ryan, Selwyn, 84

Said, Edward, 89, 232n30
Saint-Rémy, Joseph, 16–17
"Samedi Smith Song," 147, 156, 166–67, 175
Sander, Reinhard, 5, 34
Sandwith, Corinne, 198–99
Sanité and Charles Belair (Donkor), 184
Sannon, Horace Pauléus, 15–16, 25, 81, 199, 200
sansculottes, 25, 117, 119, 122, 123–24, 133, 165
Sans Souci, 167, 168
Scenes from the Life of Toussaint Louverture (Himid), 182
Schneider, Rebecca, 142
Schœlcher, Victor, 16
Schwarz, Bill, 73
Scott, David: *Conscripts of Modernity*, 5, 13, 70, 76, 94–95, 102–4, 114–16, 125, 142; on appendix, 125; on Hayden White, 140; on tragedy, 27, 87
The Seesaw Log (Gibson), 10, 145
Selden, Dan, 178

self-translation, 131, 188
Selvarajatnan, G., 75
Sembène, Ousmane, 172
Sepia Films, 203
Sepinwall, Alyssa Goldstein, 25, 235n67, 261n133
Il Sessantotto (1968), 190
Shakespeare, William, 33, 95, 203
Shango, 147. See also Lyndersay, Dexter
Short Pants [pseud. for Llewellyn McIntosh], 213
silences: in Caribbean records, 250n91
Sir George Williams University Affair, 203, 261n117
Smith, Matthew J., 200, 201
Smith, Samedi, 26, 118, 138, 139, 147, 155, 166–67, 168, 171
Soboul, Albert, 24, 87, 117, 124, 165, 243n85
Société haïtienne d'Histoire et de Géographie, 202
South Africa, 4, 12, 198–99, 202, 260n113
Soyinka, Wole, 150–51, 248n50. See also Lyndersay, Dexter; Nigeria; University of Ibadan
Spain, 110–11, 160–61, 169, 226n41
speculative thought, 27, 103, 110, 125
Spencer, Harry, 37
Stage Society, 56
Stalin, Joseph, 93–94, 191; Stalinist revisionism, 75, 93–94, 212, 238n101
State Capitalism and World Revolution (James), 3
Stephens, Michelle, 36, 225n29
St. John, Spenser, 87
Stoddard, T. Lothrop, 19, 30, 87–90, 92–93
Stone, Judy, 194, 195
Stone, Ria [pseud. for Grace Lee Boggs], 121
strong (mis-)readings 127
Sweeney, Fionnghuala, 35, 36
Sylla, 167, 168

Tacitus, 108
Talawa Theatre Company, 196
Talking History (James, Thompson), 203
Taylor, Diana, 142
Taylor, Dora, 199, 259n91. See also Parry, Benita
Teixeira Filho, Afonso, 193
text-network, 5, 102–3, 132, 178–79, 212–13
Thatcher, Margaret, 185
Theater of the Oppressed (Boal), 11, 177
third theater, 194, 257n60. See also Gibbons, Rawle
Thomas, John Jacob: *Froudacity* (1889), 30; James introduction to (1969), 30, 87, 223–24n6, 224n7
Thompson, E. P., 24, 87, 117, 165, 203, 238n106
Thucydides, 108
A Time and a Season (James, Hill), 145, 153
Tolstoy, Leo: *War and Peace*, 204
tontons macoutes, 197, 201
total history, 26, 85, 87, 70, 117, 120. See also history from below
Toussaint Bonbon Or (Duval-Carrié), 187
Toussaint Chintz (Duval-Carrié), 187
Toussaint Citron (Duval-Carrié), 187
Toussaint Fuschia (Duval-Carrié), 187
Toussaint L'Ouverture (Césaire), 124–25
Toussaint L'Ouverture (Himid), 181–83
Toussaint Louverture (James): death scene, 53–54, 81; Duke University Press edition (2013), 4, 34, 35; NALIS script, 40–48; 1936 performances of, 4, 29, 34–68; 2013 Liverpool readings of, 198; 2014 Bowdoin College readings of, 198
Toussaint L'Ouverture at Bedourete (Donkor), 184–85
Toussaint Malachite (Duval-Carrié), 187
Toussaint Noir (Duval-Carrié), 187

Trinidad, 152, 198, 201, 205, 207, 209–10, 212
Trinidad Workingmen's Association, 34
Trotsky, Leon: 69, 76, 85–87, 93, 112, 210, 236–37n84. *See also* combined and uneven development, law of; *The History of the Russian Revolution*; permanent revolution, theory of
Trotskyism, 75, 78–80, 112, 141, 189, 192, 199
Trouillot, Michel-Rolph, 22–23, 30, 88, 200, 201–2
Trujillo, Rafael, 106, 129
Turner (Spanish publisher), 191

UK Diaspora (Donkor), 184–86
Ulysse, Gina Athena, 179, 186. *See also individual works*
University of Ibadan, 4, 133, 144–52, 162, 248n53
United States. *See* America
University of the West Indies: Cave Hill, Barbados, 197, 205; Mona, Jamaica, 203, 245; St. Augustine, Trinidad, 37
unsilencing, 141–42

Valère, Gloria, 37
vanguard party, 112, 133, 141
Vastey, Baron de, 20, 221n71
Verlag Neues Leben (East German publisher), 192
vèvè, 188
Vincent, Colonel, 149, 158, 159
Vodou, 146–47, 152, 163, 180–81, 182, 186, 188, 192, 193

Walcott, Derek, 130, 263n164
Walcott, Harclyde, 11, 193, 197–98
Warburg, Frederic, 75
Watts, Nic, 188
Watts, Richard, 7, 217n20, 240n11
Webb, Constance, 36
Wesker, Arnold, 248n40

West Indies, 156. *See also* Caribbean; *individual islands*
West Indies Federation, 107, 156, 176–77; alternative federation, 131, 202; breakup of, 125–26, 130, 172, 173–74
West Indian/Caribbean history, 23, 32, 33, 59, 107, 125, 212
West Indian independence, 106, 107, 108, 125
West Indian/Caribbean identity, 73, 124, 128, 130–32, 213
West, Michael O., 73
Westminster Theatre, 56
White, Hayden, 13, 94, 115, 140, 241n51. *See also* Callinicos, Alex; narrativism; Scott, David
White, Tony, 147. *See also* "Samedi Smith Song"
Wilberforce, William, 84
Wilder, Gary, 103, 255n41
Williams, Eric: James and, 27, 66, 83, 84–85, 125; and People's National Movement, 129–30. *See also Capitalism and Slavery*; *From Columbus to Castro*
Williams, Eugene, 11, 36, 193, 195–96
Winter, Jay, 209
Wong, Ansel, 205
Worcester, Kent, 73
Wordsworth, William, 193
workerism, 190, 192, 255n44
Workers' and Farmers' Party (WFP), 143, 159, 175
World Revolution 1917–1936 (James), 3, 75, 86, 94
World War II, 126, 129, 189
Worldwrite, 204
Wright, Richard, 36

Xala (Ousmane), 172

yard theater, 194, 257n66
Young, Robert, 82

www.ingramcontent.com/pod-product-compliance
Lightning Source LLC
Chambersburg PA
CBHW070753230426

43665CB00017B/2333